INDIANA IN STEREO

Three-Dimensional Views of the Heartland

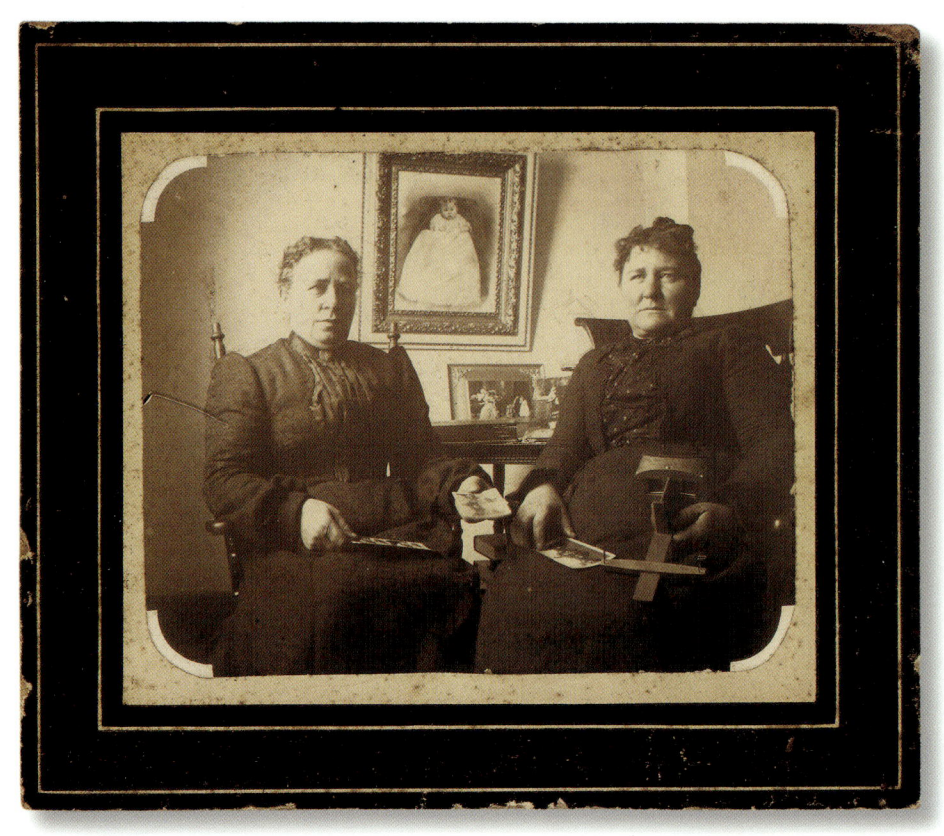

Women viewing stereographs, early 1900s. Handwriting on the back of the photograph identifies the women as Grandma Bowen and Philena.

INDIANA HISTORICAL SOCIETY PRESS

INDIANA IN STEREO

Three-Dimensional Views of the Heartland

Indianapolis 2003

EDITED BY GEORGE R. HANLIN AND PAULA J. CORPUZ

With essays by Anne E. Peterson and Joan E. Hostetler and an essay and photographs by Darryl Jones

This book is a publication of the: Indiana Historical Society Press
450 West Ohio Street
Indianapolis, Indiana 46202-3269 USA
www.indianahistory.org
Telephone orders 800-447-1830
Fax orders 317-234-0562
Shop on-line shop.indianahistory.org

The paper in this publication meets the minimum requirements of American National
Standard for Information Sciences—Permanence of Paper for Printed Library Materials,
ANSI Z39.48–1984 ∞

Library of Congress Cataloging-in-Publication Data
Indiana in stereo : three-dimensional views of the heartland / edited by George R. Hanlin and
  Paula J. Corpuz
    p. cm.
  Includes bibliographical references.
  ISBN 0-87195-165-7 (alk. paper)
    1. Indiana—History—Pictorial works. 2. Indiana—Pictorial works. 3. Stereoscopic
views—Indiana. 4. Photography, Stereoscopic—History. I. Hanlin, George R. II. Corpuz,
Paula.

F527.I57 2003
977.2'031'0222—dc21   2002191348

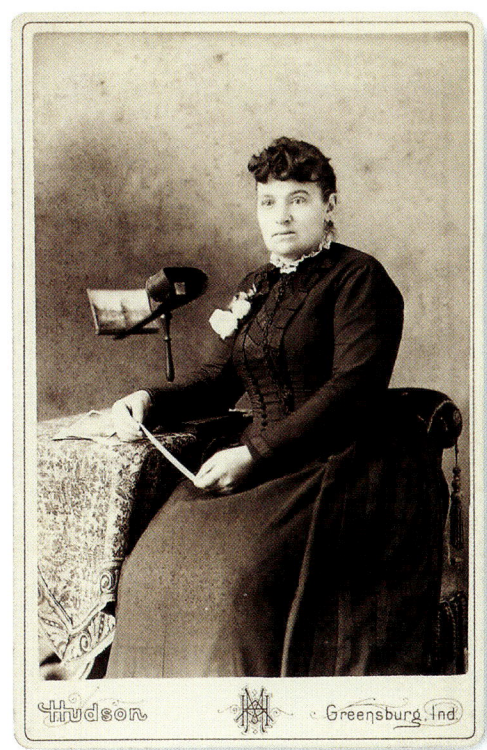

Millard Hudson, a Greensburg photographer,
took this portrait of a woman posing with a stereoscope.
The image dates to the late 1880s.

CONTENTS

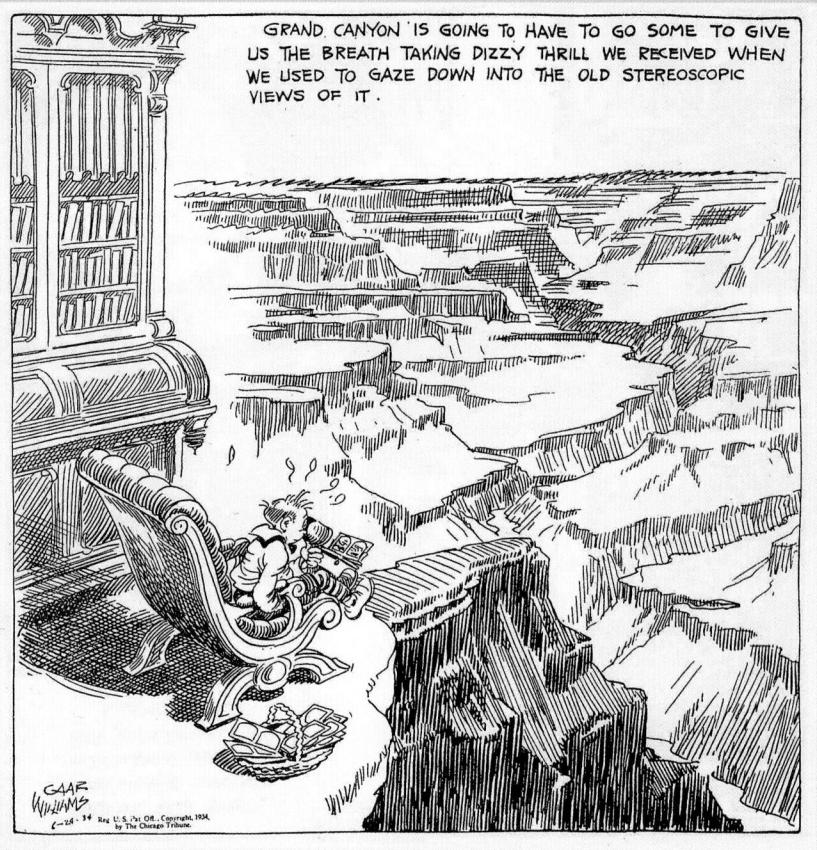

Gaar Williams, a native of Richmond, Indiana, celebrated the stereoscope in this cartoon he drew for the Chicago Tribune. *Before joining the staff of the* Tribune, *Williams worked as a longtime cartoonist at the* Indianapolis News.

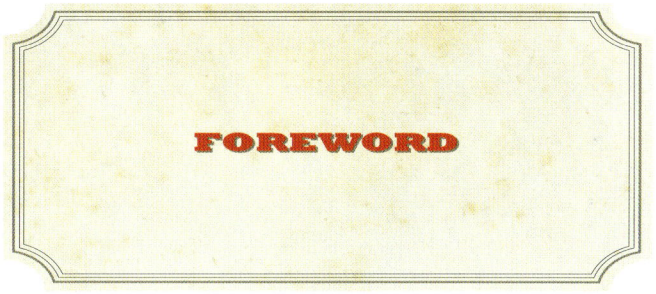

FOREWORD

FOR MANY, OLD PHOTOGRAPHS ARE FASCINATING. THEY EXUDE CHARM, INSTILL A SPIRIT OF TIME AND PLACE, AND tell intriguing stories about the past. When presented in stereoscopic format and viewed in three dimensions, they can have an even greater effect, arousing interest and offering additional insights. In an attempt to introduce readers to the history of stereographs and to capture some of their wonder, the editors of the Indiana Historical Society Press present *Indiana in Stereo: Three-Dimensional Views of the Heartland*.

The idea for this project originated with Kent Calder, former managing editor of the Society's magazine *Traces of Indiana and Midwestern History*. For several years Kent discussed publishing an article about Indiana-related stereographs in *Traces*, but for various reasons the project never advanced. After Kent left Indiana in the late 1990s (he now serves as editorial director at the Wisconsin Historical Society Press in Madison), some of the other editors at the IHS Press kept the idea in the back of their minds with plans to pursue it someday. Then a few years ago we were considering future projects, and we again revisited the stereographs. Rather than publishing just an article, we explored the possibility of expanding the idea into a book. We were aware that the University of Iowa Press had published an attractive book of Iowa stereographs, and we thought we could duplicate the efforts for Indiana.

Before proceeding, however, we wanted to know just what sort of Indiana-related stereo views existed. We suspected the large national stereo manufacturers had produced some scenes of Indiana, but we were afraid the number would be small. We were more or less correct in

GEORGE R. HANLIN

our assumptions. We were rather surprised, however, by the number of our own Hoosier photographers—both professional and amateur—who produced stereoscopic images in Indiana in the late nineteenth and early twentieth centuries. In the collections at the Indiana Historical Society we found hundreds of views created by dozens of photographers, and we learned that local historical societies across the state held even more. Relatively speaking, Indiana-related stereographs still remain scarce, but we nevertheless had sufficient material to produce our book.

The next challenge was to decide what views to include. When choosing, we considered three factors: the technical quality of the image, the interest level of the subject matter, and the location. It was difficult to balance these three factors, and often we had to sacrifice one of them for the sake of another. For example, we include in the book a view of a canal boat. The image is faded, and it does not have much three-dimensional effect, but because it is a unique scene, we decided to include it. In other instances we chose to forego technically superior views, often of Indianapolis, in favor of less impressive views of small towns, all for the sake of geographic diversity. (Indianapolis still dominates, though, and understandably so given its size and the number of photographers and patrons in the city.)

We also include in the book contemporary views of Indiana by well-known local photographer Darryl Jones. A few years ago the Society hired Darryl to take photographs for our book *Destination Indiana*, which highlights twenty-five historic sites around the state, and he did much of the work in stereo. When Darryl told us that he had been shooting other Hoosier scenes in stereo over the past few years as well, we decided to include some of them here. These modern views demonstrate stereography's continuing relevance as a form of communication and art, and we hope our readers find as much value in them as they do in the historical views.

So that readers may enjoy the three-dimensional effects of the stereographs, we have included in the back of the book a plastic handheld viewer. This viewer cannot begin to replicate the effect of looking at cards in an actual stereoscope, but it does at least allow readers to see the images in depth. To use the viewer, place it against the bridge of your nose. Lay the book flat on a table or hold it in front of your face, about nine to twelve inches from your eyes. Adjust the distance as necessary until your eyes merge the two images into one. When that happens, you should see the image in three dimensions. Patience is necessary, as it can take a while to find the right distance and to let your eyes relax. Once you are able to do this, though, it becomes easier on subsequent tries and soon becomes second nature.

IT REQUIRES MANY PEOPLE TO PUT TOGETHER A BOOK such as this, and we take the opportunity to thank them here, beginning with our contributors. Anne E. Peterson and Joan E. Hostetler, both excellent photographic historians, provided the introductory essays and went above and beyond our expectations. Anne helped with the bibliography and the glossary, and Joan assisted with the selection of the images and provided the list of Indiana stereo photographers. As mentioned, Darryl Jones provided the contemporary views for the book and wrote an informative essay on taking stereo photographs. All three contributors were delightful to work with, and we appreciate their efforts.

Many thanks are owed to Stephen J. Fletcher, former curator of visual collections at the Indiana Historical Society. Unless otherwise noted, the historical stereographs published in this book come from the Society's William Henry Smith Memorial Library, and Stephen was chiefly responsible for collecting them. The editors are grateful for his work in preserving these images and for his help in making them available to us. Producing transparencies of almost two hundred stereographs and other images takes a lot of work, and we appreciate the dedication of Susan L. S. Sutton, who helped coordinate the reproduction efforts, and Kim Charles Ferrill, who provided his photographic services.

Several people at institutions across the state, the nation, and even the world helped with illustrations. Among them, the editors thank: Sandra Spikes, *Chicago Tribune*; Ruth Cash and Charity Mitchell, Decatur County Historical Society, Greensburg, Indiana; Wesley Wilson, Archives and Special Collections, DePauw University, Greencastle, Indiana; Tina Mellott and Diana Zornow, Elkhart County Historical Museum, Bristol, Indiana; Linda Badger and Jeff Tenuth, Indiana State Museum, Indianapolis; Dennis Vetrovec, Cunningham Memorial Library, Indiana State University, Terre Haute; Susie Richter, La Porte County Historical Society, La Porte, Indiana; June Felton, Marion Public Library, Marion, Indiana; Corrie Cook, Morris-Butler House, Indianapolis; David Haberstich, National Museum of American History, Smithsonian Institution, Washington, D.C.; Matthew Bailey, National Portrait Gallery, London; Mary Leitch, Noble County Historical Society, Albion, Indiana; Chuck Poehlein, Perry County Museum, Cannelton, Indiana; Venita Paul, Science and Society Picture Library, Science Museum, London; Paul Schueler, Tippecanoe County Historical Association, Lafayette, Indiana; and Jan Livingston, Wayne County Historical Museum, Richmond, Indiana.

At the Indiana Historical Society Press, many staff members assisted with this book, including Managing Editor Ray E. Boomhower and Assistant Editors Kathleen M. Breen and

Judith Q. McMullen, who helped review text and other materials. The editors also extend their appreciation to Brenda Myers, Catherine F. Bennett, and Rachael Vaught, who offered valuable advice and assistance with marketing.

Final thanks go to Patricia Prather and her coworkers at Dean Johnson Design in Indianapolis. Pat designs many books for the Society and always amazes us with her creativity and professionalism—not to mention her good nature. Once again she worked her magic on this book and has come up with a design we feel complements the text and images, telling well the story of Indiana's stereographs.

To these people and others unmentioned we extend our gratitude, and to our readers we offer our appreciation. Have fun exploring *Indiana in Stereo*!

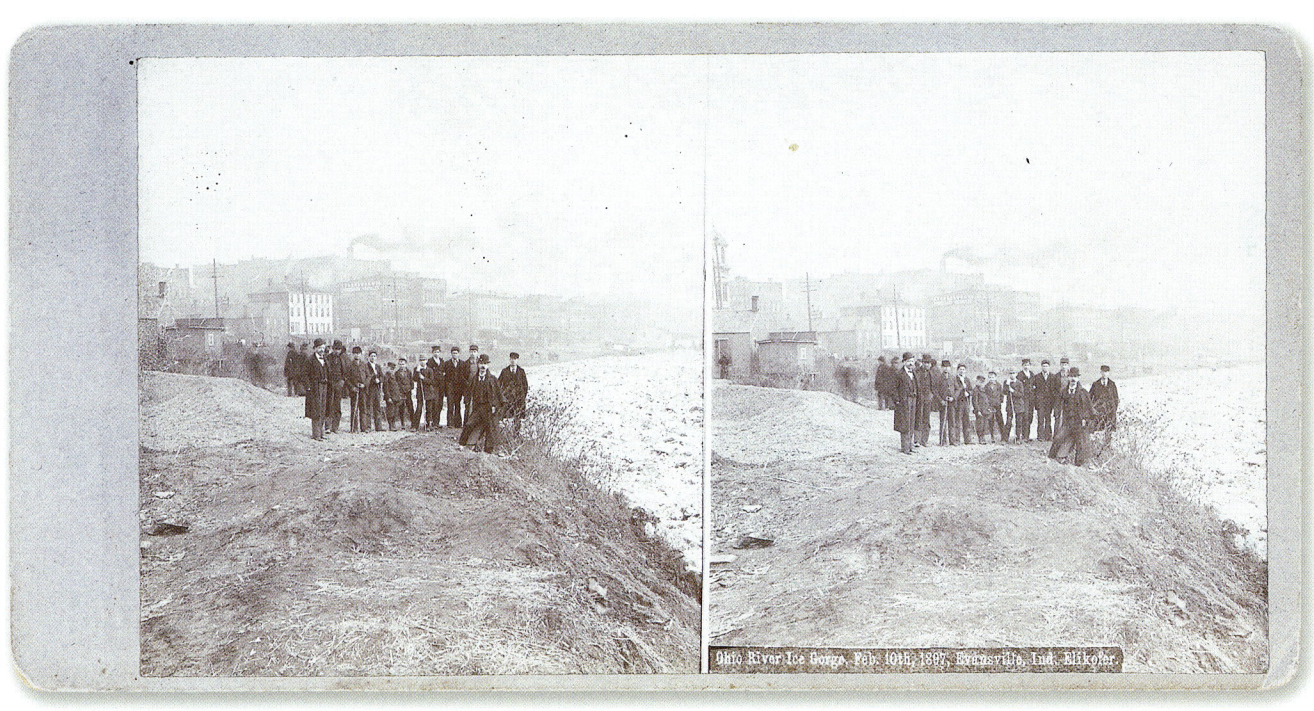

Ohio River Ice Gorge, Feb. 10th, 1897, Evansville, Ind. Elikofer.

Ice gorge on the Ohio River, Evansville, 1897. Photographed by Fred Elikofer.
Other views of the gorge appear on pages 126 and 143.

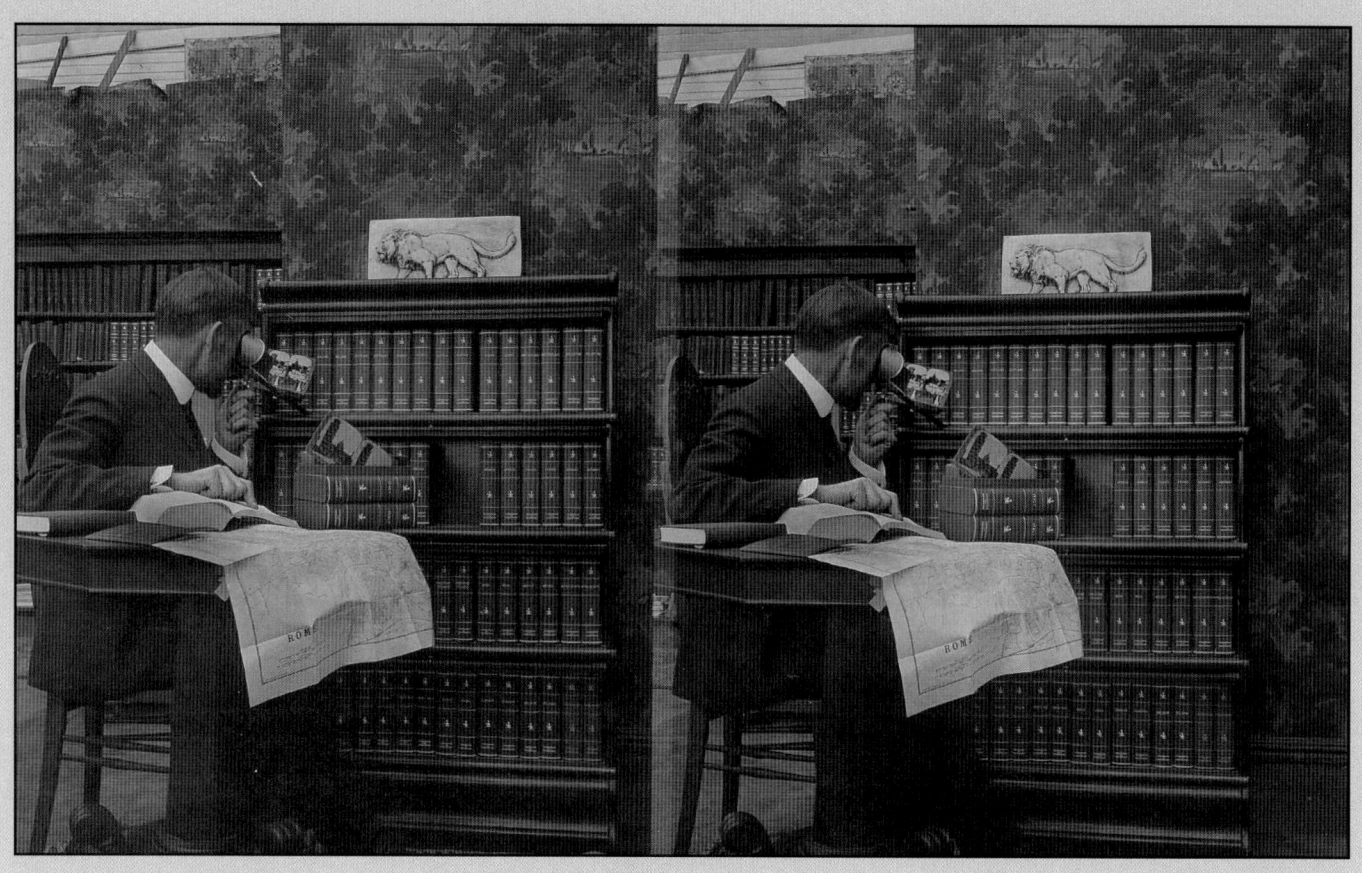

In this view created by Underwood and Underwood, a man examines stereo images and learns more about them by studying reference materials—including, no doubt, an Underwood guidebook and map.

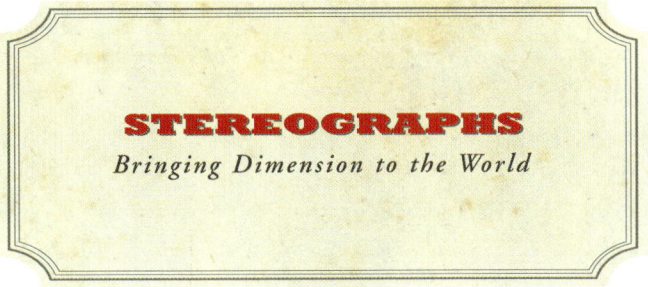

STEREOGRAPHS
Bringing Dimension to the World

IN TODAY'S WORLD, AMERICANS SEEM CONSUMED BY TECHNOLOGY, MUCH OF IT OBSOLETE ALMOST AS SOON as it comes on the market. Most households have a computer, often more than one, and these are quickly upgraded and replaced. Consumers depend on cell phones, e-mail, and the Internet to keep them connected and up to date by the minute with the latest news and with their business associates, friends, and family. It is somewhat difficult, then, to imagine the impact on individuals when stereographs became available in the mid–nineteenth century. With no movies, television, radio, telephone, or computers, the advent of the stereograph was groundbreaking in terms of home entertainment—akin to the introduction of television a century later. The industrial revolution that had started in the eighteenth century was firmly established by 1850, and with it had come significant changes in the American economy, advances in transportation, and increased immigration and urbanization, which in turn brought sociological change. The growing middle class had more leisure time, and for this curious public, stereographs became the first mass medium for visual information and entertainment.

EARLY DISCOVERIES A stereograph—also known as a stereoscopic photograph, stereo view, stereogram, card view, or simply a stereo—usually consists of a pair of almost identical paper photographs mounted next to each other on heavy card stock. The illusion of a single three-dimensional image is created when the stereograph is viewed through the stereoscope, sometimes simply called a stereo viewer. The principles of stereoscopy were known even before the first photographic processes had been published. Scientists and artists since the time of Euclid in ancient Greece had some understanding of how human beings see depth. Then in the nineteenth century, British physicist Sir Charles Wheatstone (1802–1875) invented a stereo viewer to illustrate these concepts. Wheatstone conducted experiments on the theory of human binocular vision and built the first reflecting-mirror stereoscope in 1832.

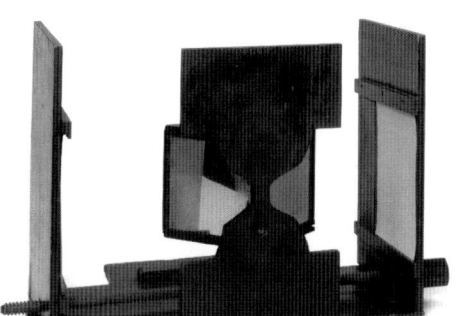

Wheatstone's original stereoscope.

Wheatstone recognized that each eye has a slightly different perspective and that the brain merges the two views into a single three-dimensional image. He presented a paper that explained the phenomenon of binocular vision to the Royal Society in 1838. He also coined the term "stereoscope," roughly translated from the Greek as "solid figures." Because photographs were not yet available, he demonstrated his theories by using two slightly different geometric drawings to represent what would be seen by each eye. He placed these drawings in his stereoscope, and the mirrors reflected them and merged them into one view.

Although Wheatstone published his findings that same year, more than ten years passed before stereoscopes were generally available to the public. The delay was largely due to the cost and difficulty of the early photographic processes and the awkwardness of Wheatstone's experimental stereoscope.

The stereoscope became linked to photography practically from the beginning. Several inventors had been working separately with photographic processes in France, England, and elsewhere. The first to make his photographic process public was Frenchman Louis-Jacques-Mandé Daguerre (1787–1851). On 7 January 1839 the secretary of the Academy of Science in Paris announced Daguerre's success. Later that year the daguerreotype was made available to the public, and photography for the masses was born. There were limitations, however, to Daguerre's process. The daguerreotype is a direct positive process on photosensitized metal made with no negative. Having a unique image from which copies could not be made was

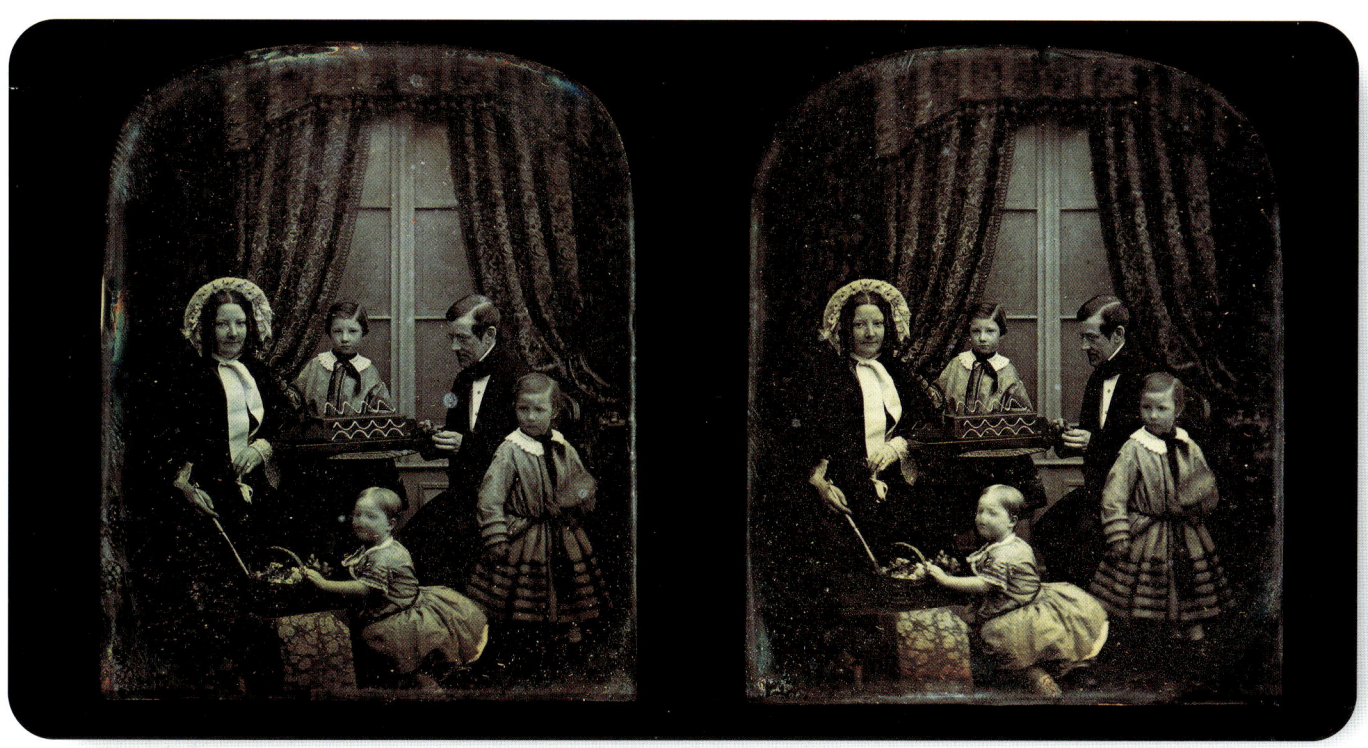

Sir Charles Wheatstone, inventor of the stereoscope, with his family. This stereoscopic daguerreotype was taken in the early 1850s.

not ideal. Daguerreotypes were expensive, fragile, and subject to tarnish, and the highly polished mirrorlike surface made them difficult to view. But the images were astonishingly clear, and they portrayed the most minute detail. Because of its precise representation, for the next twenty years the daguerreotype dominated the field of portrait photography in America.

At the same time Daguerre was conducting his experiments, William Henry Fox Talbot (1800–1877) was working independently in England on another somewhat different photographic process. His was a paper-negative and print process more directly related than the daguerreotype to the photographic processes used today. Talbot was astounded by the announcement of the daguerreotype because of the similarity to his experiments. By the end of January 1839 he described to the Royal Society his first photographic process, which he called photogenic drawing, and presented samples of his experiments. Photogenic drawing was a printing-out process, meaning that the paper was developed by direct exposure to light—for as long as an hour—and not by chemical treatments. In September 1840

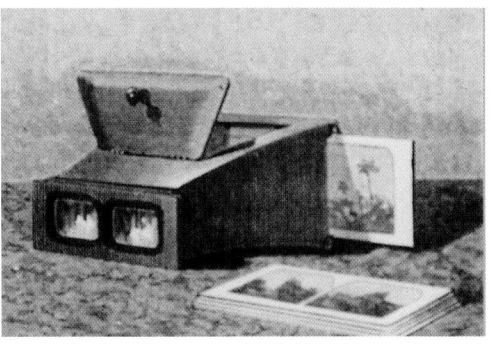

In the early decades of stereoscopy, the Brewster viewer was among the most popular stereoscope models.

Talbot introduced improvements to the process that utilized chemical baths for development, reducing exposure times. Photographs made by this revised method were later called talbotypes in England and calotypes elsewhere. There were inherent problems, however, with the calotype. Paper negatives did not yield sharp definition, and the prints often had little contrast, were somewhat uneven in their tonal range, and tended to fade quickly. In addition to the imperfections of the calotype, Talbot took out restrictive patents that severely curtailed the use of his invention. This was particularly true in the United States, where as a result of patent restrictions the daguerreotype achieved greater popularity. Still, despite the limitations of Daguerre's and Talbot's processes, photography gained immediate widespread appeal, and soon cameras and other photographic equipment were being made and commercially sold to the public.

Shortly after the introduction of photography, inventors began utilizing it for stereoscopic applications. In 1840, at Wheatstone's request, Talbot made large-scale calotypes of statues, buildings, and people for use in Wheatstone's stereoscope. Talbot's images, then, are the earliest known stereo photographs, but soon daguerreotypes were also made available to Wheatstone for viewing in the stereoscope.

Improvements to the stereo viewer were most important in bringing the rise in widespread popularity of the stereograph. A Scottish scientist, Sir David Brewster (1781–1868), became interested in binocular vision and began experimenting with improving the stereoscope for use with images smaller than those used in the Wheatstone instrument. In March 1849 Brewster spoke to the Royal Scottish Society of the Arts and described several lenticular stereoscopes he had developed. His viewers were wood or metal pyramid-shaped boxes with twin lenses instead of mirrors. The lenses were spaced two and a half inches apart, which is the normal distance between the eyes, and were mounted at the smaller end to see the images at the bottom of the case.

Brewster had stereoscopes made in Scotland and Paris. A Brewster lenticular stereoscope made by the French optical firm of Duboscq and Soleil for viewing daguerreotypes was displayed in 1851 at the Great Exhibition at the Crystal Palace in London. Conceived as a showcase for Great Britain's role as leader in the Industrial Revolution, the huge glass-and-iron palace housed more than thirteen thousand exhibits, and more than six million visitors came from all over the world to view them. Brewster's stereoscope attracted the attention of Queen Victoria at the exhibition, and he then presented her with a beautiful Duboscq instrument. This began a craze for stereographs. Neither Wheatstone nor Brewster had taken out patents on their stereoscope models, and opticians in London and Paris freely began to manufacture stereo equipment. Thousands of Brewster viewers were sold, which in turn created an even larger market for stereo views. The first commercially produced stereo views were daguerreotypes, and stereographs with mounted paper prints were available by 1852. By the next year shops in major tourist cities such as London, Rome, and Paris offered stereo views to visitors.[1]

One of the earliest publishers of stereographs was the London Stereoscopic Company, which started large-scale production in 1854. Because of its marketing techniques and mass production, by 1858 the firm had a list of more than 100,000 stereo views available for sale. Its slogan was, "A stereoscope for every home."[2]

STEREOGRAPHS IN AMERICA

Although the new photographic processes had quickly spread to America, the general popularity of the stereograph came a bit later to the United States. Initially, wealthy American tourists

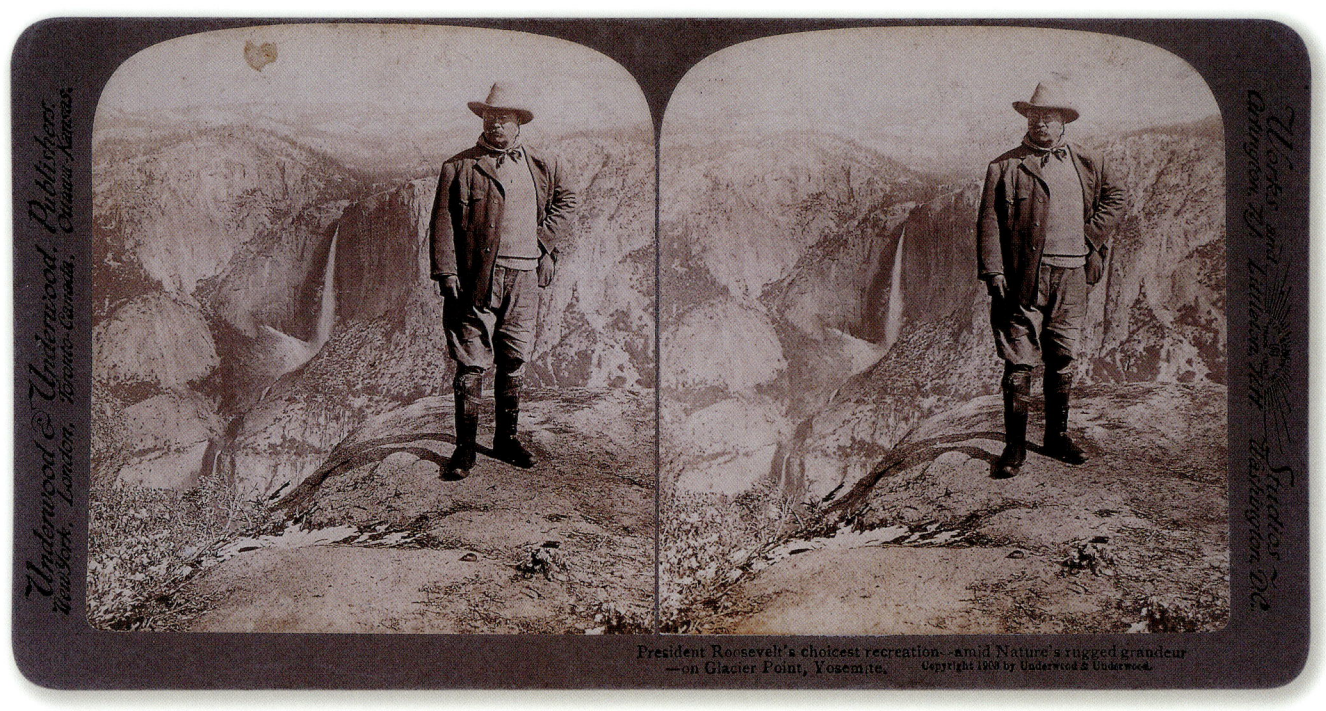

President Roosevelt's choicest recreation—amid Nature's rugged grandeur —on Glacier Point, Yosemite. Copyright 1903 by Underwood & Underwood.

This 1903 view by Underwood and Underwood shows President Theodore Roosevelt at Yosemite. Well-known figures were popular subjects for stereographs in the late nineteenth and early twentieth centuries.

traveling abroad bought Brewster viewers and stereographs in Europe and brought them home. By 1852 D. Appleton and Company offered European stereographs for sale in New York, and starting in 1853 optical shops in the United States sold Brewster stereoscopes, some of them locally made.[3] Brothers Frederick and William Langenheim of Philadelphia were pioneers in the field of publishing and were the first to issue views of American scenery in addition to European views. In 1854 they started to produce glass and paper stereographs of American landscapes from Pennsylvania and the Niagara Falls region. They first attempted to market their stereographs in the form of glass slides that could also be used in magic lanterns, but these were not successful.[4]

Over the next few years many other companies began producing stereo views. One of the largest early publishers of American stereographs was the New York firm of E. and H. T. Anthony, which also sold a full range of photographic equipment and developing materials. By 1860, as the popularity of stereographs increased, at least two hundred American photographers were making them.[5]

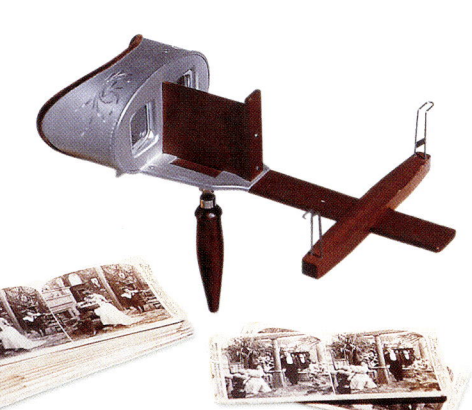

In the 1860s the Holmes stereoscope revolutionized the world of stereoscopy. It was inexpensive and easy to use, and it helped broaden interest in stereographs worldwide.

Oliver Wendell Holmes (1809–1894) did much to advance the popularity of the stereograph in America. The Harvard physician, teacher, poet, and essayist was an enthusiastic stereo collector who personally owned about one thousand views. He wrote about the unique possibilities for education through the stereograph and discussed the benefits of stereo libraries.

He published two important articles on stereoscopy in the *Atlantic Monthly* in 1859 and 1862, marking a new era of popularity in photography for the burgeoning American consumer market. Besides his endorsement of the medium, Holmes made two other significant contributions to the world of stereographs: he coined the word "stereograph," and he invented the mass-produced handheld viewer.

There were notable distinctions in Holmes's new viewer. His stereoscope design had a hood that fit around the eyes—for comfort in holding it up to the face while viewing—and a handle to balance the instrument. Because the stereograph was placed in front of the lenses and not enclosed, it received more light and was easier to see than in the Brewster viewer. Holmes tried to find someone to manufacture his invention in Boston, then Philadelphia and New York. He found no one interested in making the viewer even though he did not want to take any profit from it for himself. Finally in the early 1860s Joseph L. Bates in Boston—to whom Holmes had demonstrated his model—started making Holmes stereoscopes. Bates had a shop where he sold a variety of decorative items, and the Holmes viewers sold well. Bates made a few alterations to Holmes's initial design by adding a sliding cross piece to adjust the focus and also attaching metal card holders to it.[6] The Holmes stereoscopes were significantly cheaper, lighter, and easier to use than the more cumbersome and expensive Brewster models. The handheld viewer substantially expanded interest in stereographs worldwide and pushed the Americans to the forefront as leaders in stereo activity.

STEREO PHOTOGRAPHY

The cameras used to make stereographs were another arena for invention in the nineteenth century. Initially stereographs were made in two ways. After making an exposure, photographers could simply move a camera holding a single plate over the distance of two or three inches (the average distance between the eyes) to expose a second plate from a slightly different angle. Alternatively, two cameras could be carefully placed next to each other to make a pair of negatives. It was, however, difficult to get the exact distance and angle required to make the photographs truly stereo when viewed. In addition, the scene often did not remain static, especially outdoors, and in the time it took to move the camera, there might be, for example, the intrusion of an animal or person into the view. English optician John B. Dancer (1812–1887) worked on a single stereo camera. He is credited with designing perhaps the first practical stereo camera with mounted twin lenses in 1851. His cameras were not produced for public sale, however, until 1856.

Two advancements in photography ensured that paper-print stereographs became by far the most popular format. In England, Frederick Scott Archer (1813–1857) announced the perfection of the collodion or wet-plate process in 1850. In this process, collodion, which is a mixture of guncotton, alcohol, and ether, was used to coat glass plates. The plate was sensitized in a darkroom just before exposure. The negative then had to be developed immediately after exposure. While incredibly cumbersome, having a sharply defined negative from which to

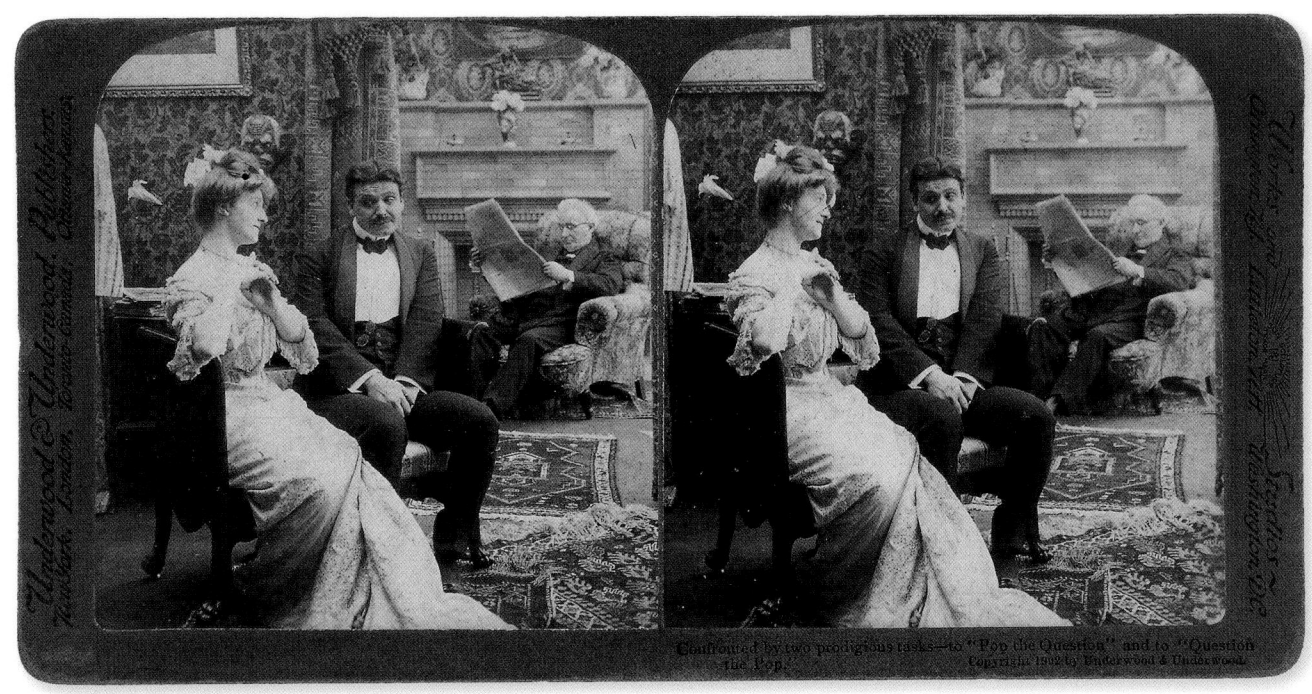

Confronted by two prodigious tasks—to "Pop the Question" and to "Question the Pop."

Copyright 1902 by Underwood & Underwood

Stereograph publishers sold many cards with comedy scenes such as this. The scenes were often part of a small series that told a story.

make prints made the process popular until the advent of dry plates in 1880. At about the same time as Archer's discovery, Frenchman Louis Désiré Blanquart-Evrard (1802–1872) developed the albumen-print process, an improvement over the old calotype process. Prints were made on paper coated with egg whites and sensitized with silver salts. The prints were characterized by their sharp definition and rich, purplish-brown cast. These improvements ensured the success of the paper stereograph in dominating the commercial scene for years to come and ushered in the golden age of stereoscopic photography.

The aesthetic quality of a stereograph depended in great part upon the eye and skill of the cameraman. The subject, angle, lighting, distance, and framing were all up to his interpretation and creativity. The advent of the wet-plate process, even as cumbersome as it was, gave the photographer much more flexibility than before in terms of mobility and thus also in subject matter. Finished views were ultimately distributed by publishers, and sometimes the publisher and the photographer were one and the same. More often, though, especially as stereographs gained popularity, publishers hired photographers to make views or bought views made by photographers out in the field. In addition to obtaining stereo negatives from professionals, publishers also purchased them from itinerant photographers and amateurs.[7]

Initially photographers made the same type of views as had daguerreotypists—that is, portraits, statues, and other still lifes. As they recognized the potential for more diverse subject matter, however, photographers began to venture out into the world during the 1850s and thus broadened their field. They then concentrated on five subject areas that appealed to Victorian tastes: architecture, the natural environment, still life, sculpture, and pictorial groups.[8]

The largest number of stereographs made in the early years were scenic views. These romantic views idealized nature with pastoral scenes that mirrored subjects of contemporary landscape painters. Naturally, architecture from tourist spots was popular both in terms of education and as evidence of travel. Classic antiquities of Italy, Greece, and the Middle East were of great interest as were views of European cathedrals, palaces, and government buildings.

Stereographs illustrating sculpture were particularly popular with Victorian patrons because they appreciated the artwork and because they often associated the piece with a particular museum or place. Because photography could now record detail in minutia, photographers sought to copy artistic still-life groupings in pleasing arrangements just as painters had before them.[9] Pictorial groups were also vastly popular, and thousands were made even in the early years. These genre compositions of two or more persons told a story and allowed great potential for creativity. The pictorial-group stereos featured humor, allegory, history, religion, sentiment, and even eroticism. These views could come in the form of a single card, illustrating children at play, for example, or in the form of a series, perhaps showing a couple before and after marriage or featuring satirical scenes illustrating women's rights.

While the popularity of the stereograph was immediate and widespread, another mid-nineteenth-century photographic innovation temporarily stalled its growth. In 1854 André-Adolphe-Eugène Disdéri (1819–1890) patented the carte-de-visite portrait format in France. As the name suggests, the carte de visite was a photograph glued on a mount similar to the size of a calling card. It was inexpensively reproduced and therefore effectively brought an end to the use of the daguerreotype process. The rise of "cardomania" was meteoric, and by 1860 the carte de visite was embraced worldwide. Family and friends exchanged cards, and publishers marketed portrait cards of the famous and other subjects as well. The family album into which these cards were placed became a fixture in every middle-class Victorian parlor, as did the stereoscope and stereo views. In the end, though, the interest level of the stereograph perpetuated its popularity. A family album could be pored over only so often,

whereas a stereograph library illustrating everything from foreign scenes to comedy held continued long-term interest. The fact that stereographs became three-dimensional when viewed through the stereoscope made them additionally appealing.

The stereograph was the world's first visual mass medium, and stereoscopic photographers quickly understood the potential for news coverage. Naturally, war and conflict were among the first newsworthy events to be documented. The camera had been used to a limited degree in the Mexican War (1846–1848), the second Opium War (1856–1860), and the Indian Mutiny (1857–1858). The Crimean War (1853–1856), however, commanded the first intensive photographic scrutiny.

The scale and degree of civilian interest in the American Civil War (1861–1865) and its photographic documentation, however, was unprecedented. In terms of casualties, Civil War battles were the only ones of any large-scale significance ever fought on American soil. More men died as a result than in all other American wars combined. The Civil War has been called the first "living-room" war because of its mass public exposure in a variety of formats such as newspapers, magazines, and stereographs. Most photographs made during the war were individual portraits intended to record the likenesses of soldiers and their families. In addition, stereographs and carte-de-visite portraits of government leaders and officers were also made. Because of the cumbersome equipment, length of exposure time, and dense smoke around the fighting, battle scenes were not recorded. Photographers often were not near the fighting, and the dead were buried within two or three days; actual casualties, therefore, were seldom caught on film. When photographers did record battlefields after the fighting, they did so most often with stereo cameras. Stereographs sold better than the larger views, and a stereo negative could also be printed as a single carte de visite.[10] The first photographs of the war were taken at Fort Sumter by Charleston photographers, and some of these early images were stereographs.[11] Mathew Brady and his studio employees are the best known of the Civil War photographers, and the northern effort was well recorded.

The aftermath of the Civil War and events of the next few decades had a pronounced effect on American life. Reconstruction, political corruption, and financial instability made the late 1860s tumultuous. The South did not economically recover from the war for another fifty years. The panic of 1873 led to an economic depression that lasted for several years and no doubt affected the field of photography. The late 1860s and 1870s, however, was also a period of new growth in the United States, and Americans moved west and began settling territories. In 1869 workers completed the

transcontinental railroad, connecting East Coast consumers with the western states that produced such raw goods as mineral ores and cattle. Photographers documented this new western territory, often traveling with the United States Geological and Geographical Survey and other expeditions, making photographs in a variety of sizes, including stereographs.

The late 1870s brought advancements in photography that vastly improved the ease with which photographers worked and greatly increased their mobility. British physician Richard Leach Maddox (1816–1902) invented what came to be known as gelatin dry plates. These plates were already sensitized and could be carried out in the field without requiring the portable darkroom necessary for wet collodion plates. By 1880 dry plates were being mass-produced and sold commercially. The 1880s saw other innovations that helped bring photography to the masses. Transparent roll film came into use, and George Eastman (1854–1932) introduced the Kodak, the first truly portable handheld camera. These developments opened up photography to amateurs worldwide.

A NEW ERA OF STEREOGRAPHY

The end of the nineteenth century brought rapid technological advancement and social change. As industrialization affected all aspects of American life, the stereograph came into a new era in the 1880s—a period sometimes called the second golden age or renaissance of stereography. New publishers came to the forefront of stereo sales and employed innovative sales techniques.

One of the leading stereo publishers was the Kilburn Brothers firm of Littleton, New Hampshire, which operated from 1865 to 1909 manufacturing large quantities of views in a variety of subject areas. The company's innovative sales and marketing techniques set it apart and led the way for other stereo publishers to follow. Starting in 1879, Kilburn Brothers salesmen aggressively distributed the firm's views throughout New England and beyond. Although there had always been itinerant peddlers in the United States, the Kilburn Brothers approach was novel in terms of modern merchandizing, and it dramatically increased sales.

The largest and most innovative of the late-nineteenth-century firms was Underwood and Underwood. In 1880 the Underwood brothers of Ottawa, Kansas, began distributing views made for other companies. Eventually they produced their own views and had several offices nationwide as well as overseas. By 1901 Underwood and Underwood published 25,000 views a day and made 300,000 stereoscopes a year.[12] The firm was noted for its refinements in door-to-door sales techniques and for creating the boxed stereograph set and the collection of sets known as the Underwood Stereographic Library. Each boxed set featured a group of stereographs—100 views of Italy, for example—and included a map as well as an optional guidebook. The company also sold smaller sets in slipcases that looked like books from the outside.

Other publishers followed Underwood and Underwood's lead. The Keystone View Company, for example, started operating ten years after the Underwoods and rivaled them in scope and production by the turn of the century. Large manufacturers also included B. W. Kilburn, Griffith and Griffith, and the H. C. White Company. In the early twentieth century these five major stereograph publishers eventually had trade lists of more than 10,000 views each—and some significantly more. With their high production levels and advanced sales techniques, they eventually overtook the smaller firms.

The size, color, and mounting of stereographs also evolved over the years. Although some larger formats were occasionally used, the standard-size card was $3^{1}/_{2}$ by 7 inches. Initially the mounts were flat, but by around 1890 most publishers had begun using a curved mount, which was supposed to improve the stereo effect. Publishers printed their own logos on the cards to identify and advertise the source. In addition, they often included one-line titles or specific information about the view on the bottom of the right-side photograph, on the lower-right corner of the mount, or on the back of the card.

Although the cost of stereographs went down as companies used more mass-production techniques, for some the price was still too high. The public's desire for expanded horizons seemed universal, and even those from lower-income families wanted to experience the broader world view and access the information provided by stereographs. Around the turn of the century, publishers began producing lithoprint stereographs, a new, cheaper way to make stereos. Whereas traditional stereos featured actual photographs mounted on cards, lithoprint views were made by photomechanically reproducing the stereo images and printing them directly on the cards in the form of small color dots. These color-printed stereo cards were not sold by salesmen but were available at such less-expensive retailers as Sears, Roebuck and Company, at drugstores, and at bookstores. They were even given away as premiums in cereal boxes.

During the period from 1890 to 1920 the range of stereograph topics was enormous. The stereograph became a vehicle

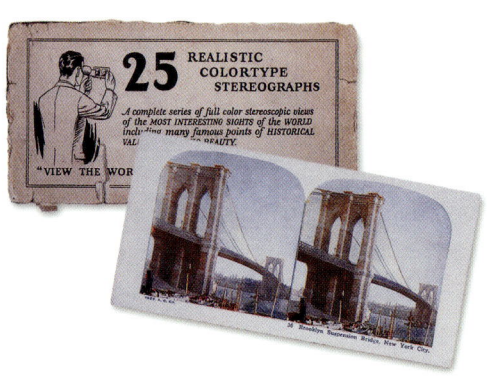

By the early 1900s publishers could produce stereo views cheaply, printing images directly on cards and packaging them for sale.

for the dissemination of knowledge unlike any before. Viewing became a vicarious form of entertainment, education, and travel.

Stereograph publishers continued to focus on the five subject areas established in the Victorian era but expanded into such topics as world agriculture, industry, the environment, and news events. American consumers continued to be fascinated with their own native scenery, especially the western landscape, and with natural disasters and catastrophic newsworthy events. Earthquakes, floods, tornadoes, volcanic eruptions, urban fires, and shipwrecks—along with wars—could now be witnessed firsthand in three-dimensional "reality" from the safety of a parlor. The large boxed sets produced by Underwood and Keystone offered new broad-based, worldwide coverage of such educational subjects as industry and agriculture, natural resources, and native peoples, as well as comprehensive studies of urban scenes, government, and public and commercial buildings. Stereographs of prominent figures and their homes, conventions, parades, sporting events, transportation, resorts, and world exhi-

14

bitions fed public interest, and humorous series foreshadowing television comedies of the twentieth century were popular too. As the first mass-entertainment medium, stereographs covered a range of topics in a manner that was truly encyclopedic.

Other forms of mass communication were on the rise, however. As such alternatives as motion pictures, illustrated magazines, and radio entertainment became available, the quickly changing world these stereograph companies illustrated became accessible in other more immediate mediums. Even the sale of tourist views was affected as postcards began competing with stereographs. With interest in stereographs waning, the Keystone View Company bought out its competitors, and by 1920 Keystone had the stereograph market all to itself. Keystone continued to sell large, educational series to schools, libraries, and individuals into the Great Depression years. In 1939, however, even Keystone stopped producing stereographs for all practical purposes.

Over the years the historical significance of the stereograph has been undervalued. Though many stereo photographers intended their views to serve only as entertainment, they unwittingly recorded an era in pronounced transition. For nearly ninety years the stereograph documented the evolution from the days of horse travel to the modern age of automobiles and airplanes, a time incorporating great industrialization and social change. As the first mass-entertainment and educational medium, the stereograph allowed the public to explore new ideas and see new vistas, bringing to the world a new visual dimension so much taken for granted today.

ANNE E. PETERSON *is a photographic historian living in Dallas, Texas. She received her bachelor's degree in art history from the University of Texas and her master's degree from George Washington University. She serves as curator of photographs at Southern Methodist University's DeGolyer Library, a special-collections library with 400,000 photographs concentrating on the American West and transportation worldwide. She is a former curator of photographs at the Louisiana State Museum in New Orleans and also worked with the Underwood and Underwood Glass Stereograph Collection at the Smithsonian Institution's National Museum of American History.*

Peterson thanks her family—especially Clayton and Nick Westmeier and Barbara and John Chamberlin—and her friends for their sustained interest in her photography projects. For their help with specific questions regarding stereographs, she acknowledges the staff at the Harry Ransom Humanities Research Center at the University of Texas in Austin; the staff at the George Eastman House International Museum of Photography and Film in Rochester, New York; John Dennis, editor of Stereo World*;*

15

John Waldsmith; and Linda McShane. She extends special thanks to her colleagues David Haberstich and Will Stapp for the helpful

exchange of ideas throughout this project, and she also recognizes the support of her coworkers at the DeGolyer Library.

NOTES

1. William C. Darrah, *The World of Stereographs* (Gettysburg, Pa.: Darrah, 1977), 3.

2. Ibid., 3–4.

3. Ibid., 4.

4. Robert Taft, *Photography and the American Scene: A Social History, 1839–1889* (New York: Dover Publications, 1938), 176. The magic lantern was also known as a stereopticon, a term much confused with stereographs and stereoscopes, though it has no relationship to either. Stereopticon slides are really photographic glass transparencies. The stereopticon is merely a device used to enlarge the slides and project them onto a wall or screen.

5. Darrah, *The World of Stereographs*, 23.

6. Paul Wing, *Stereoscopes: The First One Hundred Years* (Nashua, N.H.: Transition Publishing, 1996), 86–89.

7. Taft, *Photography and the American Scene*, 184.

8. Darrah, *The World of Stereographs*, 16.

9. Ibid., 16–19.

10. Martha A. Sandweiss, ed., *Photography in Nineteenth-Century America* (Fort Worth, Tex.: Amon Carter Museum; New York: H. N. Abrams, 1991), 142.

11. Bob Zeller, *The Civil War in Depth: History in 3-D* (San Francisco: Chronicle Books, 1997), 21.

12. Taft, *Photography and the American Scene*, 502–3.

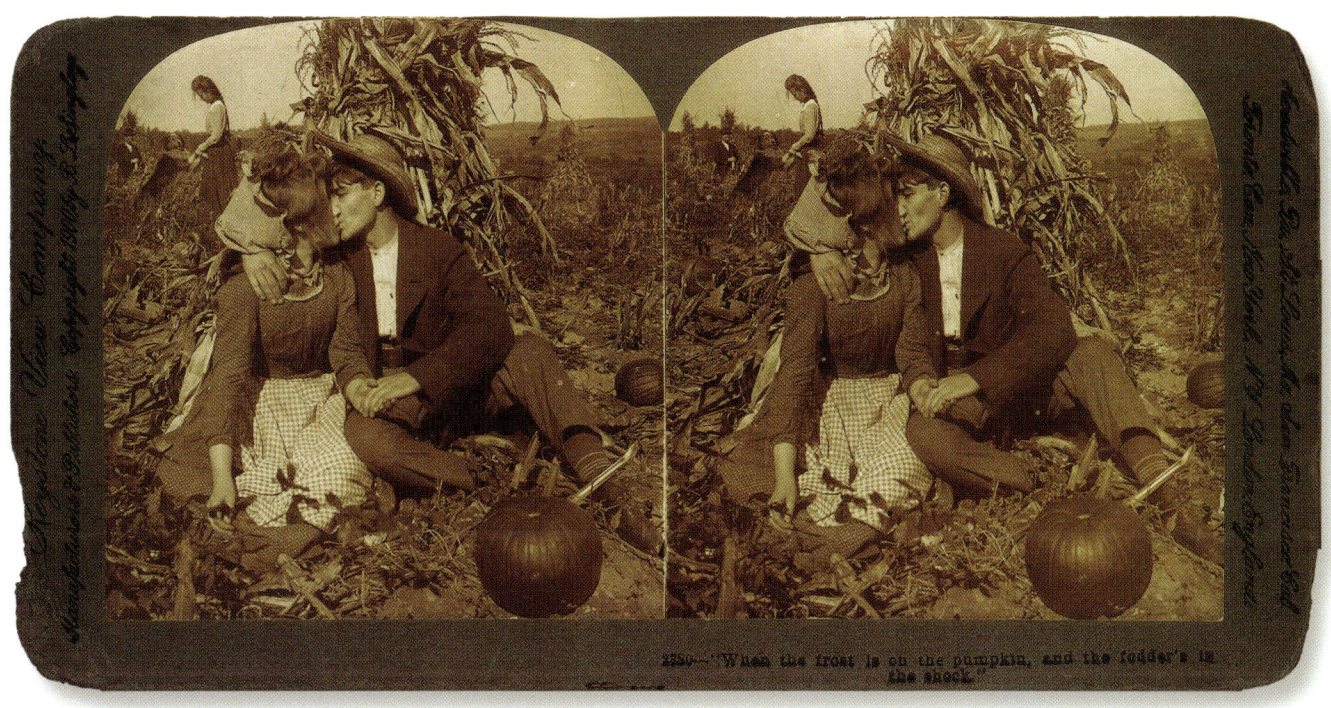

This stereograph, published by the Keystone View Company at the turn of the twentieth century,
features a popular verse by James Whitcomb Riley, the Hoosier Poet.

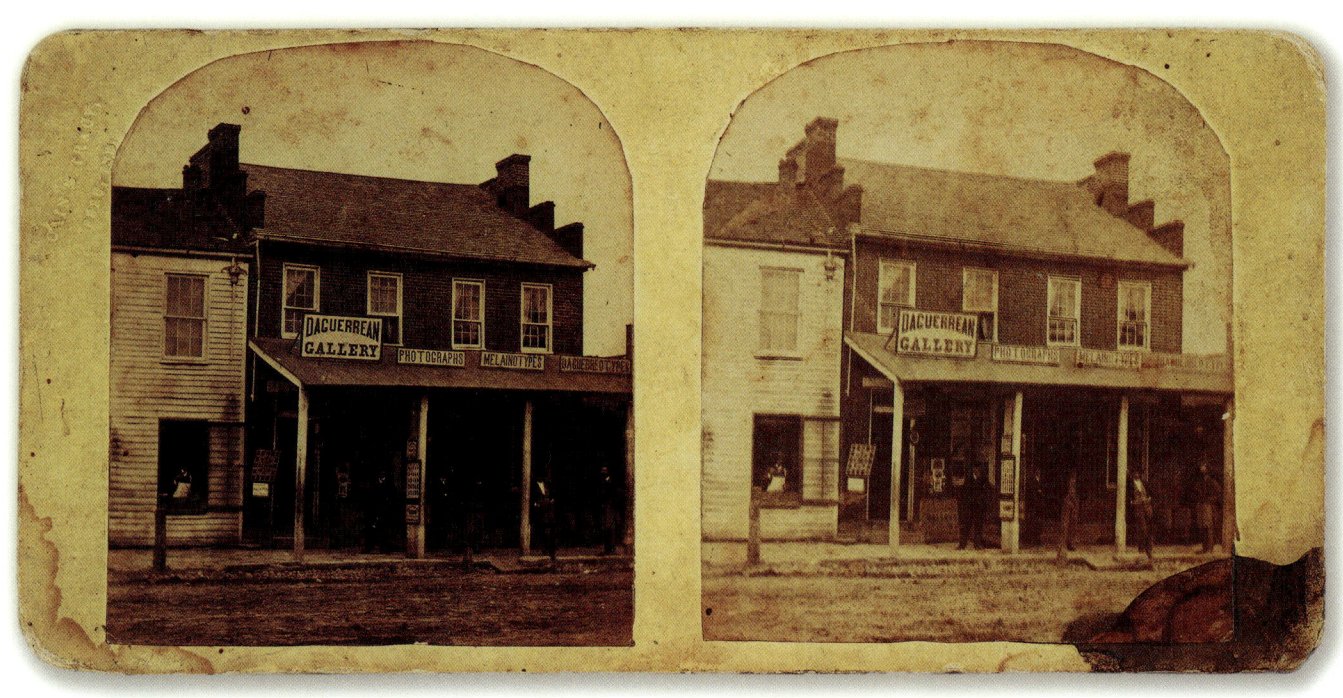

Cain and Tracy's photography studio, Peru, ca. late 1860s. Published by Cain and Tracy.

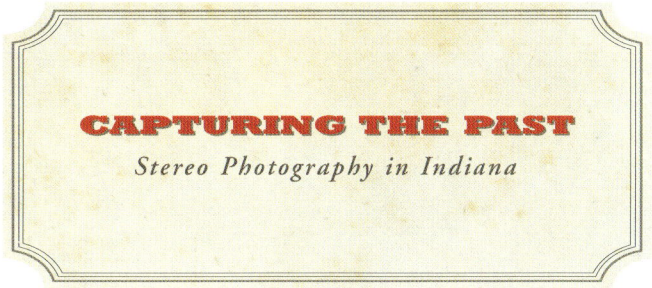

CAPTURING THE PAST
Stereo Photography in Indiana

WHILE STEREO PHOTOGRAPHY DATES TO THE 1840s, THE EARLIEST KNOWN INDIANA STEREOGRAPHS WERE taken in the mid-1860s. The hundreds of images viewed for this project indicate that stereo views were most popular in the state in the 1870s and 1880s. They continued to be made until the 1910s, with a few exceptions up to the 1930s. Photograph curators have noted the relative lack of existing stereo views of Indiana compared to other states. Perhaps the flatness of much of the landscape and lack of natural features such as waterfalls and mountains contributed to this. While images of the landscape do exist, including views of rivers, hills, ponds, and woods, the majority of Indiana stereographs document the built environment. Structures most commonly photographed are public buildings such as courthouses and educational institutions, businesses, houses (usually of the wealthy), churches, and bridges.

Very few Indiana photographers took portraits in the stereo format. When photographed, human subjects are usually secondary to buildings, often standing on front porches or looking over landscapes. Two exceptions, however, are the personal stereo views made by professional photographers and the images taken by amateur photographers. More relaxed and experimental in nature, these works often focus on loved ones. The stereographs at the Indiana Historical Society made by Marquis D. Goodlander, a Muncie photographer, appear to be from his personal collection. Among these are views of his wife and young daughter. Some of Goodlander's handwritten notes indicate that his family members may have been frequent subjects as he experimented with new techniques.

JOAN E. HOSTETLER

Stereo photographers documented numerous events and celebrations. In particular, Charles B. Ingraham captured newsworthy downtown Indianapolis activities, giving us a rare glimpse of life in the 1870s. One view shows a man looking into a large telescope, perhaps to view an eclipse or other celestial event. Another of Ingraham's stereographs, possibly taken from the roof or upper window of his gallery on East Washington Street, shows a crowd viewing the funeral procession of fire chief Daniel Glazier, who died on 11 March 1873 when a wall fell on him as he fought a fire at the Woodburn Sarven Wheel Company. Glazier's funeral cortege was the largest held in the city up to that time.[1] Other gatherings captured in stereo views include carnivals and street fairs, parades, and political rallies.

Small towns often could not support a full-time photo gallery, so photographers in communities across Indiana often relied on a second occupation in order to make a living. Markings on the backs of photographs reveal that they commonly worked as jewelers, silversmiths, dentists, and opticians.

Several Indiana stereo photographers were itinerant practitioners, traveling from town to town in wagons—or "saloons" as they were often called. In the collodion days, when photographic glass plates had to be sensitized directly before use and developed immediately after exposure, a portable darkroom or photo wagon provided mobility for the photographer. The firm of Mote and Swaine, operating in Richmond from 1868 to 1874, was so proud of its wagon that in 1871 the owners sent a photo of the wagon to the magazine the *Photographer's Friend*, which noted that "Messrs. Swain & Mote . . . send us a picture of the branch house, which is on wheels, and is a very neat looking photographic car. Evidently they believe if business don't come to them they go after it."[2] Photographers also used tents as temporary galleries, especially at fairs and in resort areas. In 1883 W. Blanch Ward of Richmond operated from the "Union View Co's Photo Pavillion," a large white tent on the shores of Lake

Setups such as the one seen here offered stereo photographers much-needed flexibility. The photographer could slide the two cameras along the crossbar to achieve an optimal stereo effect based on the distance between the cameras and the subject.

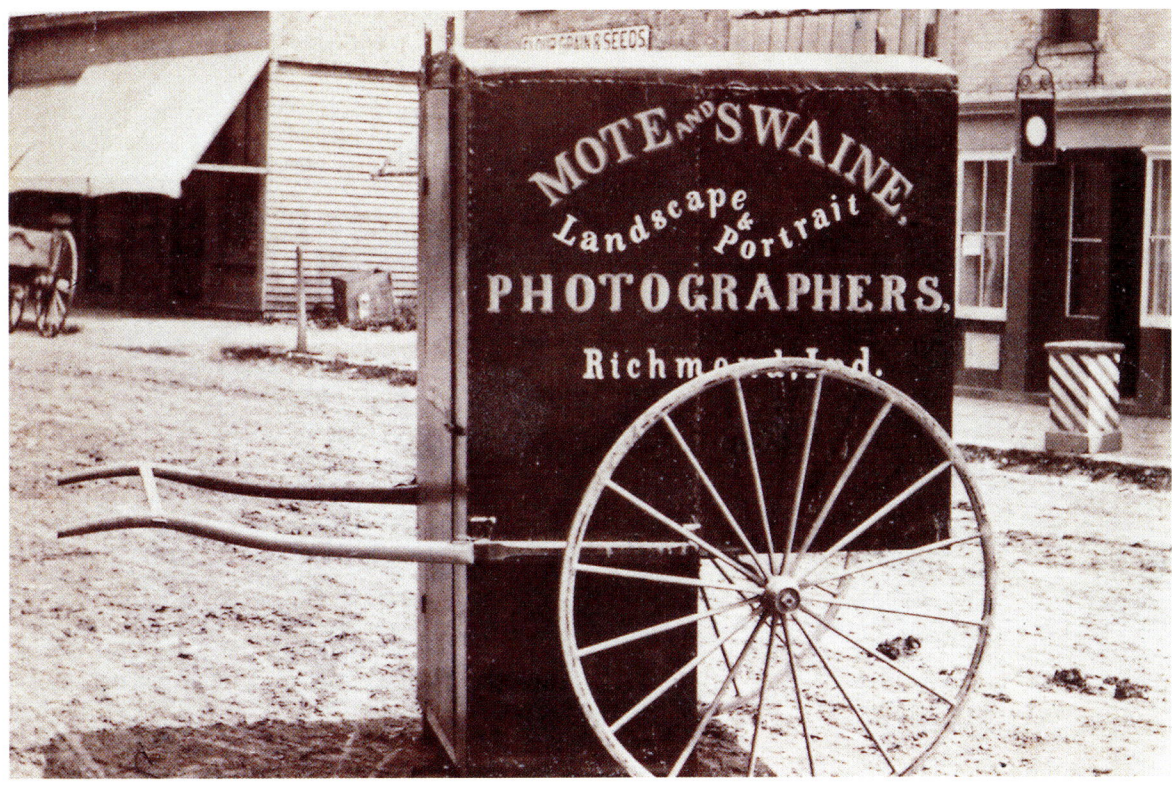

Mote and Swaine's photography wagon, ca. 1871.

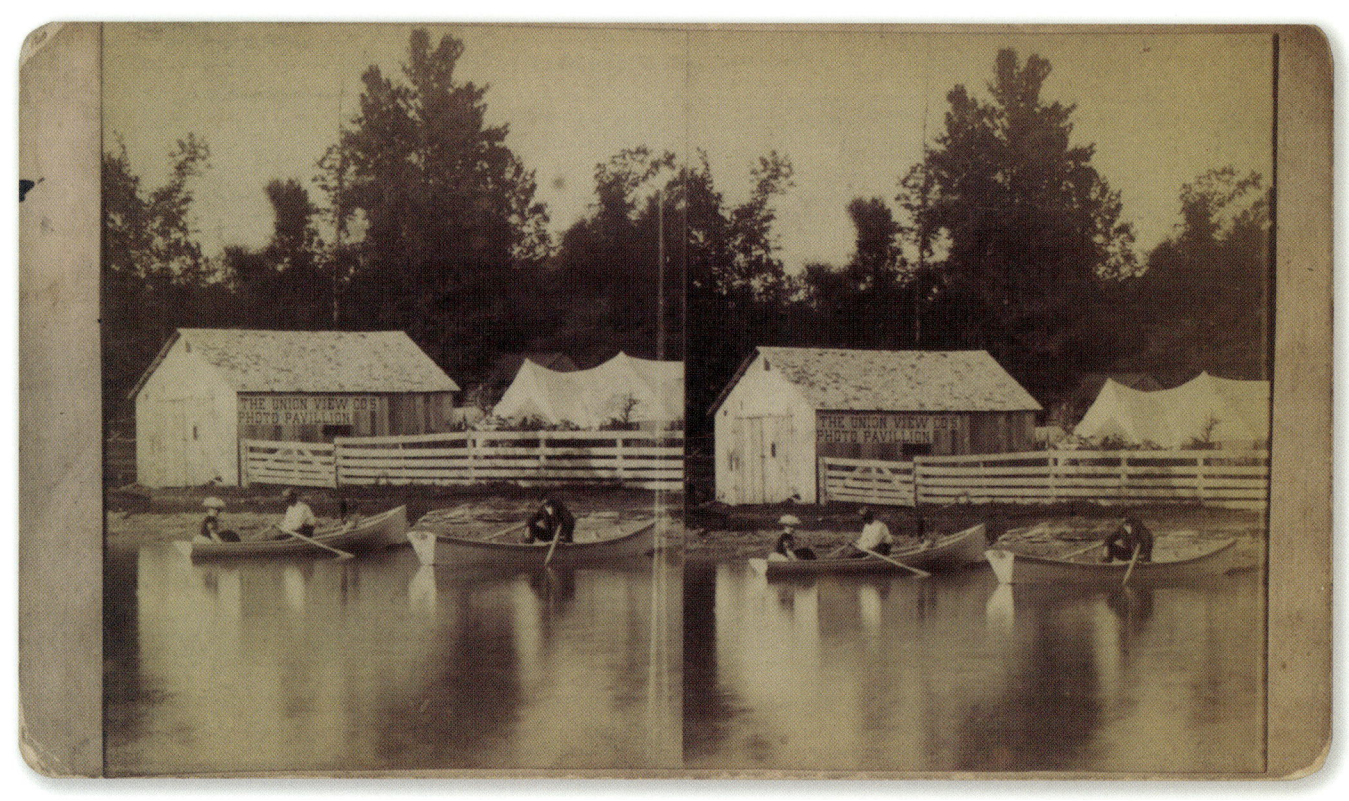

The Union View Company's photo pavilion, Lake Maxinkuckee, 1883. Photographed by W. Blanch Ward.

Maxinkuckee in Culver, and he possibly traveled to other Indiana towns as early as the 1870s. George W. Hissong, a photographer from Lagrange, made stereographs of the activities at Island Park at Sylvan Lake in Noble County for more than ten years. Research has not yet revealed just how far afield Indiana stereo photographers ventured. It is known, however, that at least three photographers traveled quite a distance to make and market their views. In 1880 the *Kokomo Saturday Tribune* reported the activities of the Eureka Photographic Company: "On yesterday, Mr. Harvey Rose, of New Castle, who has been in this city the past week soliciting orders for Stereoscopic Views, called at our office and exhibited proof pictures of several views taken in Crown Point Cemetery. These views are perfect in every particular and are finished in the highest style of the photographer's art."[3]

Stereographers sometimes made views for scientific or documentary purposes. One such photographer was Daniel R. Clark, who operated one of the most successful galleries in Indianapolis from around 1870 to 1887. In 1874 the U.S. government sent Clark to Vladivostok, Siberia, to document the transit of Venus across the face of the sun.[4] While on this trip he also made a series of images titled Clark's Asiatic and Tropical Stereo Views, depicting natives and scenes in Japan and Ceylon (now Sri Lanka). Stereographs were also used for instructional purposes. The library of the Central Indiana Hospital for the Insane in Indianapolis included medical stereographs for use by physicians.

Many photographers learned the profession as apprentices to older photographers, working from several months up to a year. Apprentices often worked as camera operators for a number of galleries before starting their own businesses, and sometimes they bought out older gallery owners. This is likely the case with the firm of Cain and Tracy, which advertised itself as the successor to Harvey G. Fetter in Peru in the late 1860s. Cain and Tracy specialized in home views and street scenes of Peru and vicinity.

Photographers kept up with the latest processes and techniques by reading professional photography magazines such as

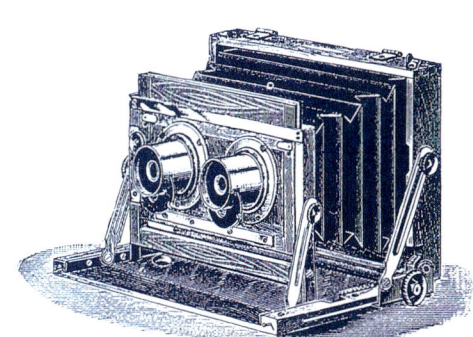

An Underwood stereo camera.

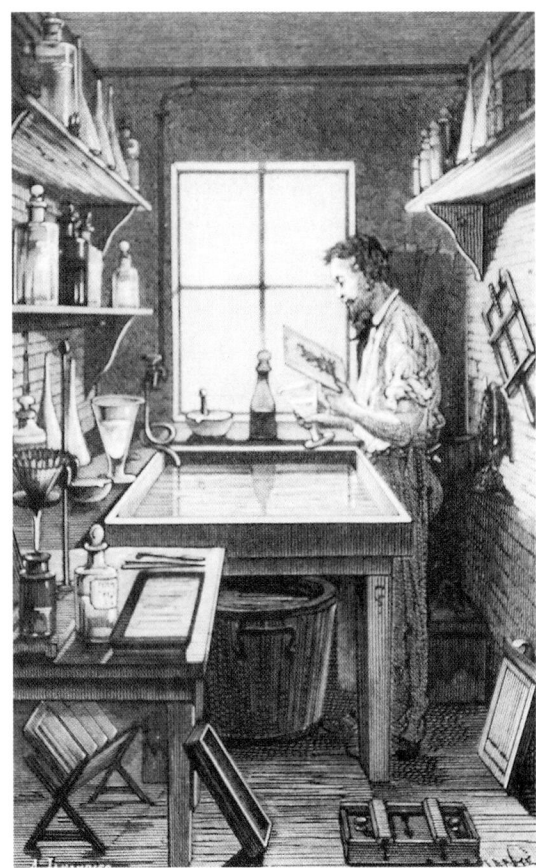

A typical darkroom, circa 1870.

the *Philadelphia Photographer* and the *St. Louis Practical Photographer*, which was particularly popular in the Midwest. Indiana photographers also contributed articles to national publications. One example is Oliver Mulvey's paper on "Stereoscopic Vision without a Stereoscope," published in *Humphrey's Journal of Photography and the Allied Arts and Sciences* in 1862.[5]

Professional conventions sponsored by the National Photographic Association provided an opportunity for photographers to attend sessions on stereo photography, learn about innovations, and view the latest equipment. During the 1870s and 1880s many of the conventions were held in the Midwest. Jacob W. Husher, a photographer from Greencastle, gave a talk on making stereo views at the 1874 convention of the NPA. Meanwhile, the Indiana Photographic Association offered assistance on a more local level. Organized in the early 1870s and comprised mainly of Indianapolis photographers, the group met monthly in members' galleries to discuss business practices, pricing, and techniques.

Few academic institutions taught photography in the nineteenth century. One school that did, however, was the Indiana College of Fine Arts and Photography, located in Wabash. At the school's opening in October 1874, it advertised that it provided facilities for the study of drawing, painting, photography, and allied branches such as optics, chemistry, anatomy, architecture, and landscape gardening.[6] Byron W. McLain served as the school's president. The thirty-year-old Civil War veteran was probably assisted by his wife, Mary Jane, who was listed as a teacher in the 1880 census. Carte-de-visite portraits and stereo views exist with "Indiana College of Fine Arts and Photography," "Indiana College of Photography," and "Byron W. McLain and Co." printed on the back. Stereograph series include the Picturesque Wabash series and the Sunset Route series featuring views of Texas. The Indiana College of Fine Arts and Photography operated through at least 1880.

Women photographers such as Mrs. McLain were common but are difficult to document today. Many wives and children of studio photographers assisted with developing negatives; making prints; mounting, coloring, and retouching photographs; and assisting customers. Surprisingly, owning a photography studio was an acceptable occupation for women because it was considered an artistic endeavor. To date, no known Indiana stereographs are marked with the name of a woman photographer, but several Indiana stereographers were known to have had wives involved with their businesses. A credit report states that Charles B. Ingraham's wife, Ellen M., was an artist and that the couple "carried on the business together."[7] In 1872 the *Indianapolis Evening*

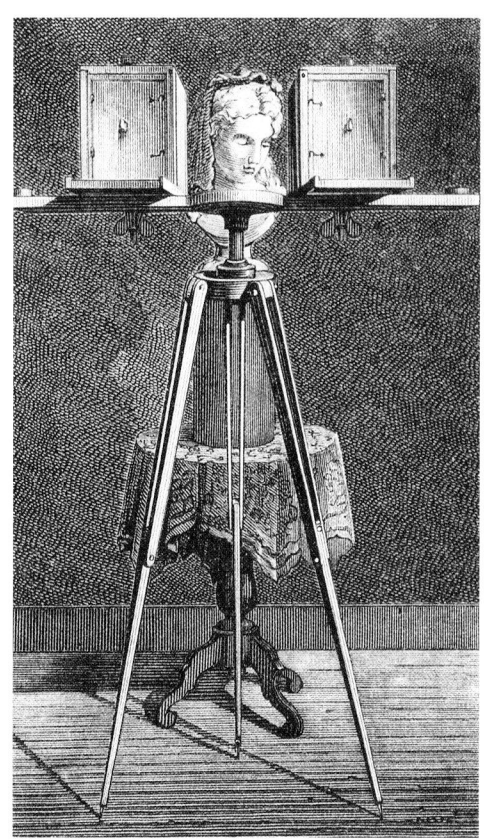

This view shows a stereo camera set up to photograph a sculpture, a common subject for Victorian stereographs.

Journal stated that the painting department at Ingraham and Claflin's Gallery of Art was "in the hands of Mrs. Ingraham whose skill as artist guarantees satisfaction."[8] Charles C. Wright, of the Lafayette firm Wright and Hartwell, most likely received assistance from his wife Sarah Ann (Judkins) Wright, who is listed in various Lafayette city directories as a photographer. Considering she came from a family of photographers, she may have even introduced him to the trade.[9] Children of photographers typically grew up in the business, as was the case with the Goodlander sisters, daughters of Marquis D. Goodlander of Muncie. H. Maude Goodlander and her younger sister Maybelle D. officially joined their father's studio by 1900 and continued operating it under the name Goodlander Sisters until the 1950s. In 1915 Maybelle was elected president of the Women's Federation, a section of the Photographers' Association of America.[10]

Stereographs were sold in a variety of places. Most photograph galleries had a reception room with cases to display the best photographs. Upon its opening in 1886, Louis Moberly's Greensburg gallery was described as a suite of ten rooms. The

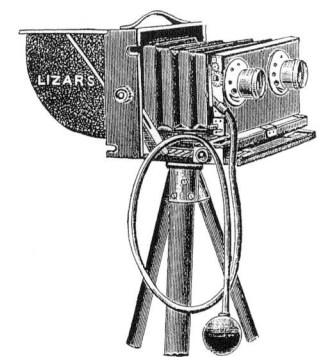

The Lizar's Challenge stereo camera was introduced in the 1890s.

eighteen-by-thirty-eight-foot reception room was floored with Brussels carpet and furnished with settees, a piano, a chandelier, and a fine pier mirror reaching from floor to ceiling. Moberly's latest work was displayed in showcases, including one revolving case that wound up like a clock and ran for twenty-four hours.[11] The idea, of course, was to entice shoppers into the studio with the hopes of selling portraits. Many photographers advertised stereographs of local scenes they had taken, as well as views made by national companies. Bookstores and stationery shops also offered stereo views to the public.

Not all stereographs were made by professional photographers. With the improvements made in photography in the last decades of the nineteenth century, including dry-plate negatives, faster exposure times, and lightweight cameras, many amateurs became photographers and built darkrooms in their homes. One such stereo photographer was Clay H. Tuttle of Hartford City. Tuttle, a shoe salesman, moved to Hartford City in 1895 and eventually owned his own shoe store. Perhaps he was mentored by his father-in-law, Phillip Covault, who had owned a photograph gallery during the Civil

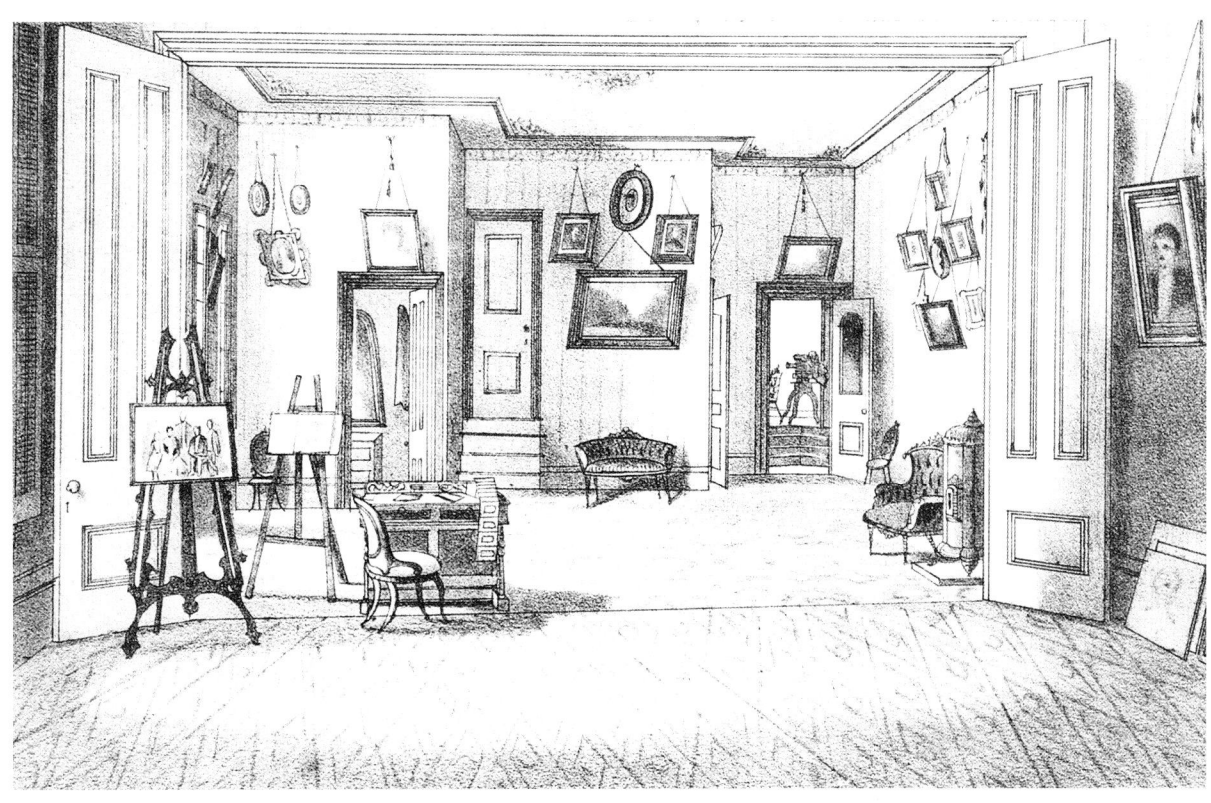

An 1875 atlas of Wabash County included this view of the Indiana College of Fine Arts and Photography.

War. While Tuttle's primary format was the photographic post-card, he made many stereographs between 1909 and 1911. His collection of photographs at the Indiana Historical Society includes fifty-four stereographs of family members, local businesses, Hartford City events, street scenes, and landscapes. He meticulously marked the backs of his images with a rubber stamp with his name and wrote the item number and date. Although Tuttle's obituary does not mention photography as a business, the professional quality of his photographs and the images of nonfamily members might indicate that he also sold stereo views to the public.[12]

Though stereo photography faded quickly after the first few decades of the twentieth century, a number of photographers, both professional and amateur, continue to pursue the art today. In Indiana, Darryl Jones, a professional photographer from Owen County, has taken an active interest in the technique. Jones discusses his stereo photography in an essay in this book and shows some of his contemporary three-dimensional views. Others across the nation also practice the craft, and enthusiasts from all walks of life join together to preserve and promote stereos through organizations such as the National Stereoscopic Association and the Stereoscopic Society of America.

Perhaps this renewed interest in stereographs will call attention to more Indiana stereo photographers and their work. Though stereo views of Indiana are not as common as views of other states, it is clear that many more exist than previously imagined. As this project unfolded, curators found and purchased for the Indiana Historical Society's collections numerous views—many through online auctions. They also discovered private collections of regional images throughout the state. The authors, editors, and others involved with this project hope this book will inspire in readers an appreciation for these documentary images and that as a result even more stereo views of Indiana will become available for the public to enjoy.

JOAN E. HOSTETLER *owns Heritage Photo Services in Indianapolis and serves as coordinator of the Indiana Photographers Project, a directory of photographers who worked in the state from 1841 through 1940. She received an M.F.A. in imaging arts from the Rochester Institute of Technology and a certificate in photograph preservation and archives management from the George Eastman House International Museum of Photography and Film. She worked with visual collections and exhibitions at the Indiana Historical Society from 1986 through 1993.*

NOTES

1. *History of the Indianapolis Fire Department: As Gleaned from All Available Sources, of the History of Indianapolis, and from Fire Department Records* (Indianapolis: Indianapolis Fire Force, 1893), 56–57.

2. *Photographer's Friend*, July 1871, p. 117.

3. *Kokomo Saturday Tribune*, 21 August 1880.

4. *Philadelphia Photographer*, July 1874, p. 213.

5. Oliver Mulvey, "Stereoscopic Vision without a Stereoscope," *Humphrey's Journal of Photography and the Allied Arts and Sciences*, 1 March 1862, pp. 322–25.

6. *Wabash Free Trader*, 18 September 1874.

7. R. G. Dun and Company Collection, Indiana—vol. 67 (Marion County), Baker Library, Harvard Business School, Boston.

8. *Indianapolis Evening Journal*, 1 October 1872.

9. Polly S. Weaver, "The Judkins Photographers," *Judkins Journal,* March and June 1991, p. 36

10. *Muncie Star Press*, 15 July 1996; *Bulletin of Photography*, 28 July 1915, p. 100.

11. *St. Louis Photographer*, June 1886, p. 175.

12. Guide to Clay H. Tuttle Collection (P282), William Henry Smith Memorial Library, Indiana Historical Society, Indianapolis.

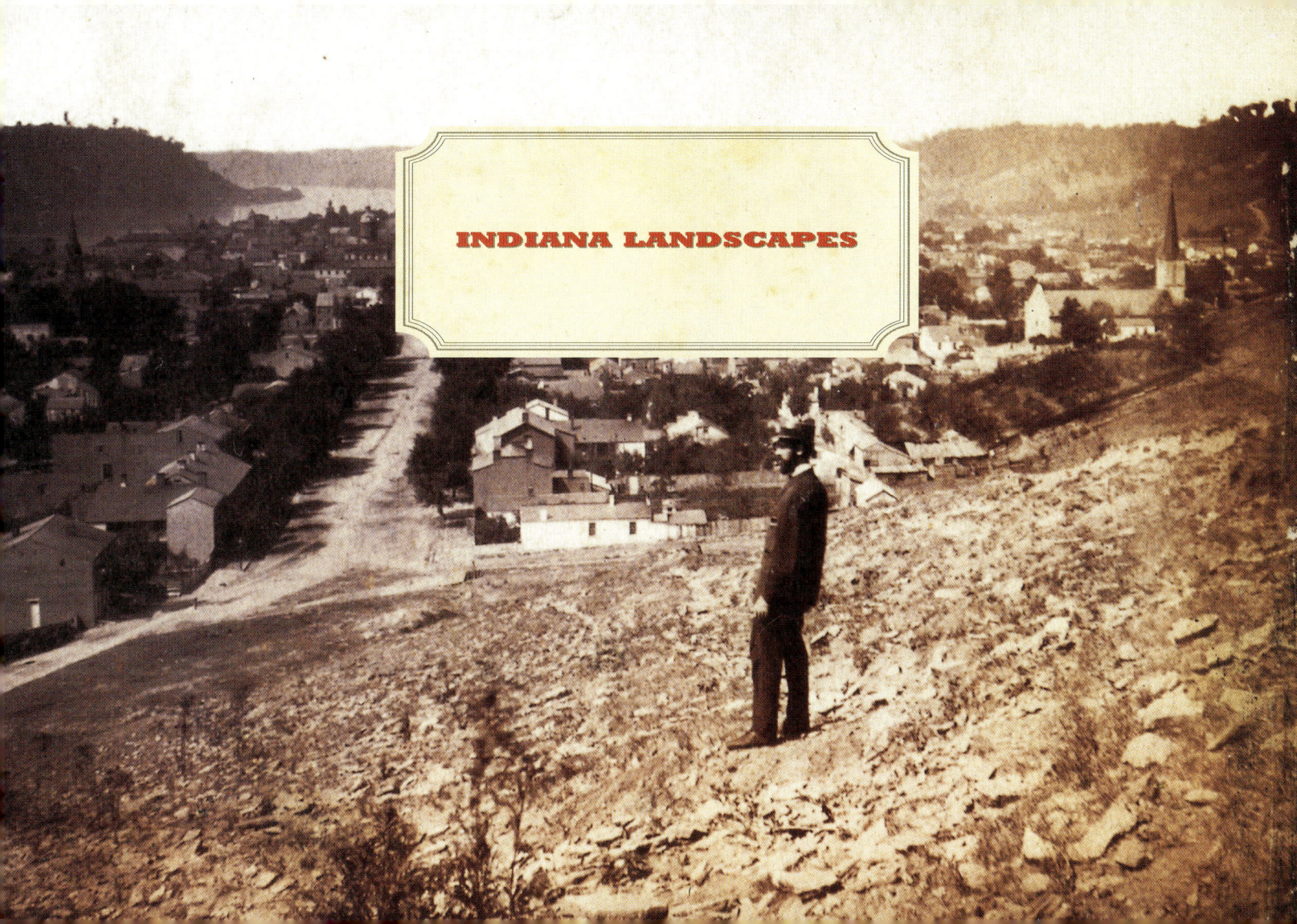

INDIANA LANDSCAPES

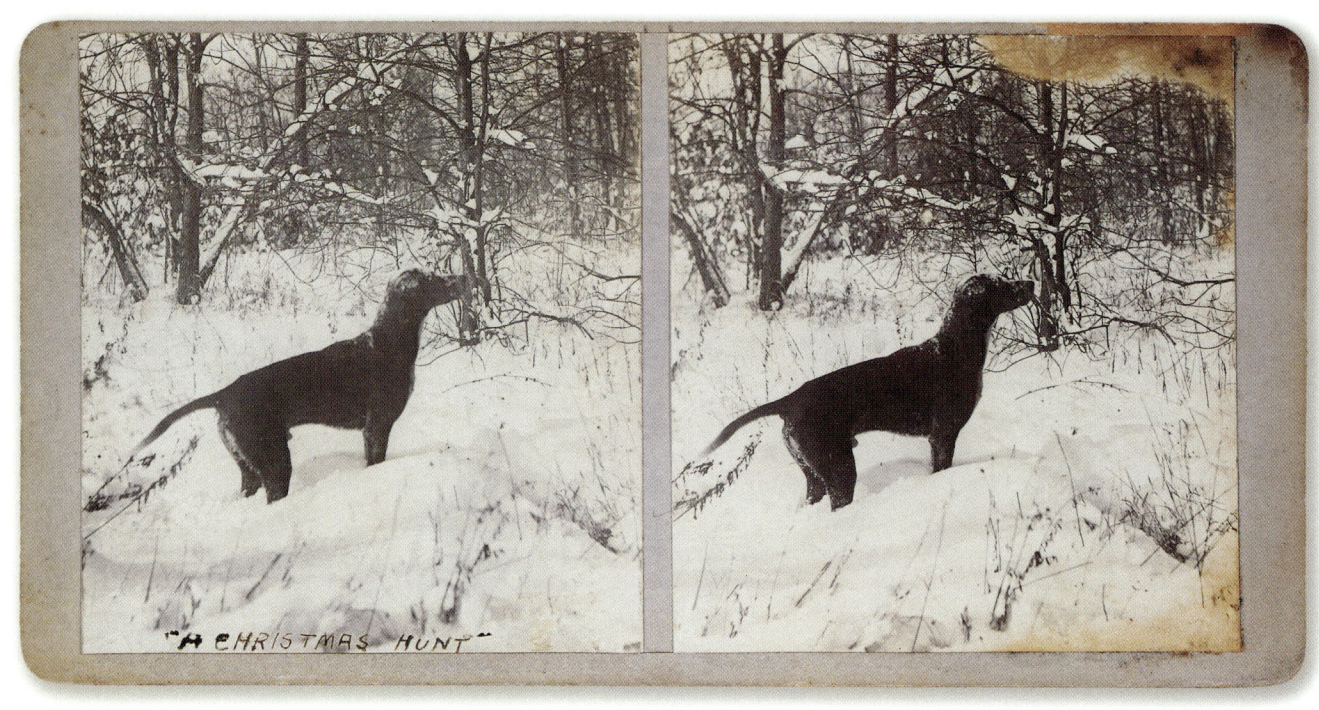

"A CHRISTMAS HUNT"

Dog in the snow, Blackford County, 1910. Photographed by Clay H. Tuttle.

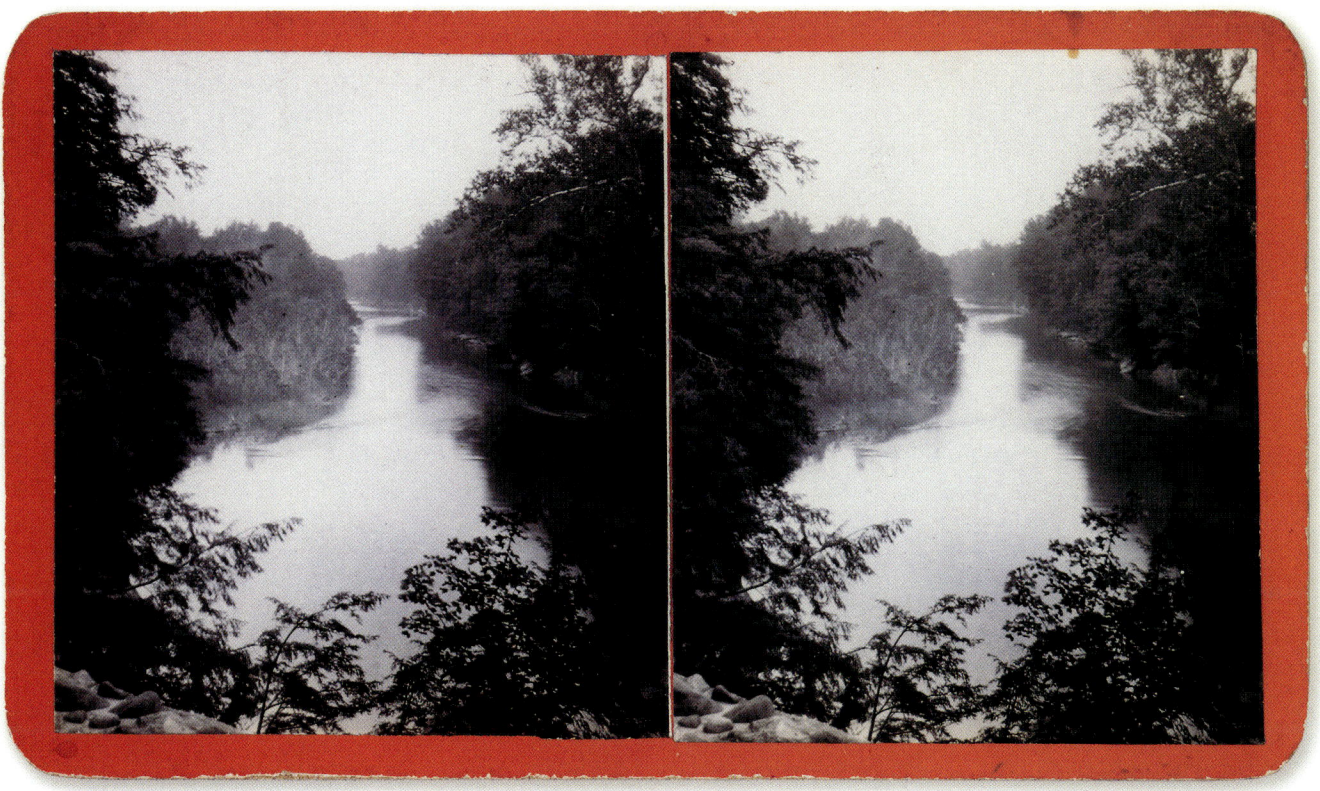

The caption on this card indicates that the scene is a river view at Turkey Run, "looking west from Stoney Point"; it was taken ca. 1880.
Photographed by M. D. Goodlander. Because Goodlander photographed scenes around Madison and Delaware Counties, the view was likely taken there
(perhaps near where the Stony Creek flows into the White River in Madison County) and not at the well-known Turkey Run area of Parke County.

34

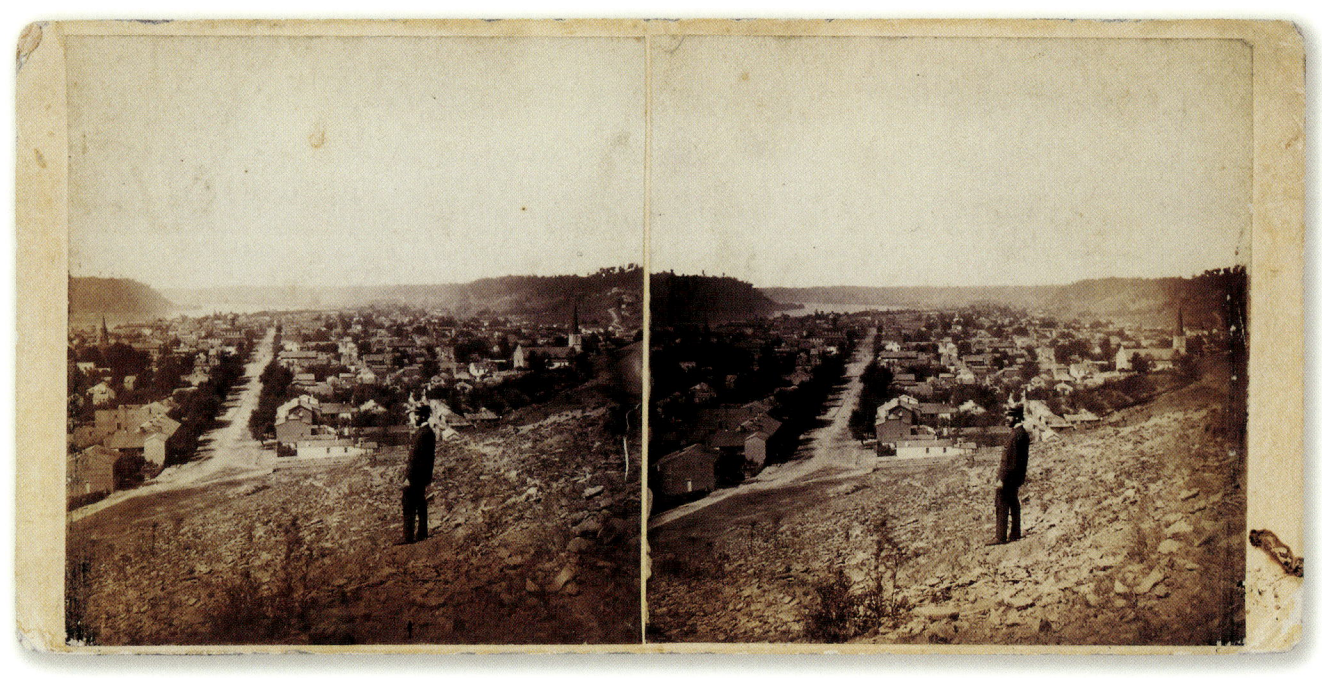

View of Madison, ca. 1870s. Photographed by Joseph Gorgas.
This view looks down Main Street and includes landmarks such as the Jefferson County Courthouse and St. Michael Catholic Church.

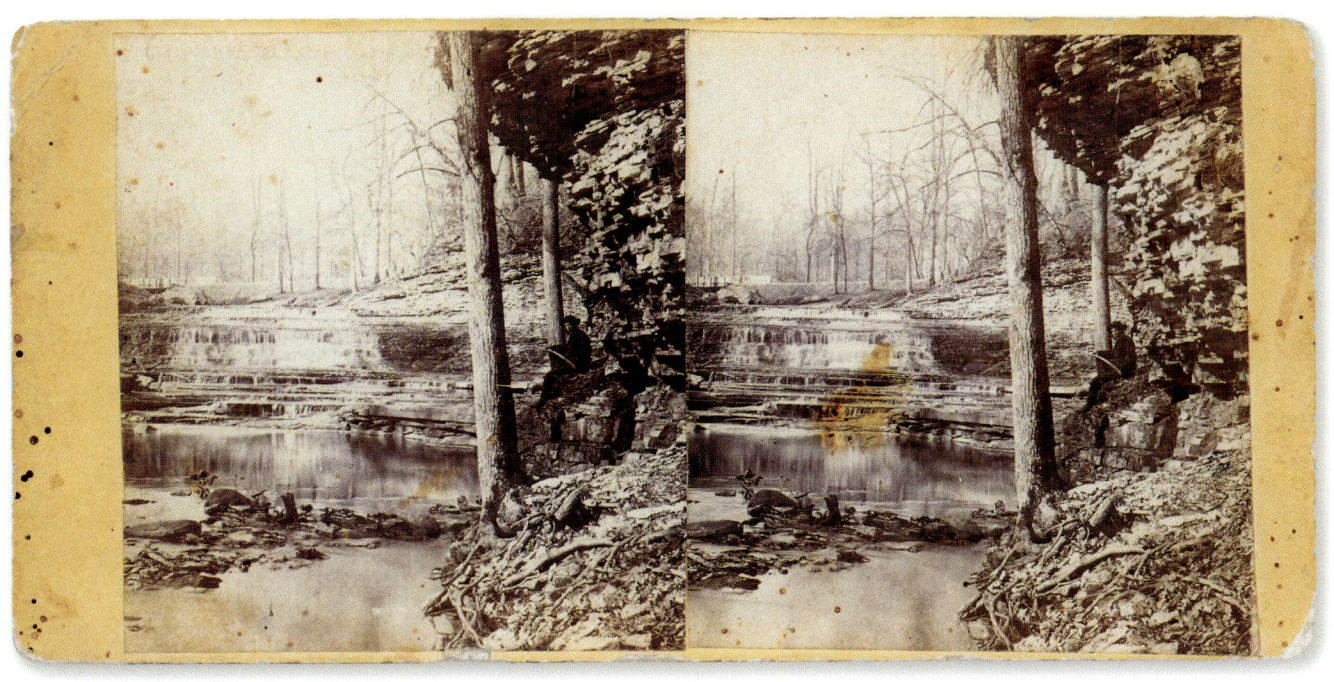

Falls at Pendleton, 1866. Photographed by B. H. Roberts.
This site along Fall Creek was a popular spot for recreation and now is part of a city park.

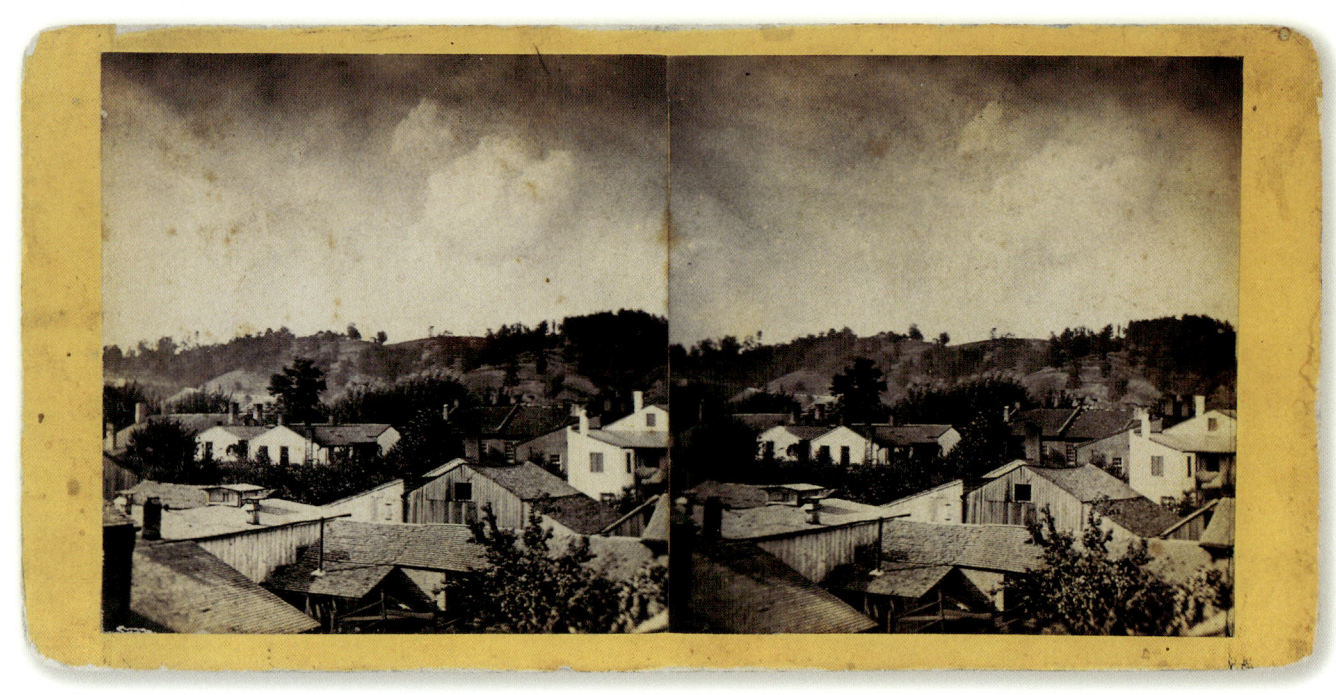

Michigan Hill at Madison, ca. 1870s. Photographed by J. R. Thorne.
This scene was taken near Thorne's photography studio.

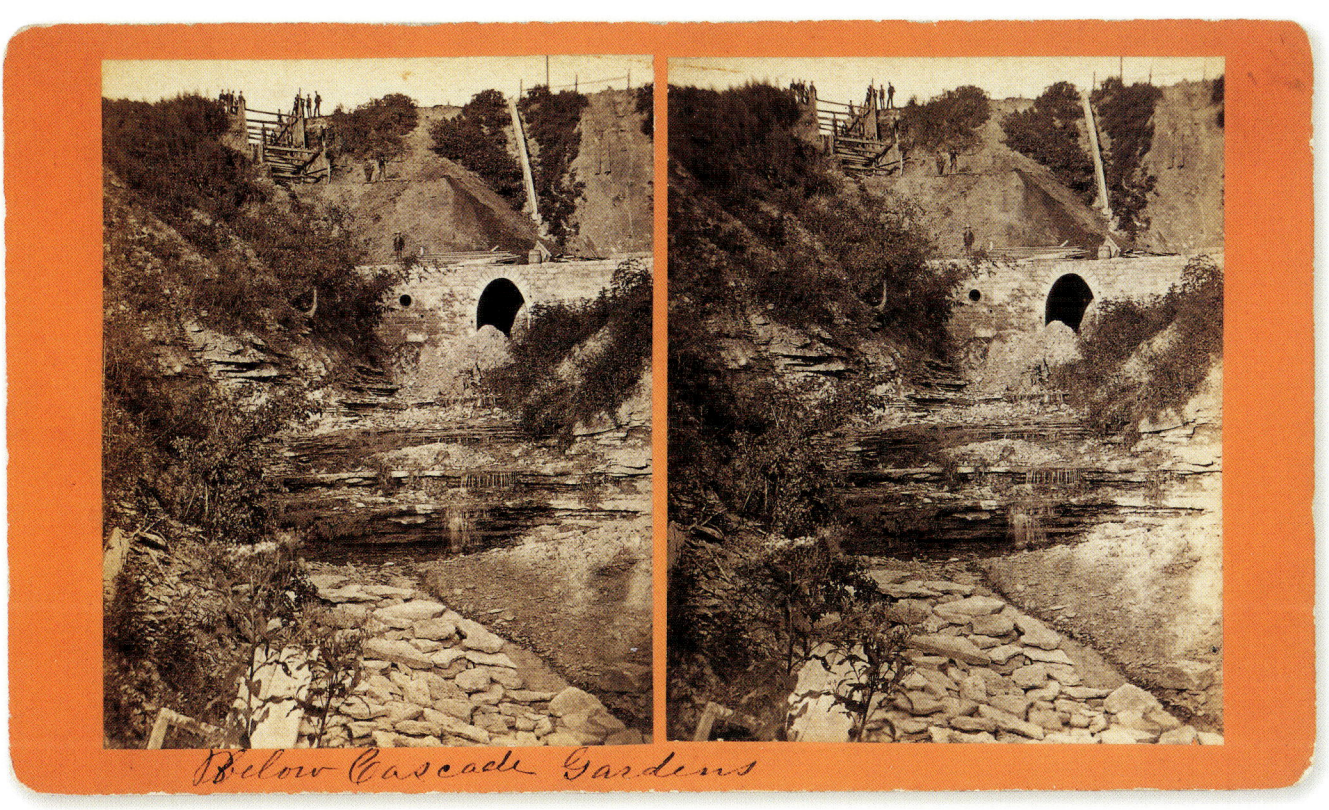

Below Cascade Gardens

View below Cascade Gardens, probably near Richmond, ca. 1870s. Published by Mote Brothers.

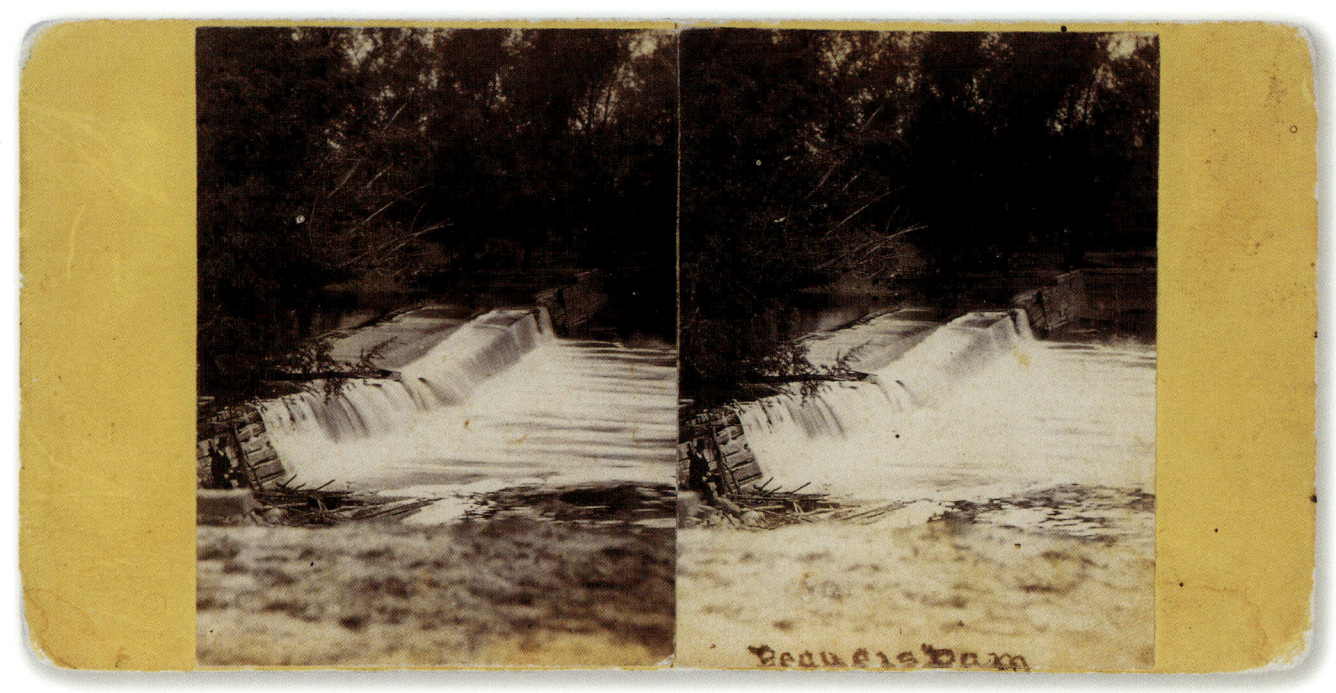

St. Joseph River, Allen County, ca. 1880s. Photographer unknown.

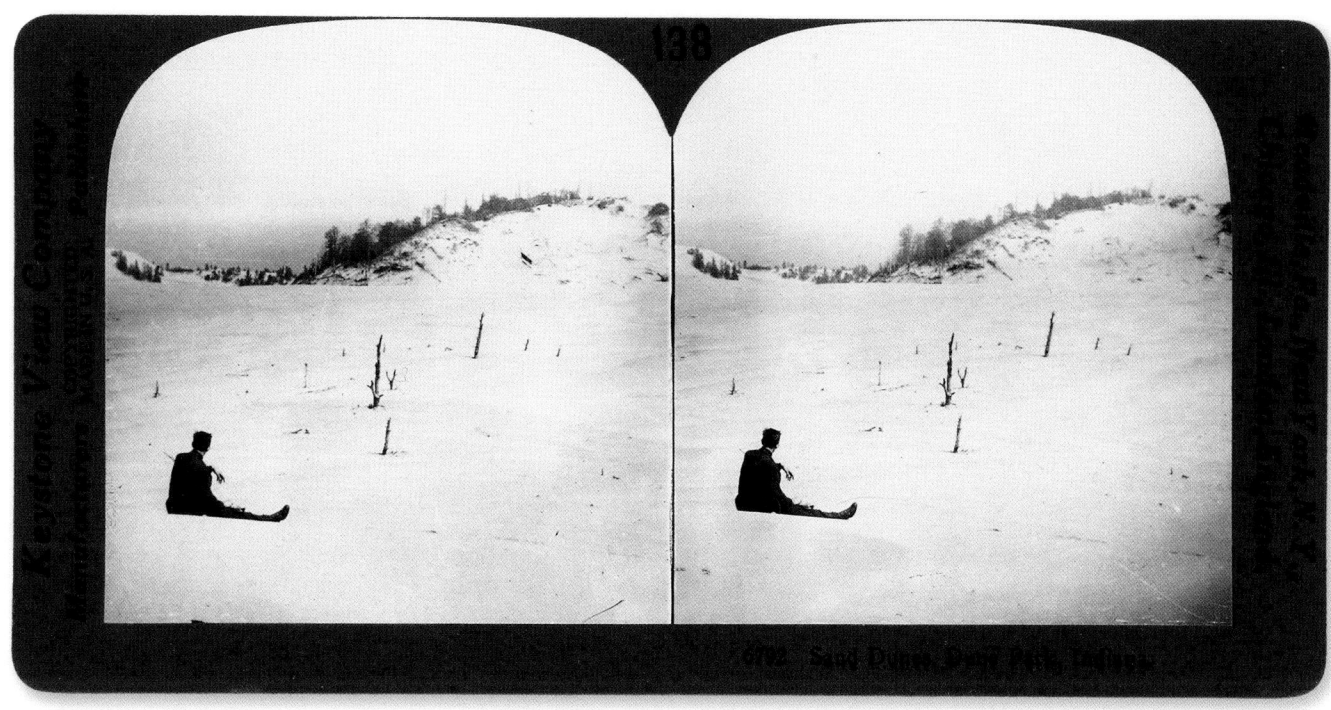

Dunes along Lake Michigan in northwestern Indiana, ca. 1920s. Published by the Keystone View Company.

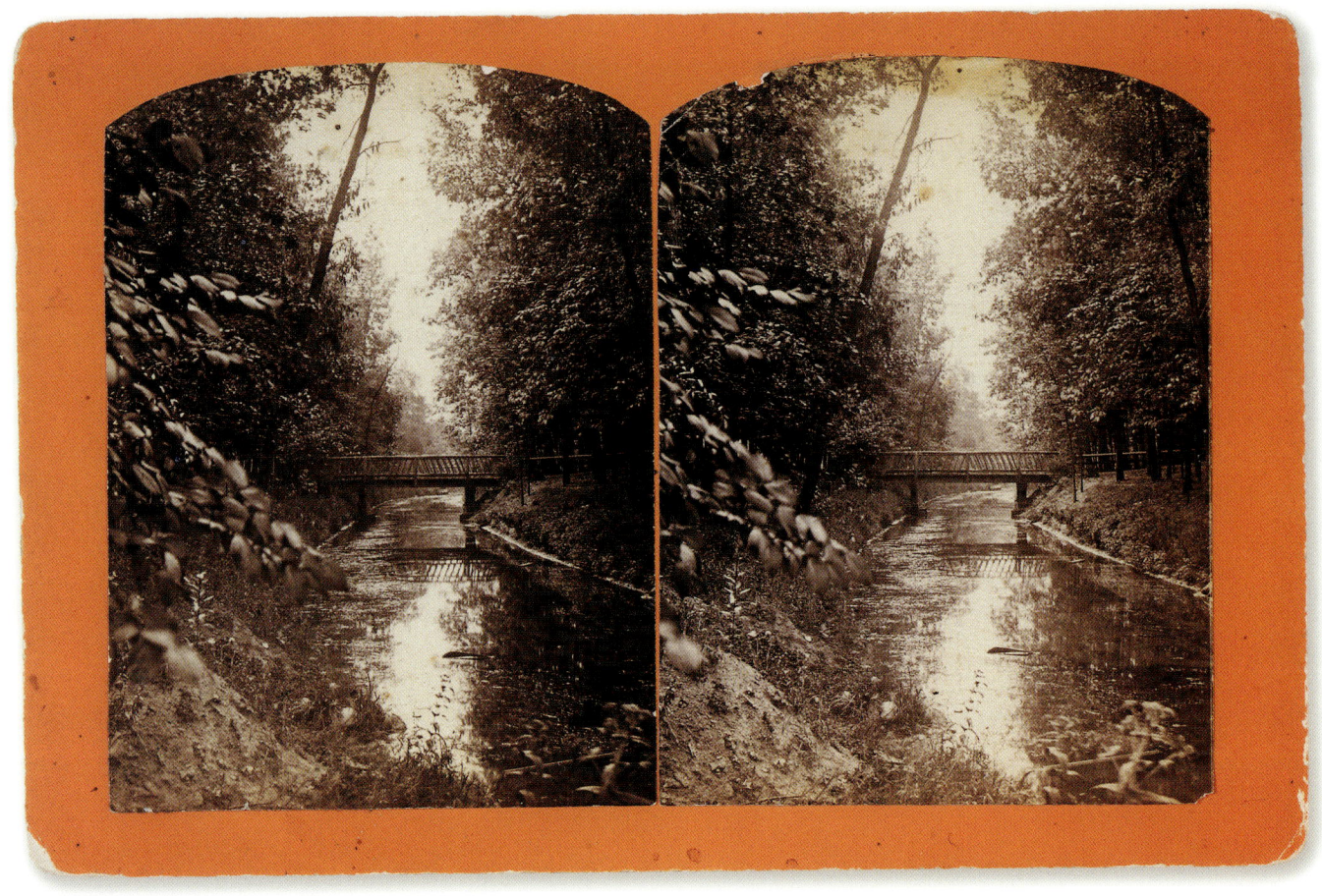

Looking down the canal on Island Park, Noble County, ca. 1880s. Published by Hissong and Son.
Island Park was located off the shores of Sylvan Lake at Rome City. The area was popular with vacationers in the late nineteenth and early twentieth centuries.

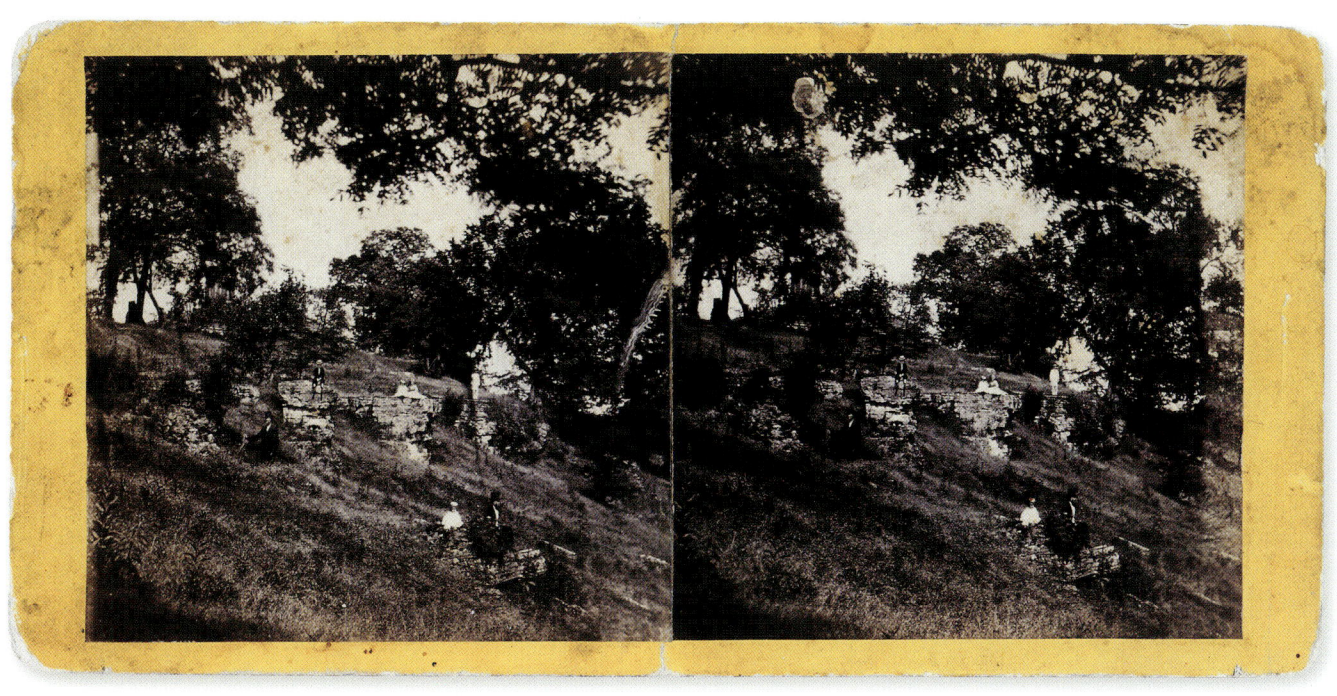

Cliffs by Hanover College, near Madison, ca. 1870s. Photographed by J. R. Thorne.

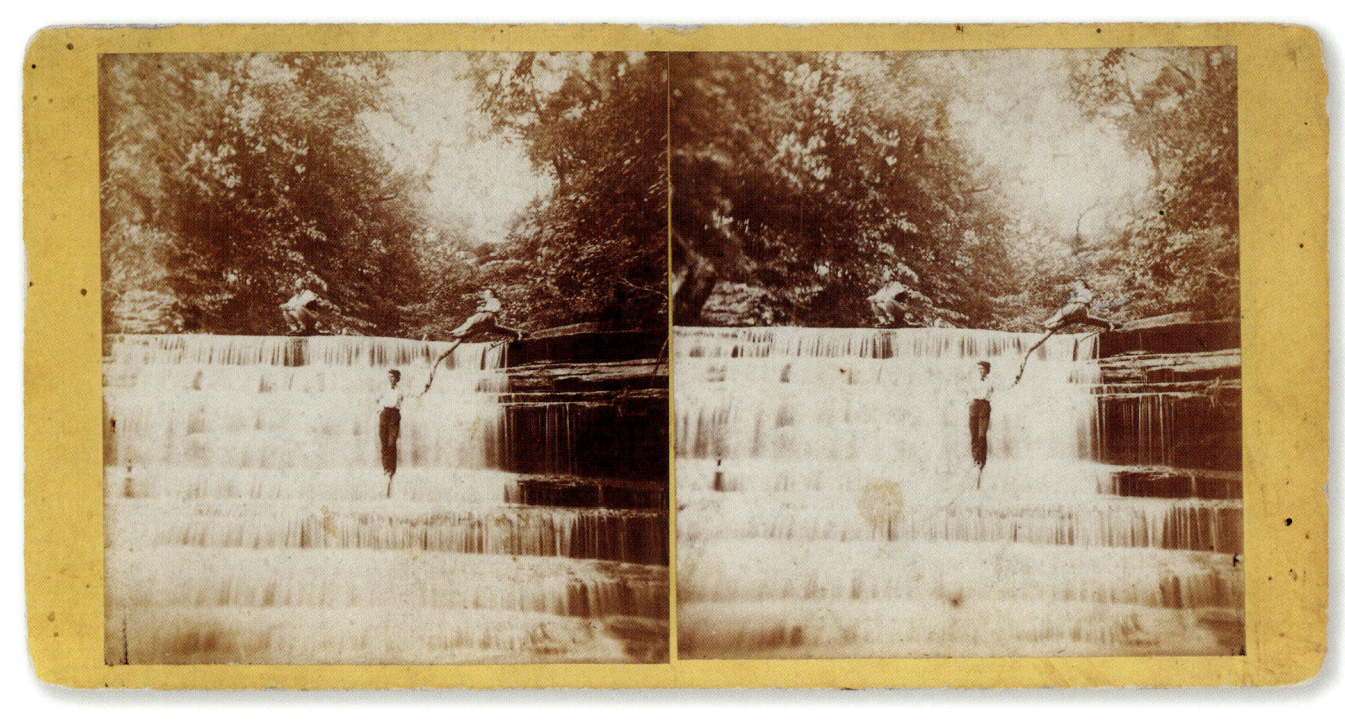

Clifty Falls, near Madison, ca. 1870s. Photographed by J. R. Thorne.

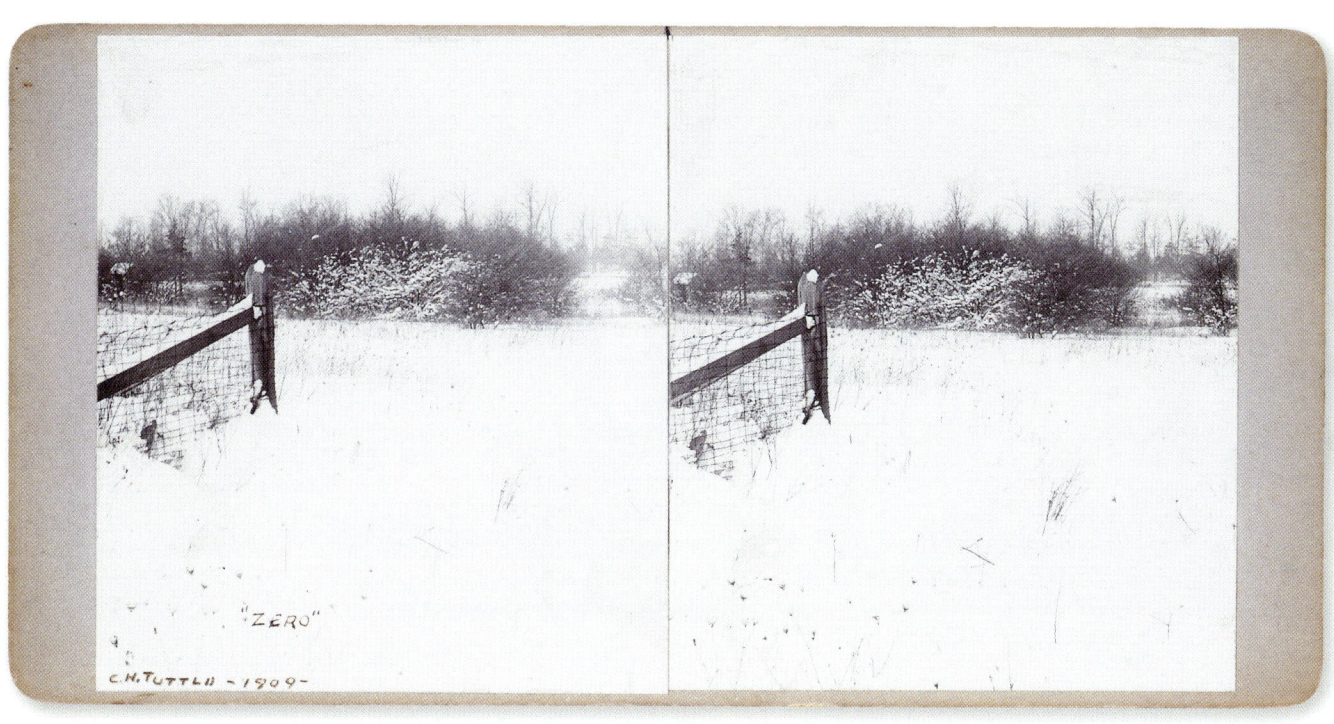

"ZERO"

C.H. TUTTLE - 1909 -

Winter scene, Blackford County, 1909. Photographed by Clay H. Tuttle.

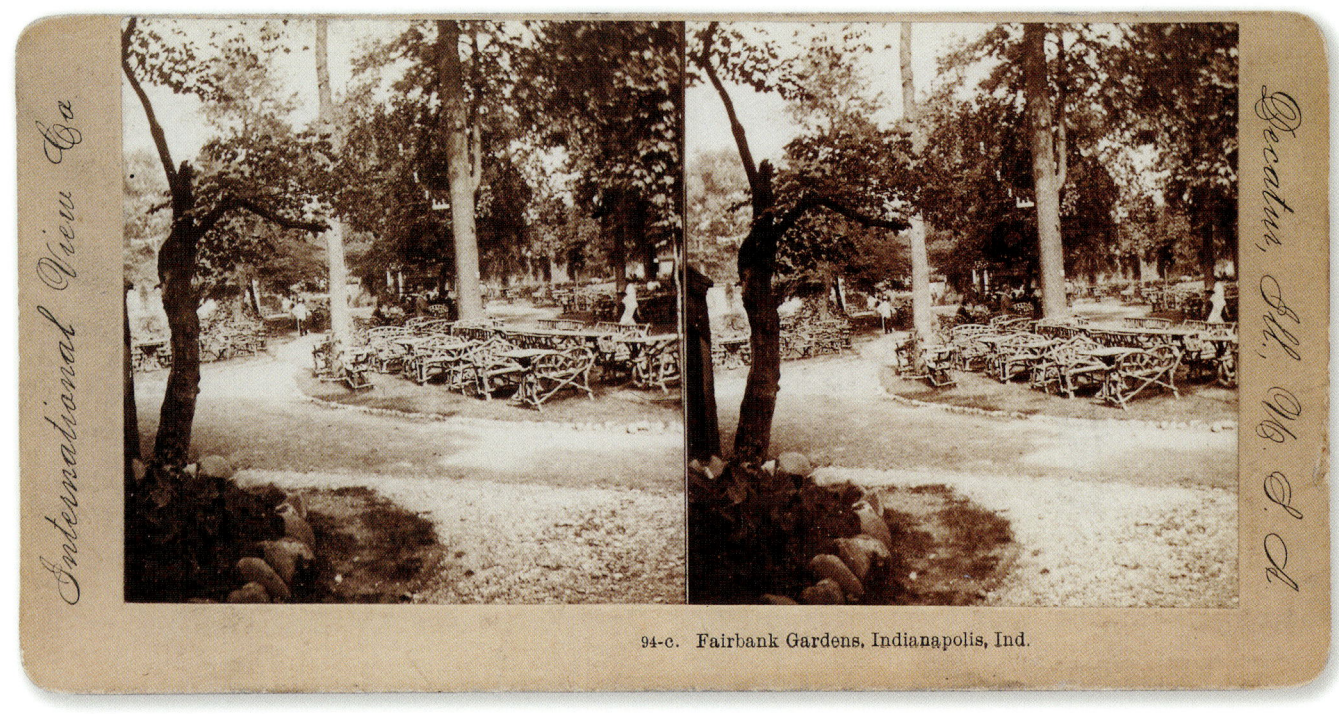

94-c. Fairbank Gardens, Indianapolis, Ind.

Fairbank Gardens, Indianapolis, ca. 1900. Published by the International View Company.
The gardens were located along the banks of Fall Creek at Illinois Street and included exotic plants, fountains, and
the café seen here. St. Vincent Hospital moved to the site in 1913.

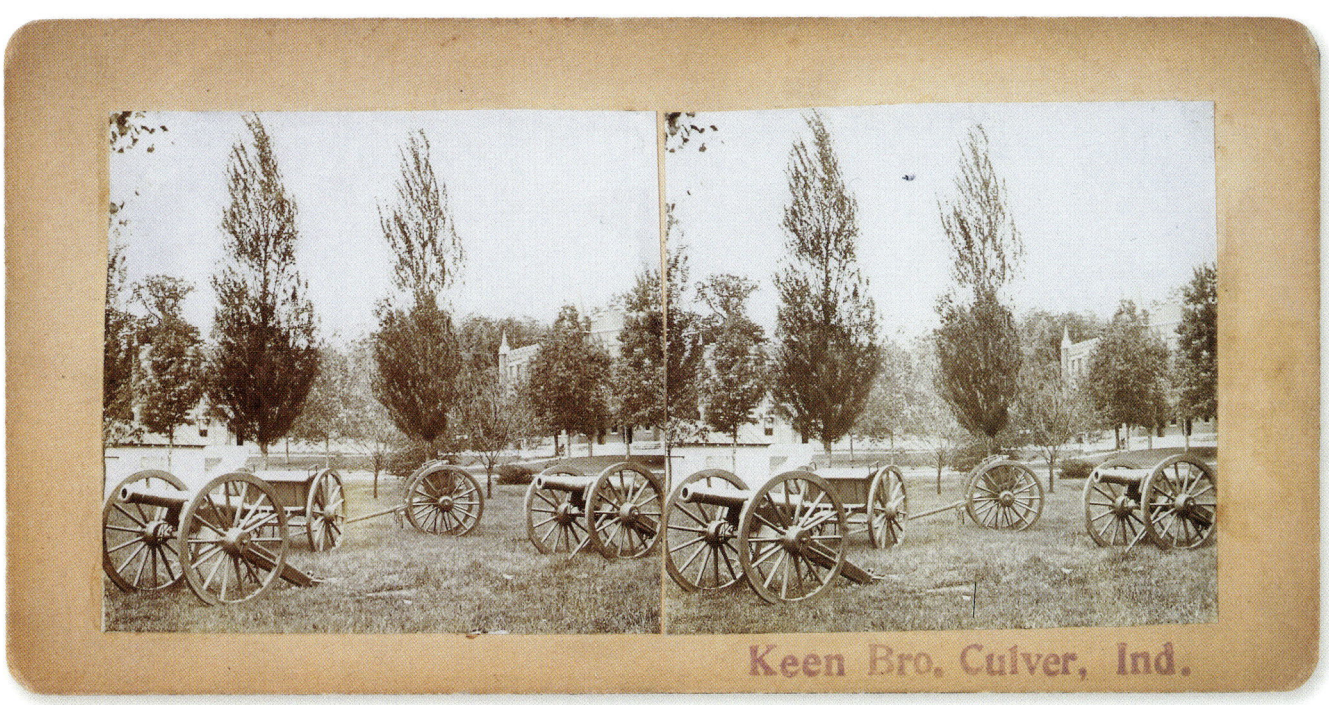

Keen Bro. Culver, Ind.

Culver Military Academy, Culver, ca. 1900. Published by Keen Brothers.
The academy, located on the shores of Lake Maxinkuckee, was founded in 1894 and today is one of the nation's leading prep schools.

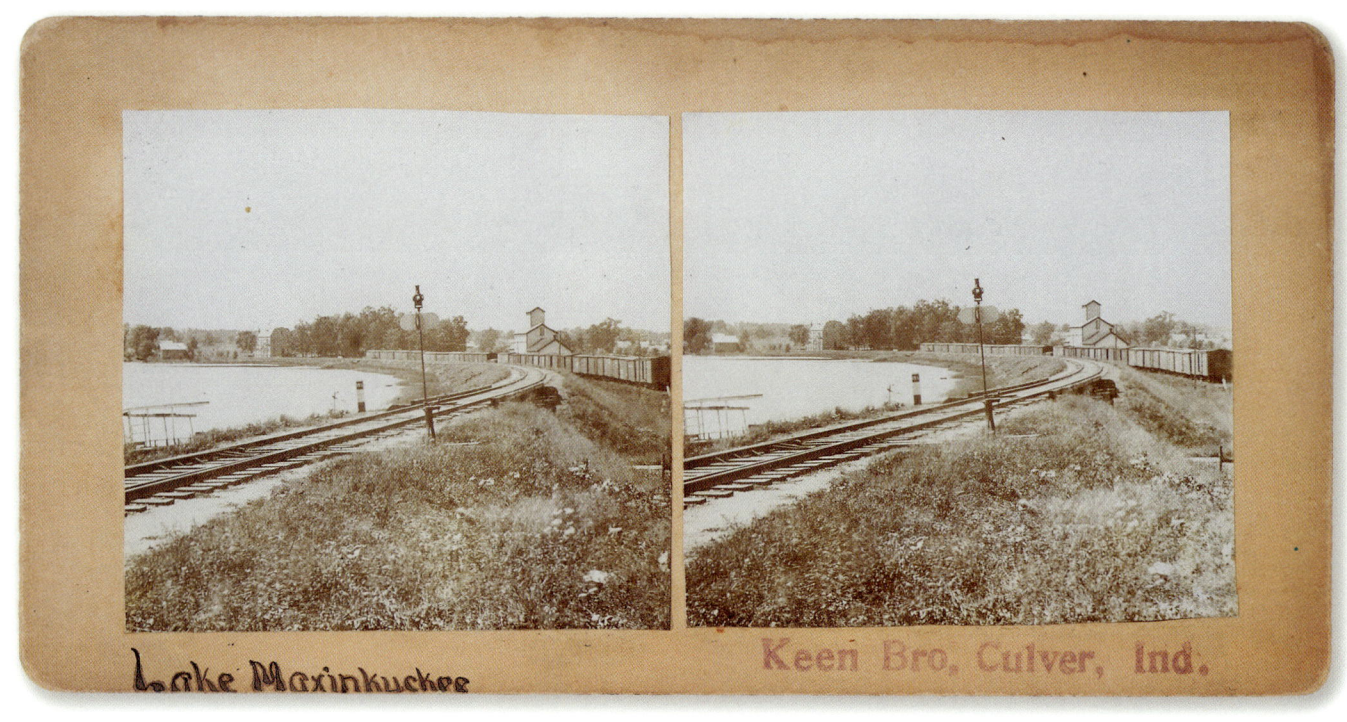

Lake Maxinkuckee, Marshall County, ca. 1900. Published by Keen Brothers.
Lake Maxinkuckee is the second-largest natural lake in Indiana.

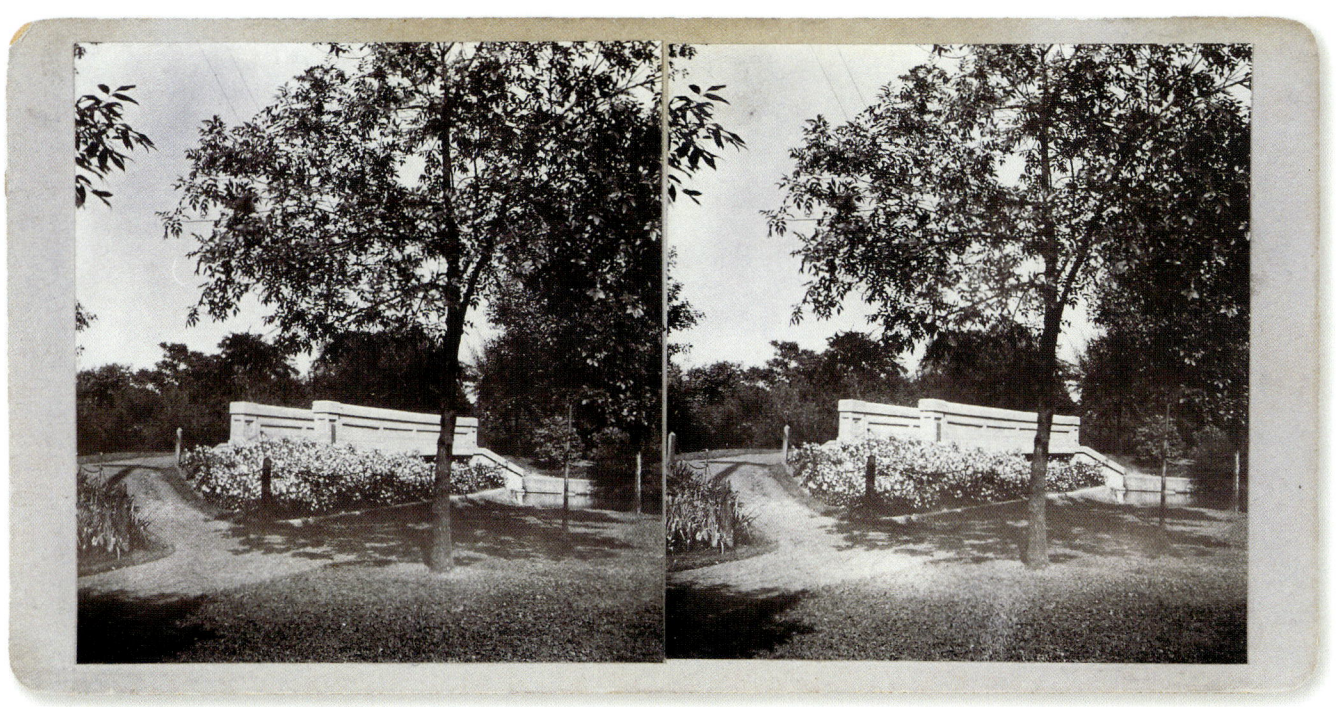

Harrison Park, Hammond, 1928. Photographer unknown.

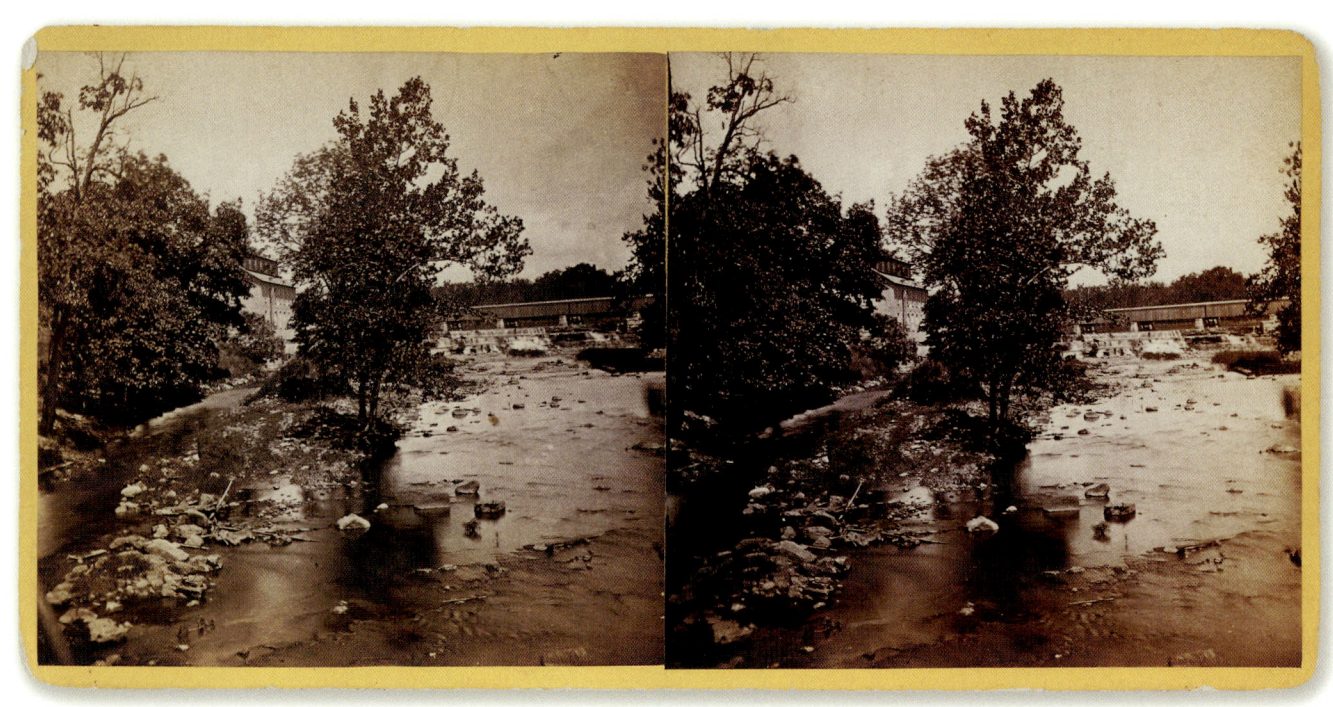

Fall Creek at Pendleton, ca. 1880s. Photographed by M. D. Goodlander.

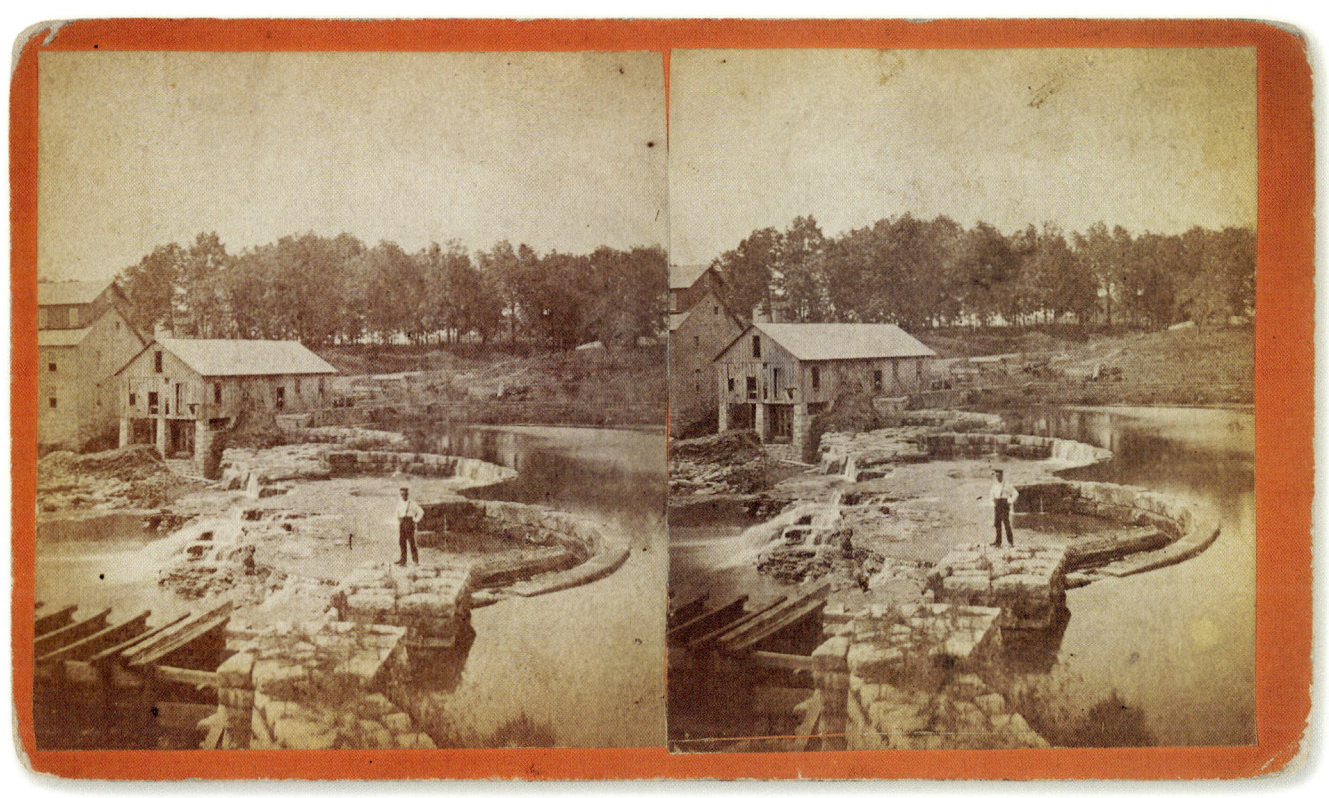

This view was likely taken along Fall Creek at Pendleton and appears to be near the same location as the scene on the opposite page, ca. 1880s. Photographed by M. D. Goodlander.

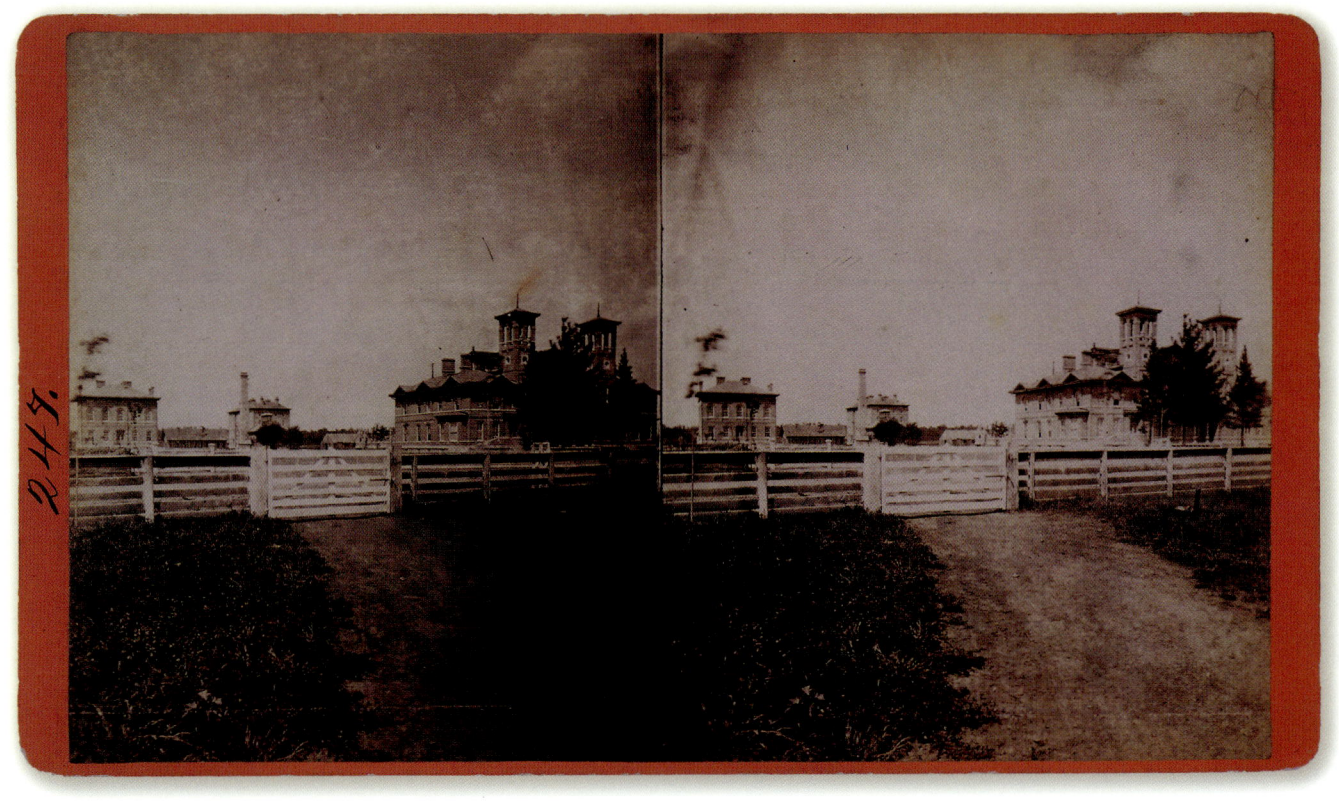

Purdue University, West Lafayette, ca. late 1870s. Published by Wright and Hartwell.
Purdue was one of sixty-eight land-grant colleges established by the Morrill Act of 1862. In 1869 the Indiana General Assembly voted to locate
the college in Tippecanoe County, and five years later it opened to students. Today Purdue is known for its agriculture, engineering, and aeronautics programs.

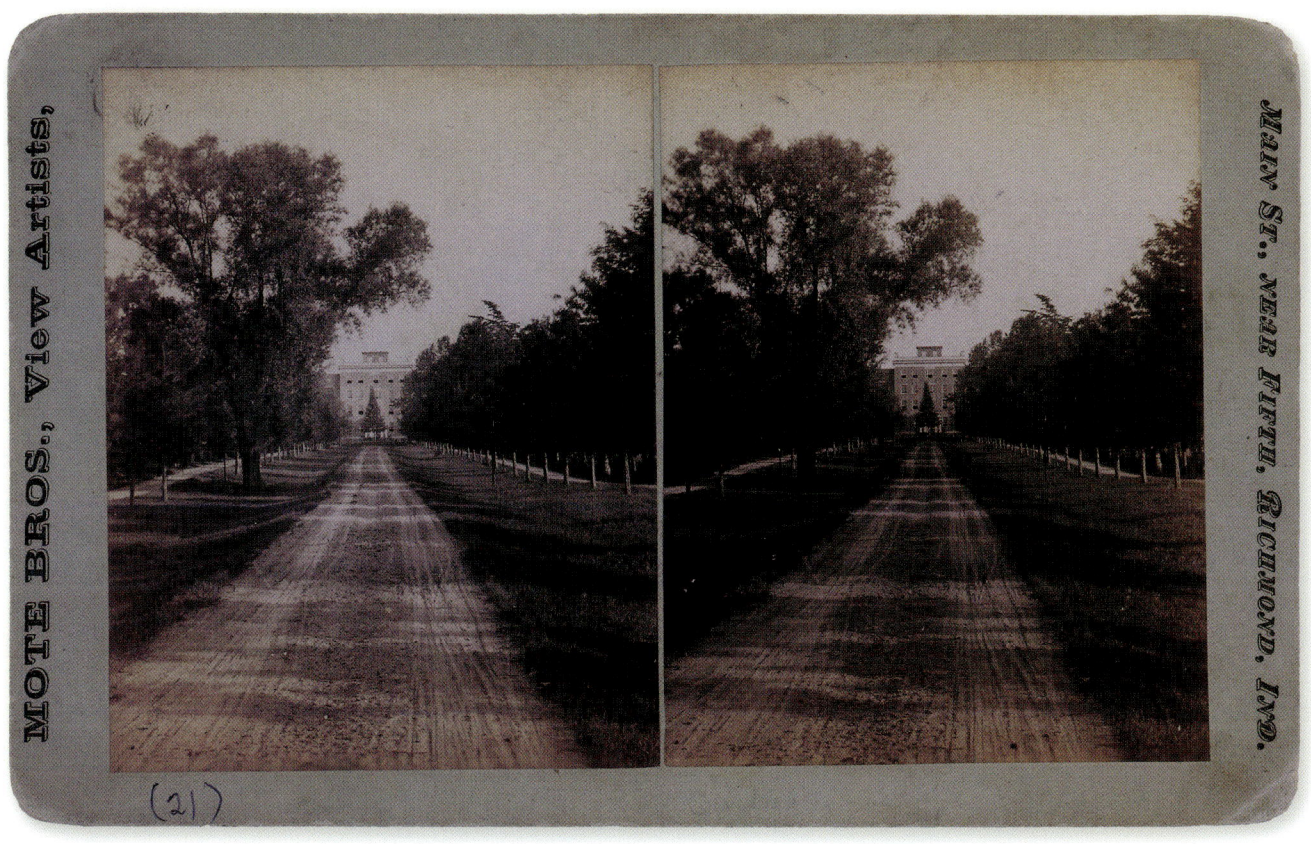

(2)

Entrance to Earlham College, Richmond, ca. 1870s. Published by Mote Brothers.
In 1847 the Society of Friends opened the Friends Boarding School in Richmond, and twelve years later the school became known as Earlham College.
The Quakers continue to operate the college today, offering strong liberal-arts programs.

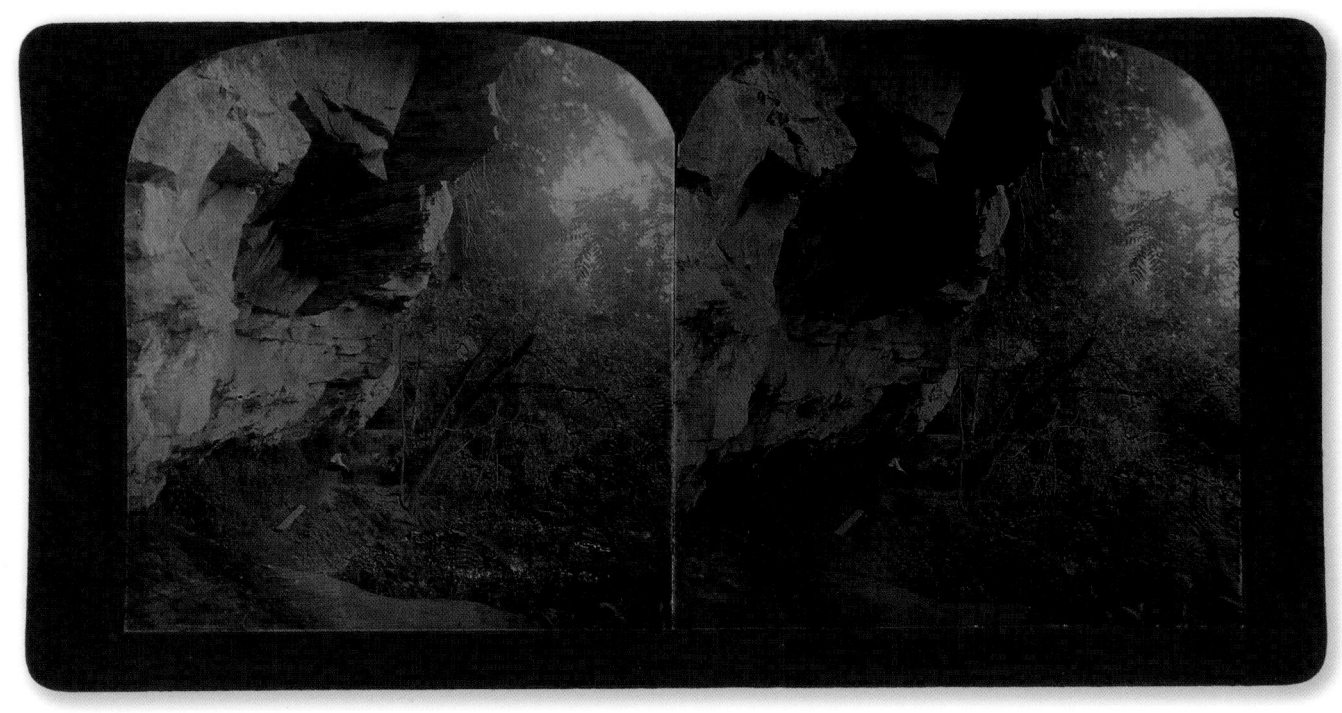

Scene along Sugar Creek, probably in Parke County, ca. 1910. Published by E. W. Kelley.
The rock formations in this view appear similar to ones found in Turkey Run State Park today, and it is likely the photograph was taken in the same area.

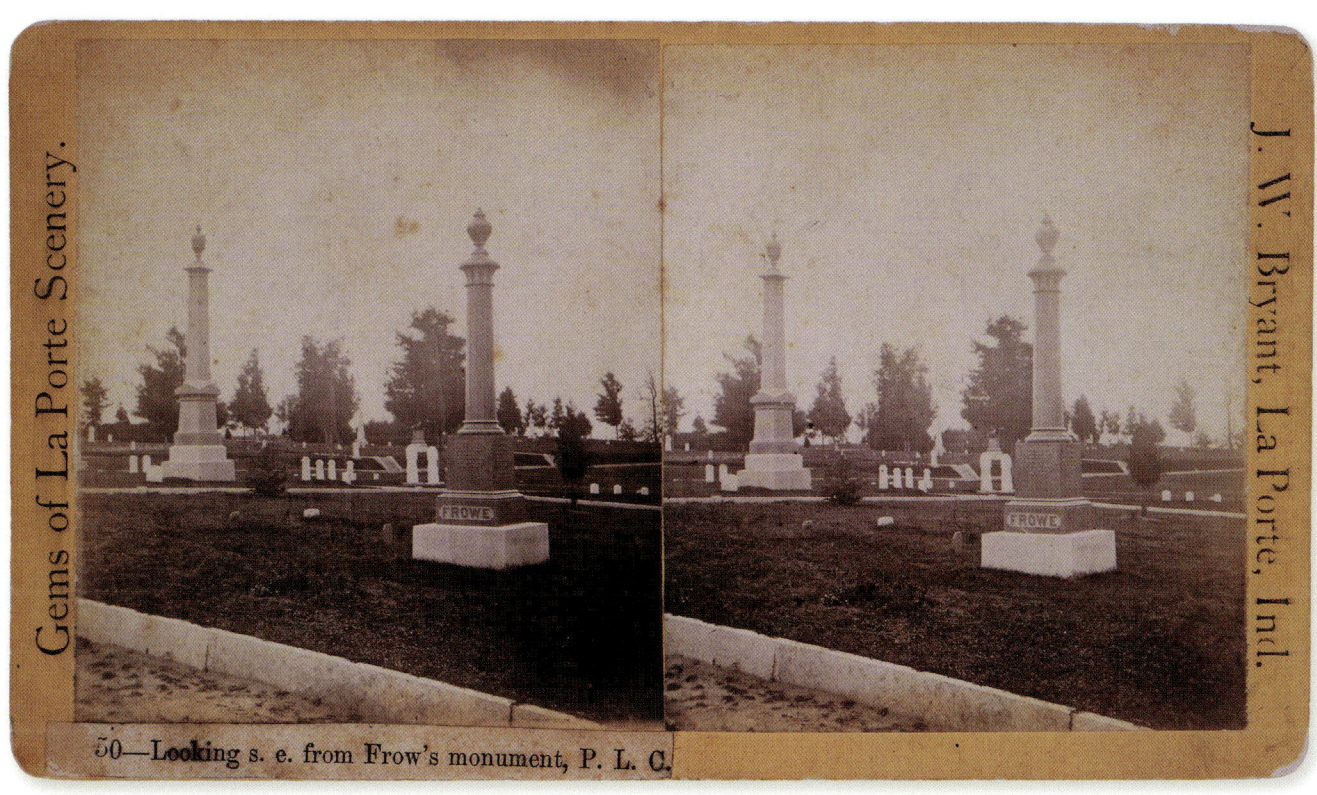

Gems of La Porte Scenery.

J. W. Bryant, La Porte, Ind.

50—Looking s. e. from Frow's monument, P. L. C.

Pine Lake Cemetery, La Porte, ca. 1880s. Photographed by J. W. Bryant.

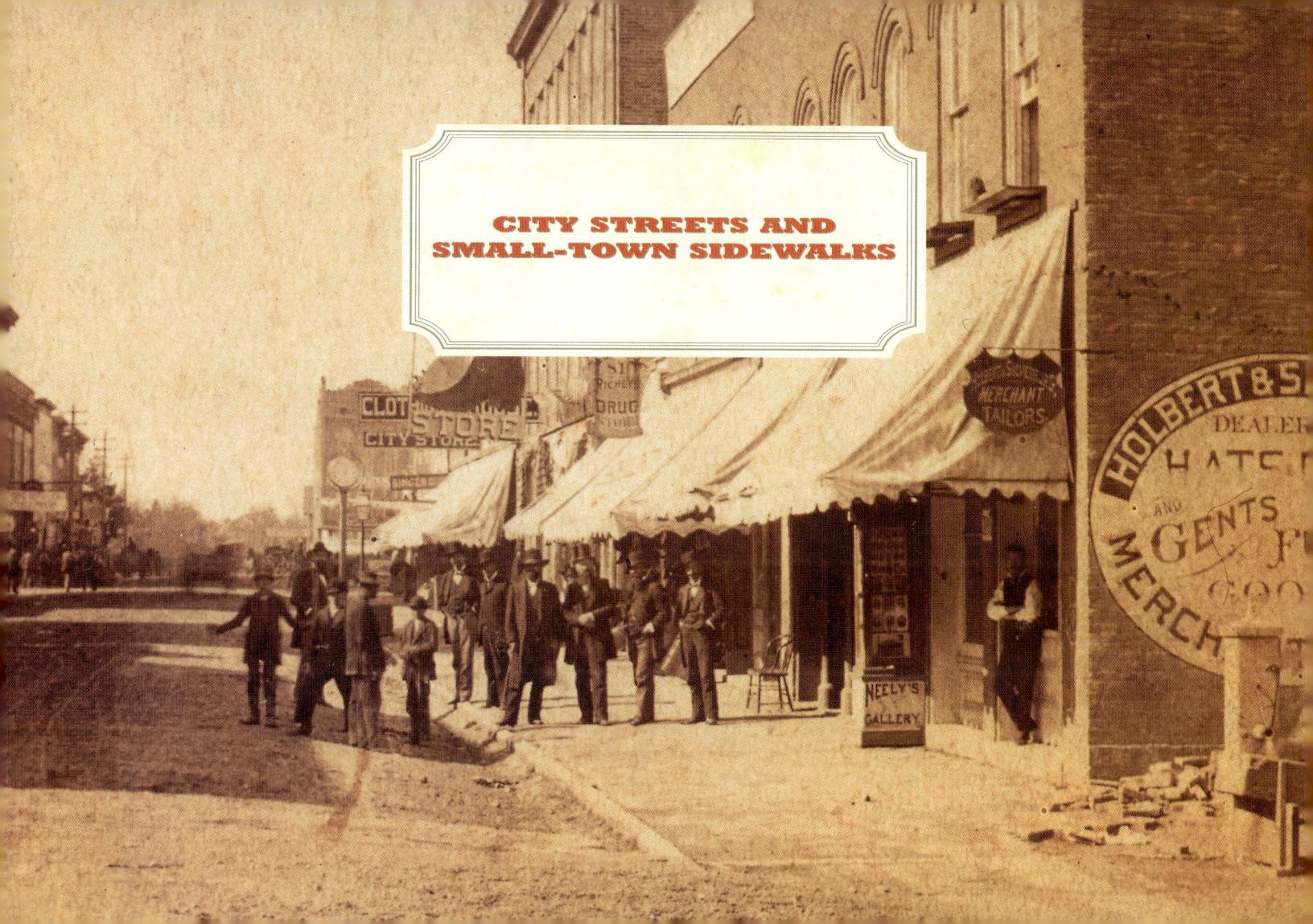

CITY STREETS AND SMALL-TOWN SIDEWALKS

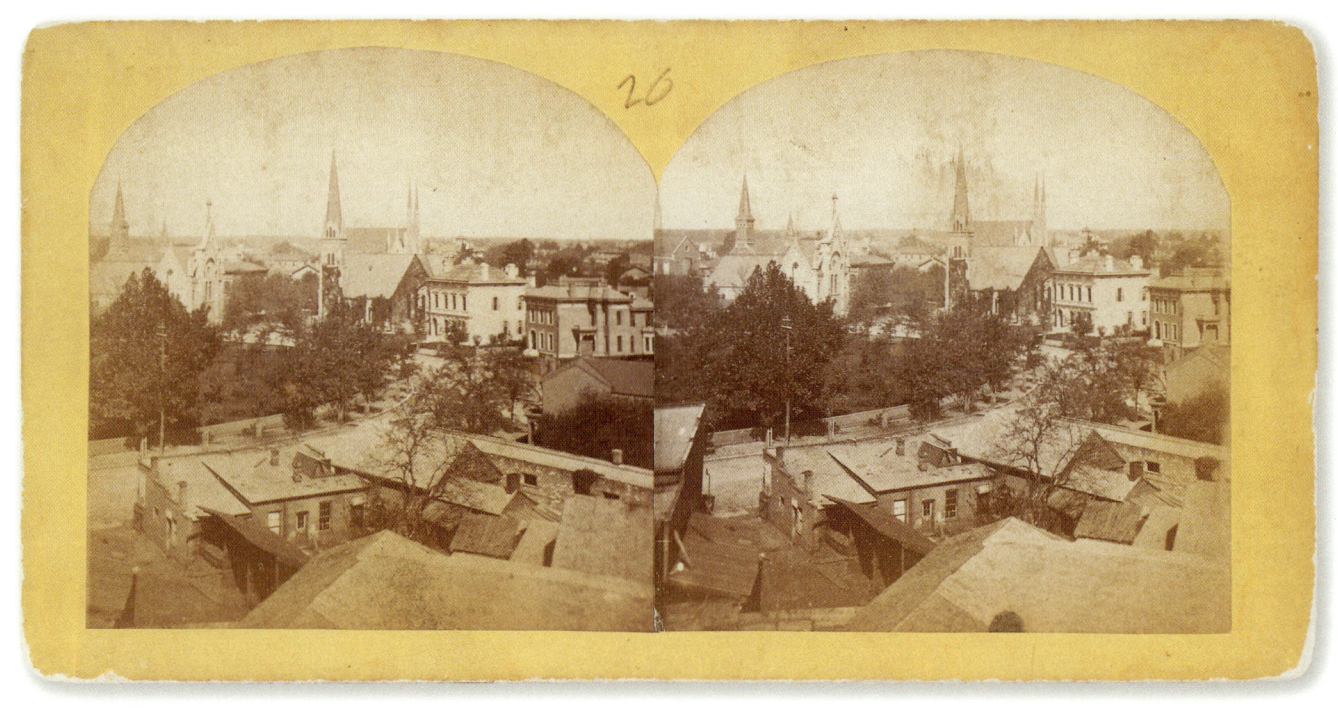

Aerial view of Circle Park, Indianapolis, ca. 1870s. Photographed by Charles B. Ingraham.
The park is now the site of the Indiana Soldiers' and Sailors' Monument, and today the area is known as Monument Circle.
The opposite page shows a similar view of the Circle taken in the early twentieth century.

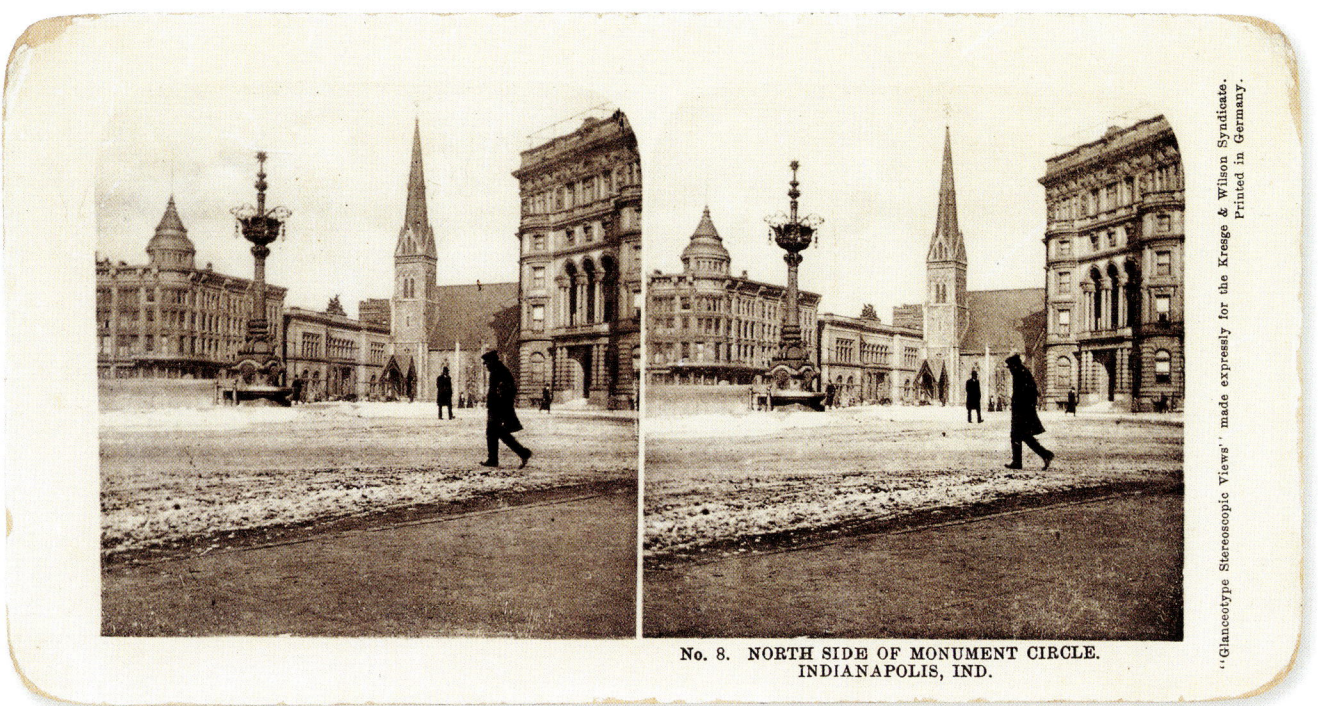

No. 8. NORTH SIDE OF MONUMENT CIRCLE.
INDIANAPOLIS, IND.

"Glanceotype Stereoscopic Views" made expressly for the Kresge & Wilson Syndicate.
Printed in Germany.

57

Monument Circle in the snow, Indianapolis, ca. 1905. Published by the Kresge and Wilson Syndicate.
This card, billed as a "glanceotype stereoscopic view," has the image printed directly on it and demonstrates the inexpensive printing methods
that became available around the turn of the twentieth century.

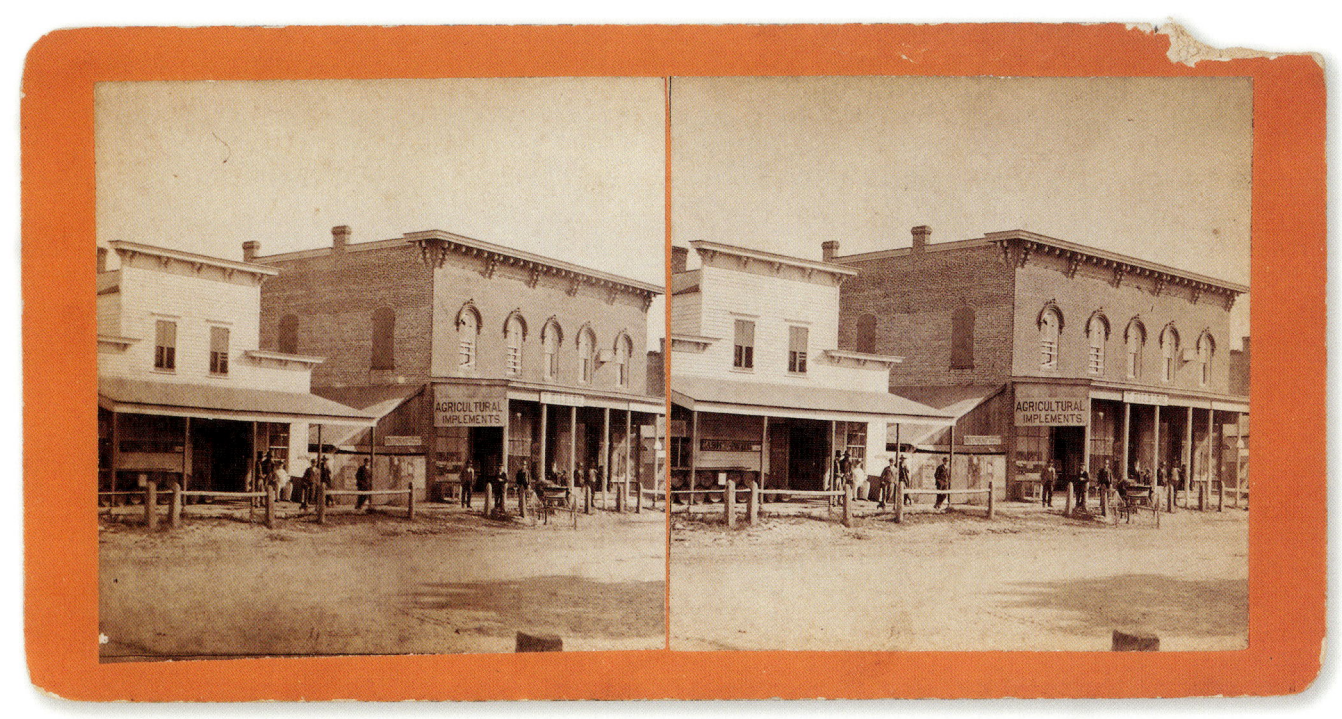

T. Hilbish's agricultural implements store, Bristol, ca. 1890s. Photographer unknown.

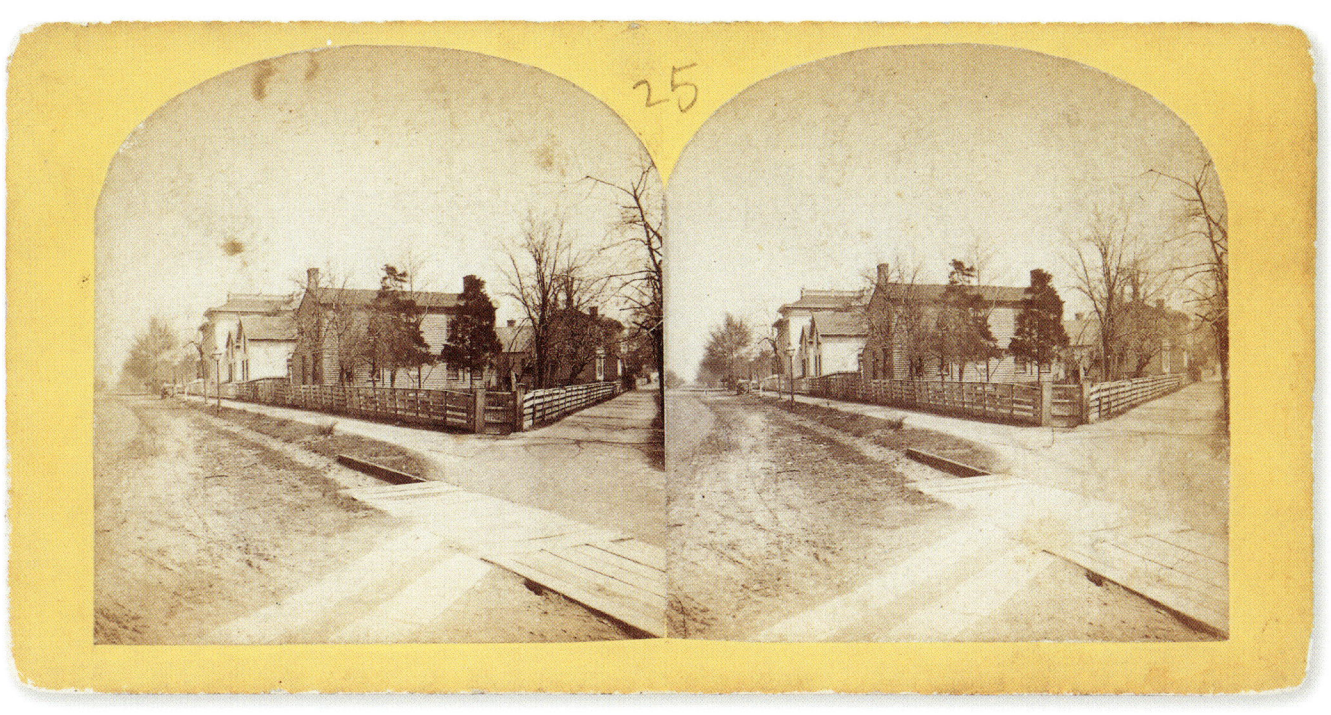

25

Unidentified street corner, Indianapolis, ca. 1870s. Published by Ingraham and Claflin.

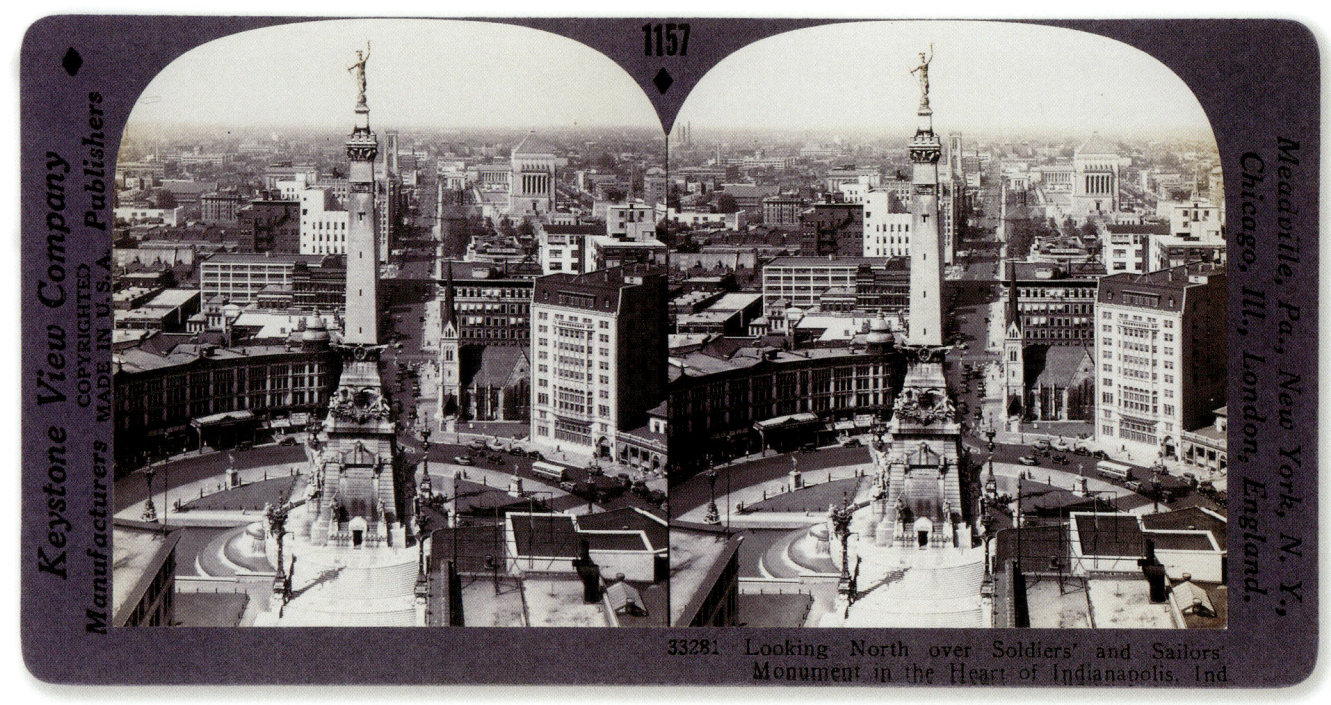

1157

33281 Looking North over Soldiers' and Sailors'
Monument in the Heart of Indianapolis, Ind

Indiana Soldiers' and Sailors' Monument and North Meridian Street, Indianapolis, ca. early 1930s. Published by the Keystone View Company.

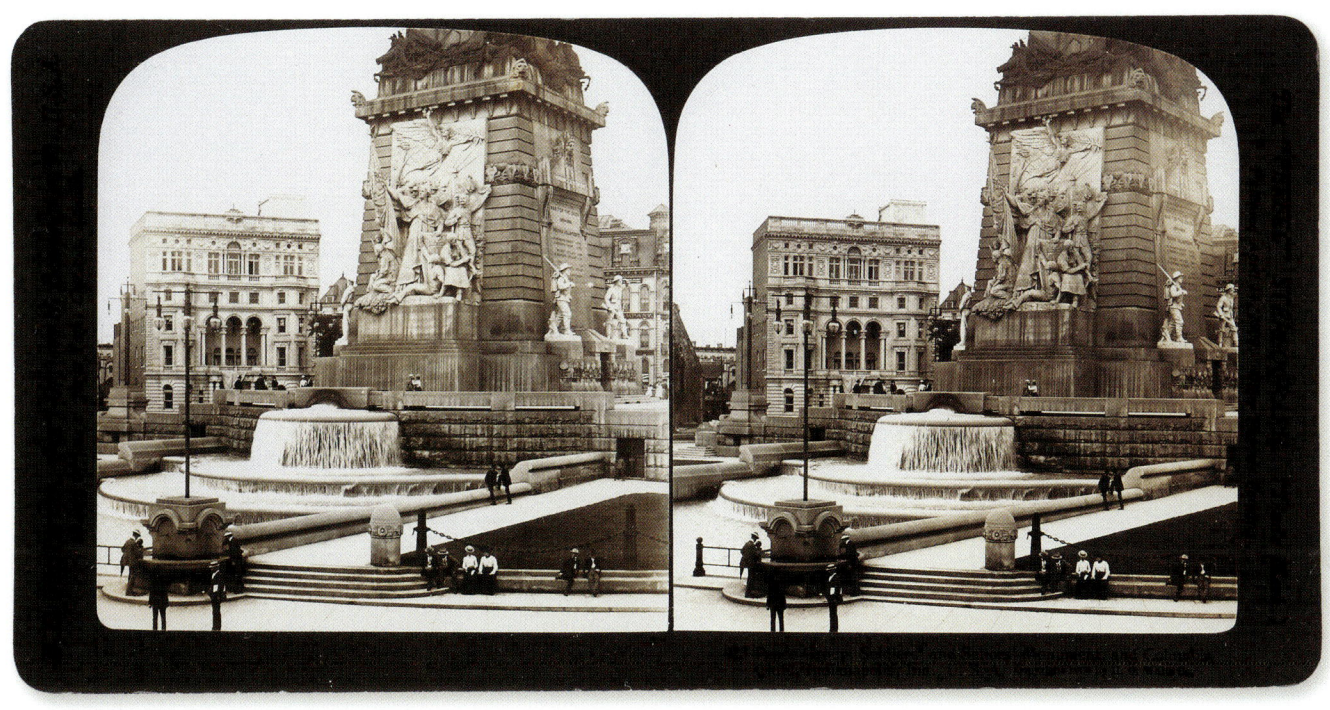

West side of the Indiana Soldiers' and Sailors' Monument, Indianapolis, ca. 1900. Published by the H. C. White Company.
The statues on this side of the monument, known collectively as the Peace Group, depict the aftermath of the Civil War, with celebrating
northern troops and a freed slave. On the east side of the monument the War Group shows troops engaged in battle.

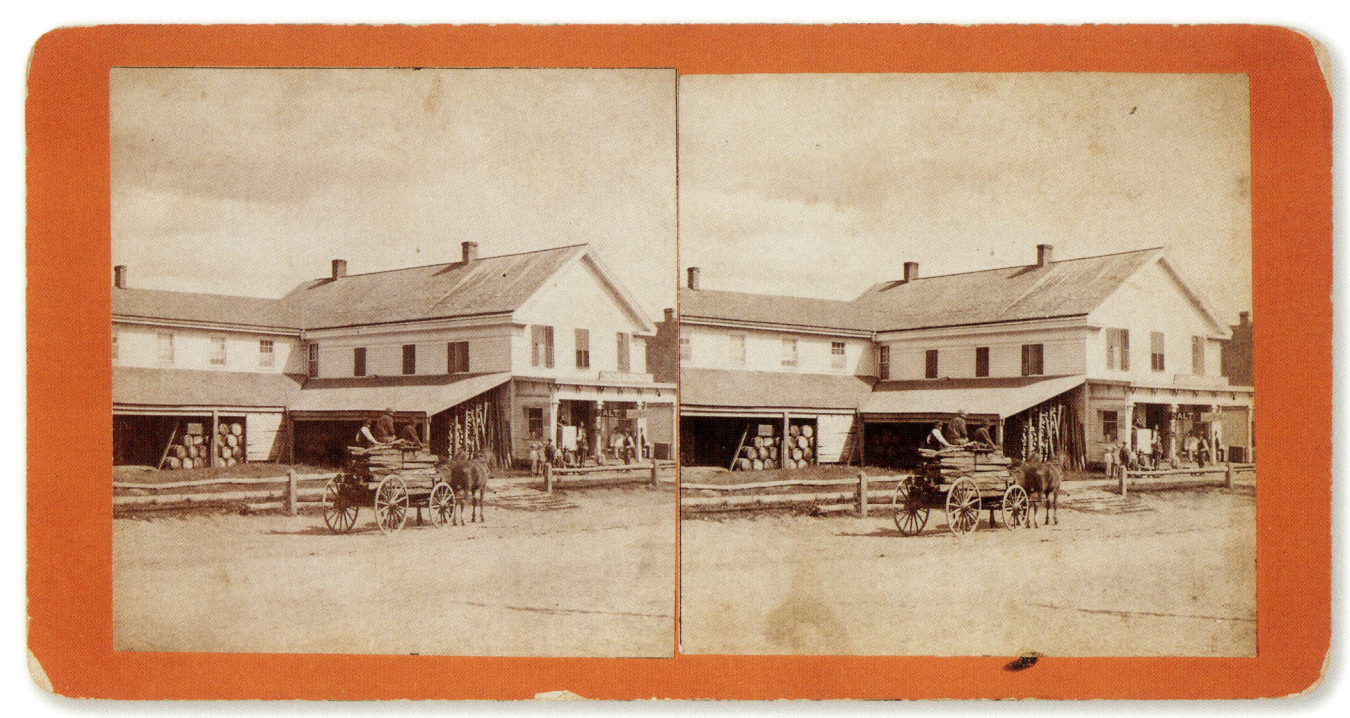

Unidentified store, Bristol, ca. 1890s. Photographer unknown.

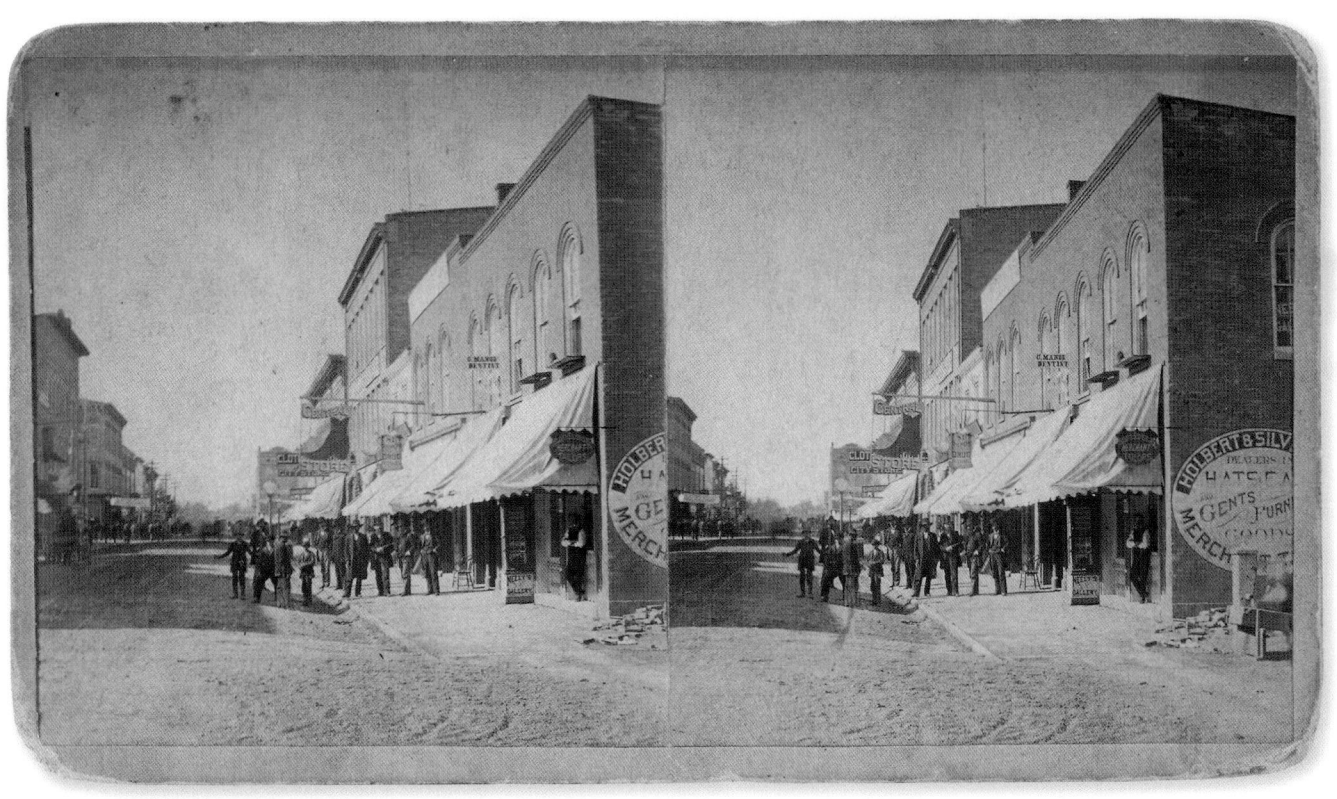

Street scene, Muncie, ca. 1870s. Photographer unknown, but possibly Lon Neely as his display case is visible in this view.

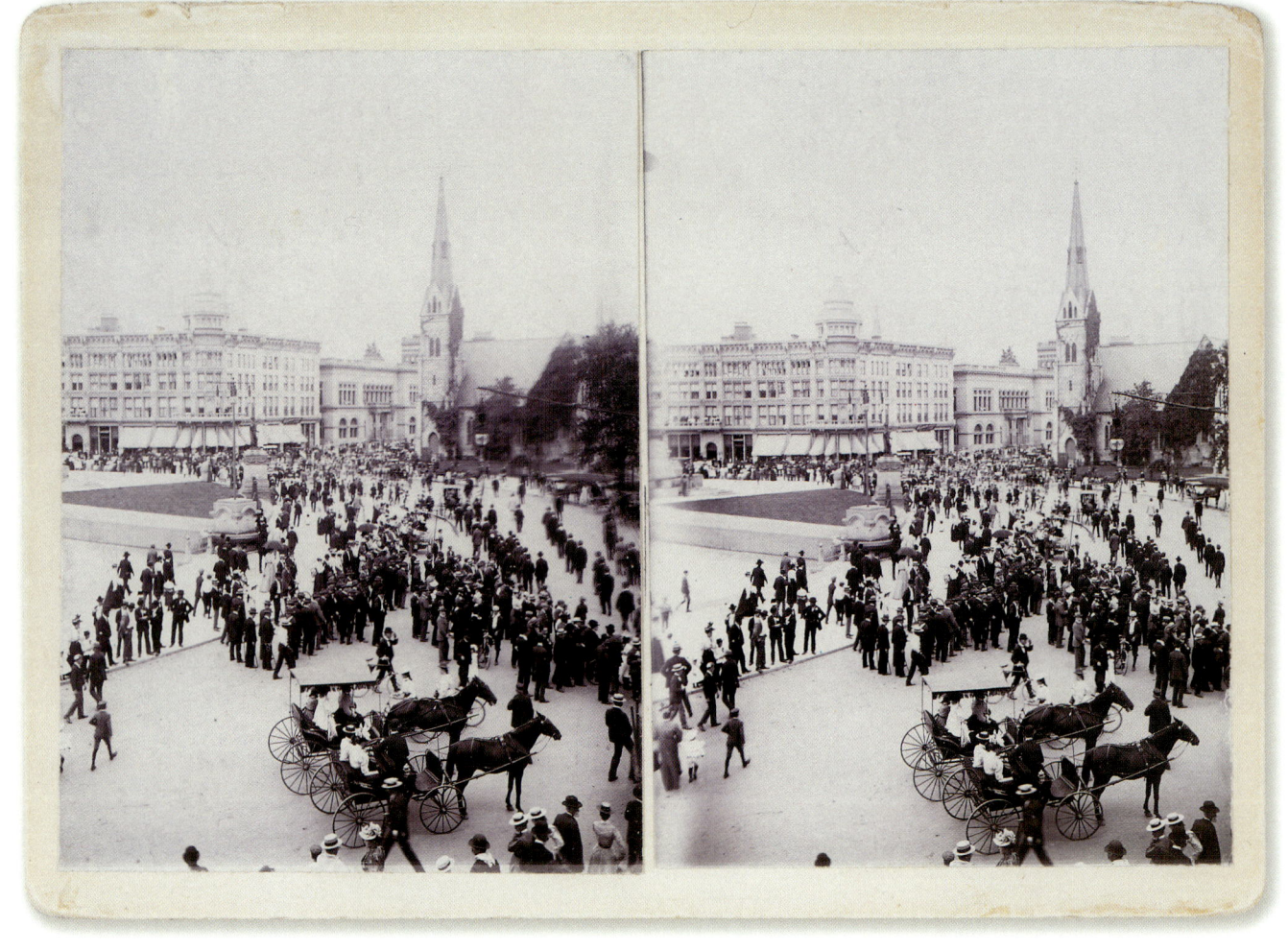

Crowd gathering at Monument Circle, Indianapolis, ca. late 1890s. Photographer unknown.
The church is Christ Church Cathedral, completed in 1859 and still standing today.

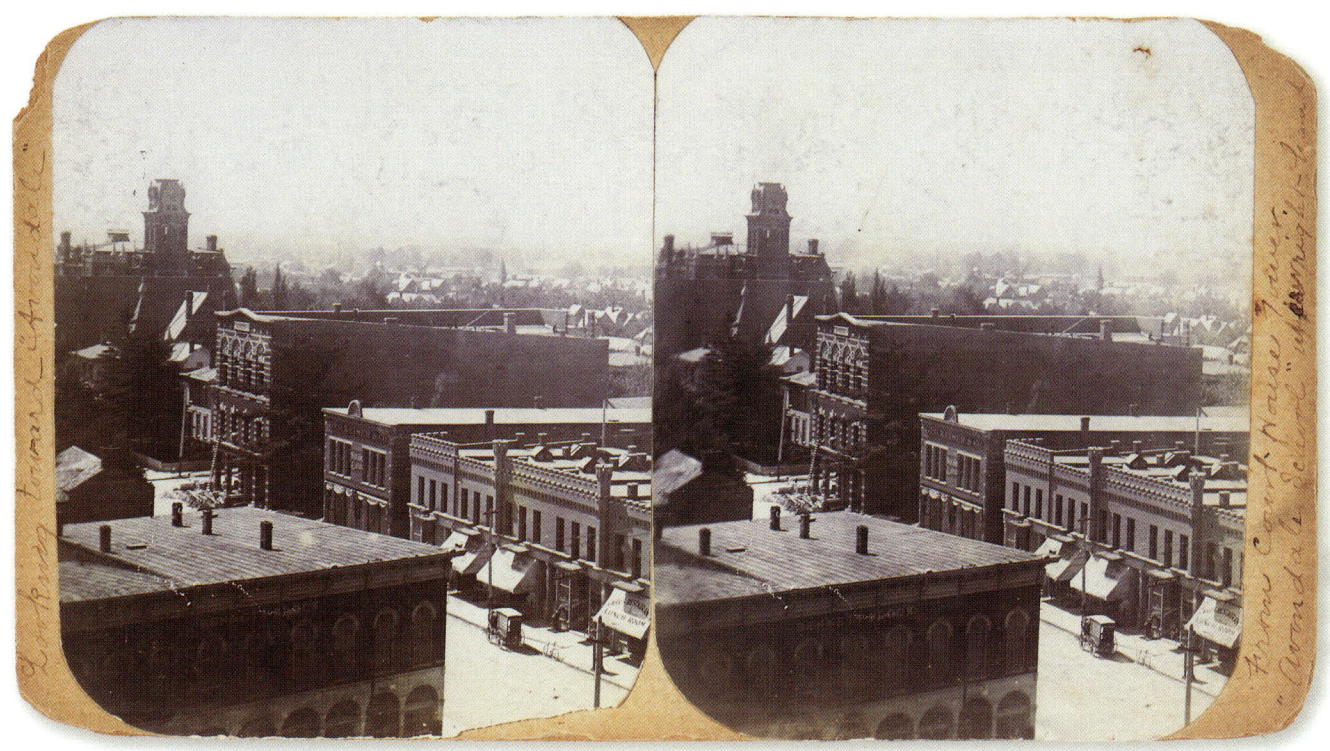

View from the Delaware County Courthouse, Muncie, ca. 1890s. Photographer unknown.
The building with the clock tower is the Muncie High School.

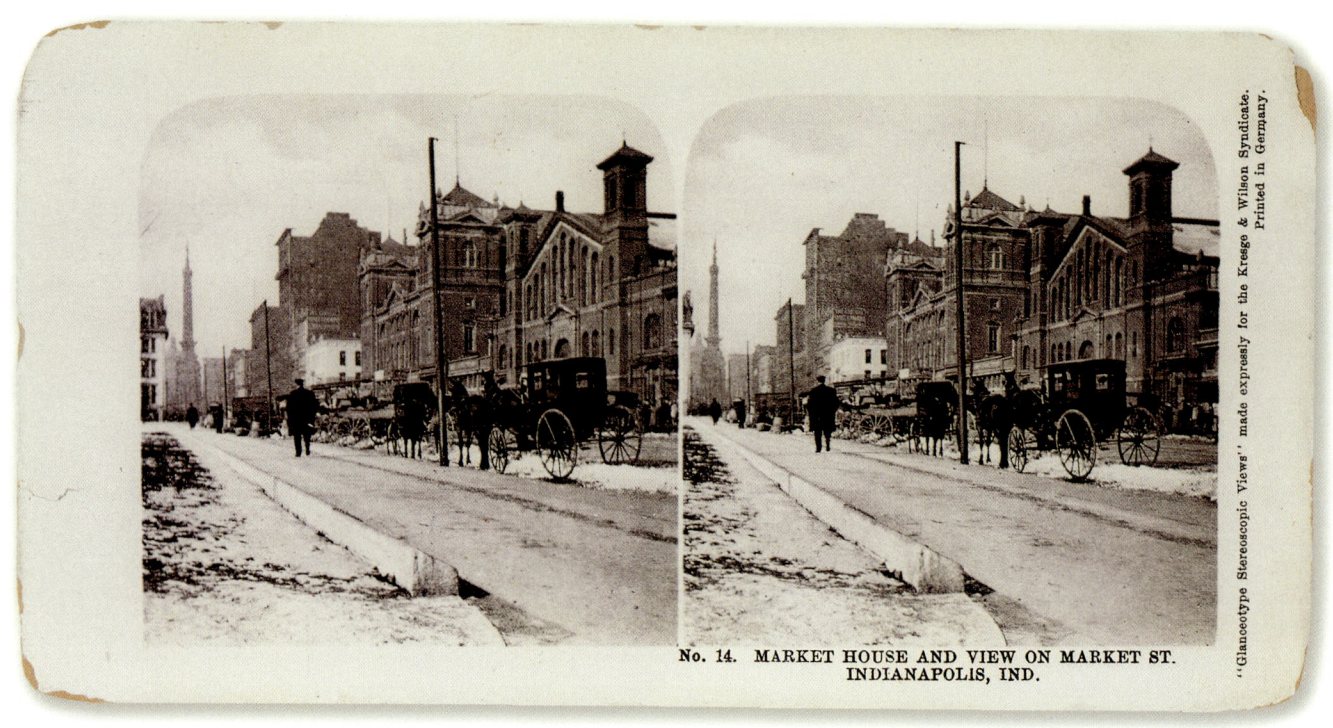

No. 14. MARKET HOUSE AND VIEW ON MARKET ST. INDIANAPOLIS, IND.

"Glancotype Stereoscopic Views" made expressly for the Kresge & Wilson Syndicate. Printed in Germany.

View of Market Street, Indianapolis, with Tomlinson Hall and the City Market in the foreground, ca. 1905. Published by the Kresge and Wilson Syndicate.

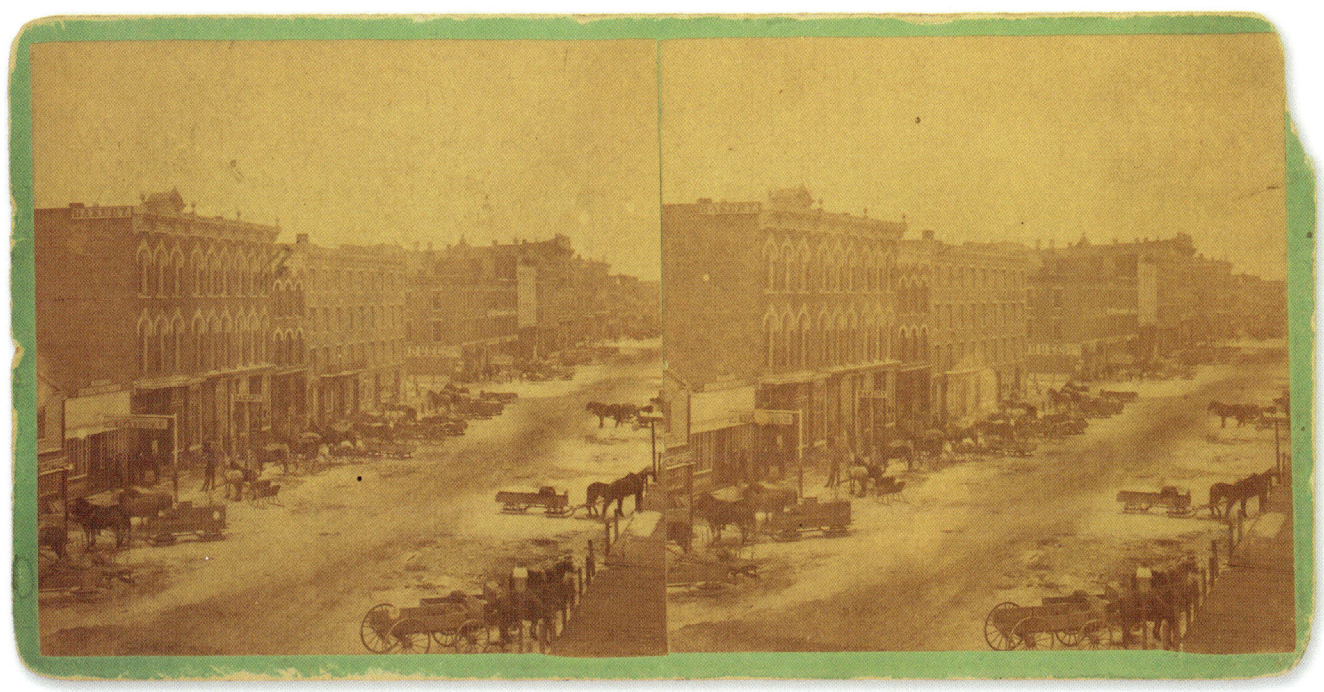

Main Street, looking northeast from the corner of Clay Street, La Porte, 1873. Photographer unknown.
Main Street is now called Lincoln Way.

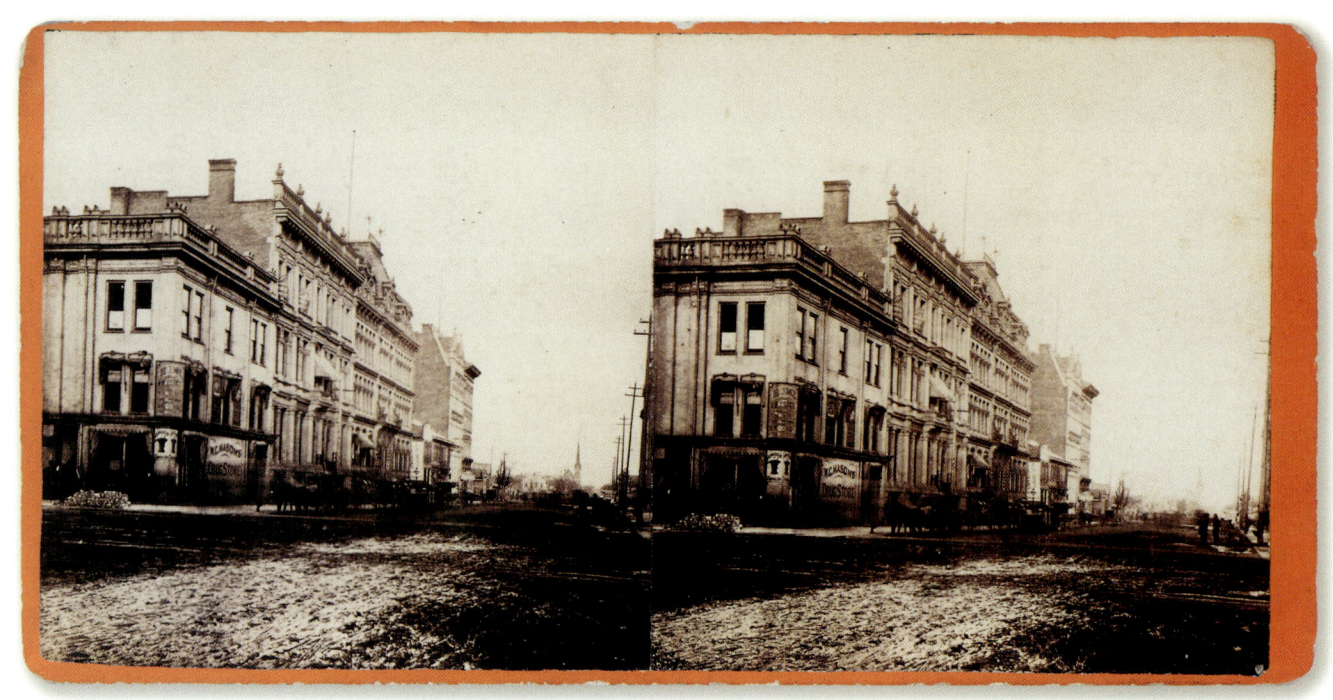

Market Street, looking east from Pennsylvania Street, Indianapolis, ca. 1870s. Photographed by J. W. Pendergast.

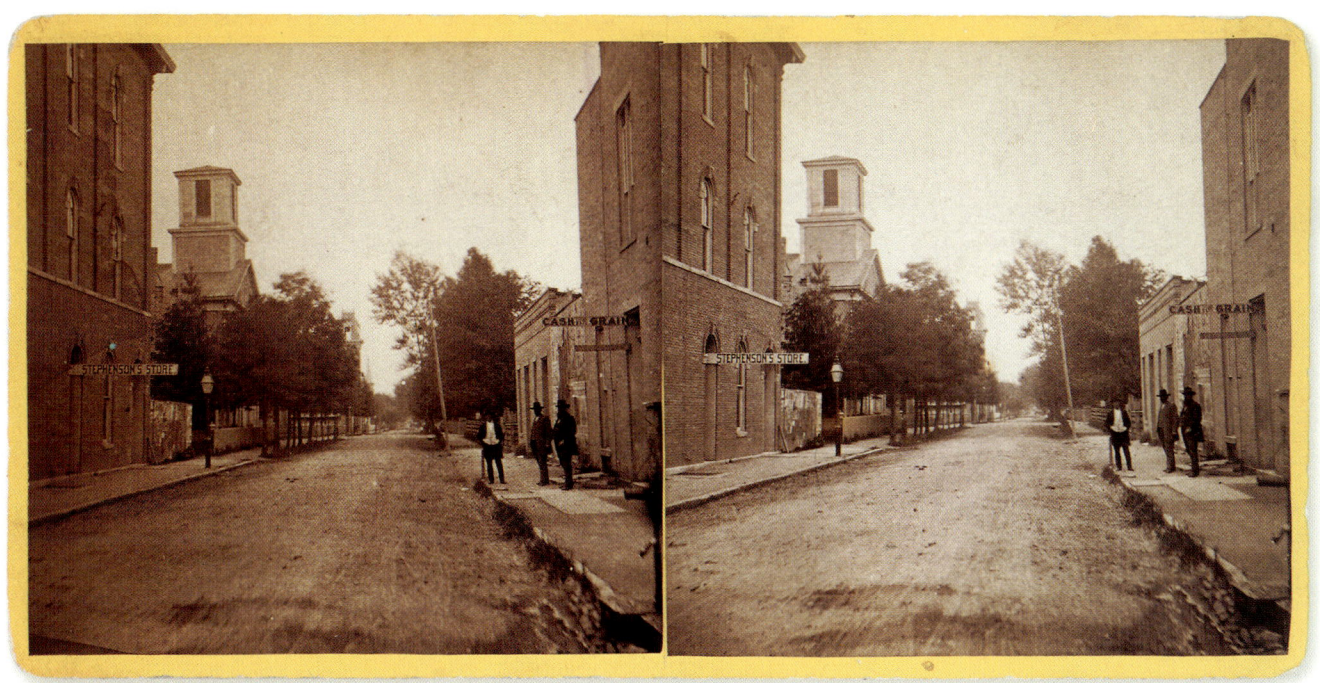

Unidentified town, ca. 1880s. Photographed by M. D. Goodlander.
This view was likely taken in either Delaware or Madison County.

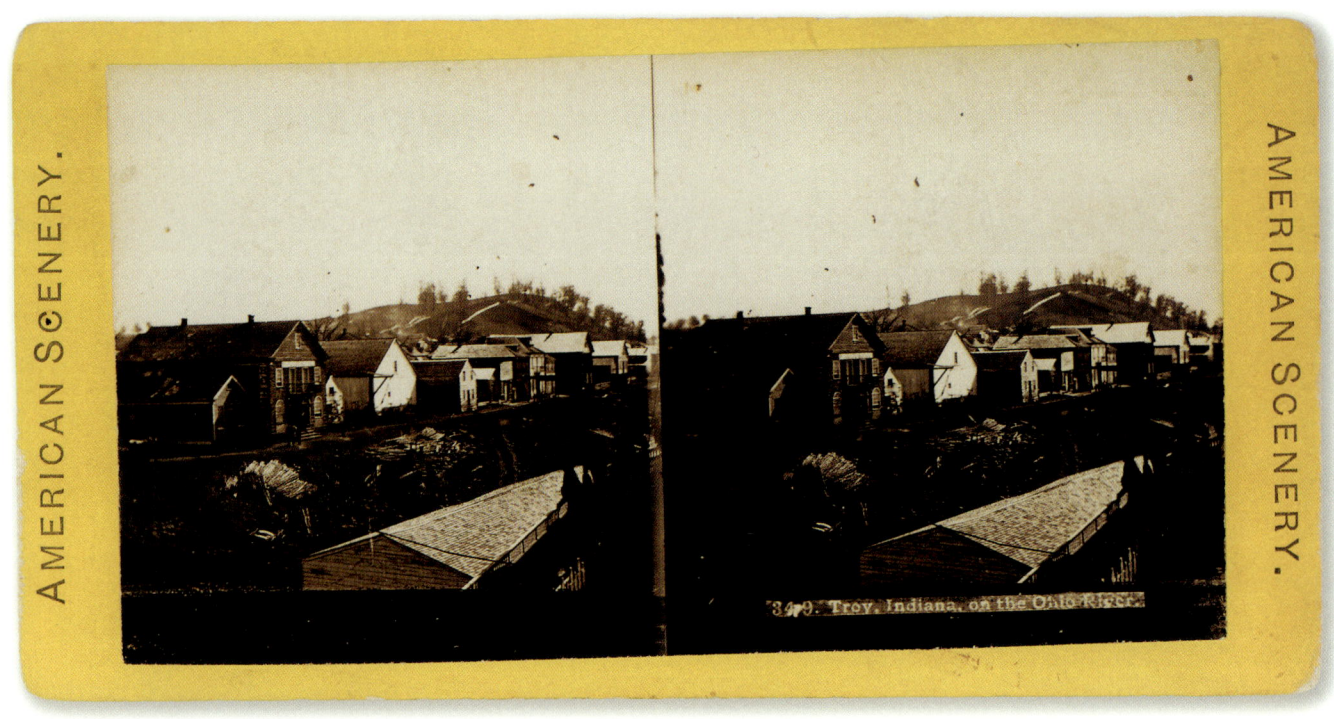

AMERICAN SCENERY.

3479. Troy, Indiana, on the Ohio River.

View of Troy, ca. 1890s. Publisher unknown.
This is an example of a copy or pirated print. It features a reproduced image on a card of inferior quality, and it includes
the generic term "American Scenery" rather than the name of an actual photographer or publisher.

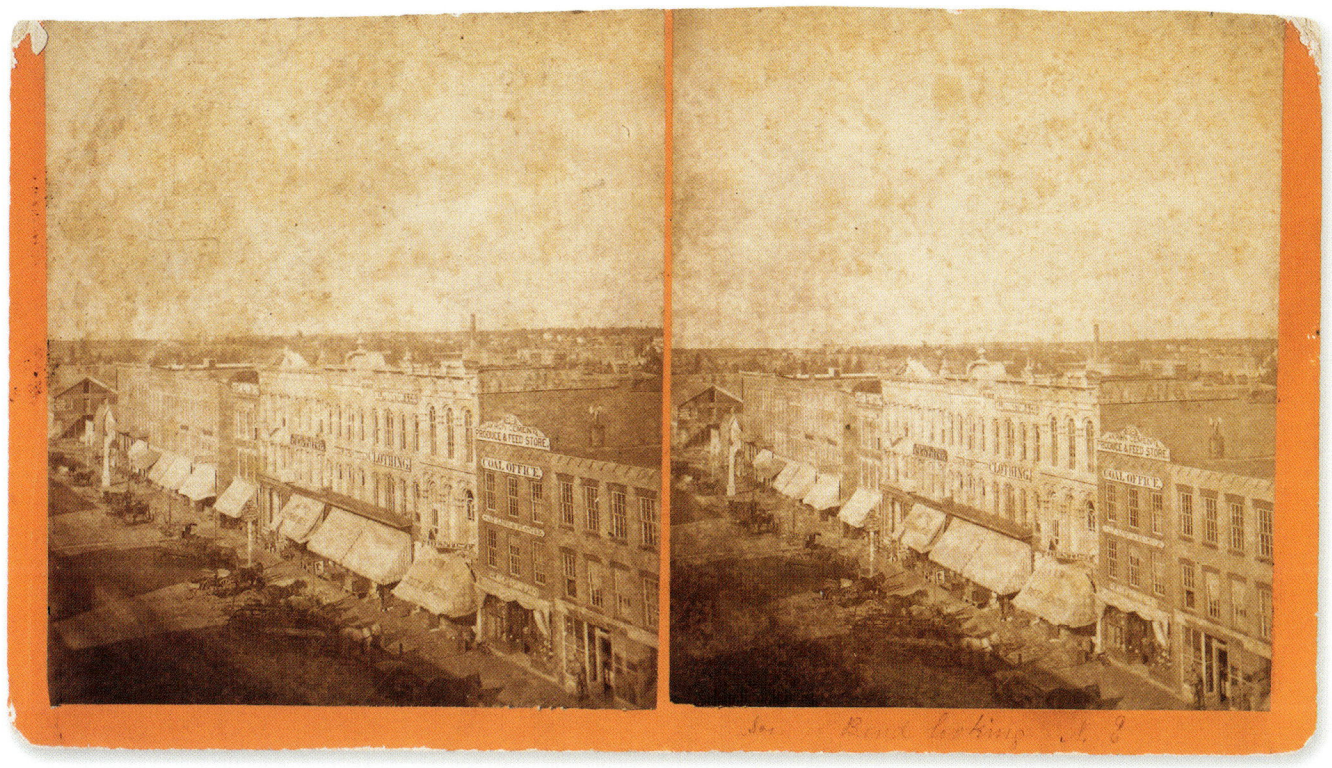

North Michigan Street, South Bend, ca. 1870s. Photographed by James Bonney.

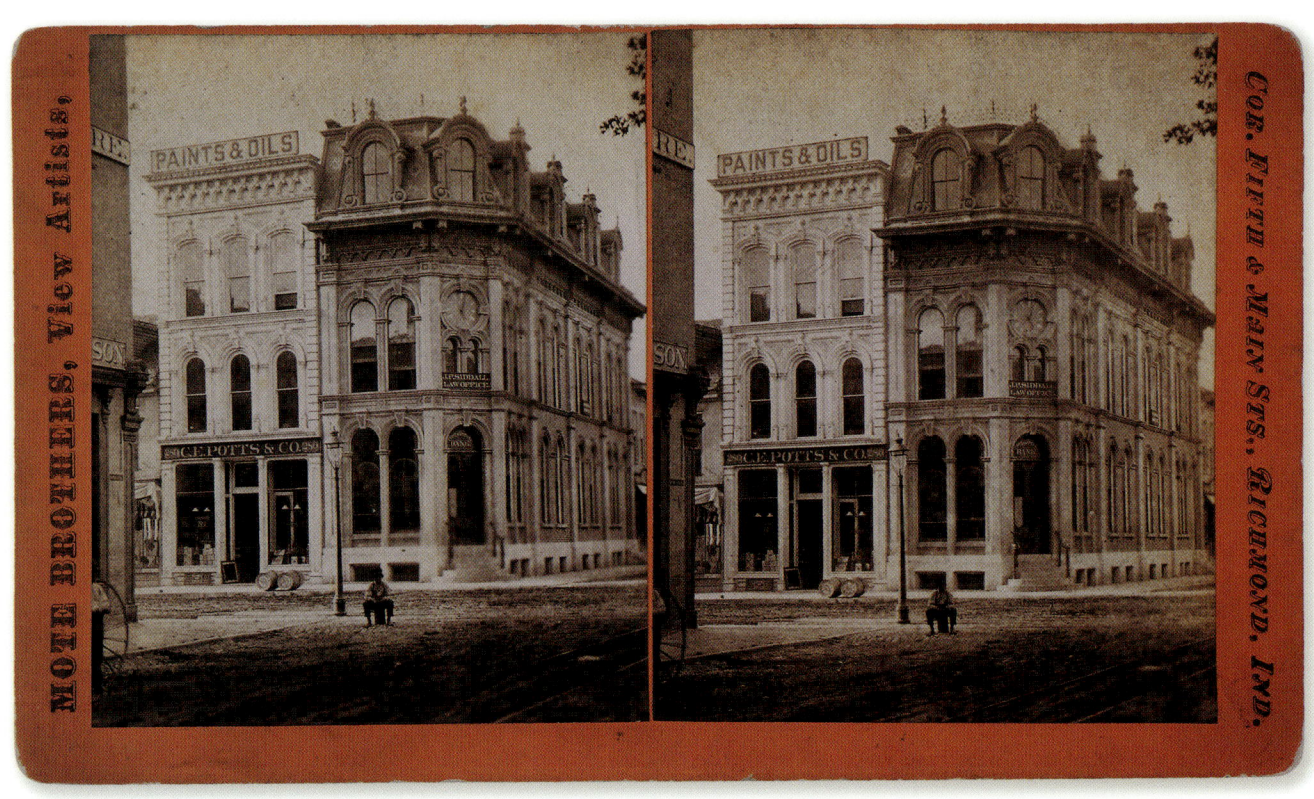

Northwest corner of Main and Seventh Streets, Richmond, ca. 1870s. Published by Mote Brothers. The building on the right was constructed in 1873 and housed the First National Bank.

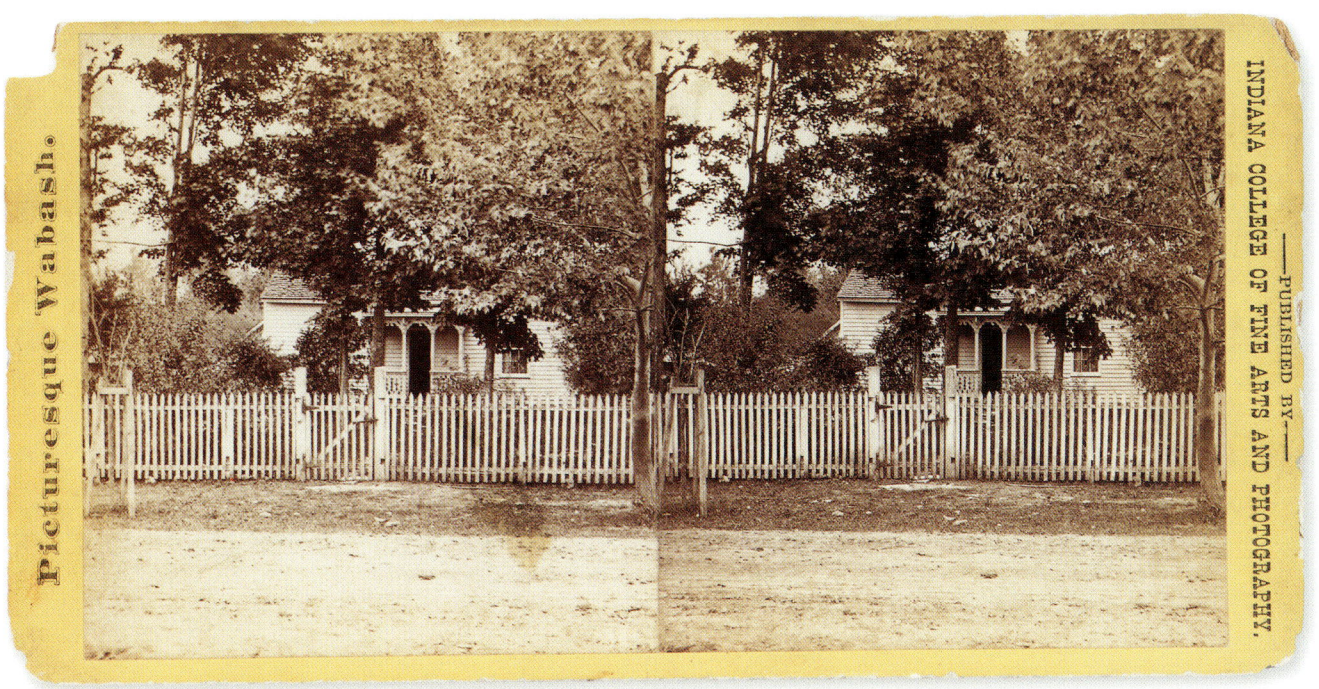

This view is presumably of Wabash, ca. 1870s. Published by the Indiana College of Fine Arts and Photography.

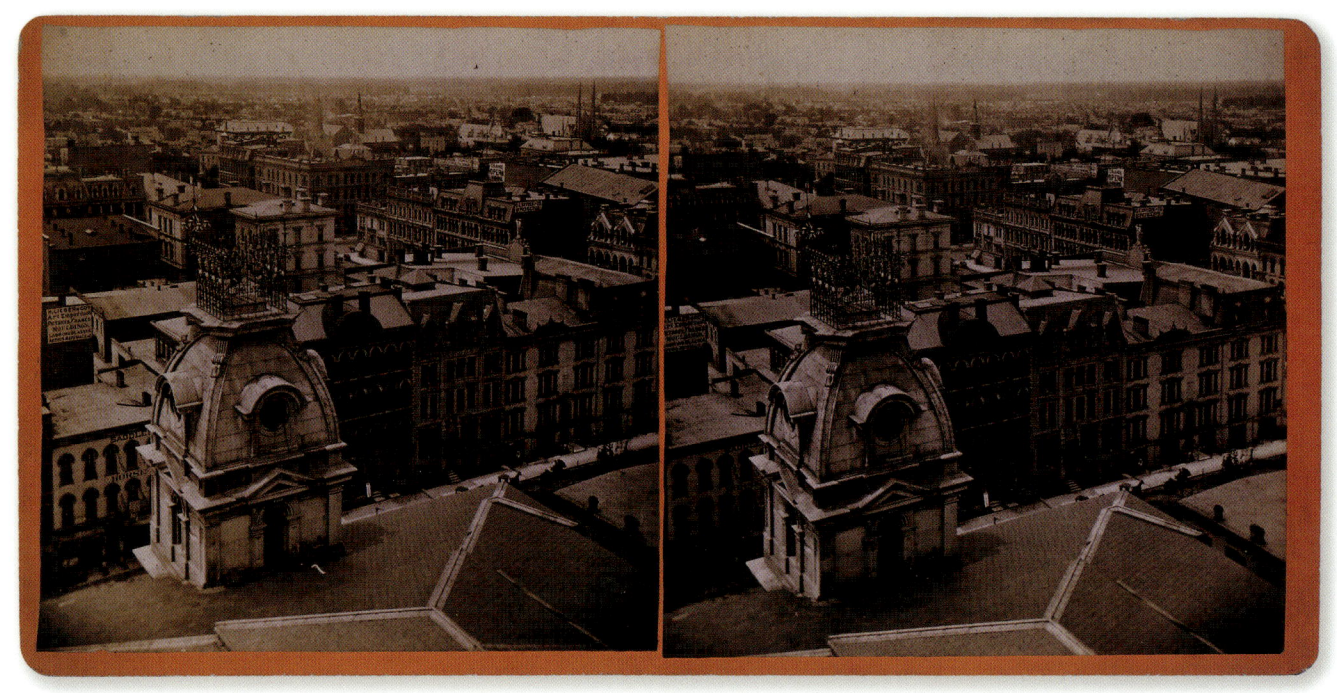

View from the Marion County Courthouse, Indianapolis, 1876. Photographed by J. W. Pendergast.
This view looks down on the west side of the new courthouse, along Delaware Street. It is one of several
Pendergast took from the courthouse as part of a panoramic series.

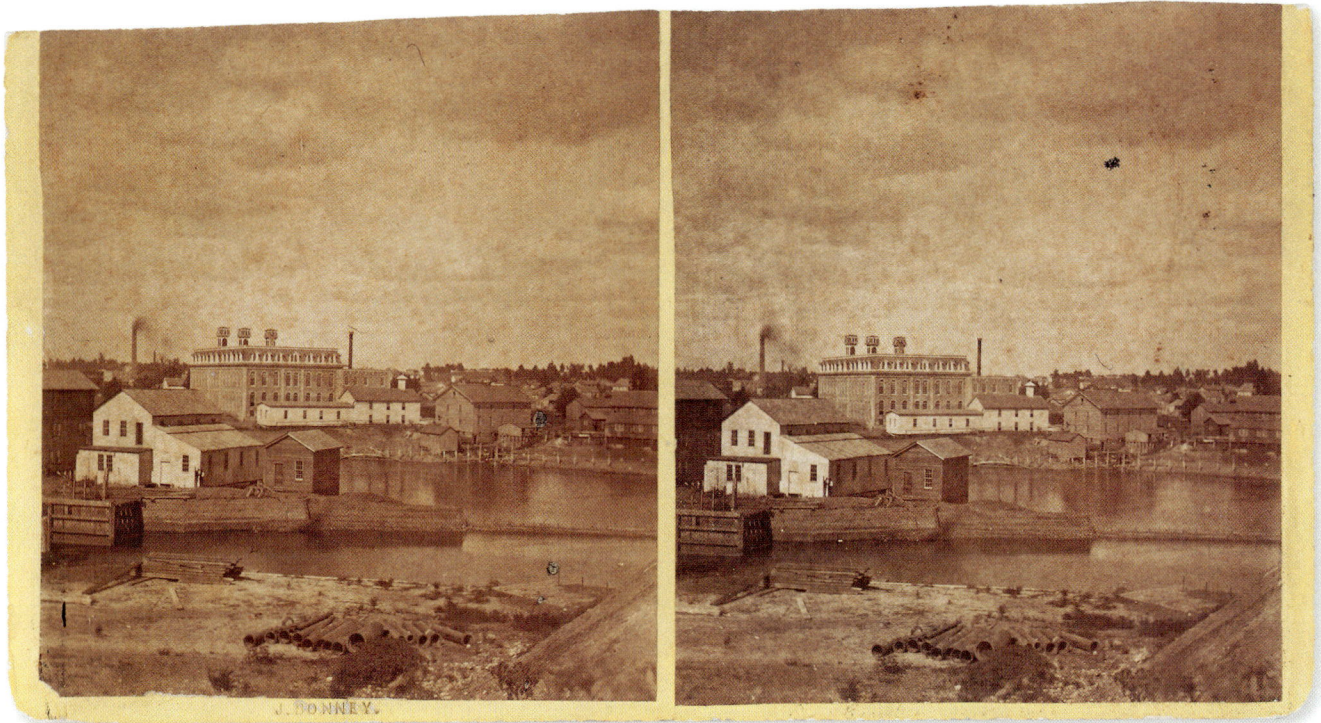

Factories along the St. Joseph River, South Bend, ca. 1870s. Photographed by James Bonney.

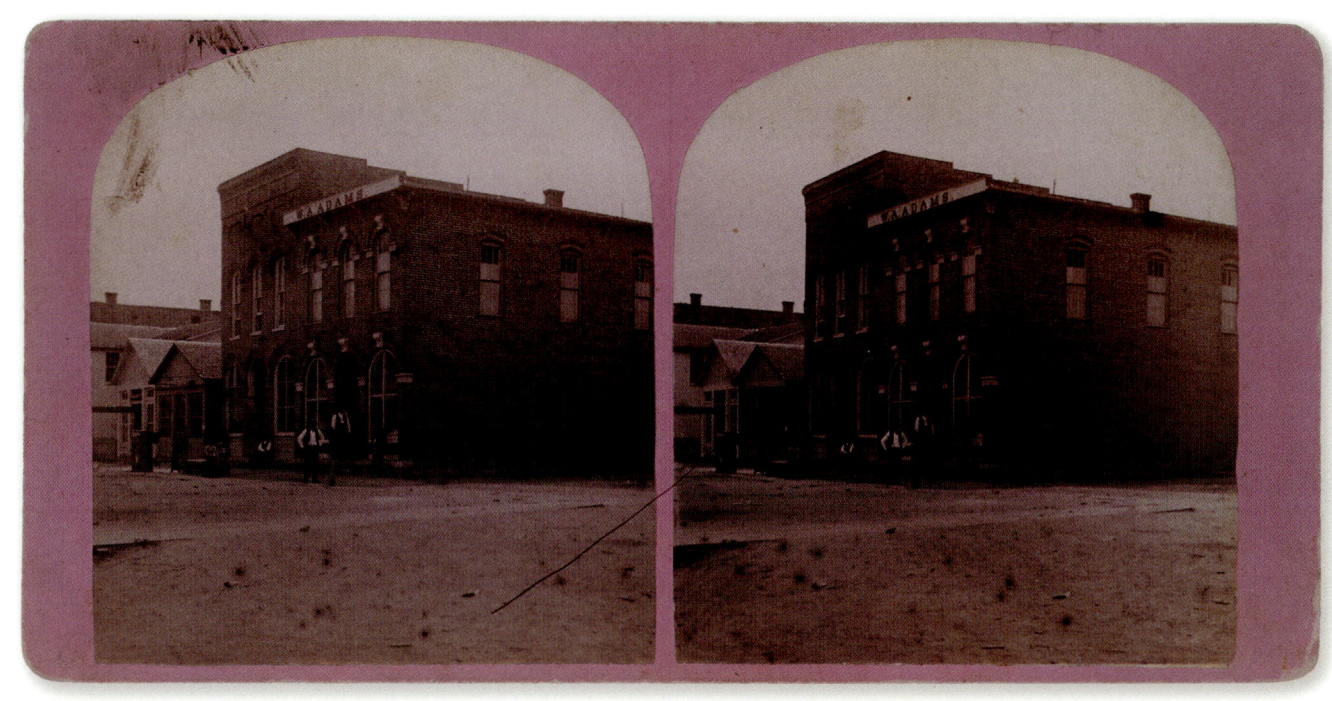

Street scene, Morgantown, ca. 1880s. Photographed by M. B. Collins.

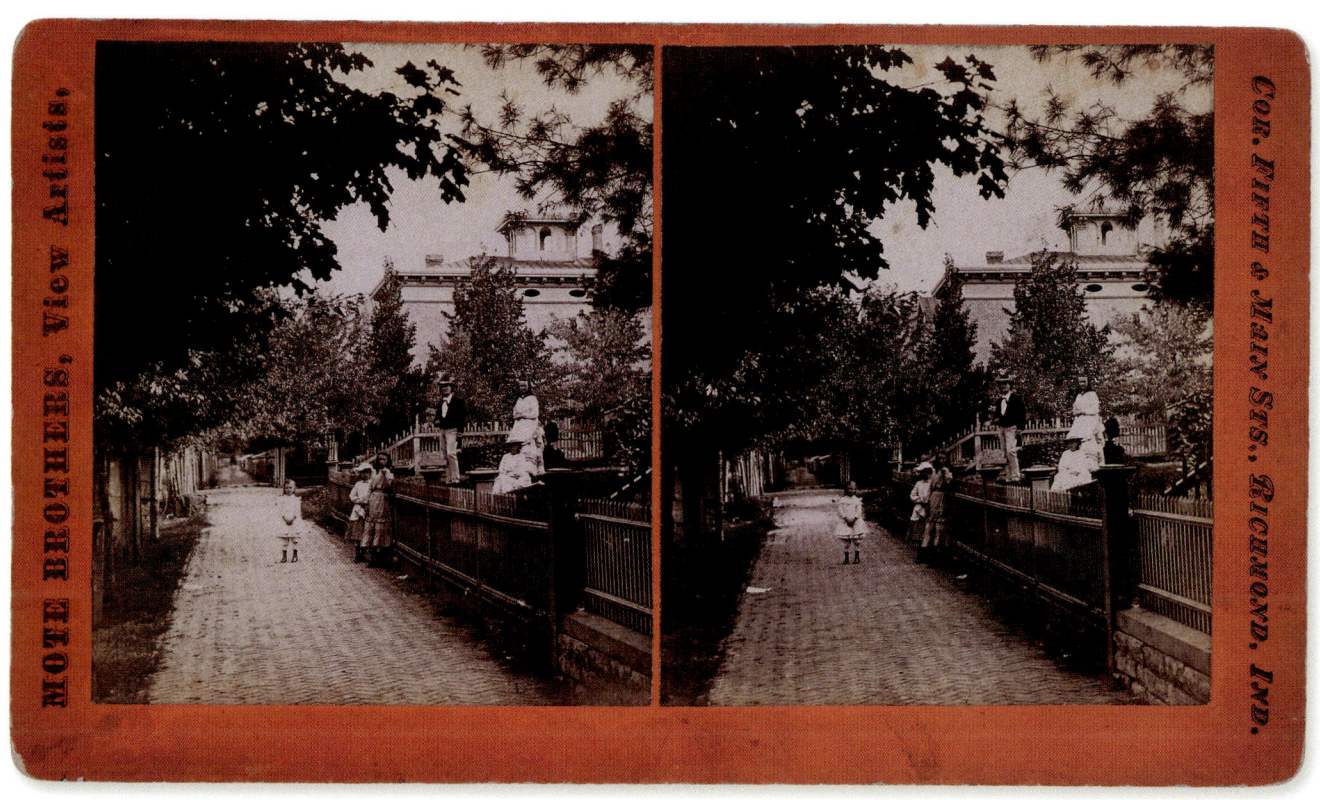

View along North Tenth Street, Richmond, ca. 1870s. Published by Mote Brothers.

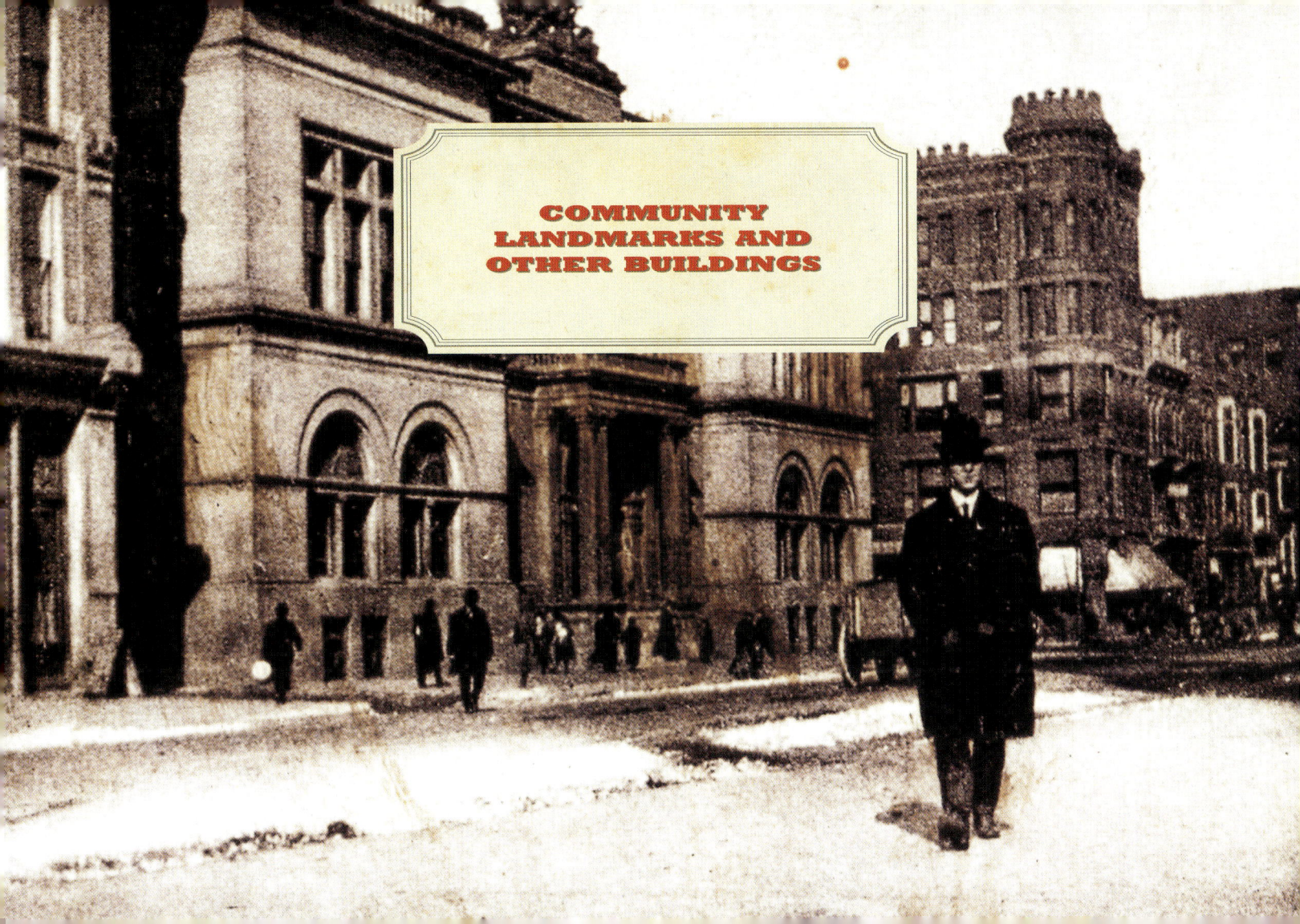

COMMUNITY
LANDMARKS AND
OTHER BUILDINGS

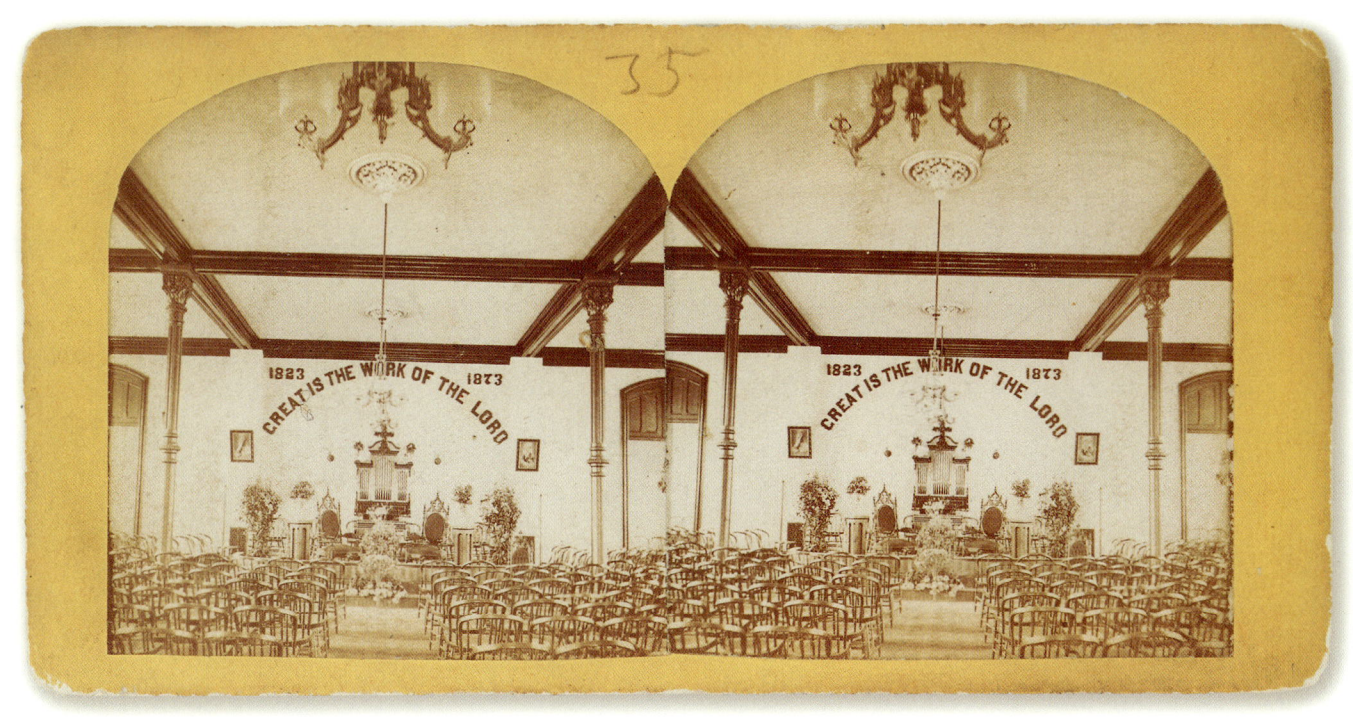

Roberts Park Methodist Episcopal Church, Indianapolis, 1873. Published by Ingraham and Claflin.
Roberts Park was celebrating the fiftieth anniversary of its founding when this photograph was taken.

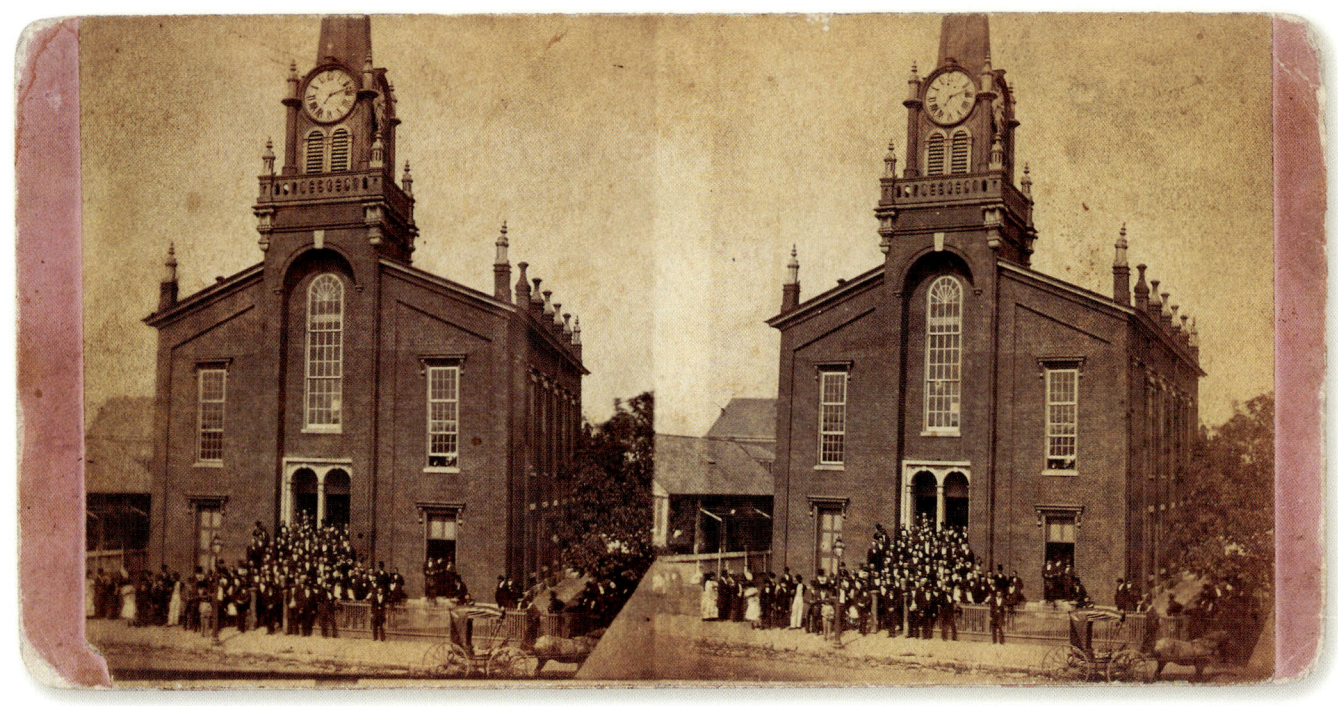

Wall Street Methodist Episcopal Church, Jeffersonville, ca. 1880s. Photographed by G. W. Finley.
Construction on the church began in 1859 and was completed by the mid-1860s. According to Baird's History of Clark County, Indiana,
the church's leaders created controversy when they included a cross on the steeple—an uncommon feature for a Protestant church at the time.

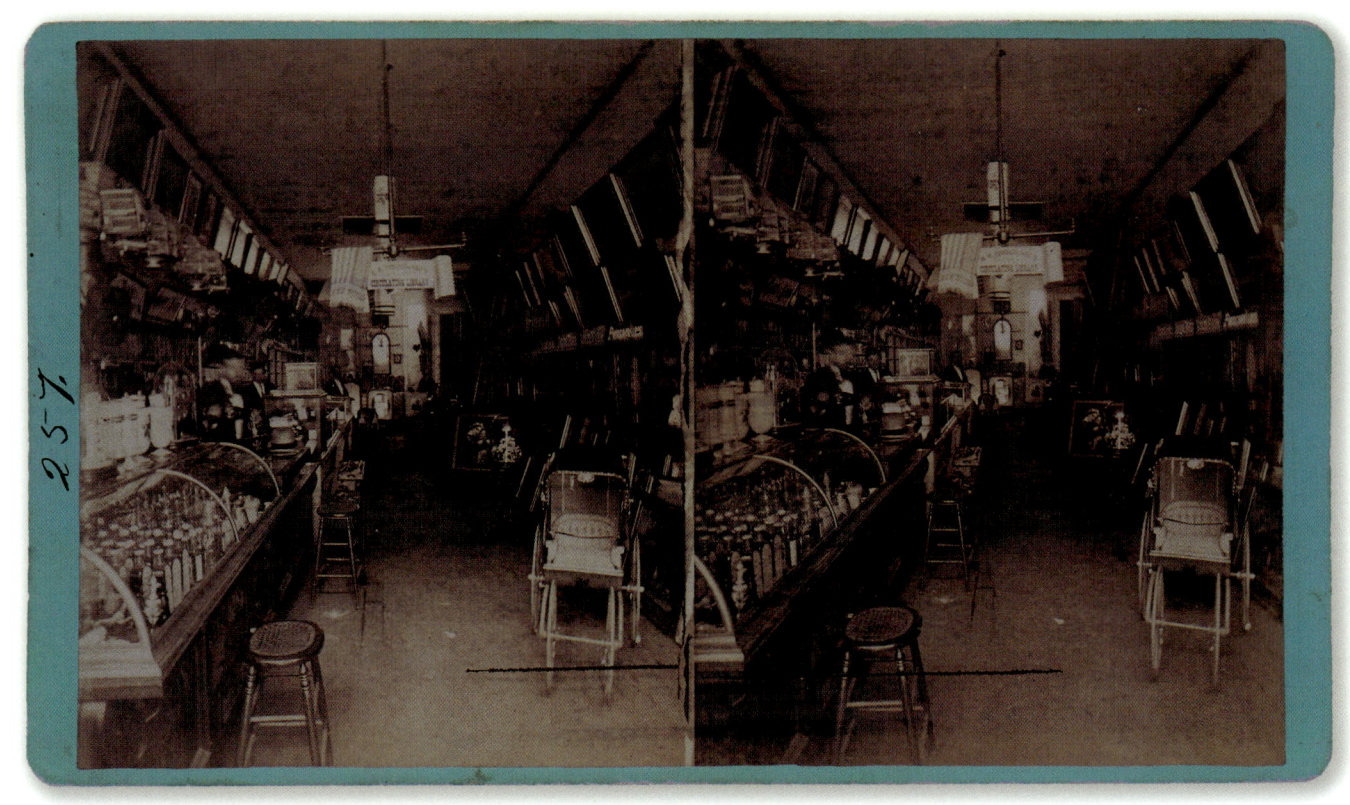

Store interior, Lafayette, ca. 1870s. Published by Wright and Hartwell.
The sign on the light fixture advertises R. C. Timberlake's circulating library.

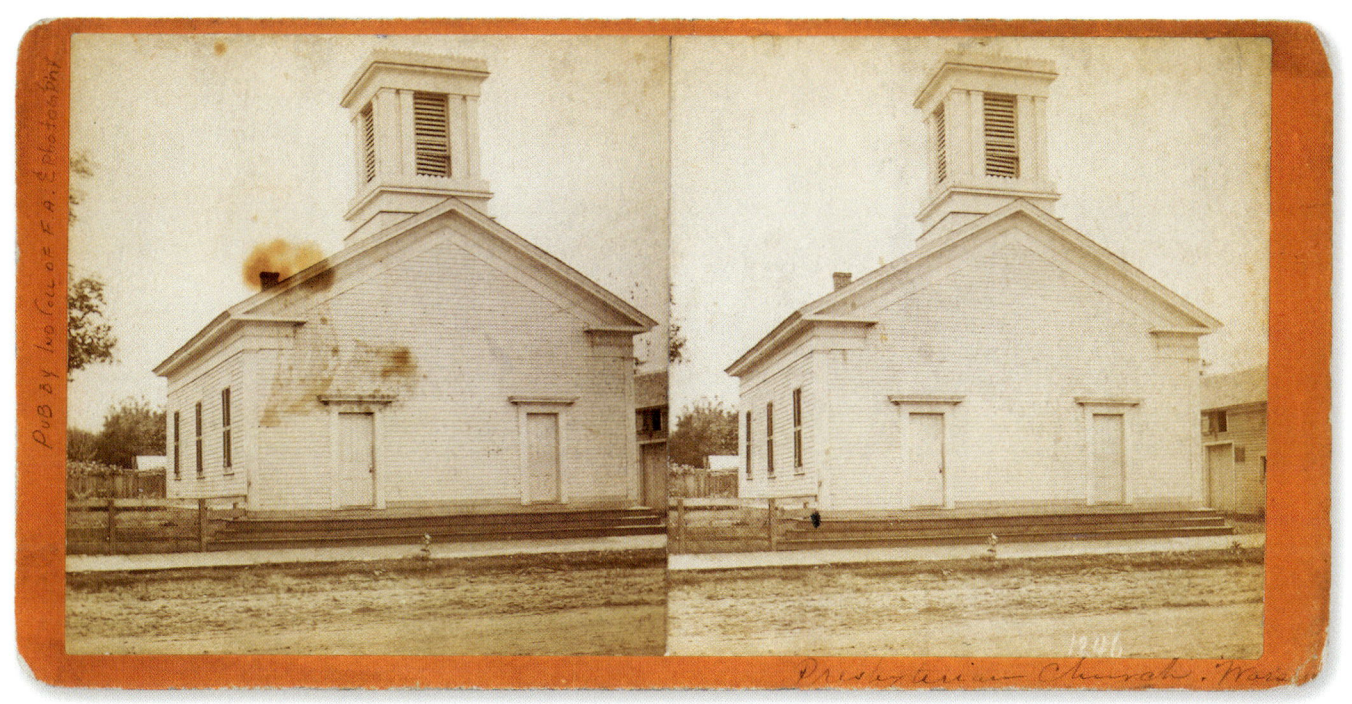

Presbyterian church, Warsaw, ca. 1870s. Published by the Indiana College of Fine Arts and Photography.

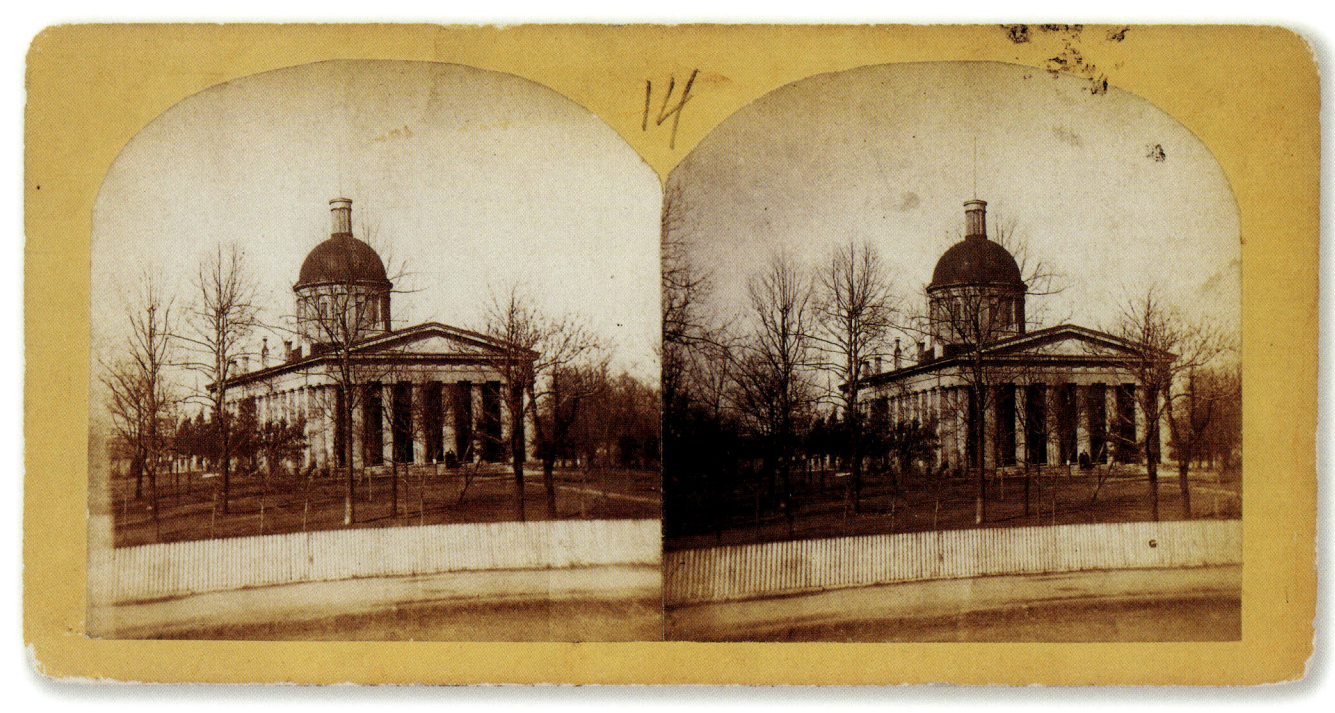

Indiana State Capitol, Indianapolis, ca. 1870s. Photographed by Charles B. Ingraham.
This building, completed in 1835, was demolished in 1877 to make way for the present-day capitol.

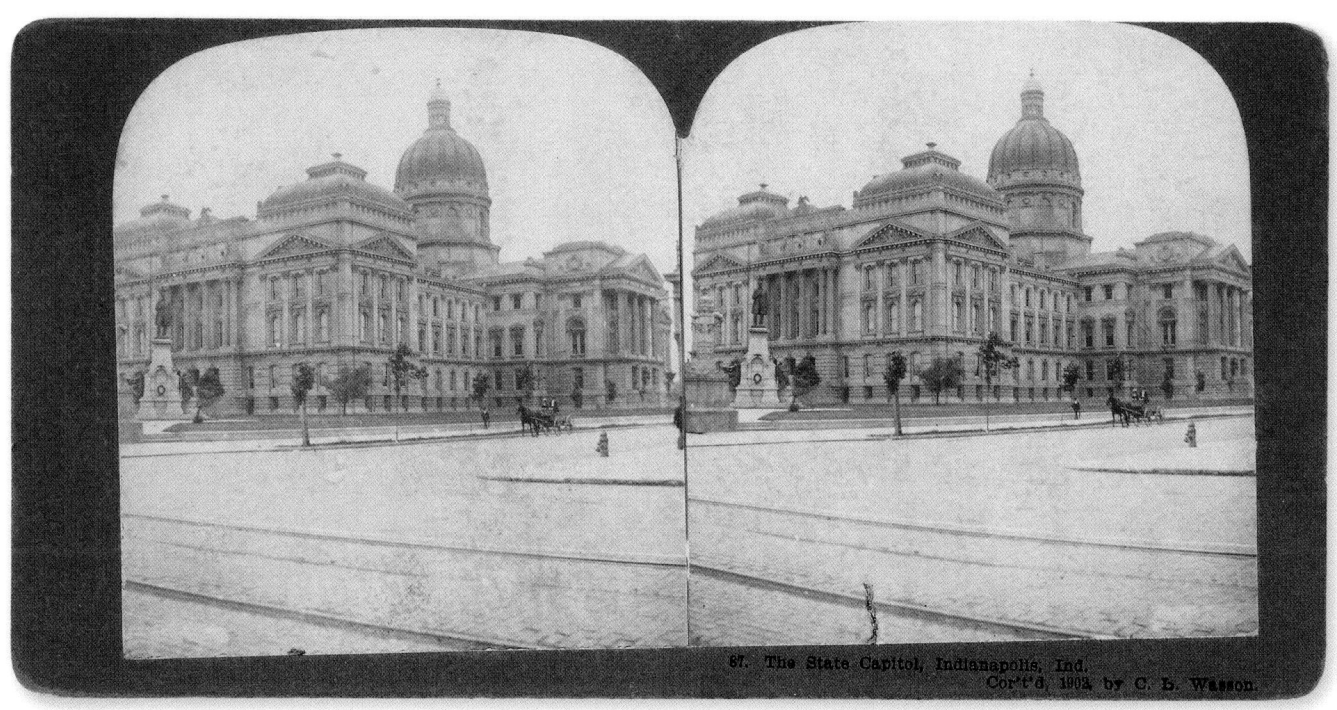

67. The State Capitol, Indianapolis, Ind.
Cor't'd, 1902, by C. L. Wasson.

Indiana State Capitol, Indianapolis, 1902. Published by C. L. Wasson.
This structure opened to the public in 1888 and still serves as Indiana's statehouse.

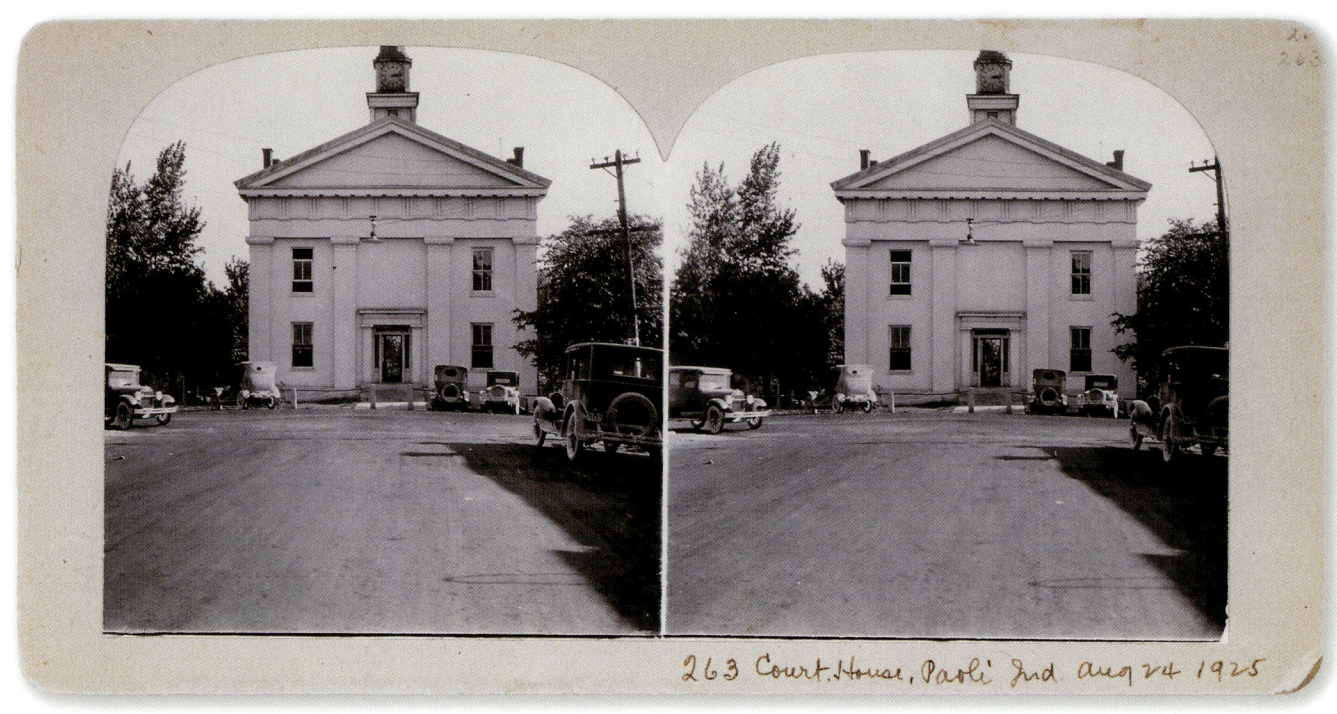

263 Court House, Paoli Ind Aug 24 1925

Orange County Courthouse, Paoli, 1925. Photographer unknown.
Built between 1848 and 1850, the courthouse is one of the oldest in Indiana still serving as a seat of government.

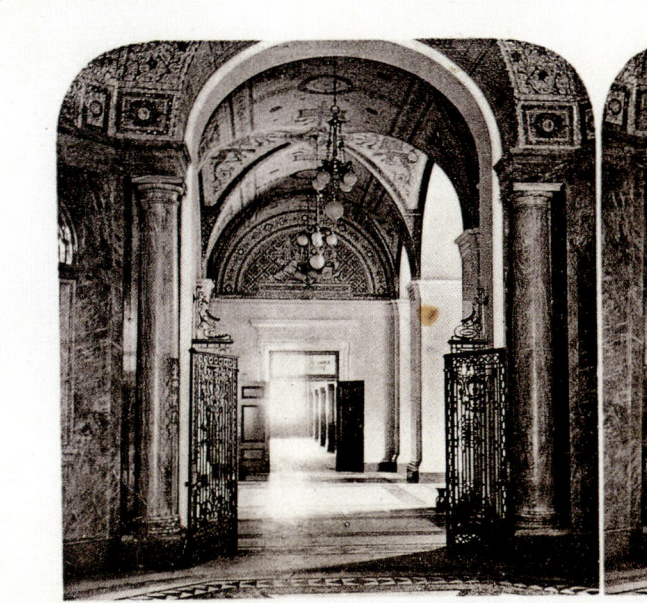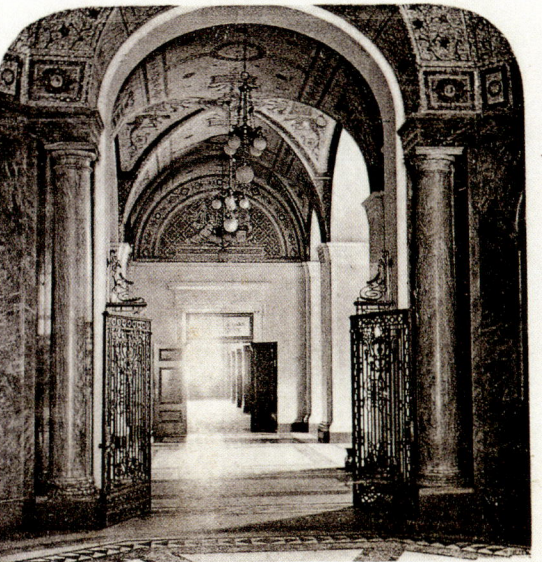

No. 6. EAST HALL OF NEW POST OFFICE. INDIANAPOLIS, IND.

"Glanceotype Stereoscopic Views" made expressly for the Kresge & Wilson Syndicate. Printed in Germany.

Interior view of the U.S. Post Office and Courthouse, Indianapolis, ca. 1905. Published by the Kresge and Wilson Syndicate. This building was completed in 1905 and served as the city's main post office until 1973. It still houses the federal courts.

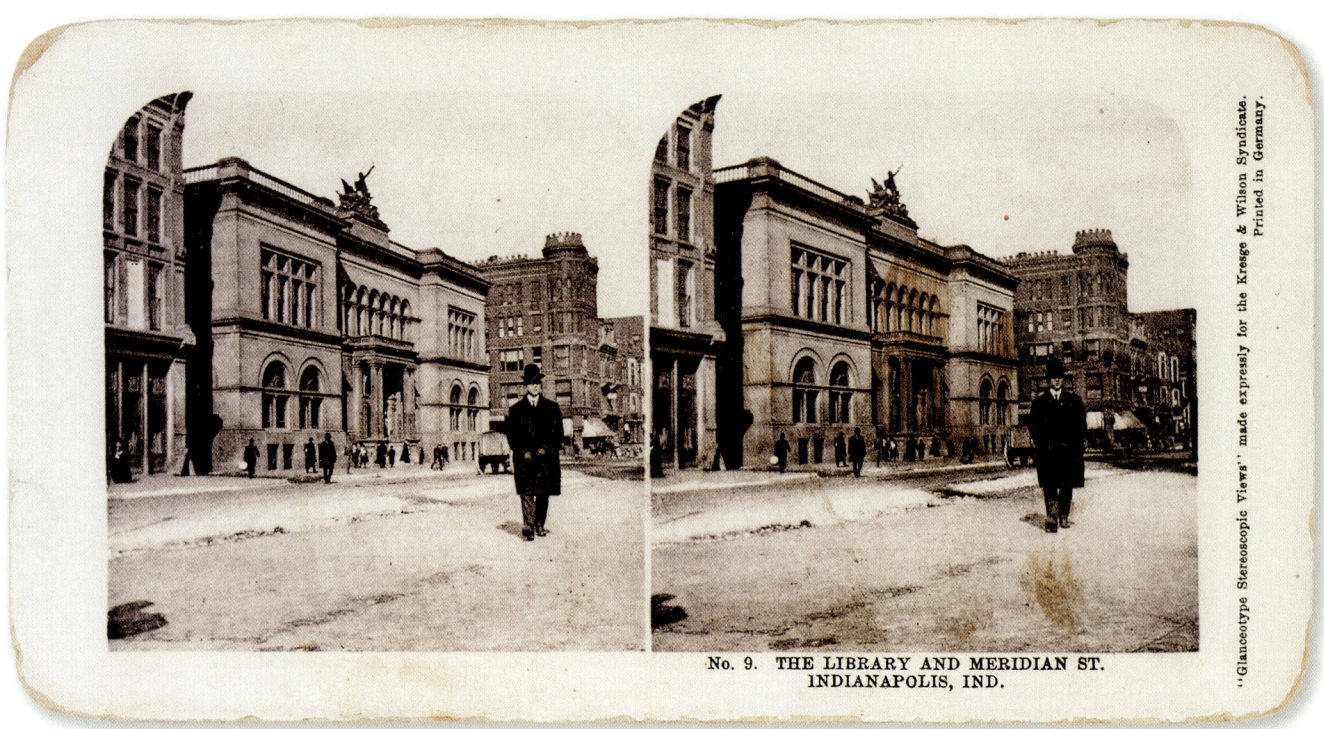

No. 9. THE LIBRARY AND MERIDIAN ST.
INDIANAPOLIS, IND.

"Glanceotype Stereoscopic Views" made expressly for the Kresge & Wilson Syndicate.
Printed in Germany.

Indianapolis Public Library, ca. 1905. Published by the Kresge and Wilson Syndicate.
The library operated out of this building, located at the corner of Meridian and Ohio Streets, from 1893 to 1917.

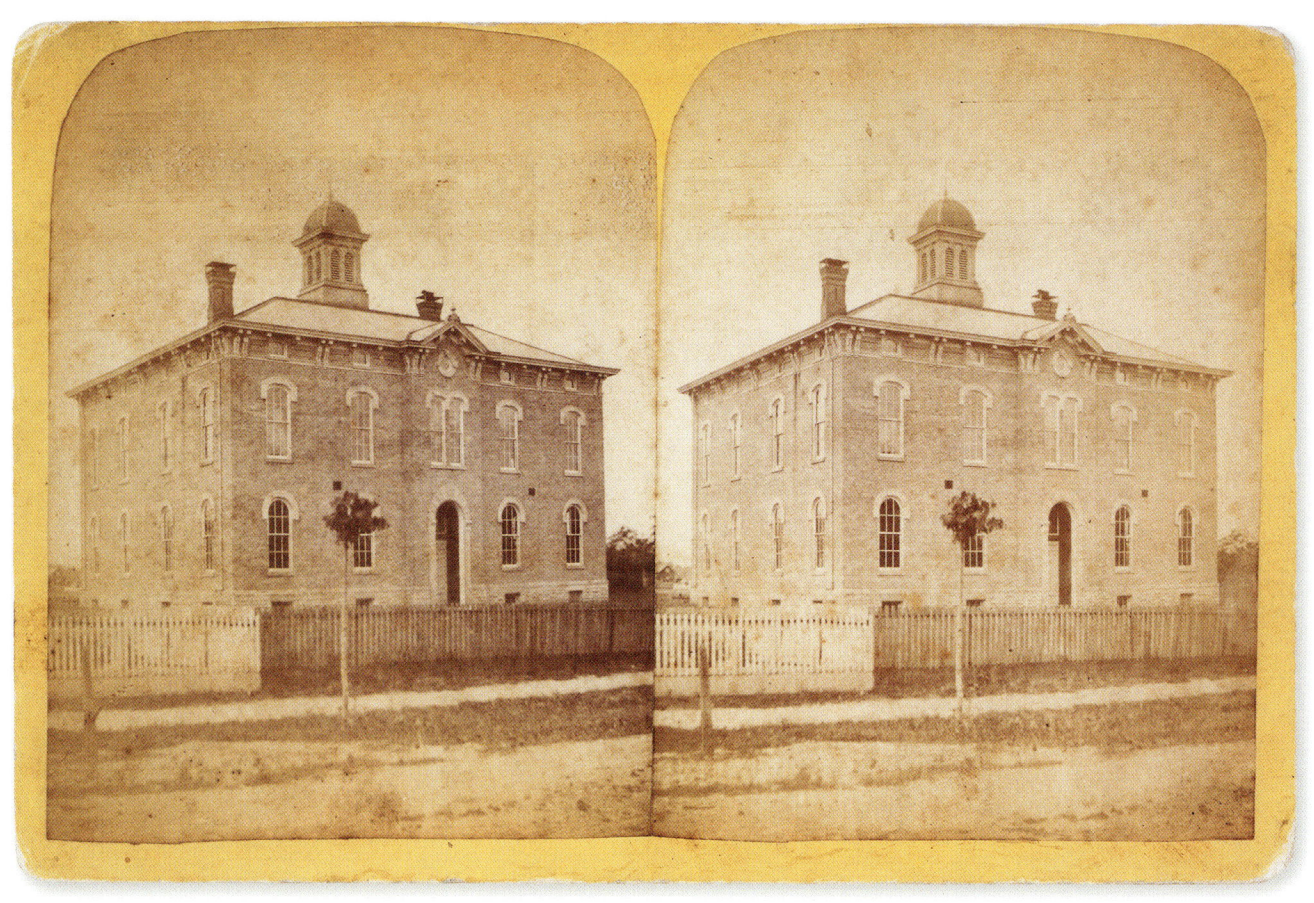

Unidentified building, location unknown, ca. 1870s. Photographed by Thomas Harrie Rose.
This structure was most likely a schoolhouse and may have been located near New Castle, where Rose operated his studio.

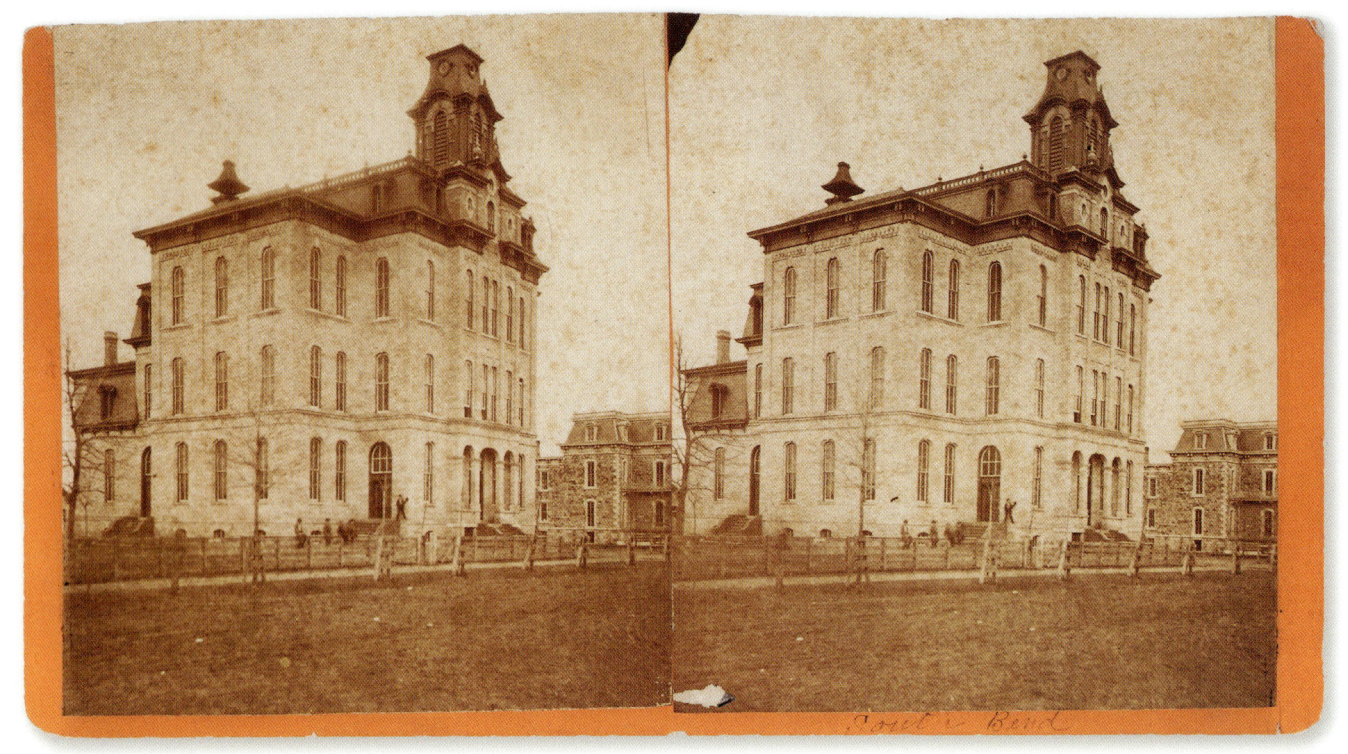

High school, South Bend, ca. 1870s. Photographed by James Bonney.
The school opened in the fall of 1873 on the site of the old county seminary, on Washington Street west of downtown.

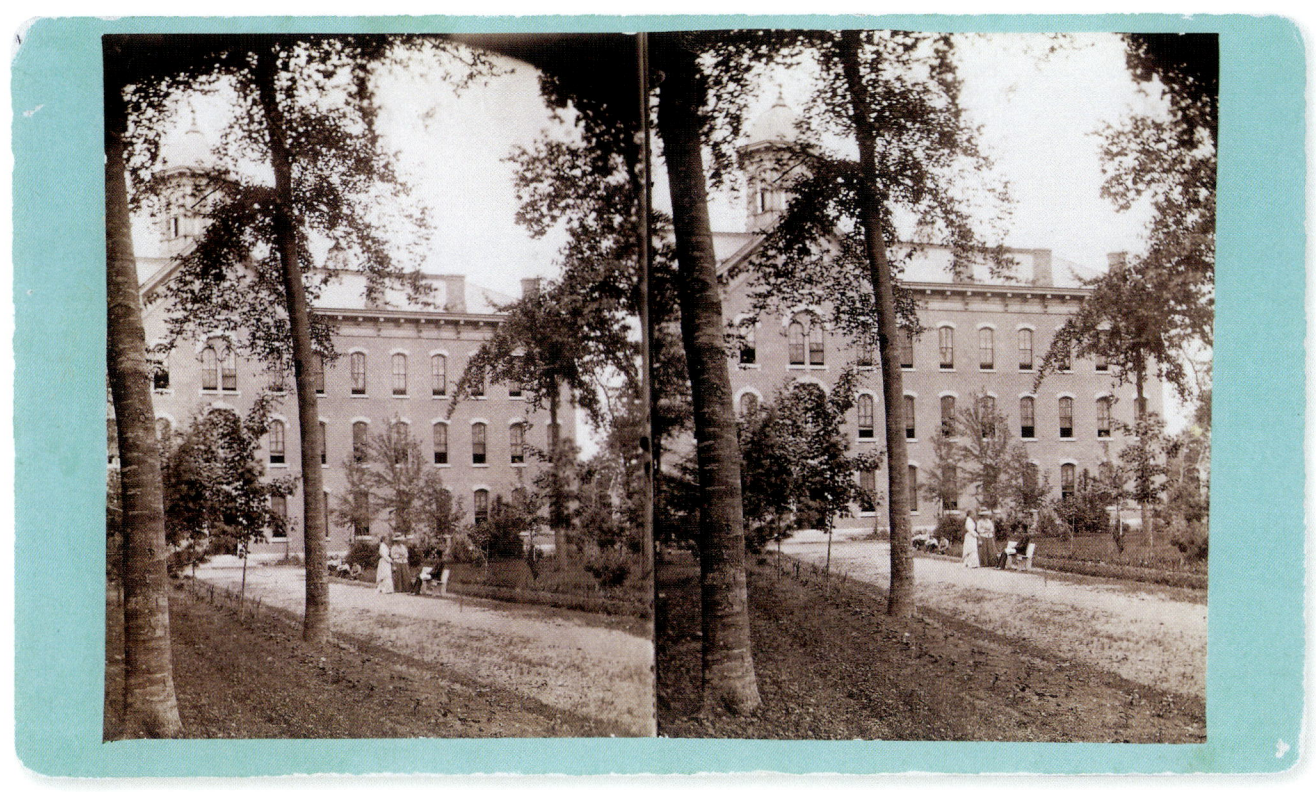

Administration Building, Indiana Soldiers' and Seamen's Home, Knightstown, 1880. Photographed by Oliver Charles.
The home originally housed disabled Civil War veterans and orphans of the war, but by the early 1870s it cared for just the children.
In 1887 its name was changed to the Indiana Soldiers' Orphans' Home, and today it is known as the Indiana Soldiers' and Sailors' Children's Home.

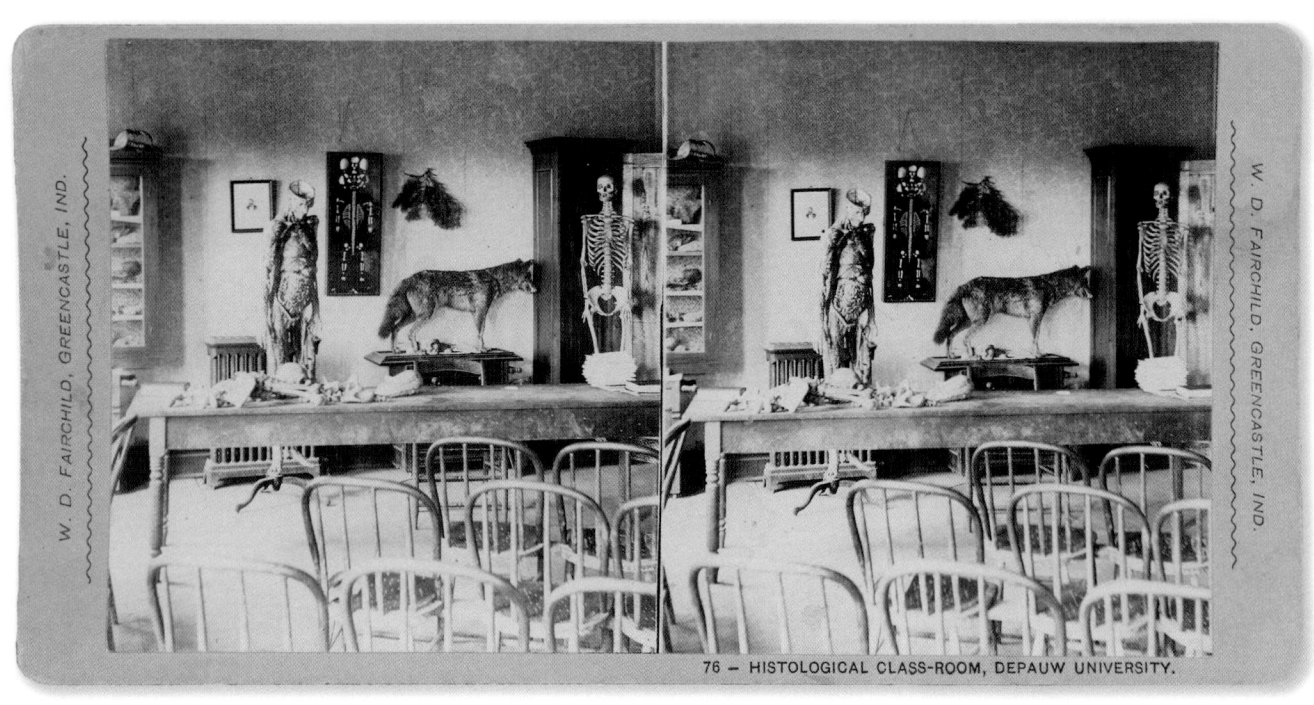

76 – HISTOLOGICAL CLASS-ROOM, DEPAUW UNIVERSITY.

W. D. FAIRCHILD, GREENCASTLE, IND.

W. D. FAIRCHILD, GREENCASTLE, IND.

Histological classroom, DePauw University, Greencastle, ca. late 1890s. Photographed by W. D. Fairchild.

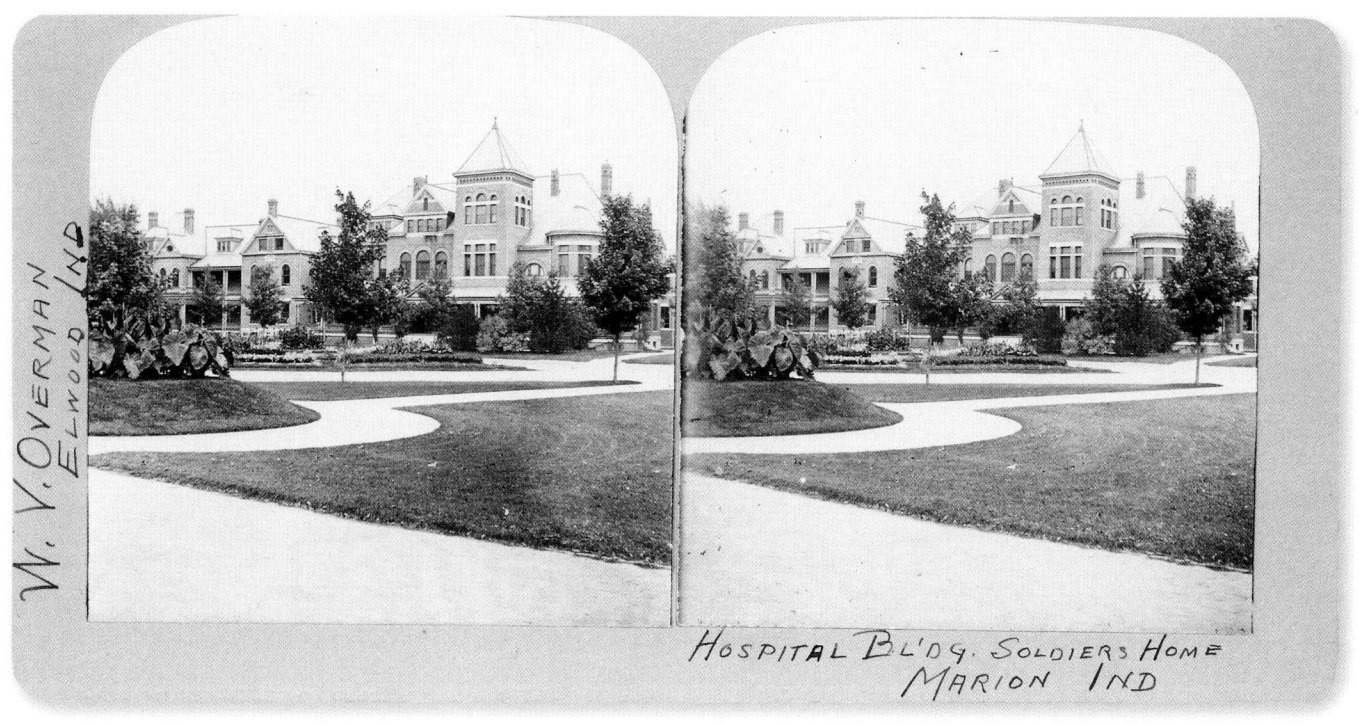

National Home for Disabled Volunteer Soldiers, Marion, ca. early 1900s. Photographed by W. V. Overman.
The Soldiers' Home, as the facility is commonly known, opened in 1890.

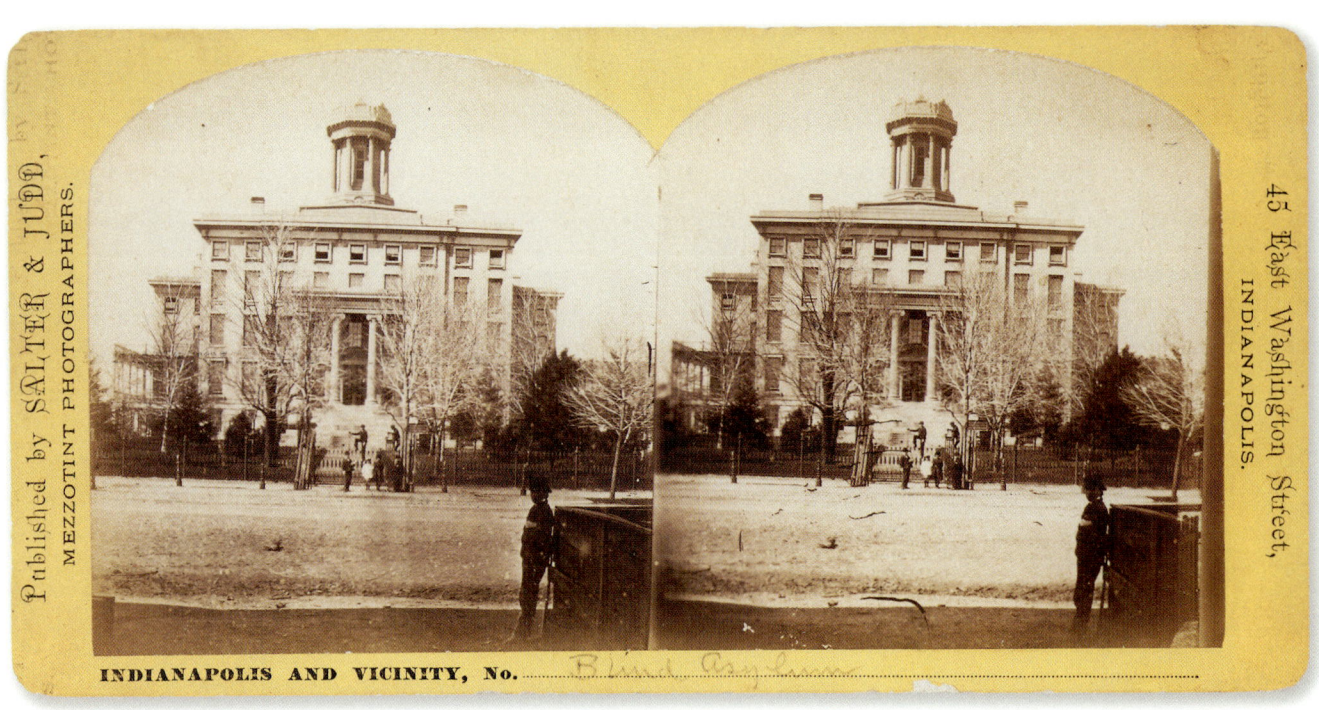

Published by SALTER & JUDD,
MEZZOTINT PHOTOGRAPHERS.

45 East Washington Street,
INDIANAPOLIS.

INDIANAPOLIS AND VICINITY, No. _____ Blind Asylum

Indiana School for the Blind, Indianapolis, ca. 1875. Published by Salter and Judd.
Architect Francis Costigan helped design the school, which stood from 1853 to 1930 on North Street between Meridian and Pennsylvania Streets.

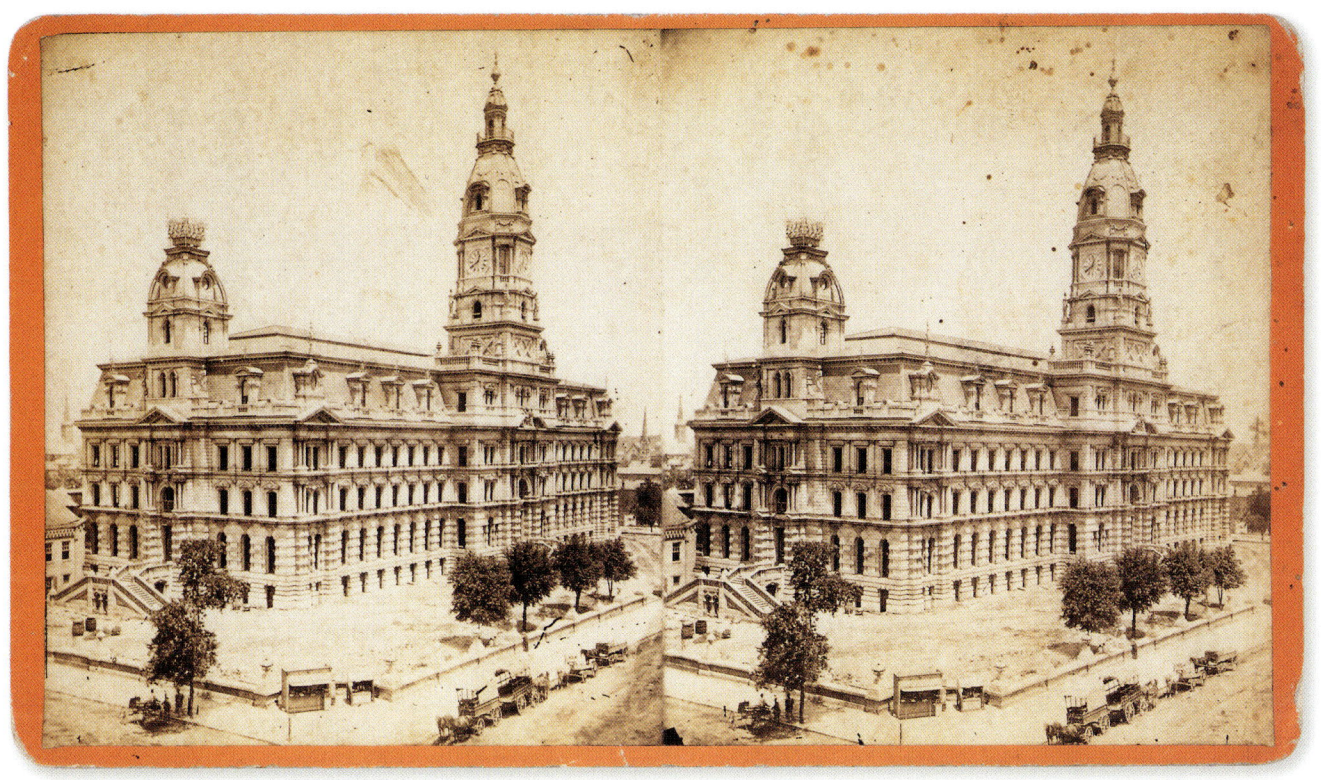

Marion County Courthouse, Indianapolis, late 1870s. Published by Pendergast Brothers.
The courthouse was completed in 1876 and served as Marion County's seat of government until it was demolished in the early 1960s.
It was located on Washington Street, just south of today's City-County Building.

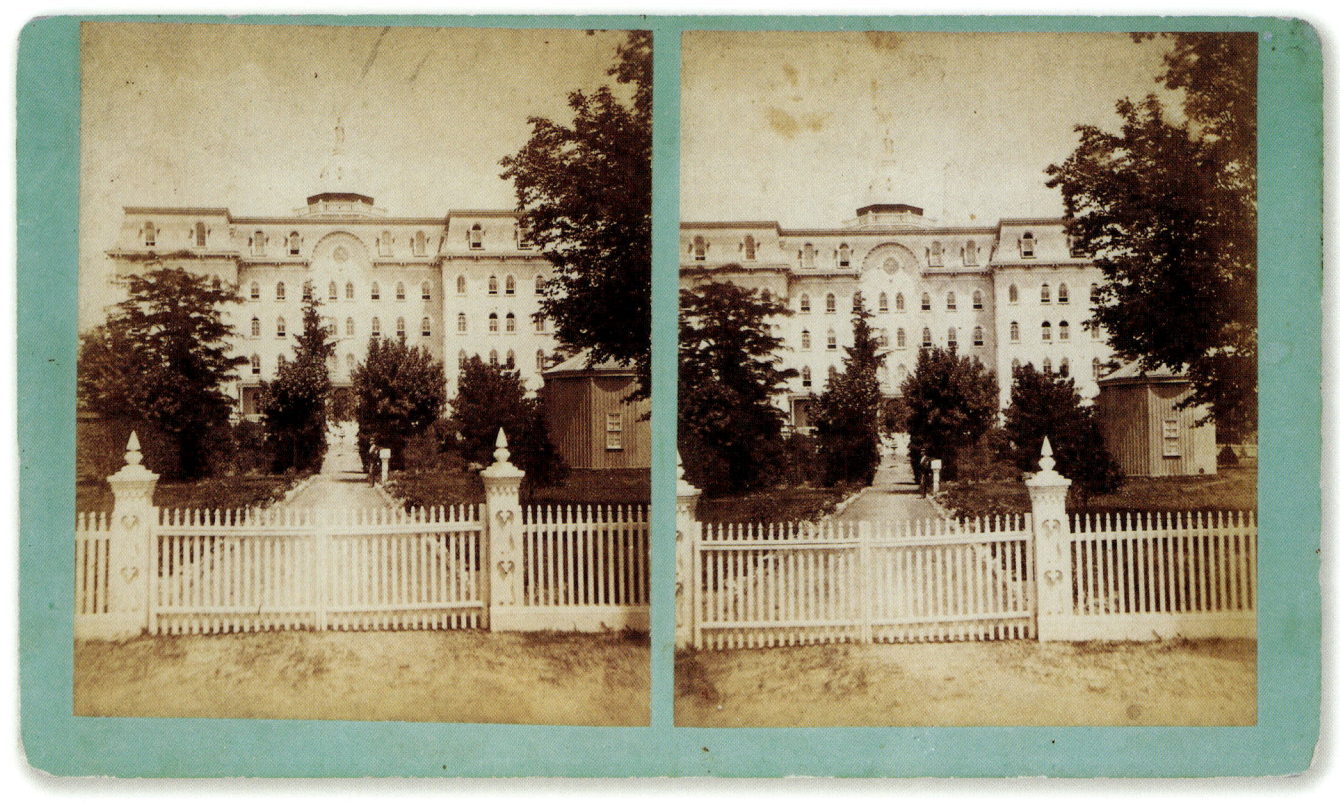

Main Building, University of Notre Dame, South Bend, ca. 1870s. Photographer unknown.
Dedicated in 1866, this was the university's second main building. Fire destroyed it (and several other campus buildings) in April 1879,
and in its place the university built a third main building—the one with the familiar gold dome, still standing today.

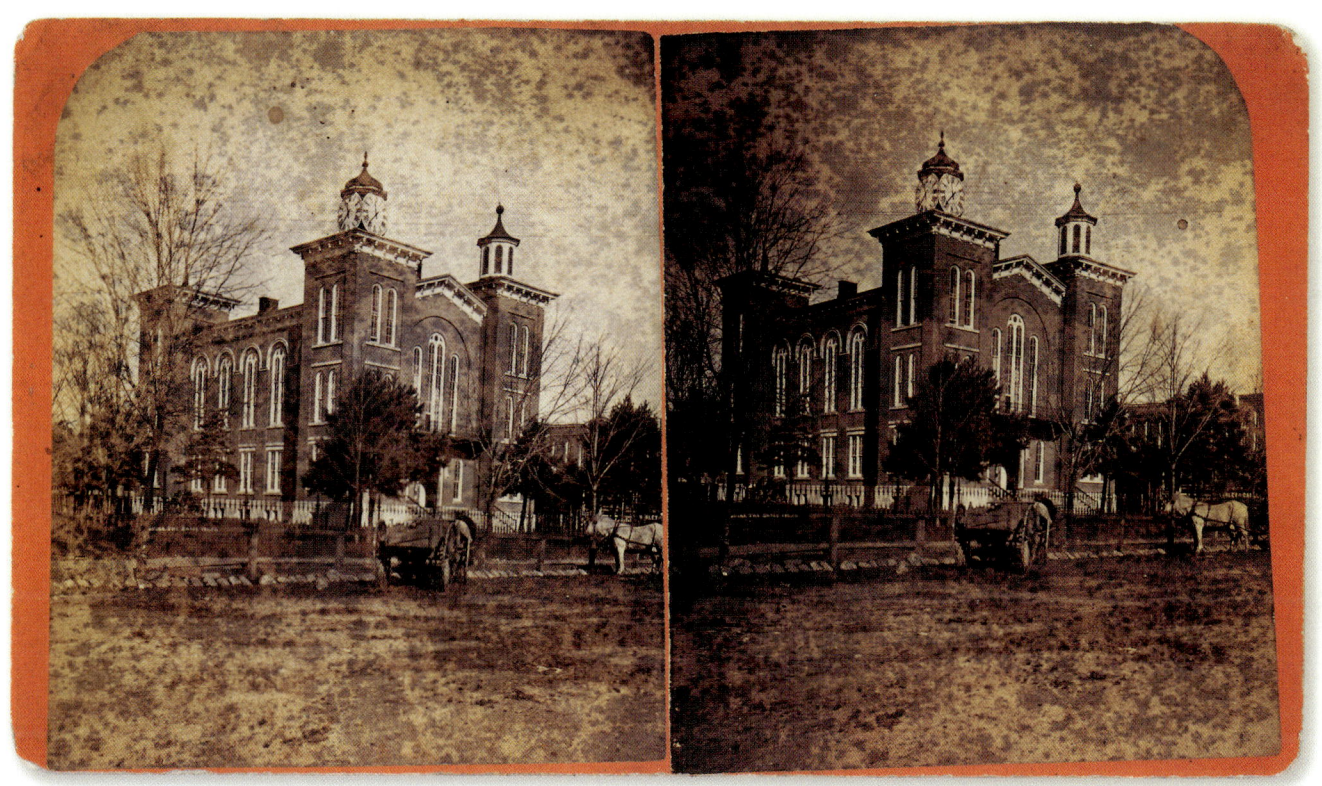

Carroll County Courthouse, Delphi, ca. 1870s. Photographed by A. W. Wolever.
This was Carroll County's second courthouse, in use from the late 1850s to 1916.

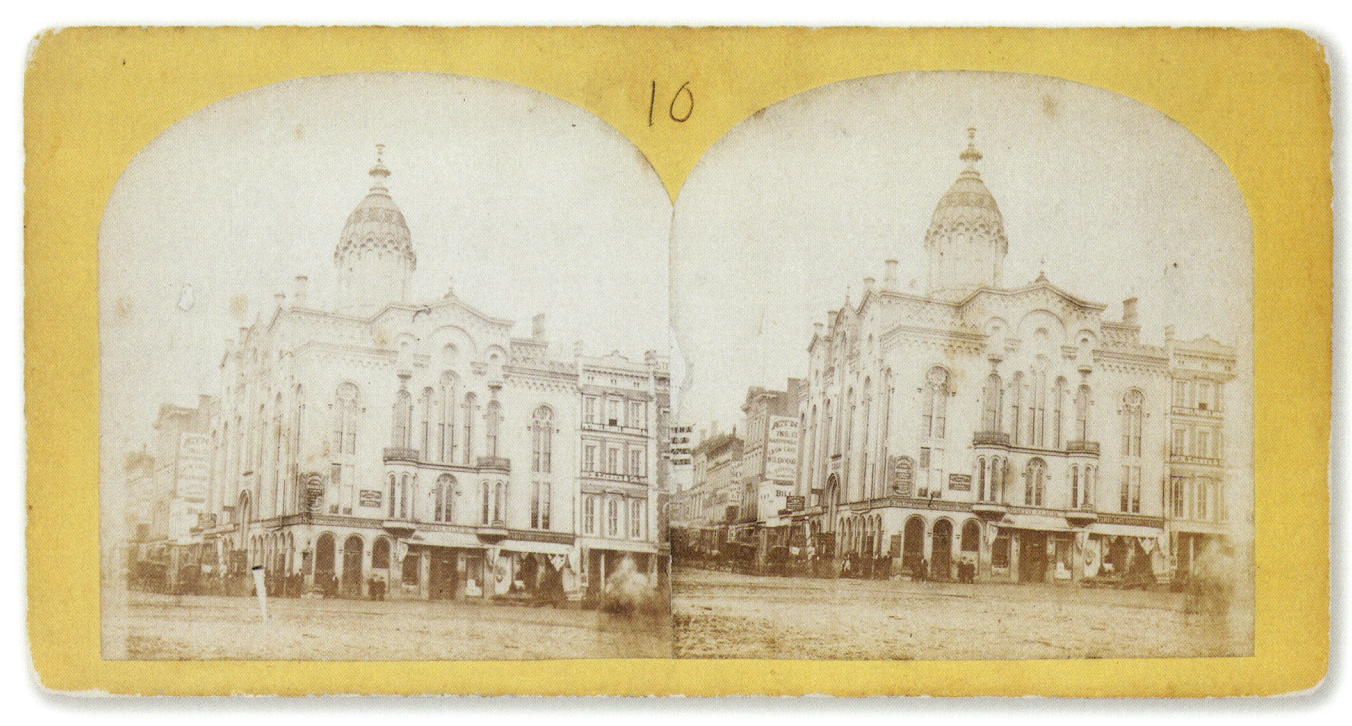

Independent Order of Odd Fellows Building, Indianapolis, ca. 1870s. Published by Ingraham and Claflin.
The popular lodge was constructed in the mid-1850s and stood on the northeast corner of Washington and Pennsylvania Streets.

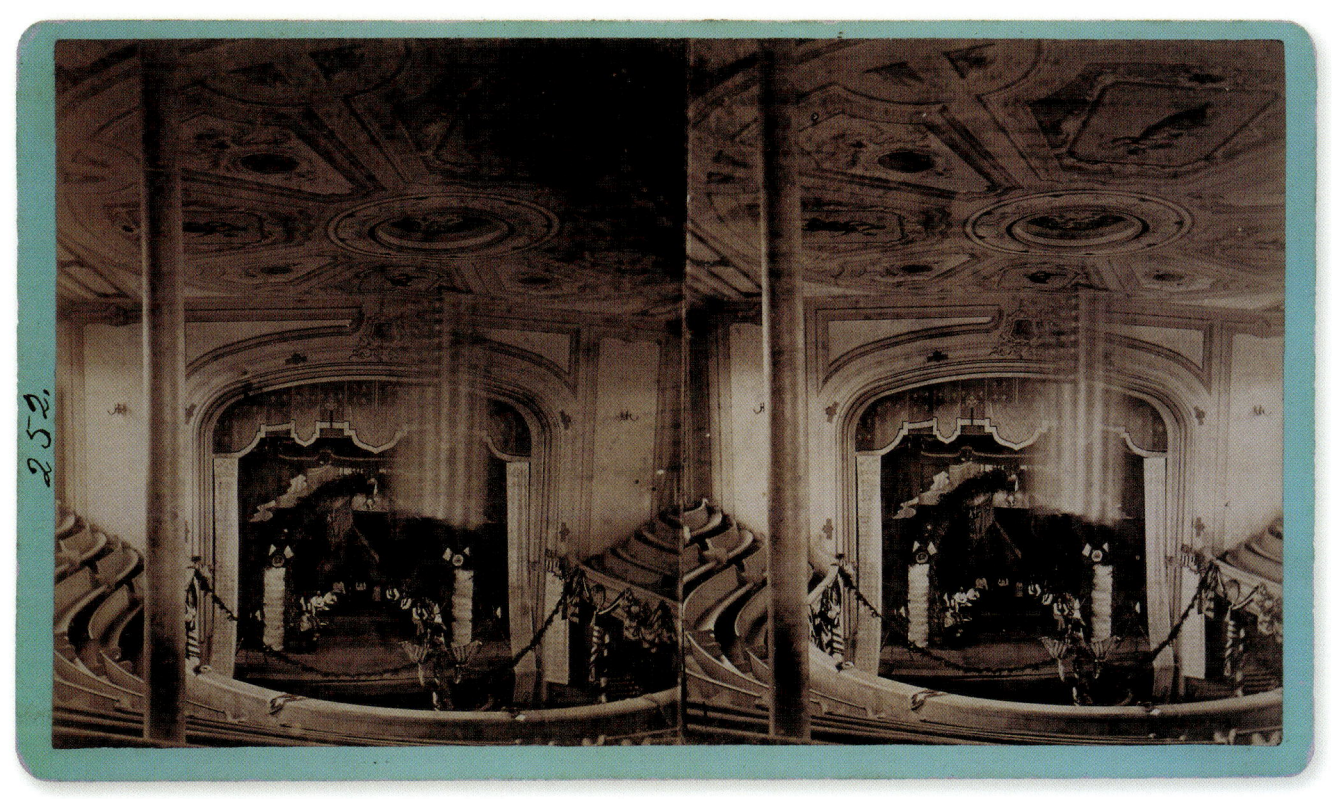

Interior of the Grand Opera House, Lafayette, ca. 1870s. Published by Wright and Hartwell.

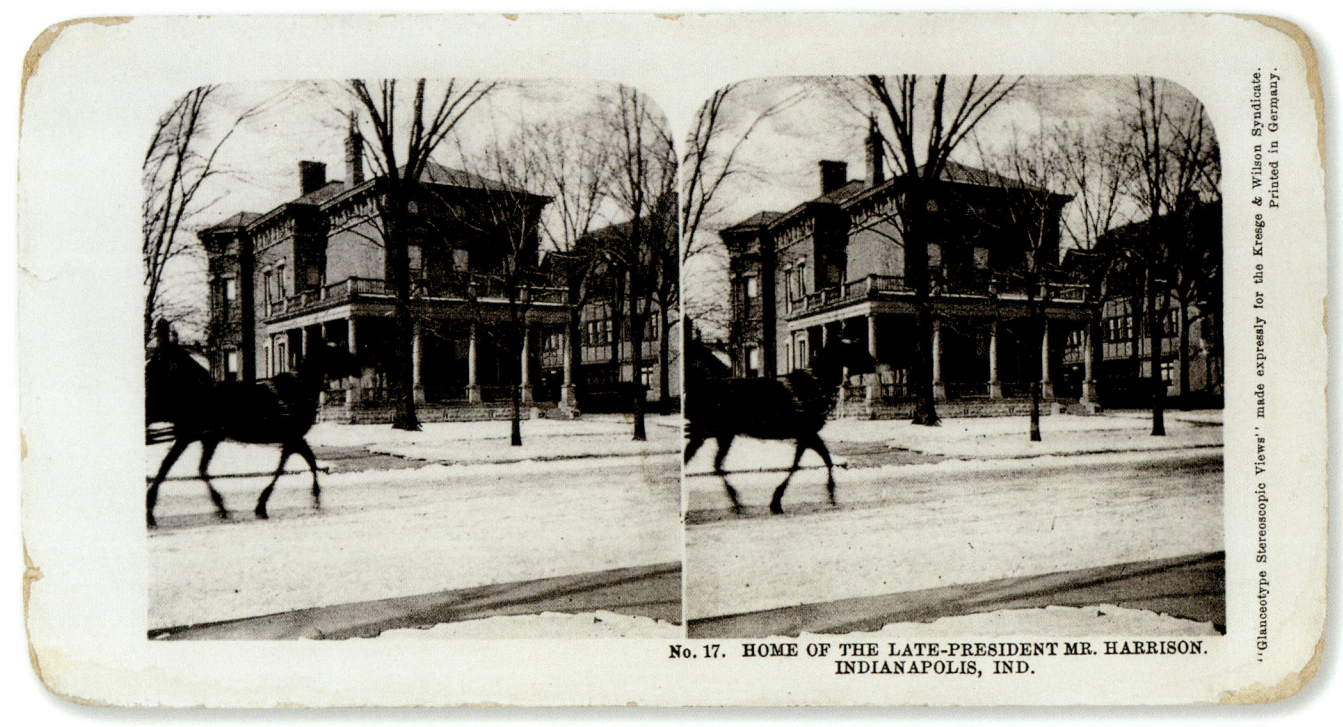

No. 17. HOME OF THE LATE-PRESIDENT MR. HARRISON.
INDIANAPOLIS, IND.

"Glanceotype Stereoscopic Views" made expressly for the Kresge & Wilson Syndicate.
Printed in Germany.

Home of President Benjamin Harrison, Indianapolis, ca. 1905. Published by the Kresge and Wilson Syndicate.
Harrison, who served as president from 1889 to 1893, lived in the North Delaware Street home from
the time of its completion in 1875 until his death in 1901.

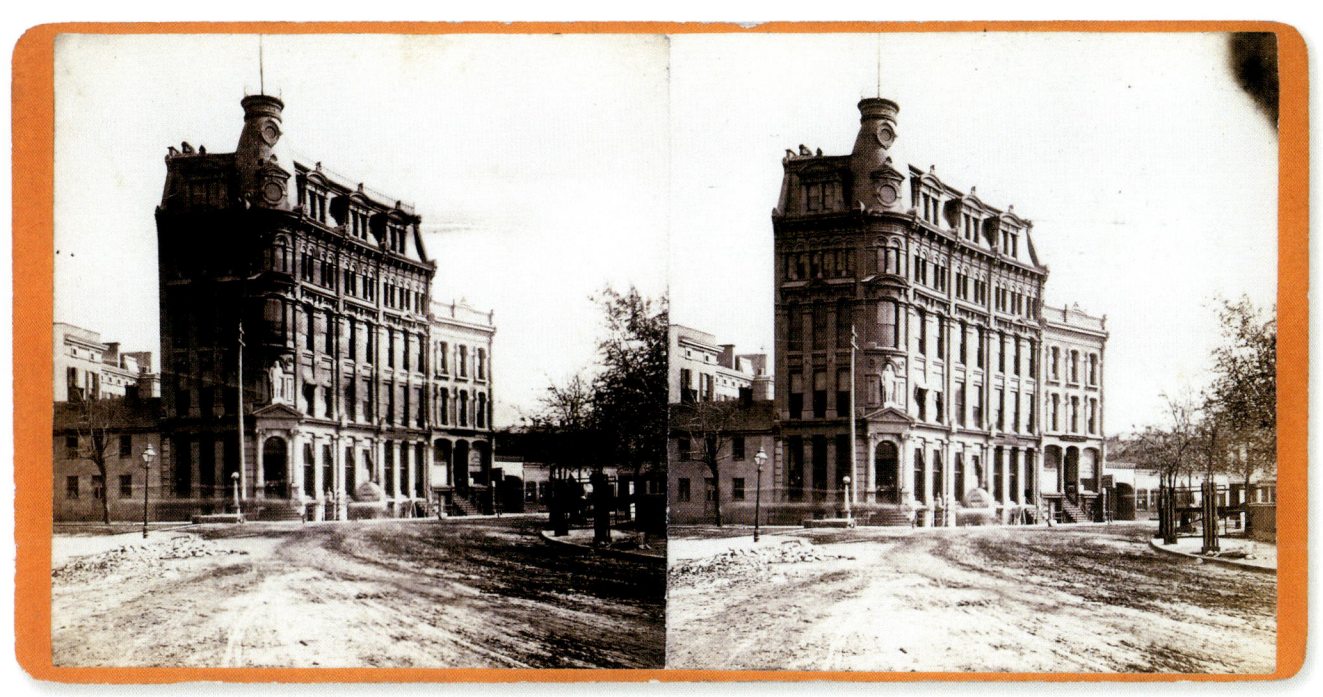

Franklin Fire Insurance Building, Indianapolis, ca. 1875. Photographed by J. W. Pendergast.
This structure stood on the southeast corner of the Circle, where the Circle Tower is located today.

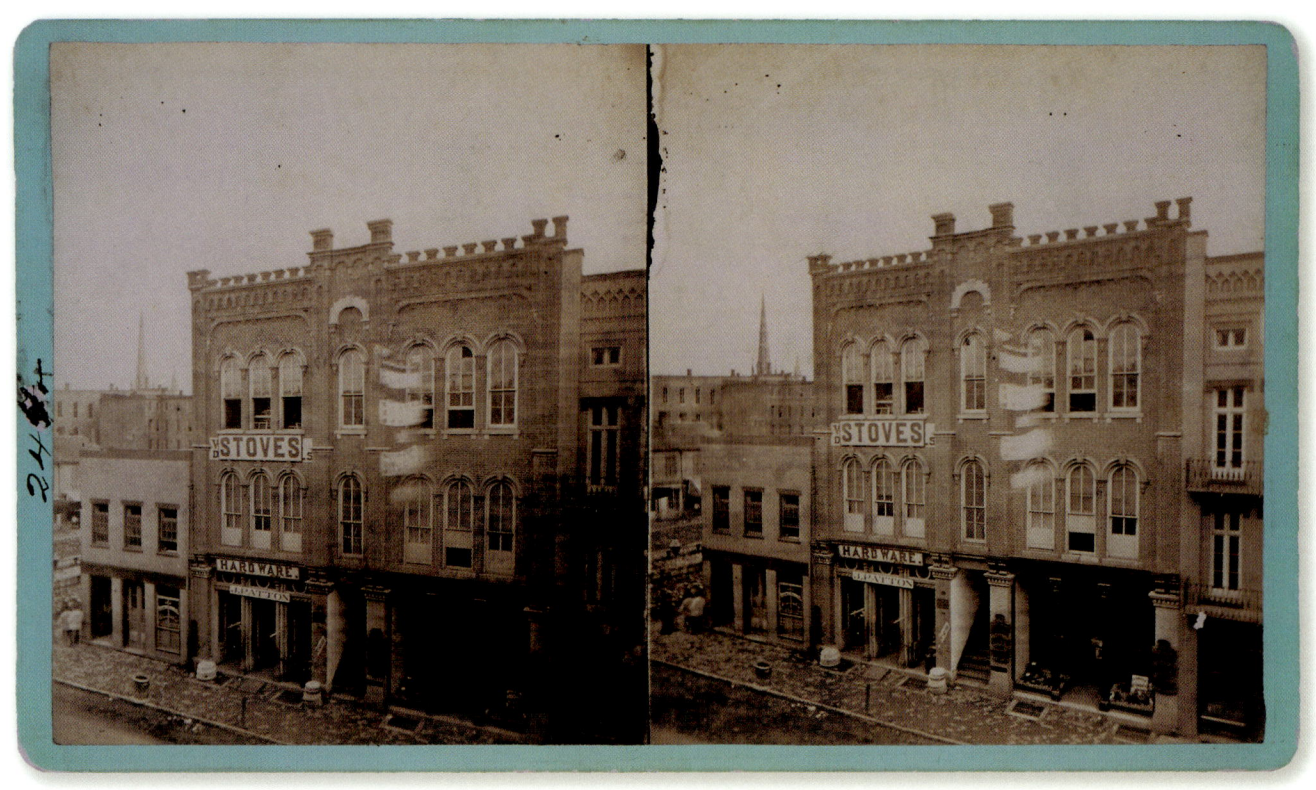

Patton Building, Lafayette, ca. 1870s. Published by Wright and Hartwell.
This building was located on Main Street, between Third and Fourth Streets.

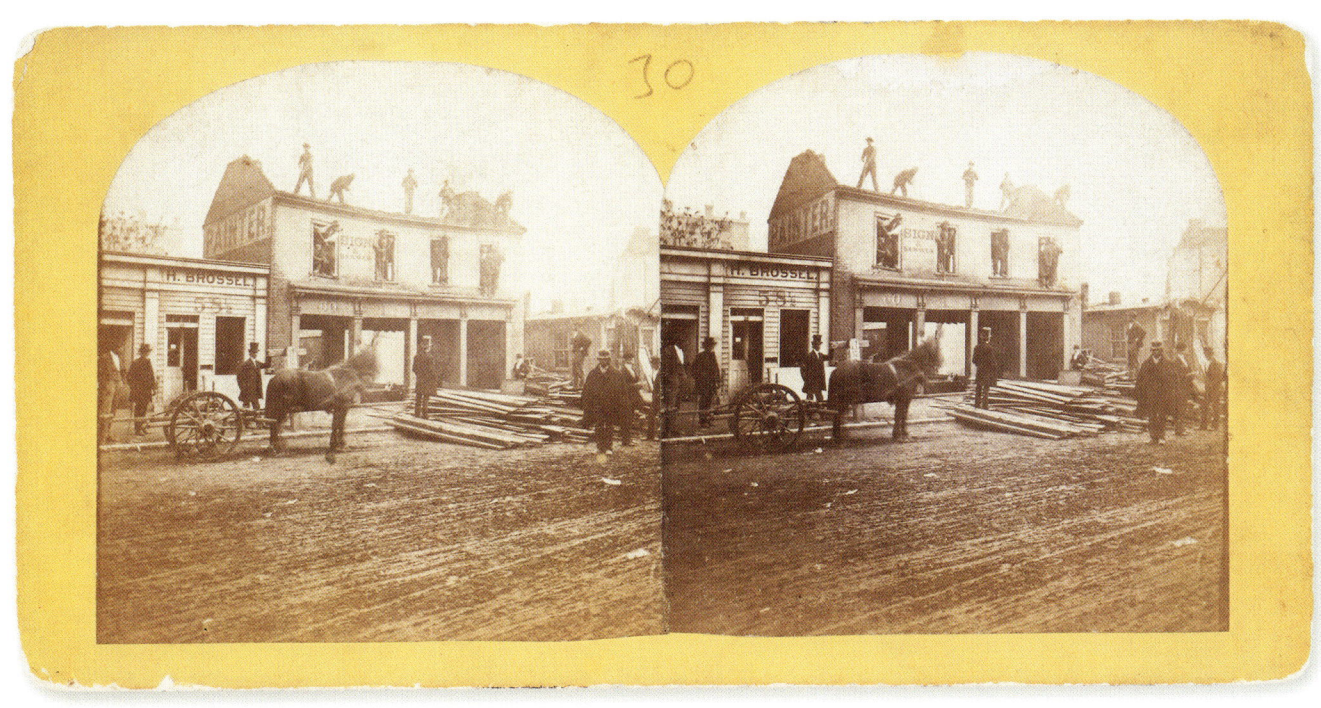

30

Brick building, Indianapolis, ca. 1874. Published by Ingraham and Claflin.
The caption on this card indicates that this structure, located at 60–62 East Market Street, was the first one constructed of brick in Indianapolis.
According to an 1870 history of the city, it was built for John Johnson in the years 1822–1823 and stood on the northeast corner of Pennsylvania and Market Streets.
In this view, workers appear to be dismantling it, no doubt to make way for new development.

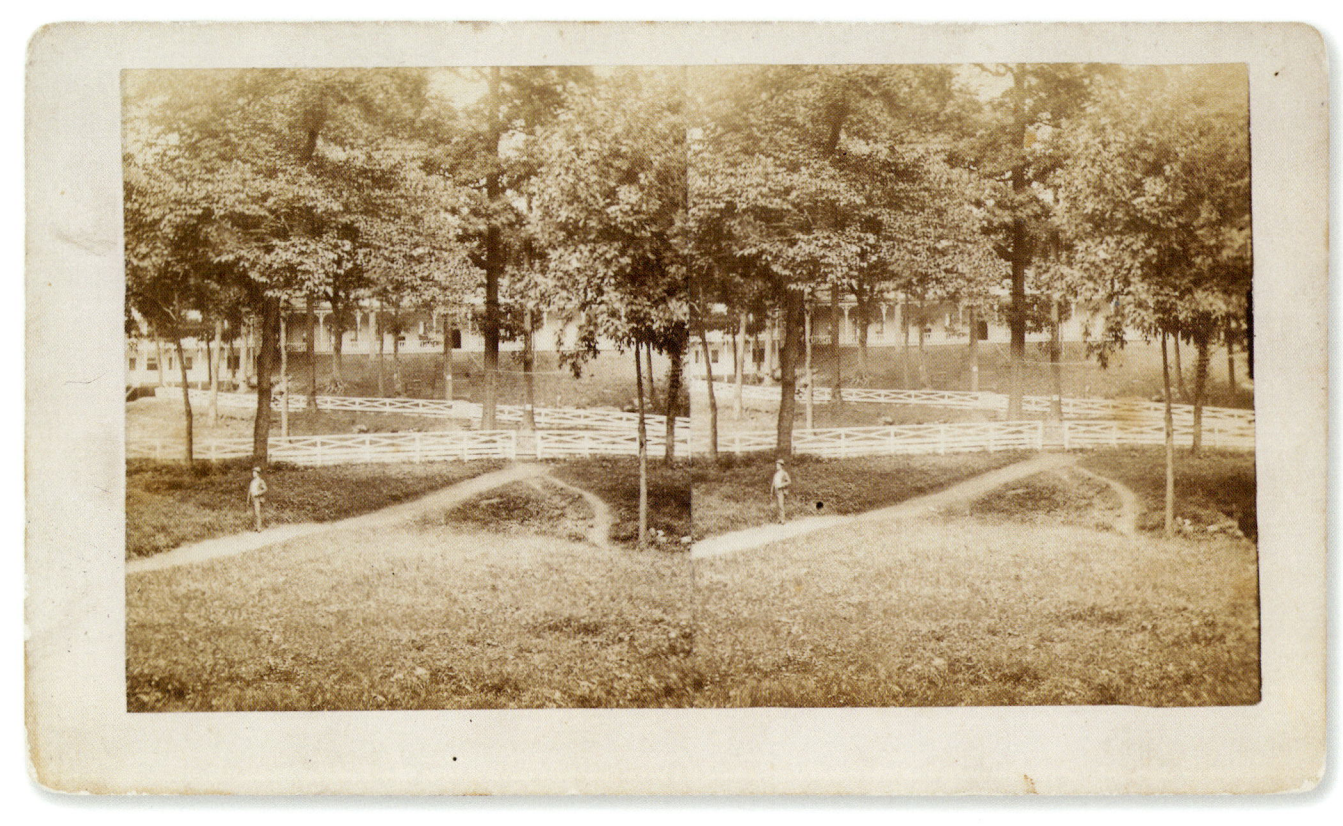

View of the West Baden Springs Hotel from Spring No. 1, ca. 1880s. Published by Weatherford and Swan.
This frame structure was built in the early 1850s and burned in 1901. In 1903 owner Lee Sinclair opened
on the same site a new hotel—the famed "Eighth Wonder of the World" that stands today.

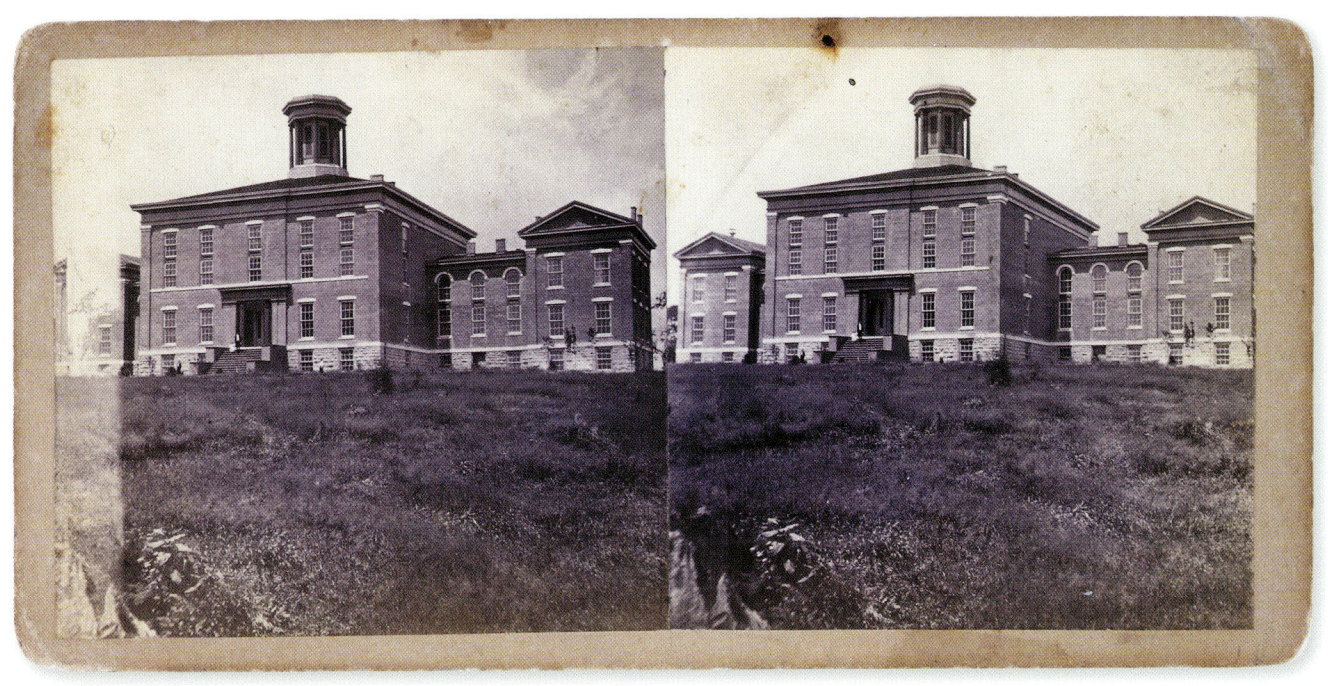

Classic Hall, Hanover College, near Madison, ca. 1870s. Photographed by J. R. Thorne.
The hall opened for classes in the fall of 1857. It remained a campus fixture until December 1941, when it burned.

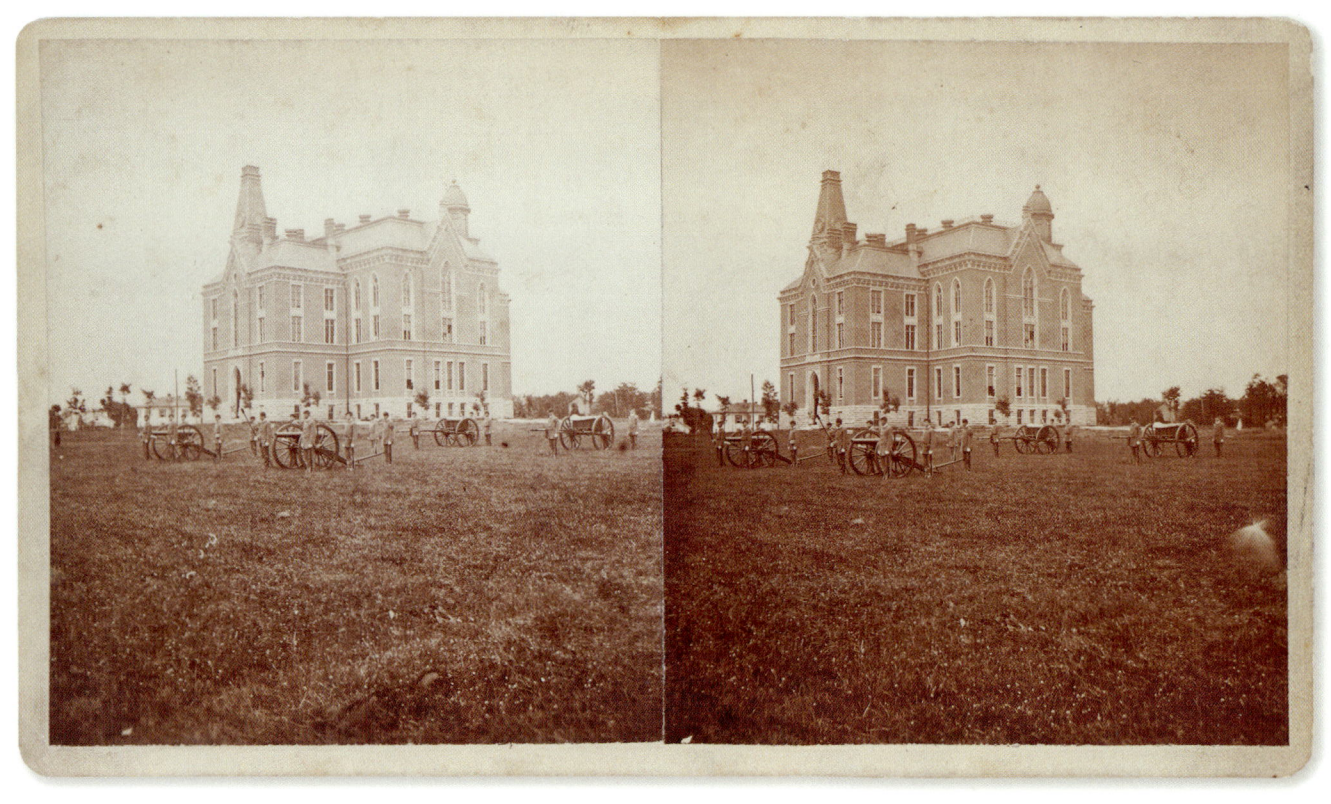

East College with cadets, DePauw University, Greencastle, ca. late 1870s. Photographer unknown.
East College is DePauw's oldest existing structure. The cornerstone was laid in 1870, and the building was dedicated in 1877.

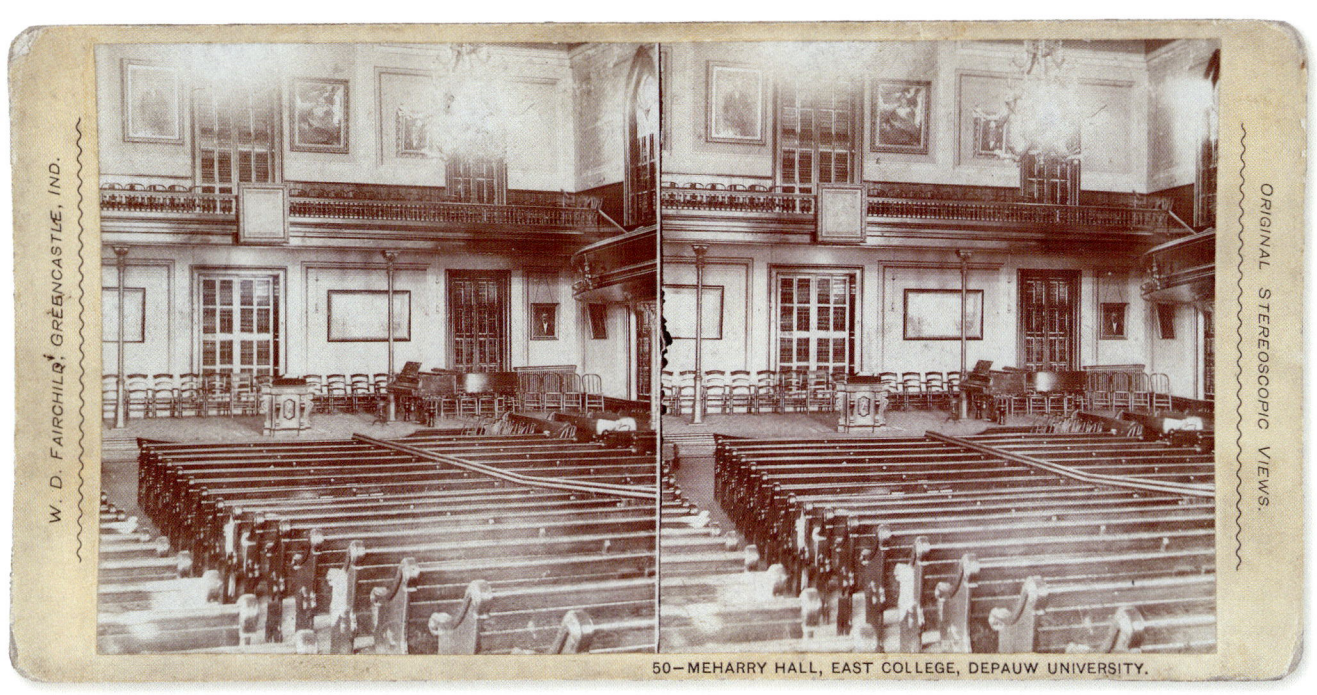

50—MEHARRY HALL, EAST COLLEGE, DEPAUW UNIVERSITY.

Meharry Hall, East College, DePauw University, Greencastle, ca. late 1890s. Photographed by W. D. Fairchild. Over the years, this room inside East College has been used for religious services, student assemblies, and lectures.

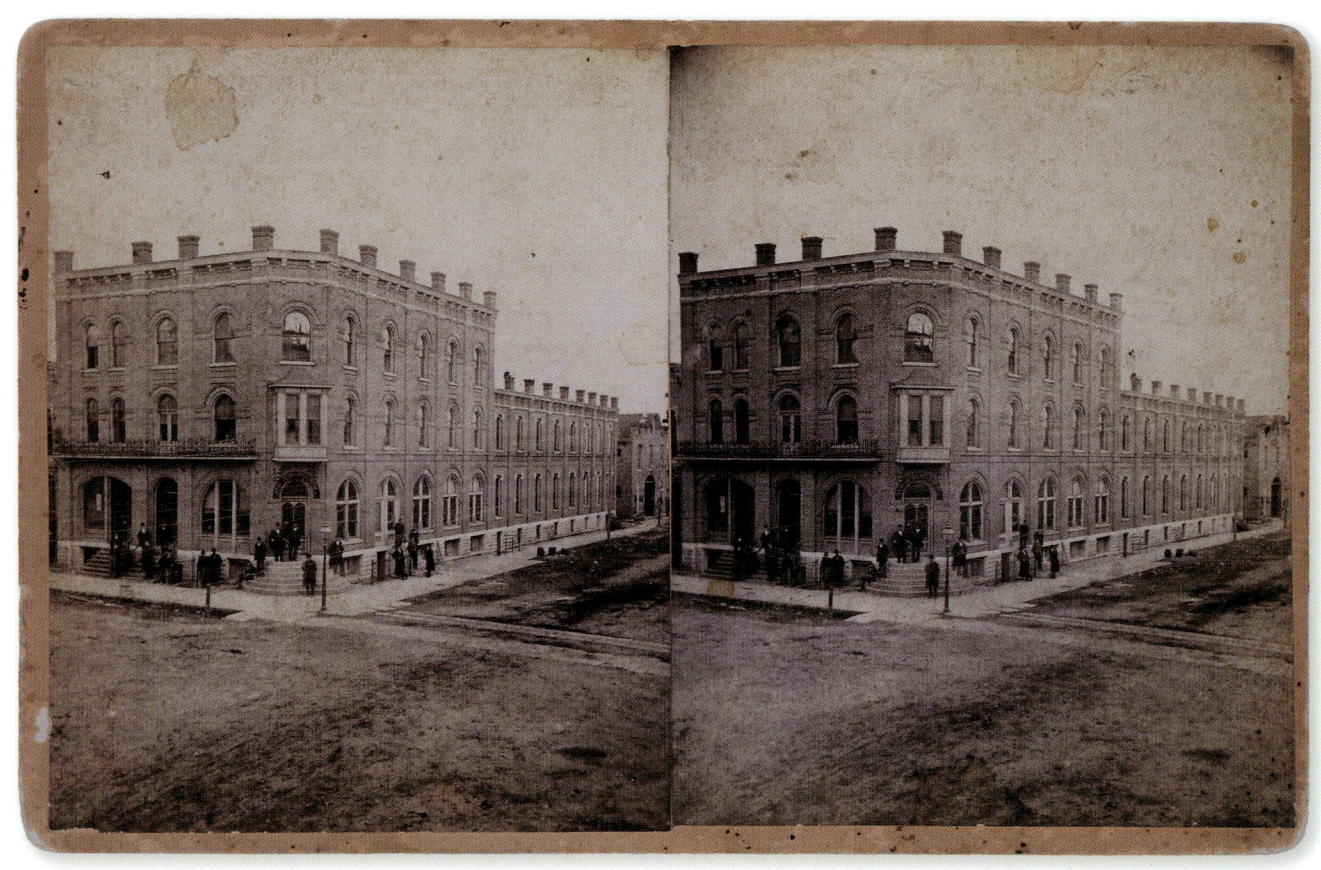

DeArmond Hotel, Greensburg, ca. 1870s. Photographer unknown.

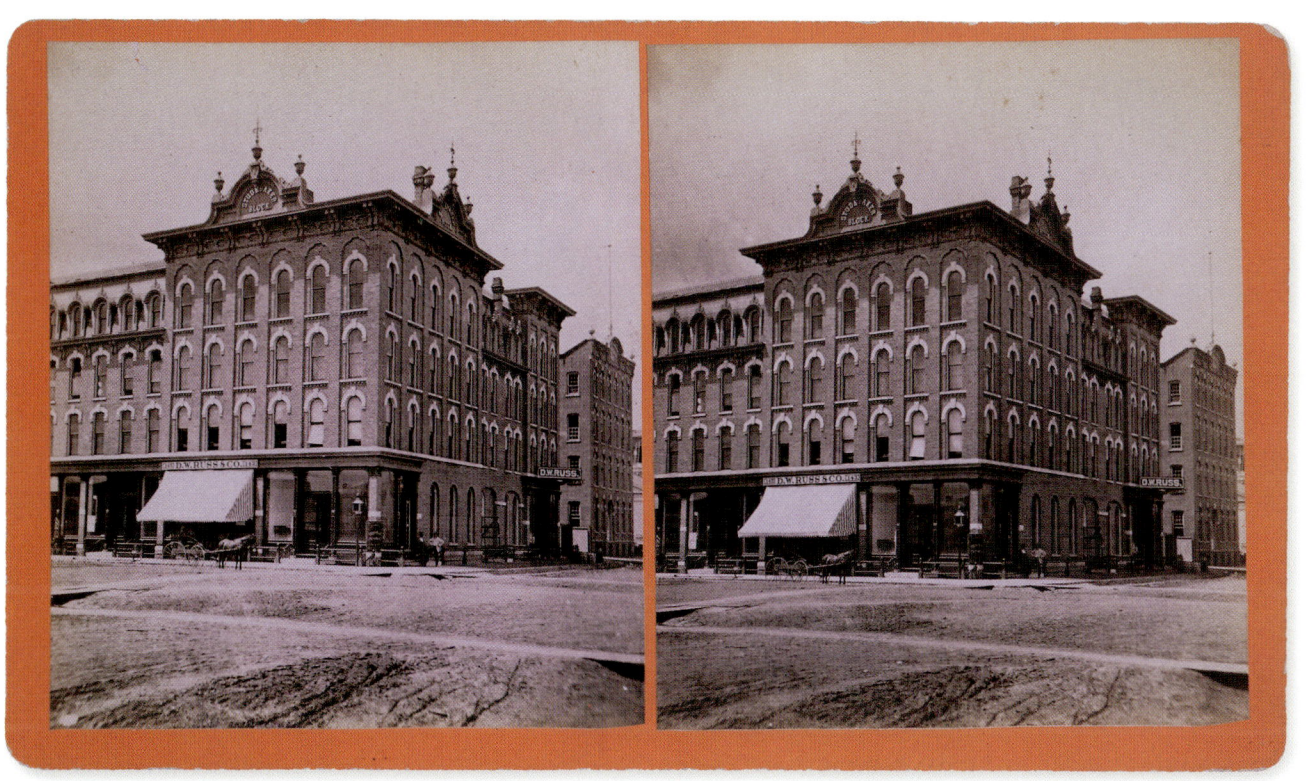

Studebaker Block, South Bend, ca. 1880s. Photographed by William G. Flanders.

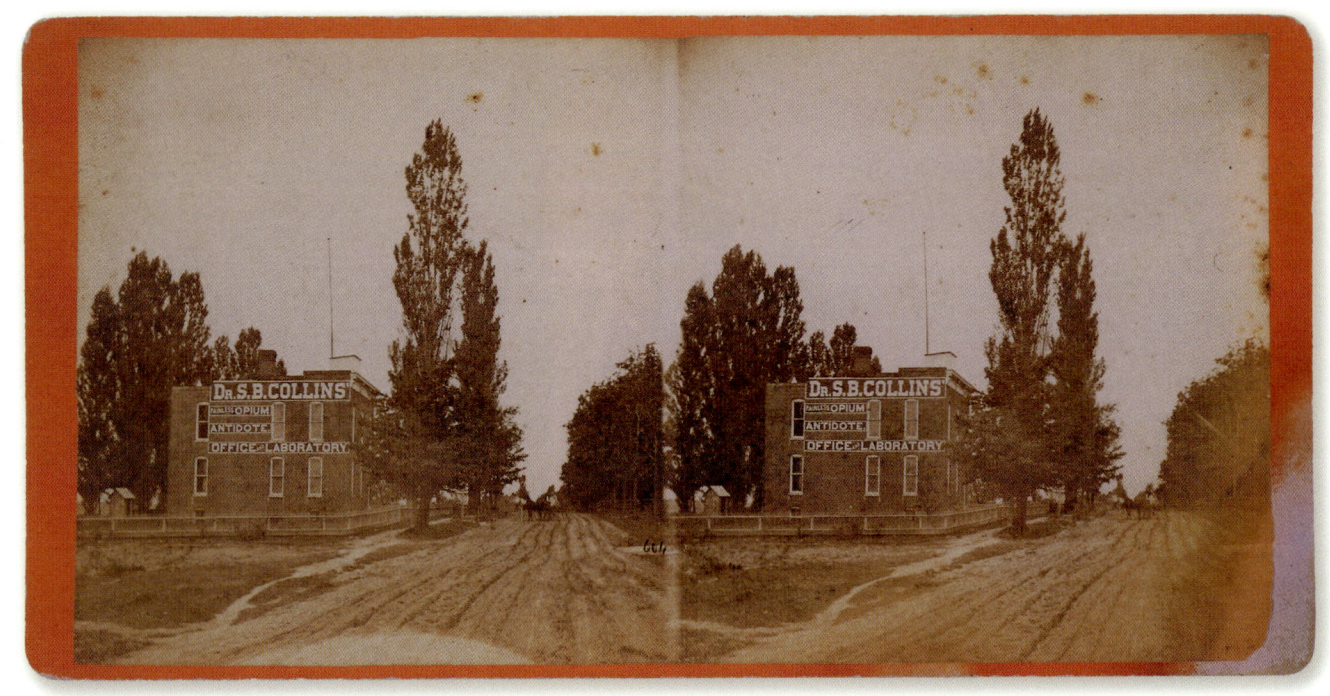

Office and laboratory of Dr. Samuel B. Collins, La Porte, ca. 1870. Photographer unknown.
Collins, a bricklayer by trade, claimed to find a cure for opium addiction in the late 1860s. Though many doubted him, patients from
both near and far came to him seeking help. Collins was so successful he was able to build a marble-fronted building in La Porte in the 1870s.

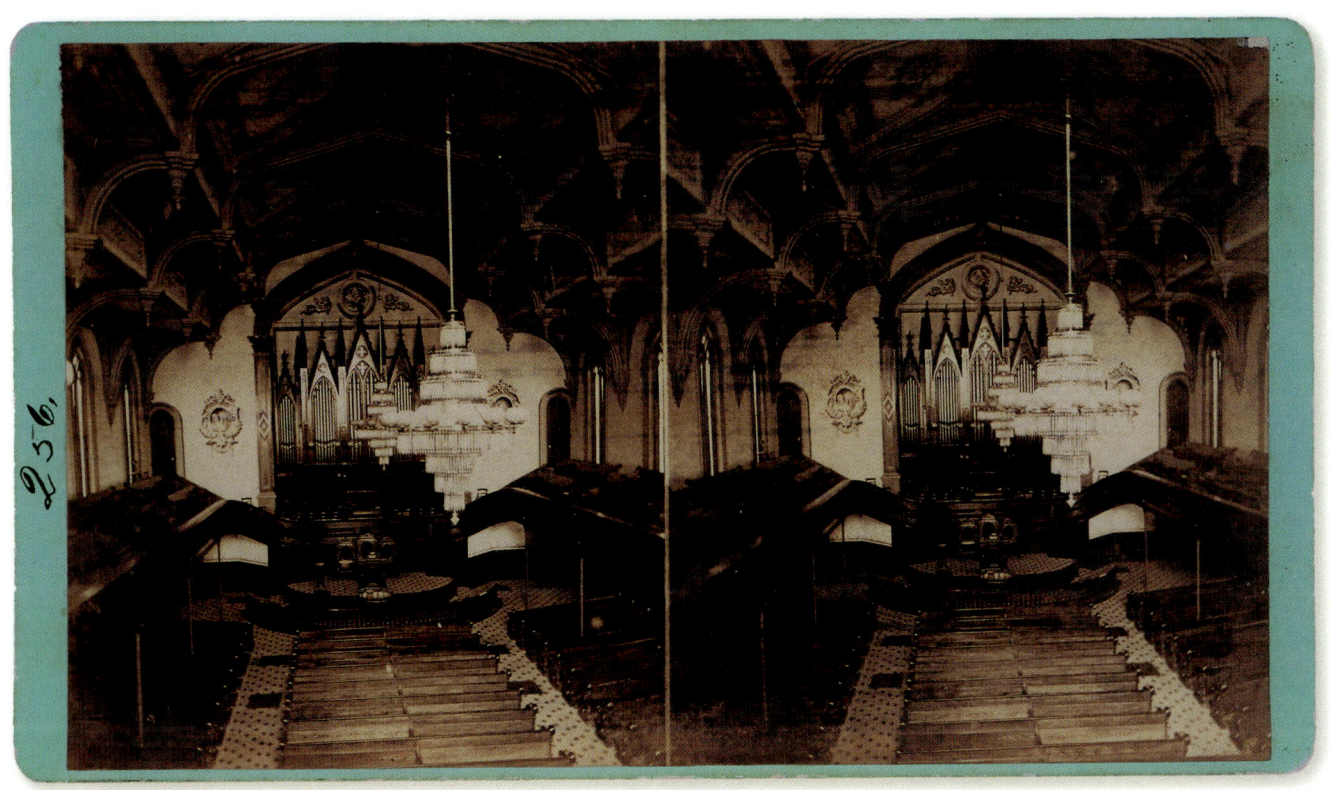

Interior of Trinity Church, Lafayette, ca. 1870s. Published by Wright and Hartwell.

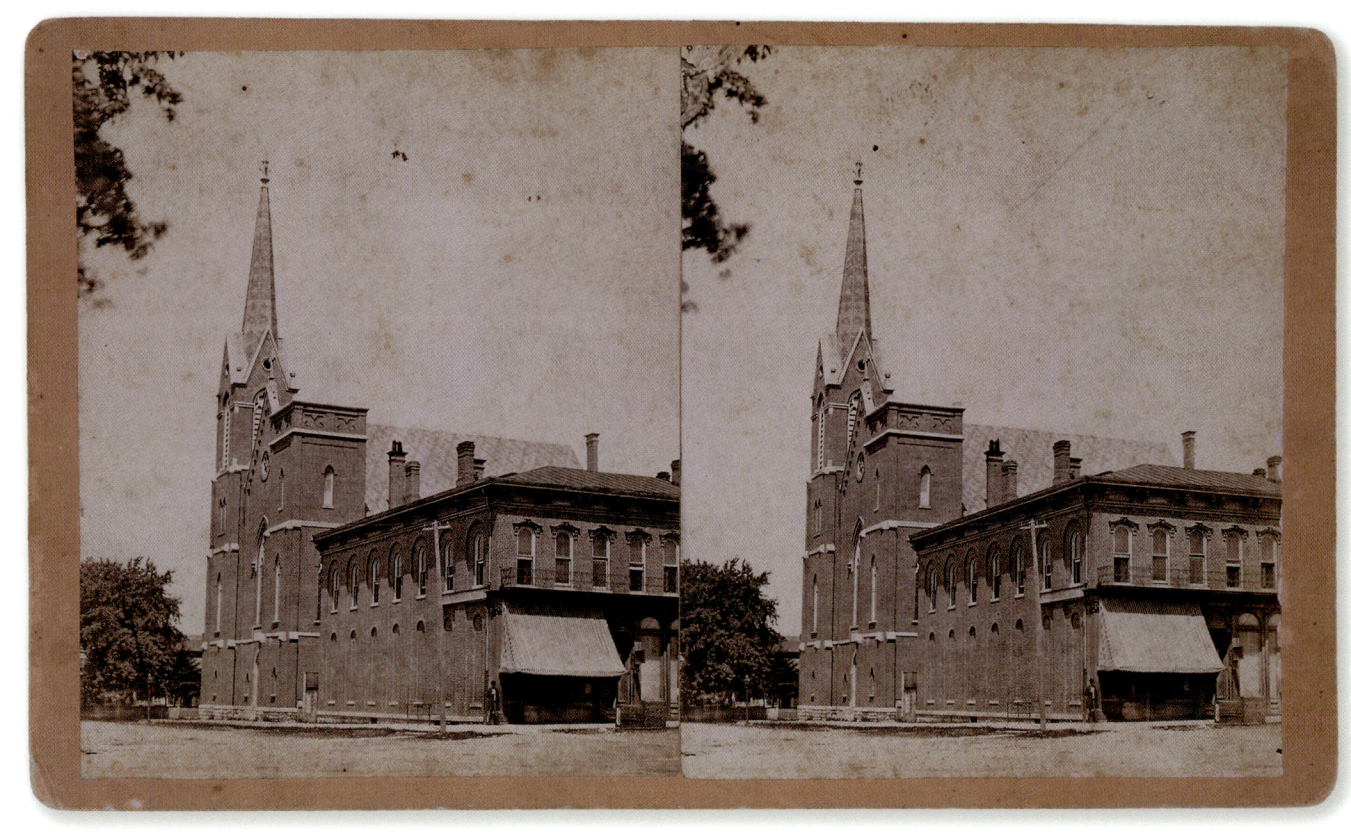

Methodist Episcopal church, Greensburg, ca. 1880s. Photographer unknown.
This church, now demolished, stood on West Washington Street.

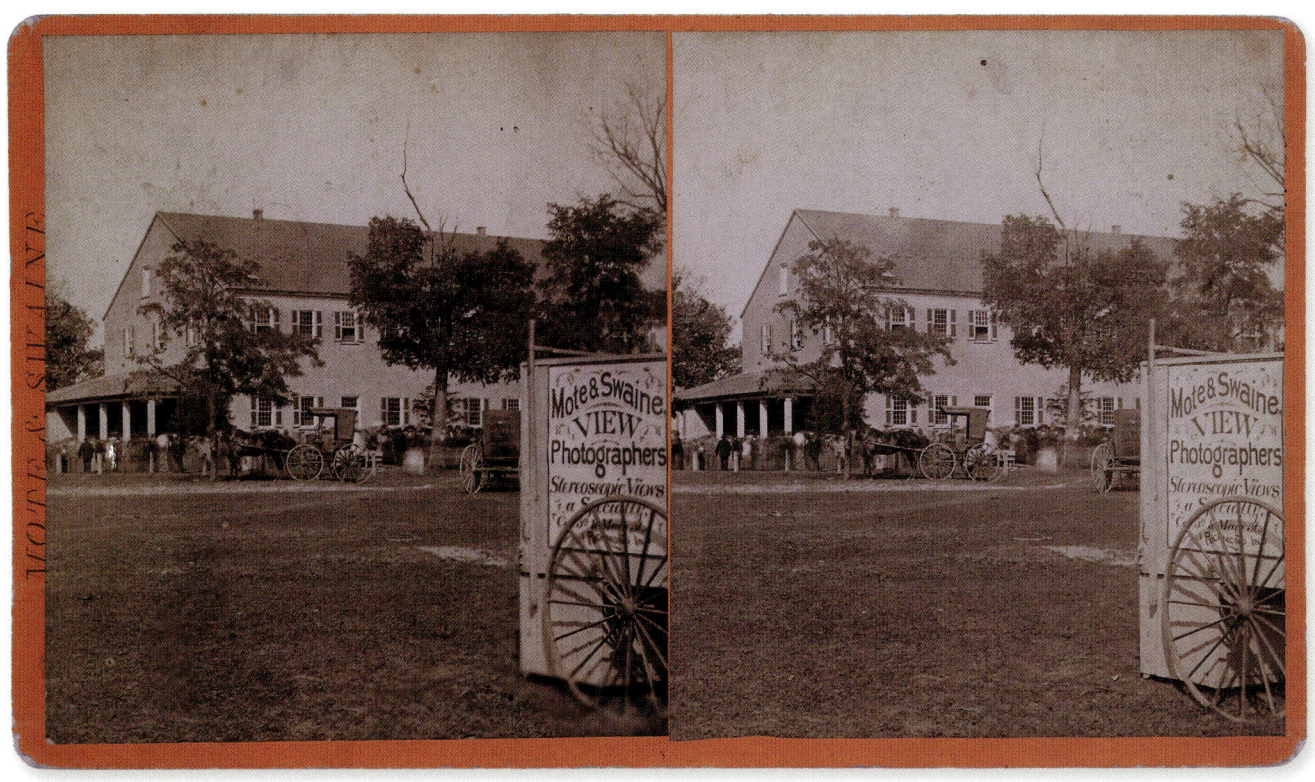

Friends Indiana Yearly Meetinghouse, Richmond, ca. 1870s. Published by Mote and Swaine.
The Quakers built this meetinghouse north of Richmond in the 1820s. Note Mote and Swaine's photography cart in the foreground.

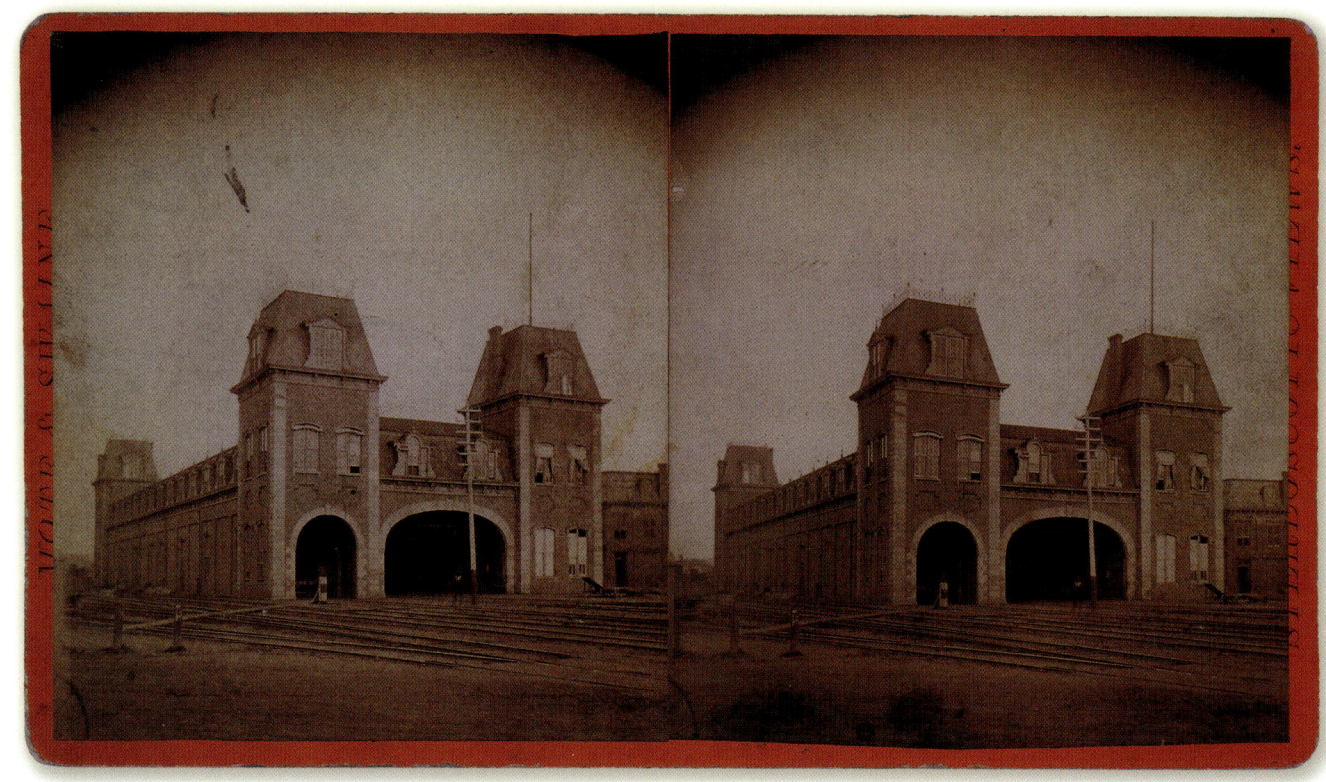

Union Passenger Station, Richmond, ca. 1870s. Published by Mote and Swaine.
This Second Empire–style train station served Richmond until the turn of the twentieth century, when
railroad officials demolished it and built a new station on the site.

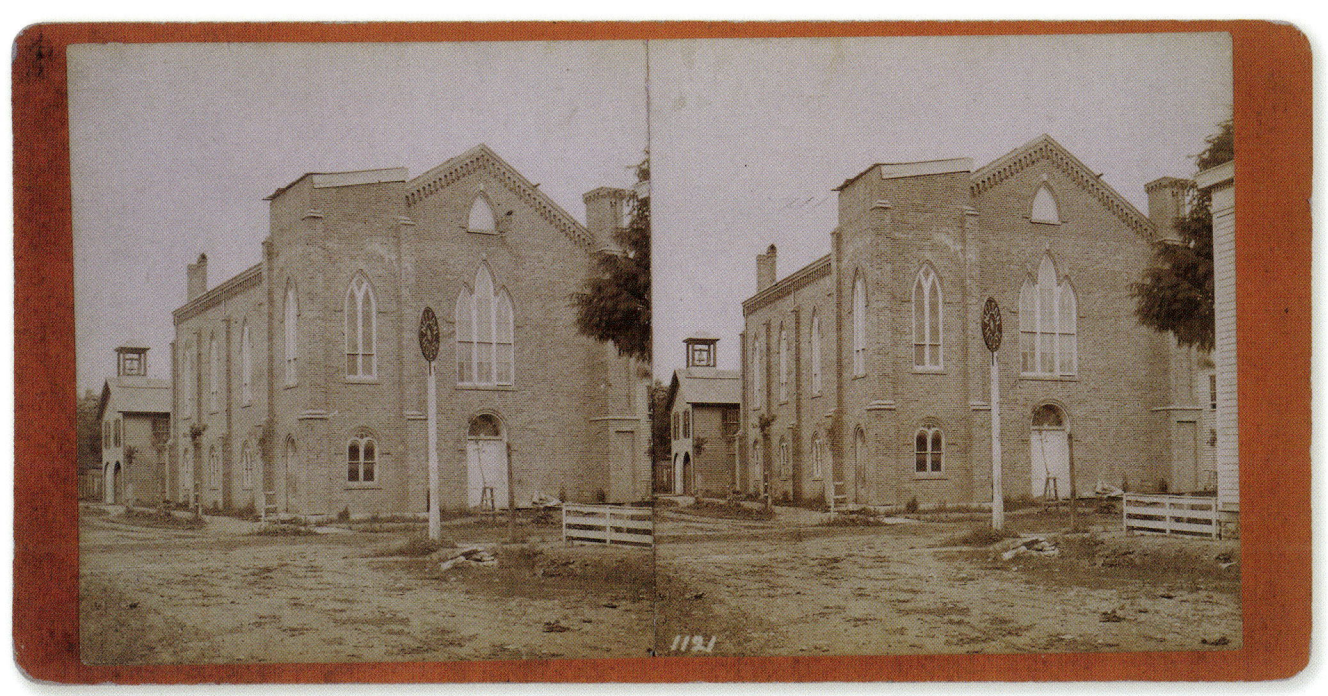

Presbyterian church, Marion, ca. 1870s. Photographer unknown.

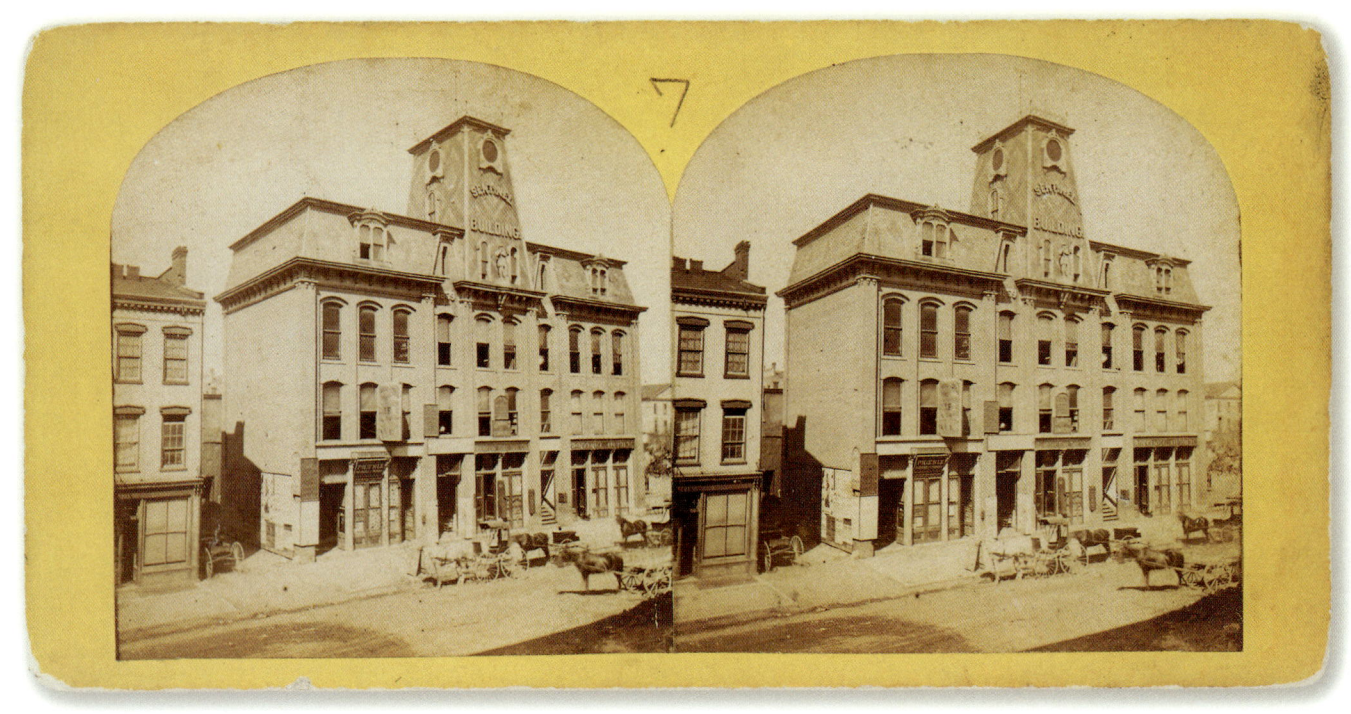

Sentinel Building, Indianapolis, ca. 1870s. Published by Ingraham and Claflin.
Completed in 1869, this building at one time housed the Indiana State Sentinel, *a long-running newspaper*
with strong ties to the Democratic party. It was located on the southwest corner of the Circle.

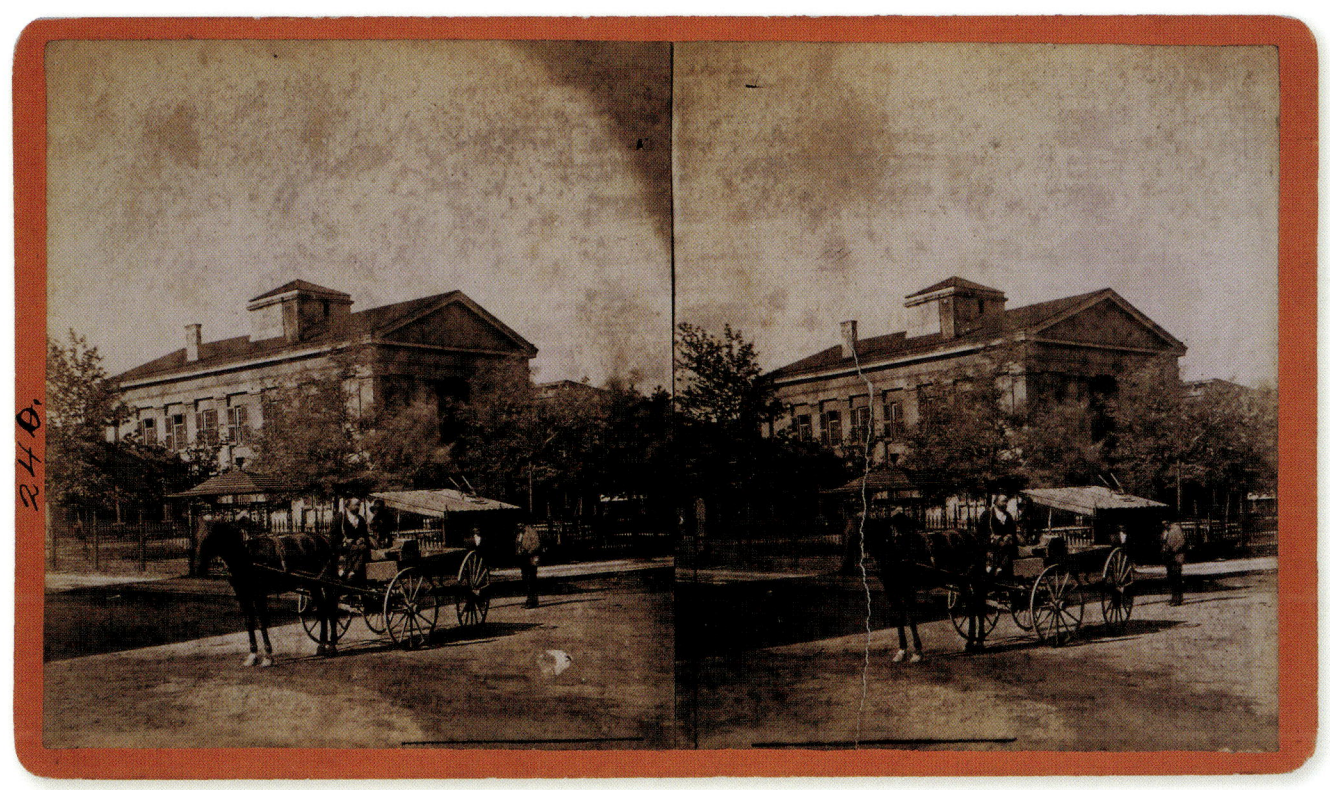

Tippecanoe County Courthouse, Lafayette, ca. 1870s. Published by Wright and Hartwell.
This courthouse was completed in 1847 and demolished in 1881 to make way for the present-day structure.

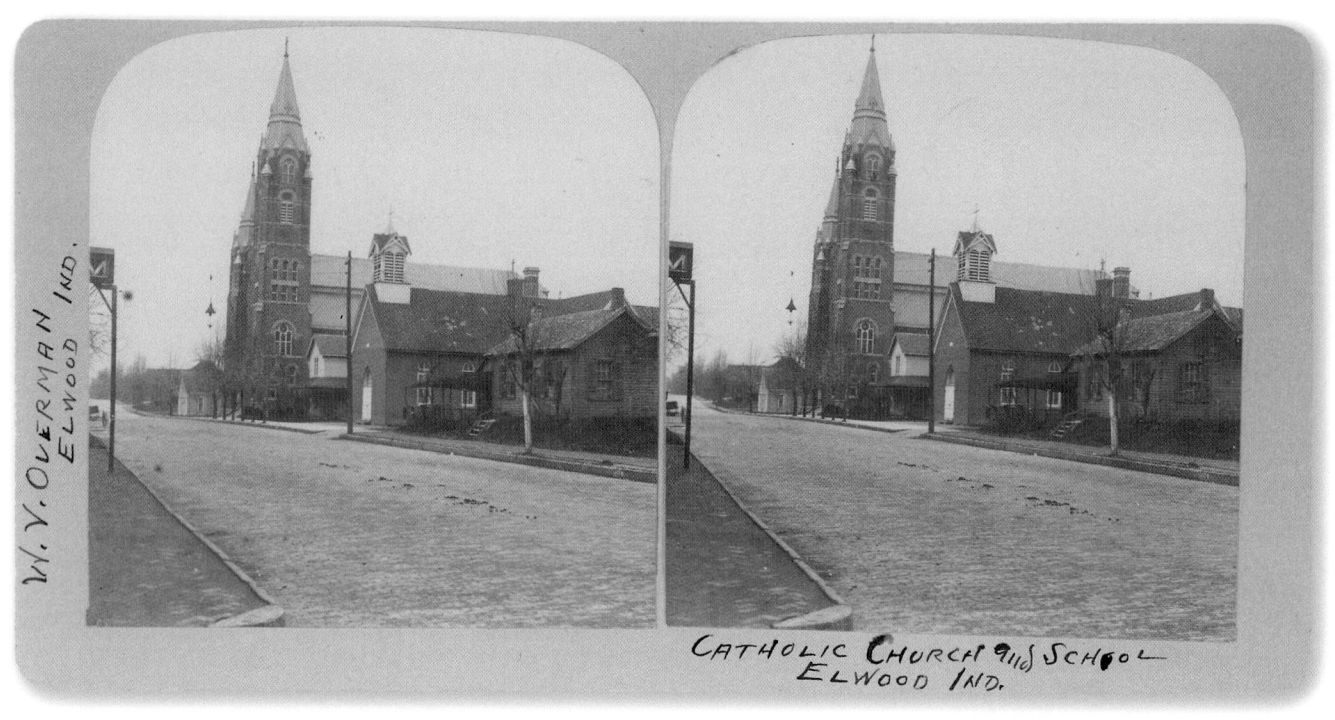

St. Joseph Catholic Church and school, Elwood, ca. early 1900s. Photographed by W. V. Overman.
The church was established in 1889.

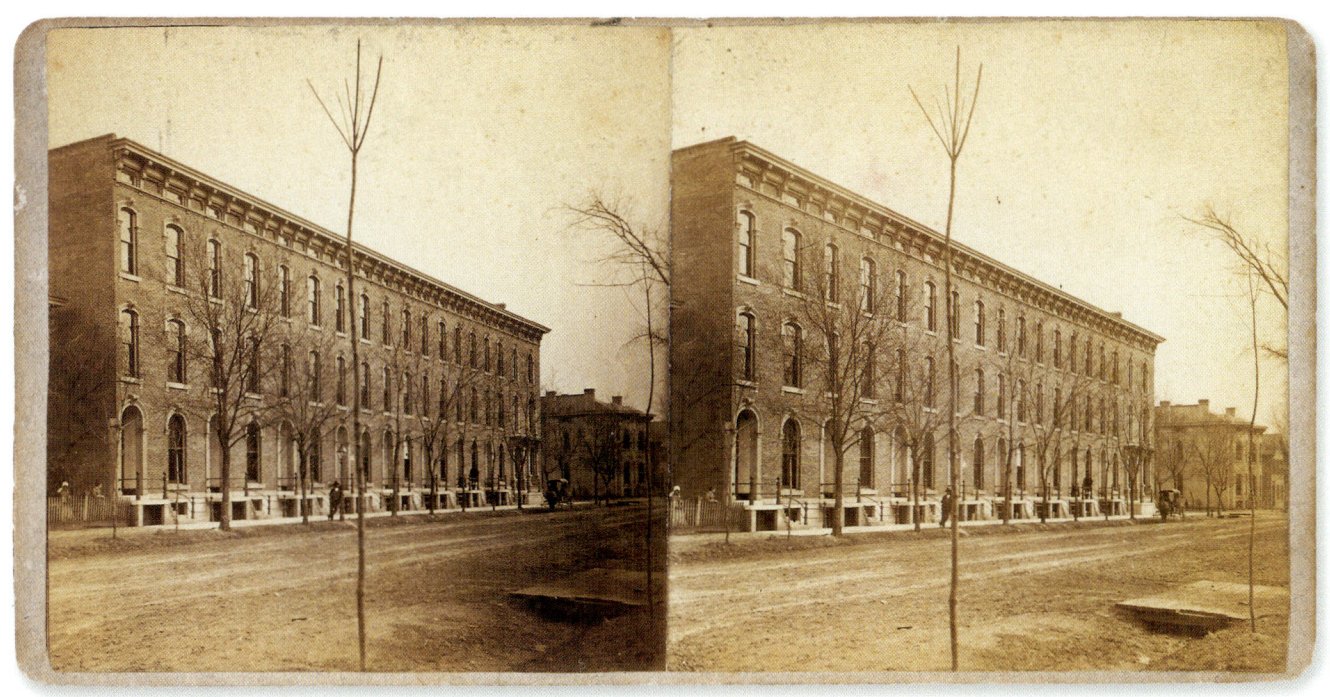

North end of the Wheatley Block, Indianapolis, 1877. Photographed by J. W. Pendergast.
The Wheatley Block was located on the northeast corner of Ohio and New Jersey Streets.

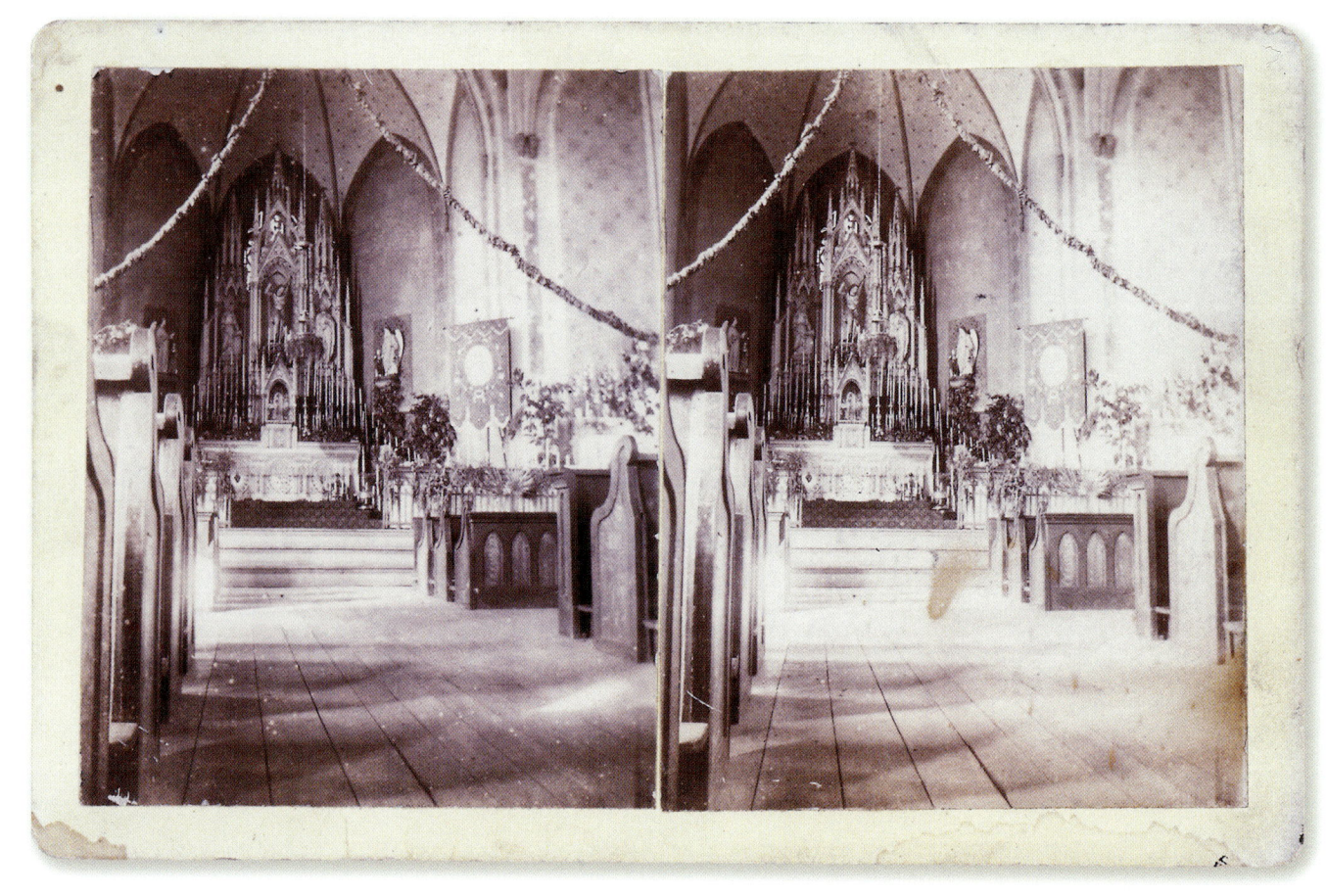

Interior of St. Michael Catholic Church, Cannelton, ca. 1880s. Photographer unknown.
St. Michael was completed in 1859 and stands today as one of Cannelton's landmarks.

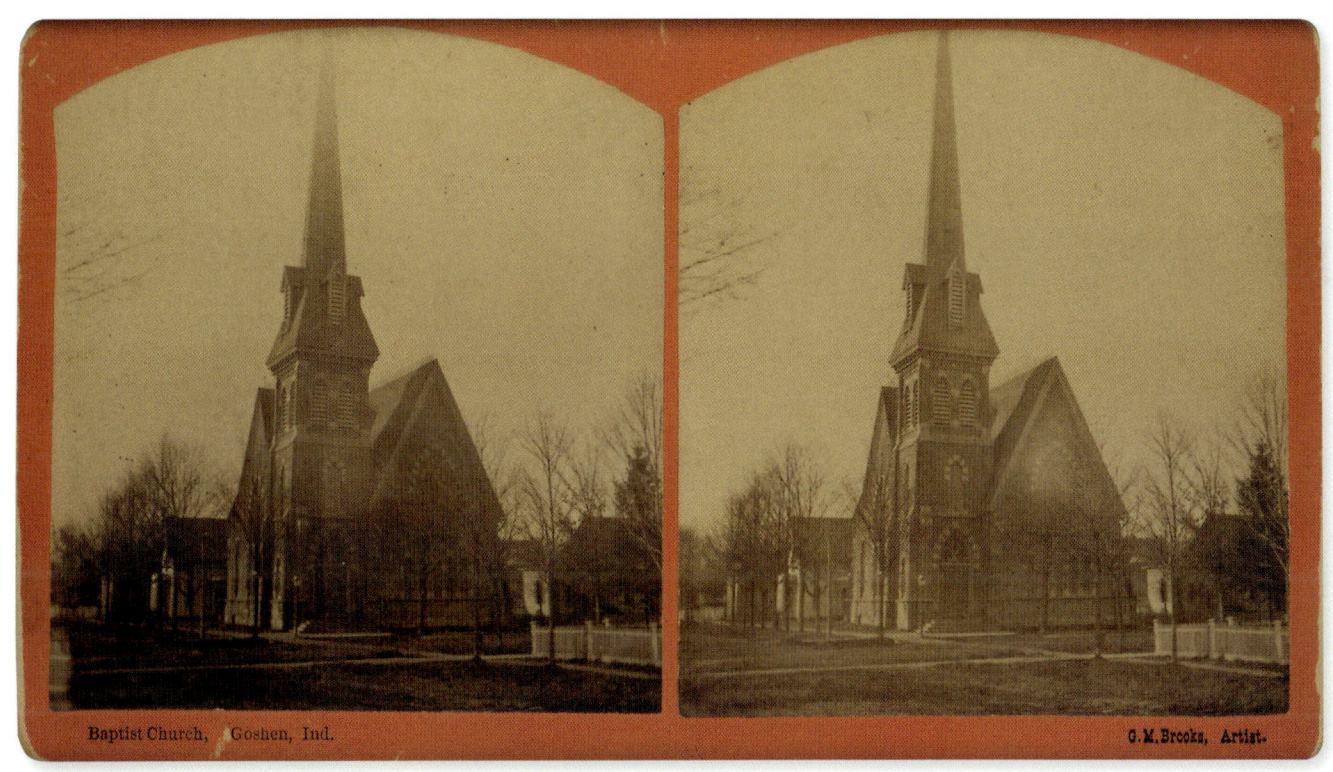

Baptist Church, Goshen, Ind.

G. M. Brooks, Artist.

First Baptist Church, Goshen, ca. 1880s. Photographed by G. M. Brooks.
This church was built in 1877 at the corner of Washington and Sixth Streets.

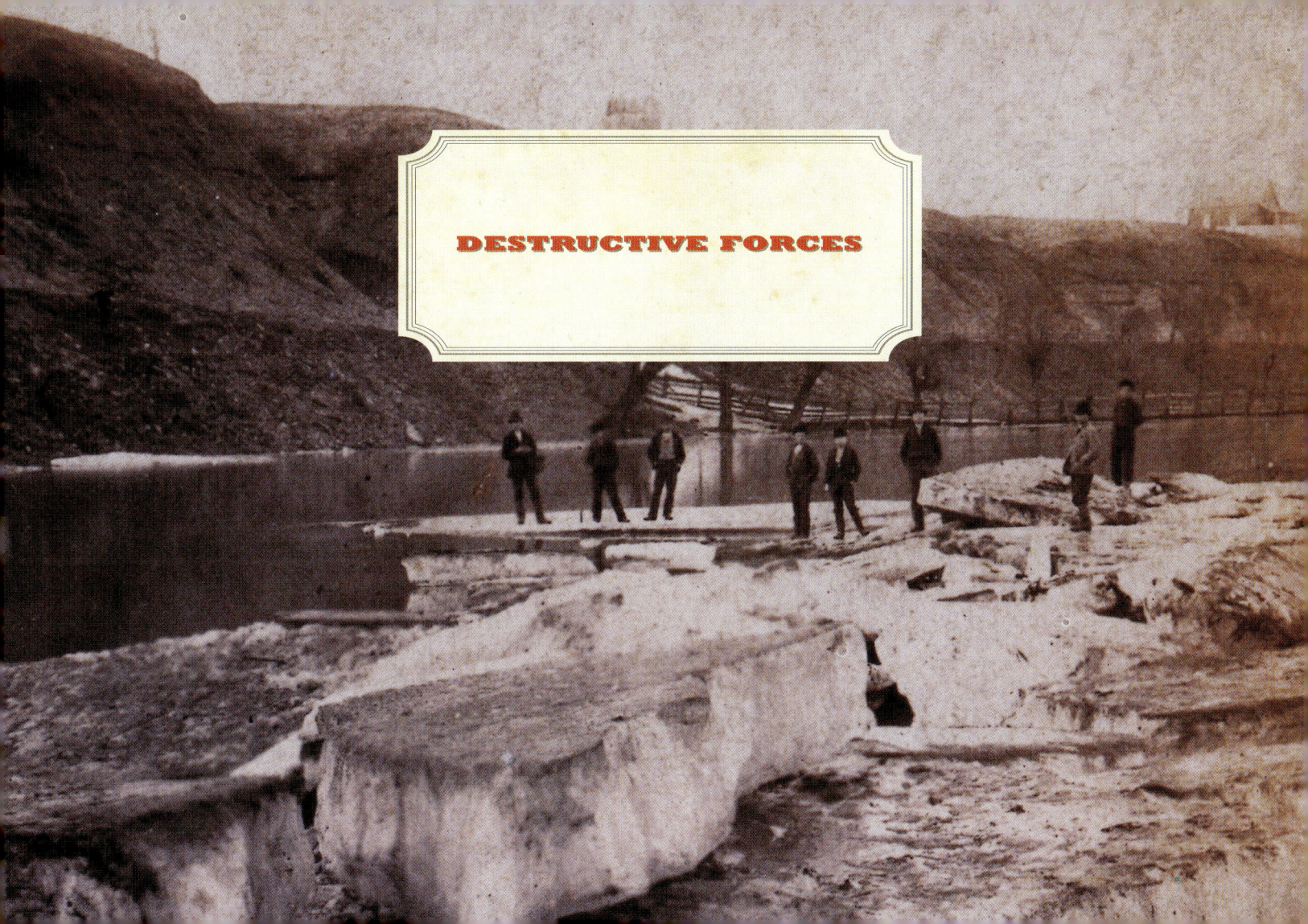

DESTRUCTIVE FORCES

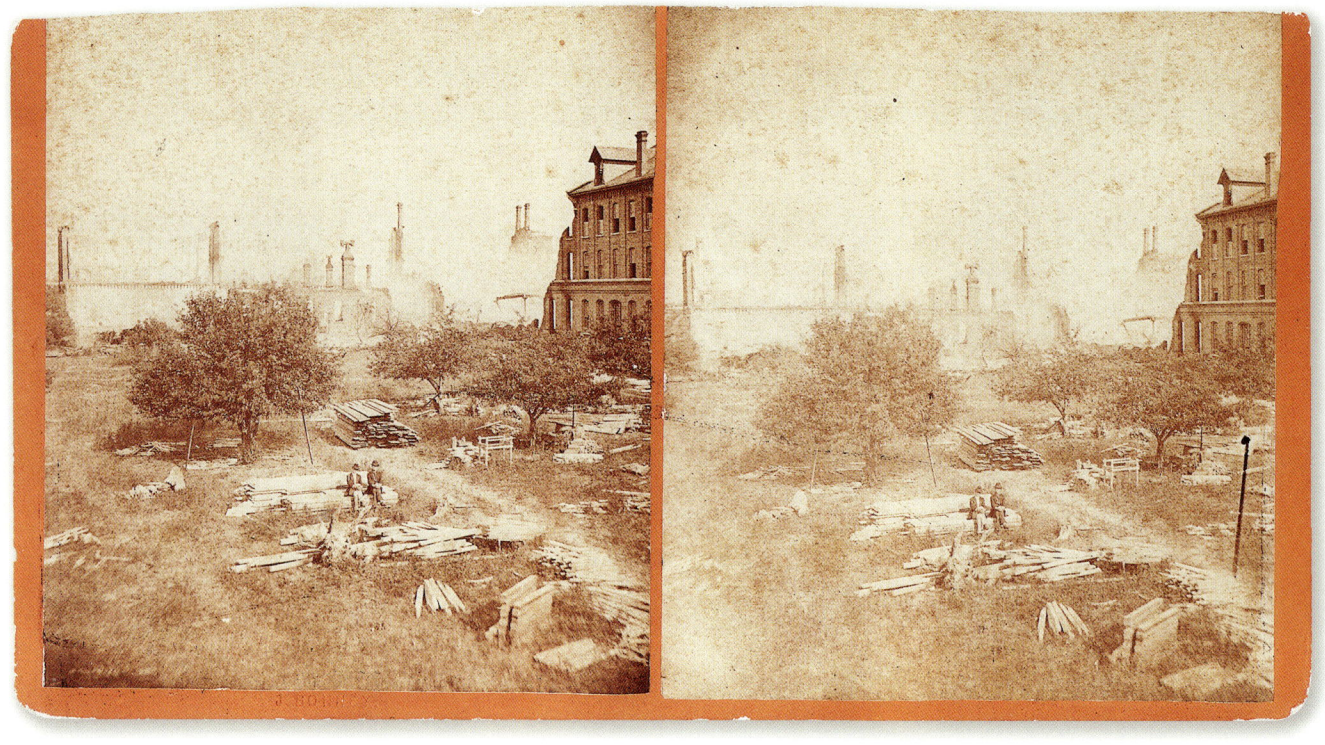

Studebaker ruins, South Bend, ca. 1874. Photographed by James Bonney.
Fire struck the Studebaker Brothers Manufacturing Company in both 1872 and 1874. This scene was probably taken
after the 1874 fire, the more extensive of the two, which destroyed two-thirds of the company's works.

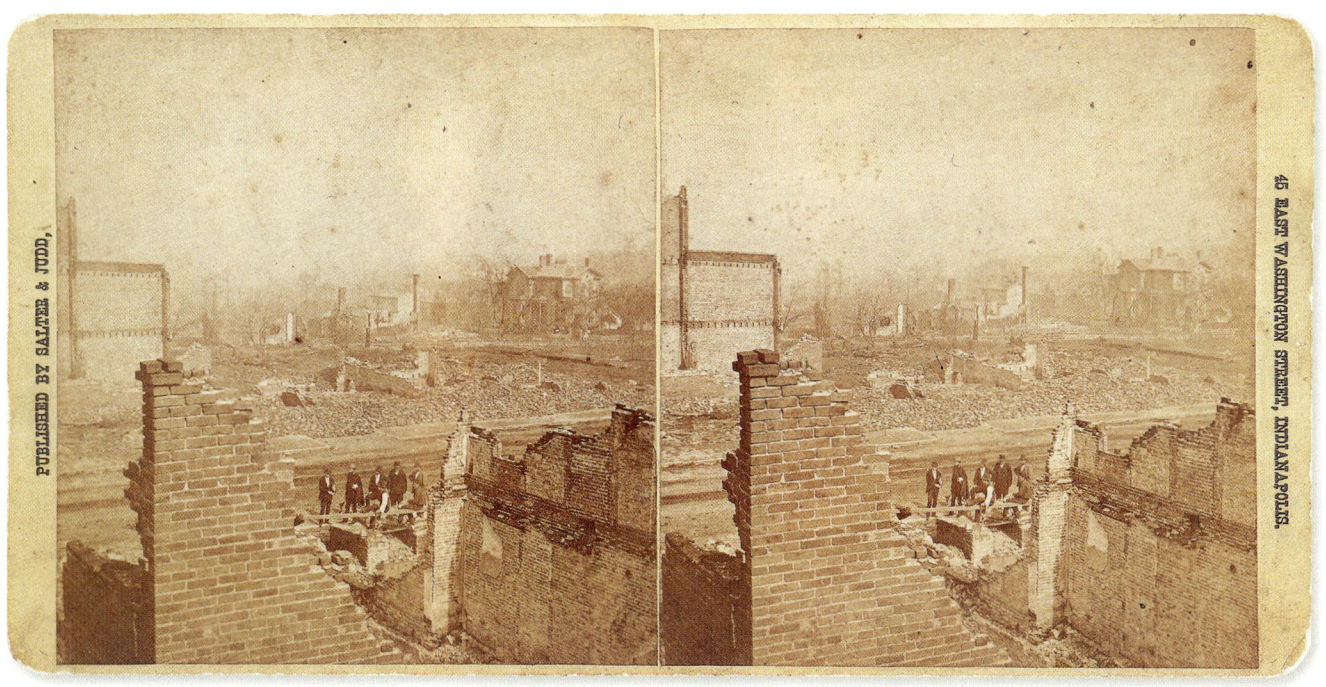

Fire destruction, Greencastle, 1874. Published by Salter and Judd.
On the night of 28 October a planing mill in Greencastle caught fire, and strong winds from the southwest spread the embers. By morning six blocks of
businesses and homes had burned. Just over four months later another fire struck, destroying the south side of the courthouse square.

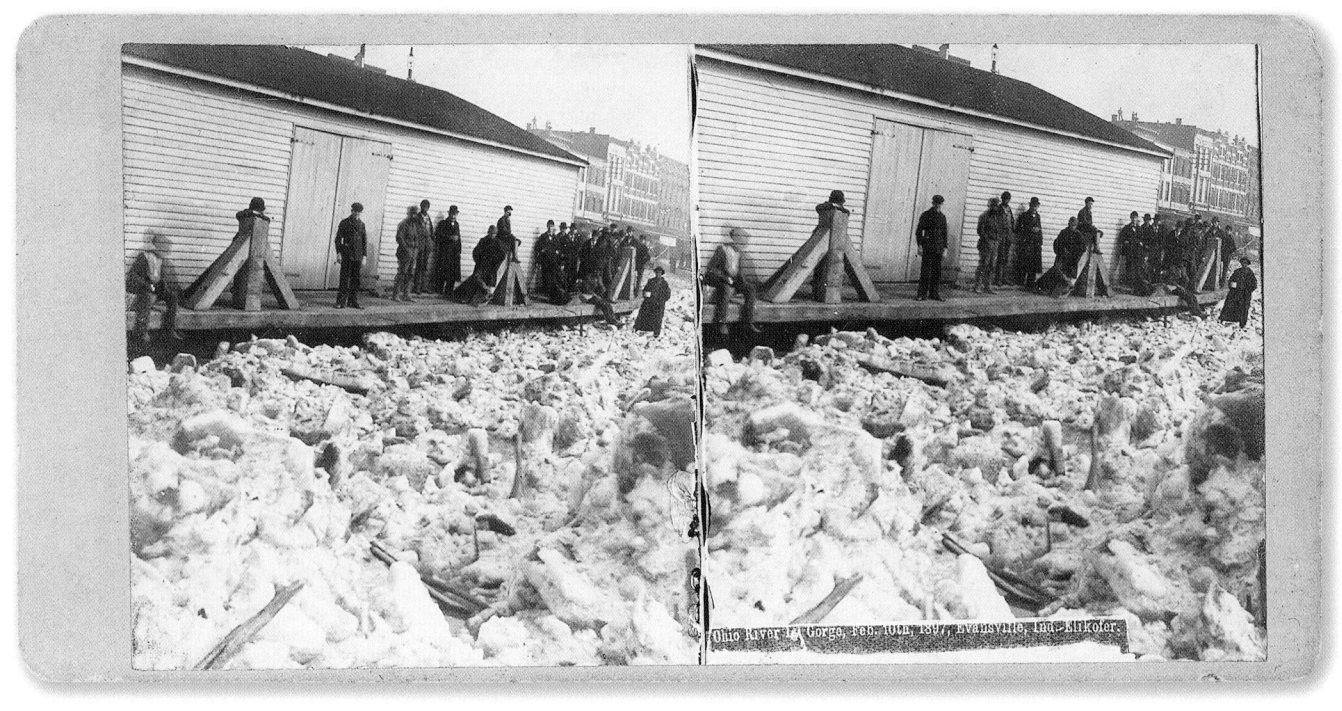

Ohio River Ice Gorge, Feb. 10th, 1897, Evansville, Ind. Elikofer.

Ice gorge on the Ohio River, Evansville, 1897. Photographed by Fred Elikofer.
The gorge formed in a narrow section of the river six miles below the city on the morning of 10 February and backed up for eighteen miles.
Thousands visited the riverbanks at Evansville to view the crests of ice. Though residents feared the gorge would last for days and cause
the river to reroute above town, it began passing by late afternoon and left behind relatively little damage.

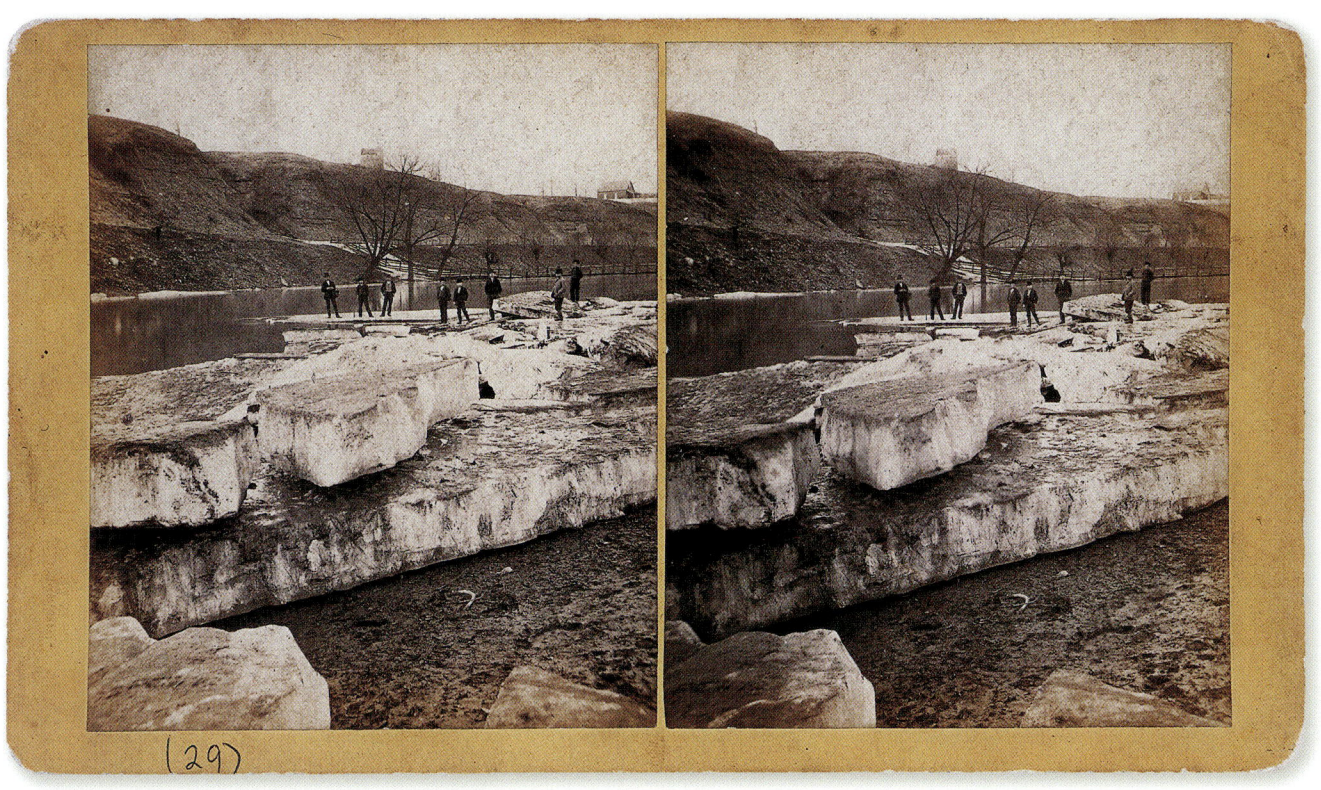

(29)

Ice on the Whitewater River, Richmond, ca. 1880s. Photographer unknown.

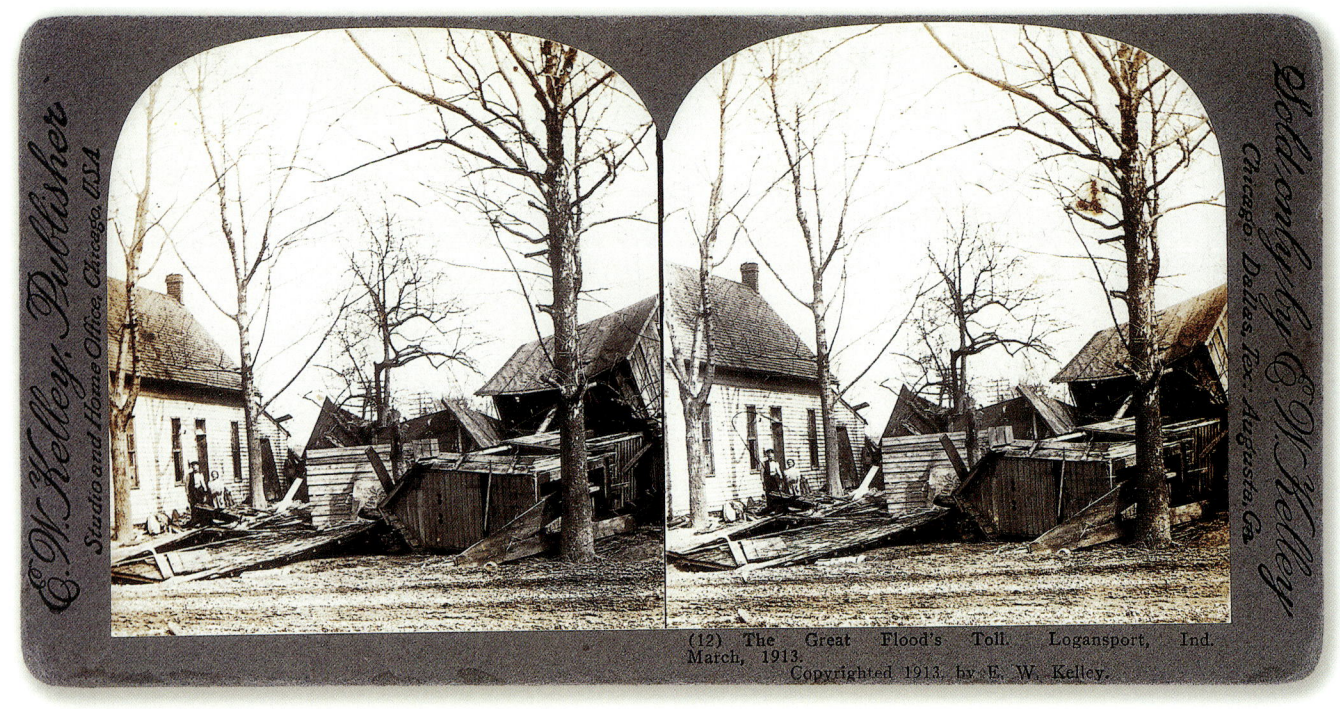

(12) The Great Flood's Toll. Logansport, Ind. March, 1913.
Copyrighted 1913, by E. W. Kelley.

Flood damage, Logansport, 1913. Published by E. W. Kelley.
Heavy rains fell across Indiana in late March, flooding the Wabash and other rivers in the region. The floods killed dozens
and caused millions of dollars of damage in towns such as Wabash, Peru, Logansport, and Lafayette.

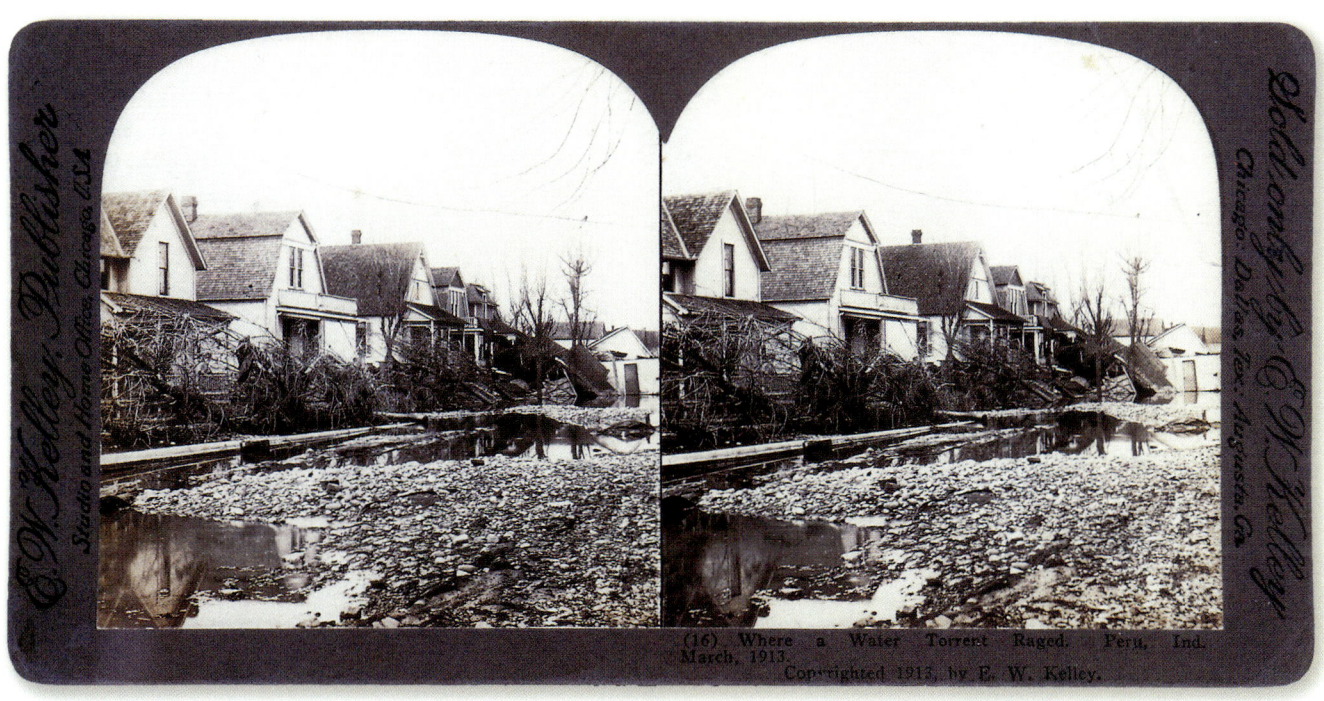

Flood damage, Peru, 1913. Published by E. W. Kelley.

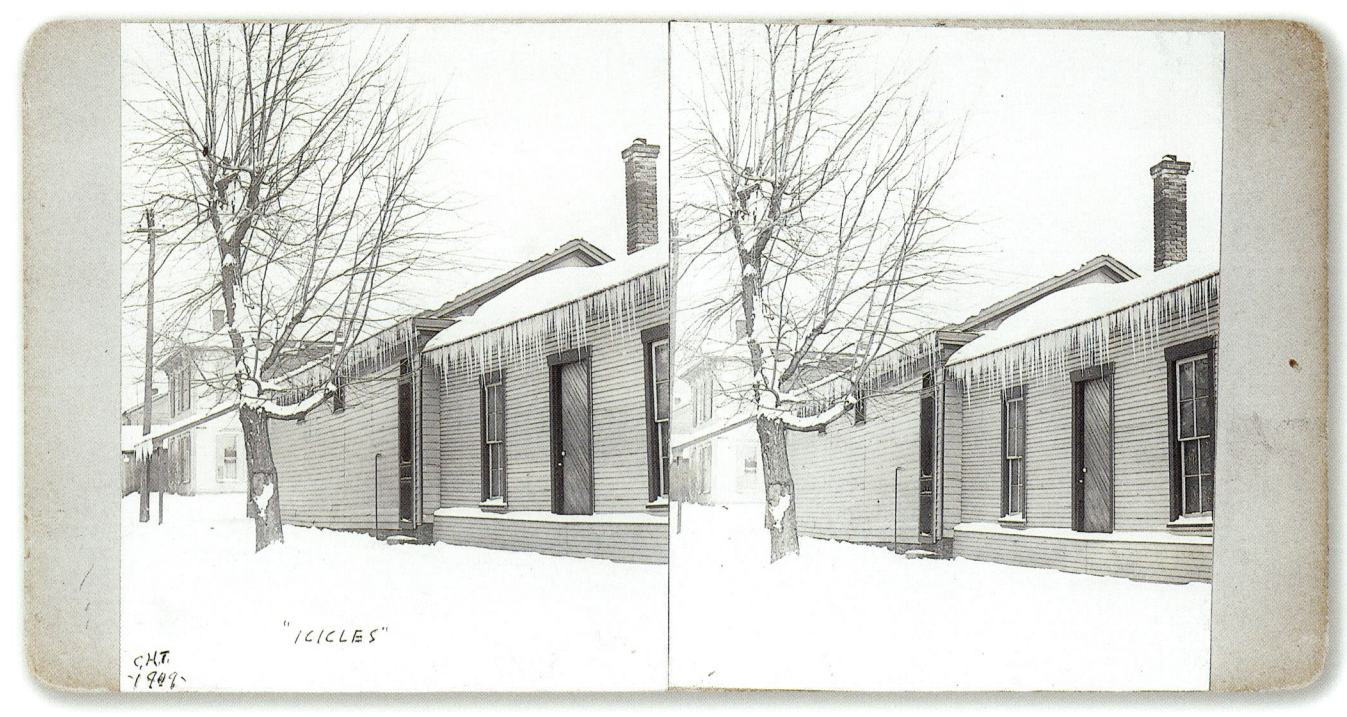

"ICICLES"

C.H.T.
1909

Icicles on a house, Hartford City, 1909. Photographed by Clay H. Tuttle.

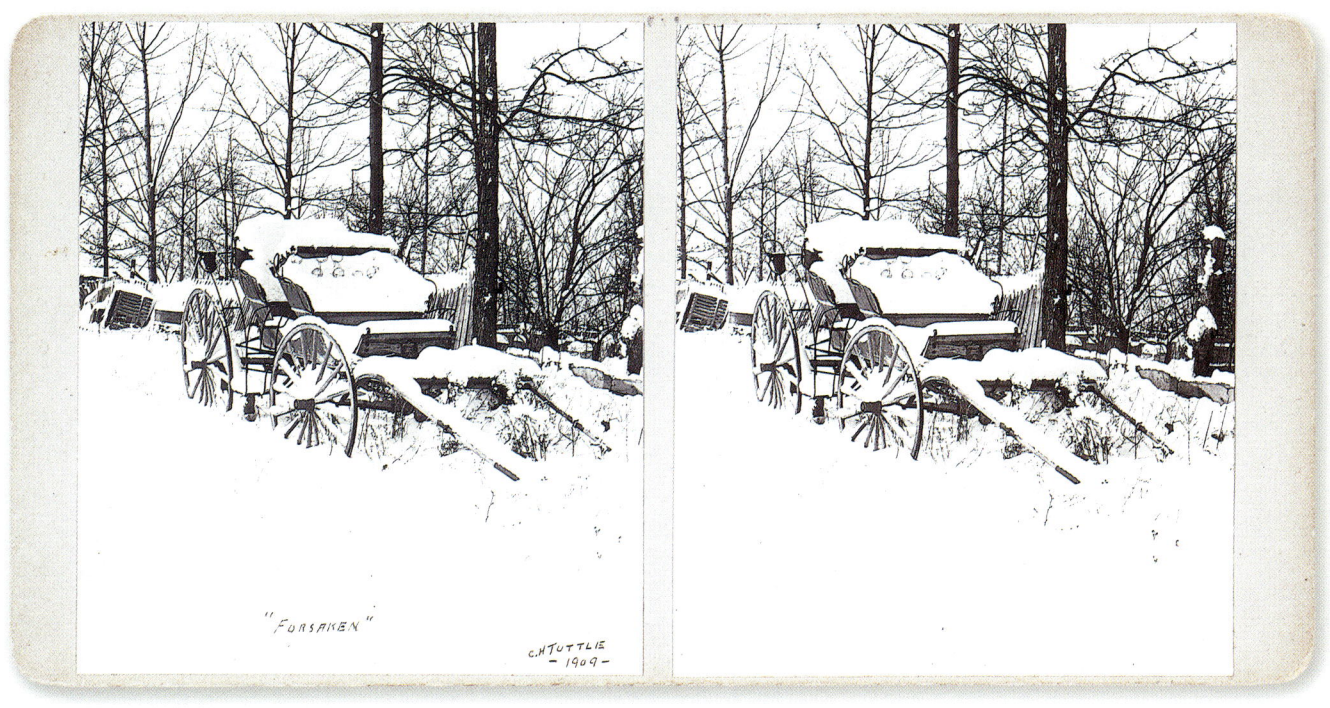

"FORSAKEN"

C.H.TUTTLE
— 1909 —

Snowfall, Blackford County, 1909. Photographed by Clay H. Tuttle.

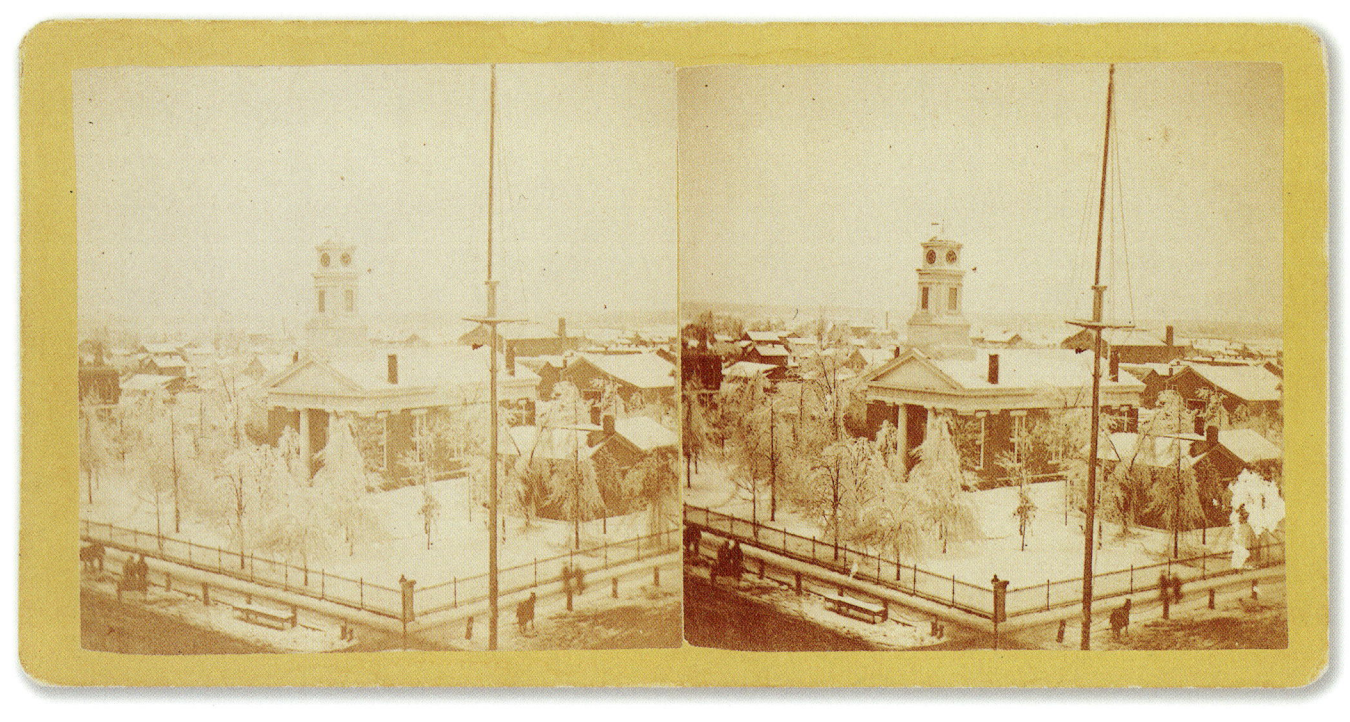

La Porte County Courthouse after an ice storm, La Porte, 1871. Photographer unknown.
This was the county's second courthouse, built in 1849 and replaced in 1892 by the current structure.

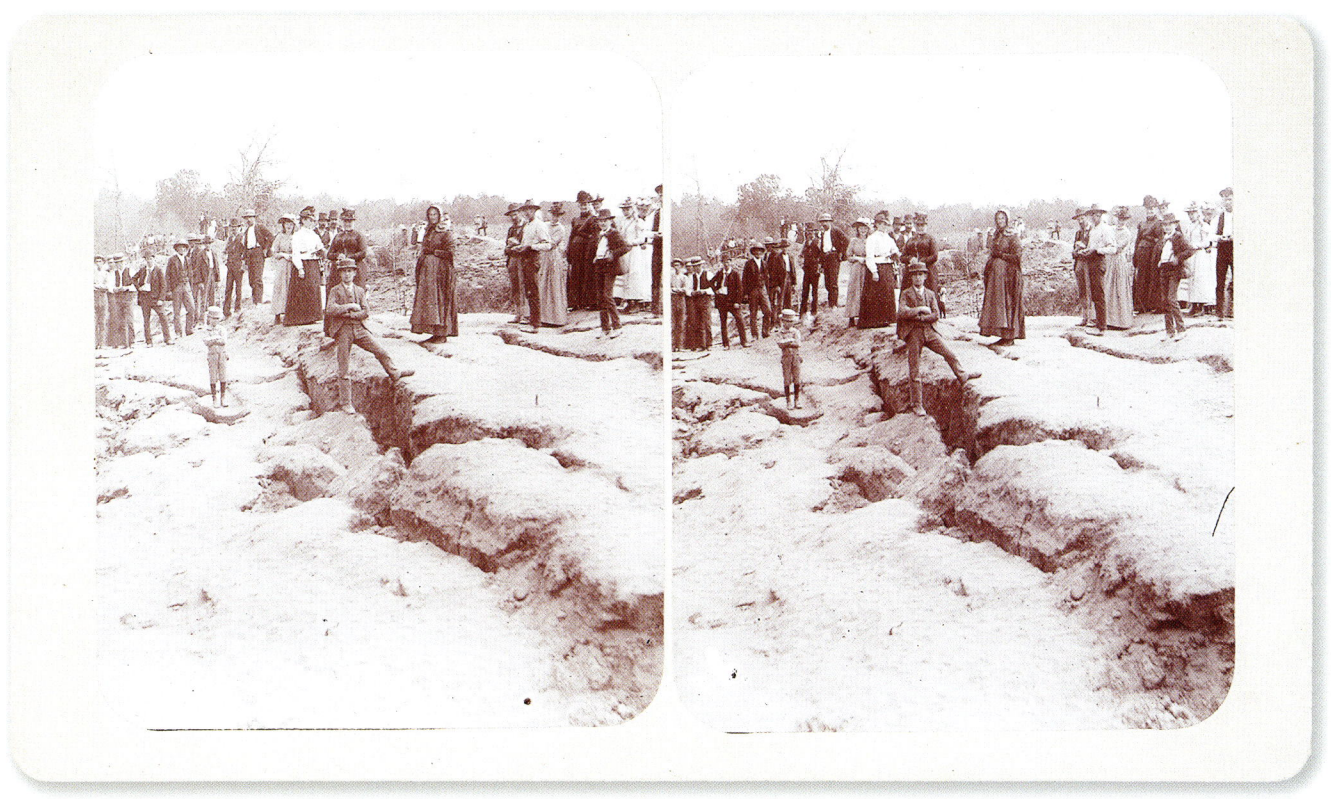

Natural-gas explosion on the Flatrock River, near St. Paul, 1890. Photographed by Julius T. Schaub.
On the morning of 11 August a pocket of natural gas near the junction of Conn's Creek and the Flatrock River exploded, destroying
some twenty acres of farmland. According to newspaper accounts, the explosion left behind large caverns that emitted gas, smoke,
and heat, as well as crevices two to fifteen feet wide and up to a half mile long.

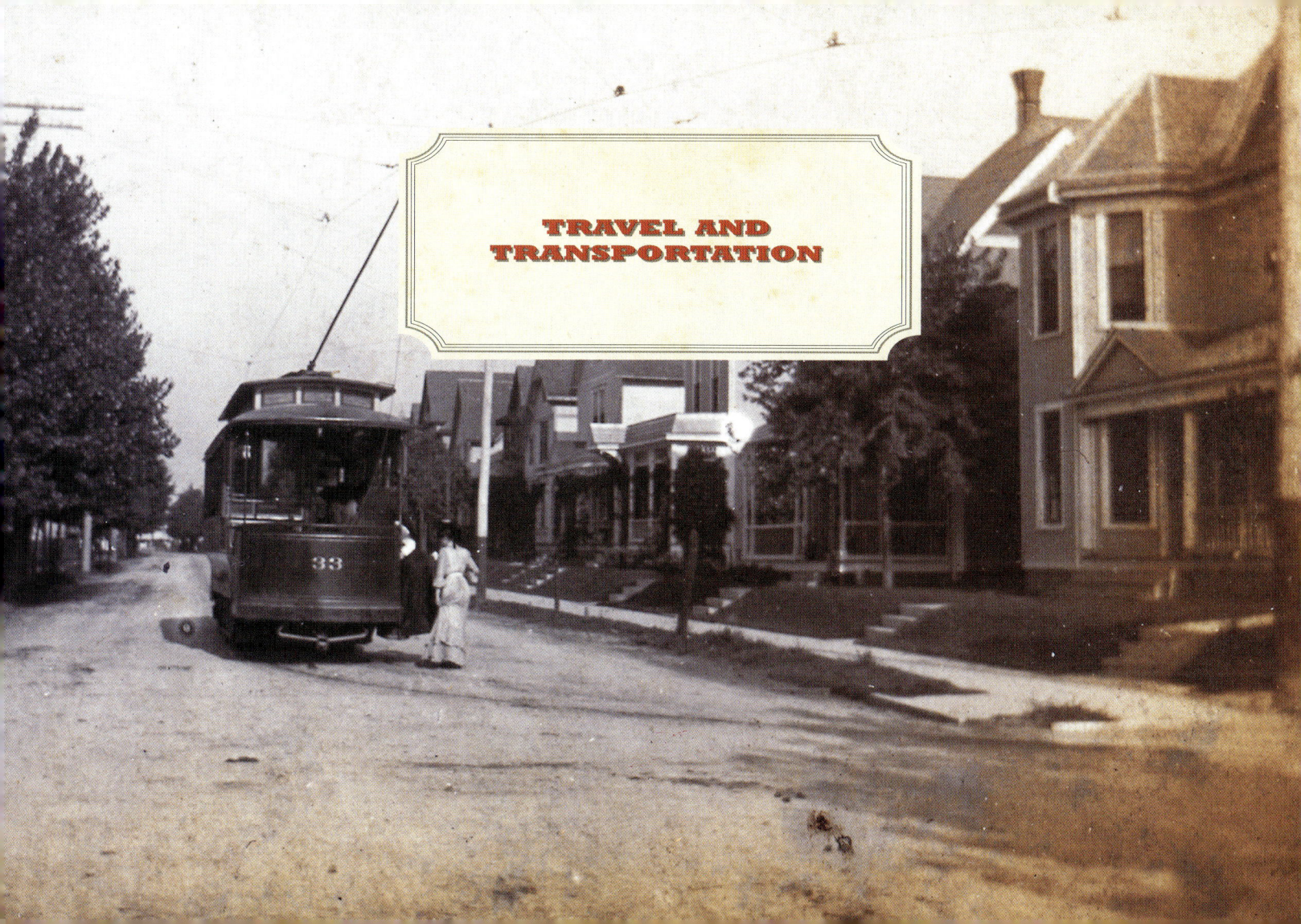

TRAVEL AND
TRANSPORTATION

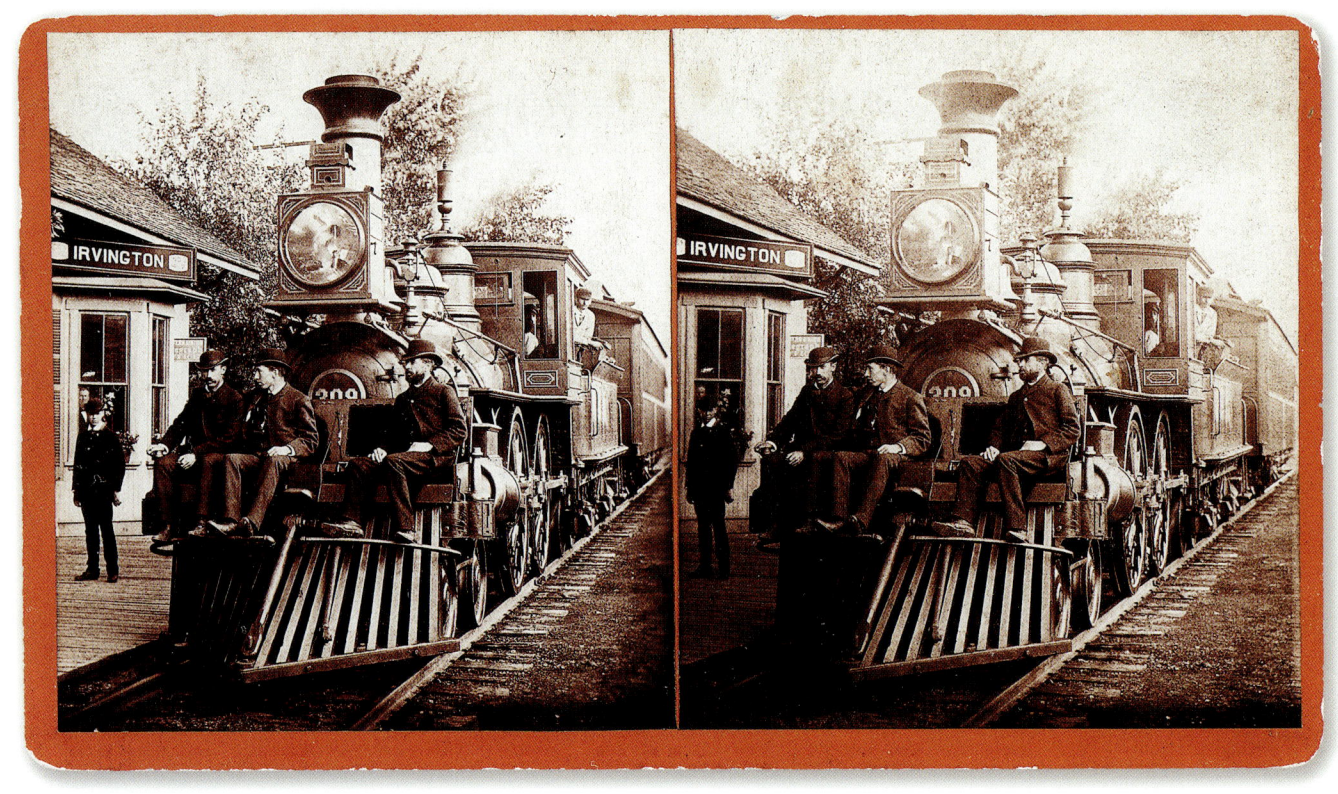

Train at Irvington station, Indianapolis, ca. 1875. Photographer unknown.
Irvington, located four miles east of downtown Indianapolis, was one of the city's first suburbs. This view looks east down the Pennsylvania tracks.

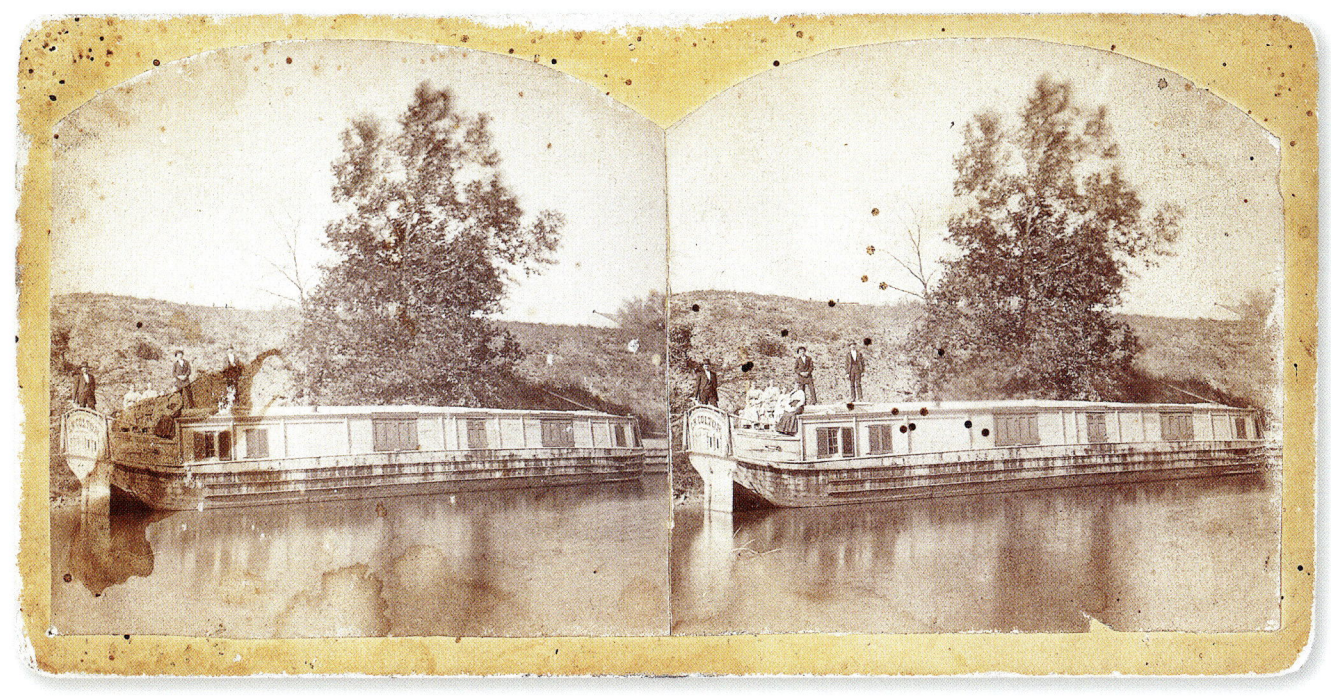

View along the Wabash and Erie Canal, location unknown, ca. 1870s. Photographed by M. D. Goodlander.
Construction on the canal began in Fort Wayne in 1832 and was completed to Evansville in 1853. The canal also ran east to Toledo, Ohio,
for a total length of 468 miles. It became an important route for shipping goods across northern Indiana.

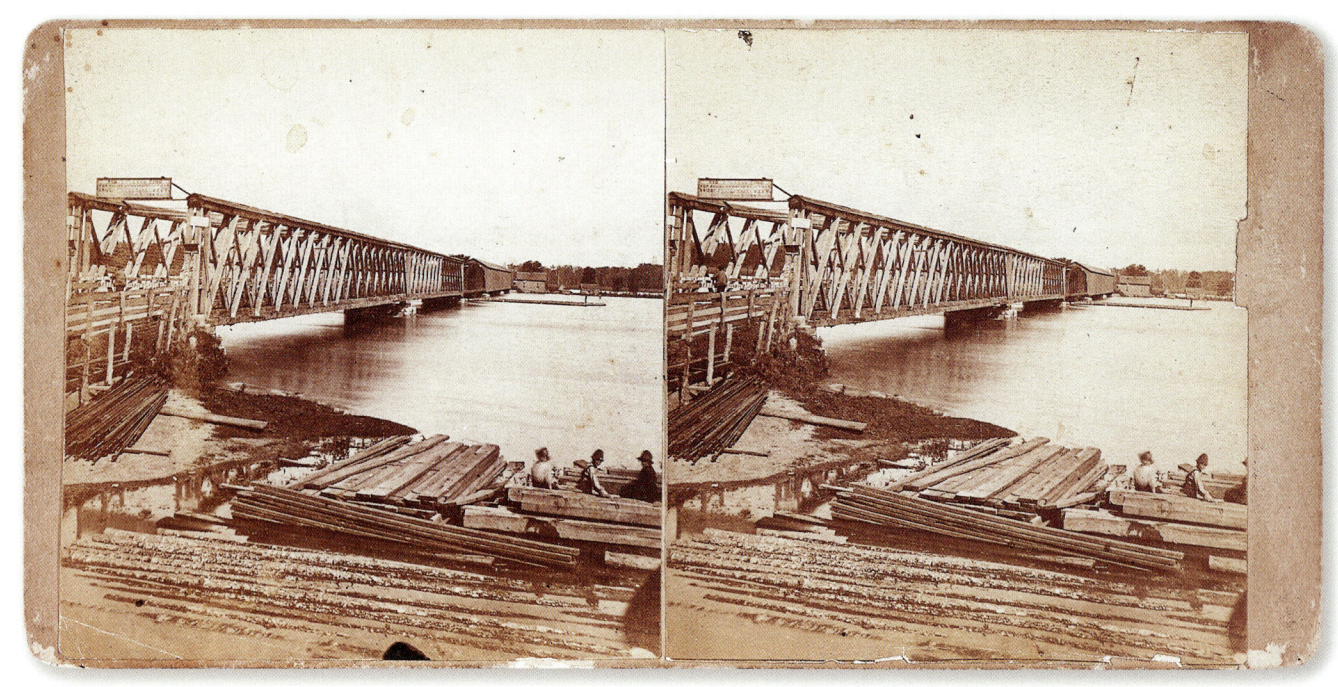

Wagon bridge, Vincennes, ca. 1880. Photographed by A. B. Craycraft.

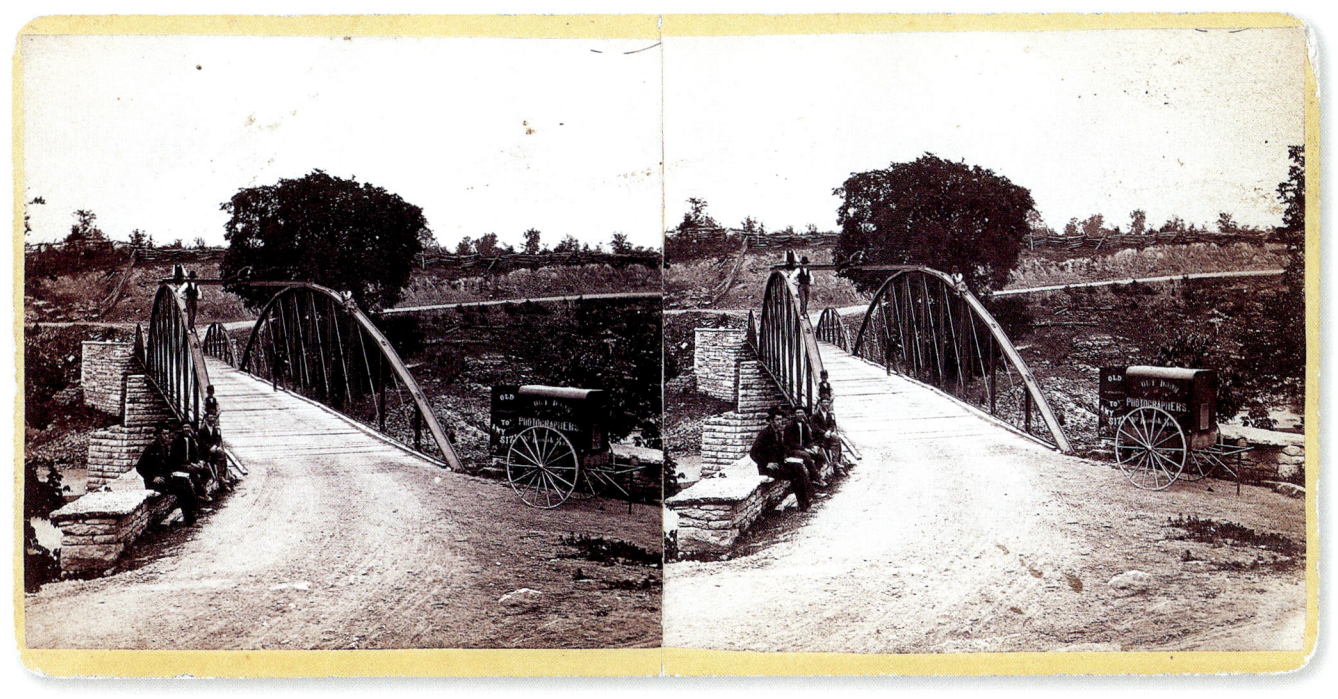

Unidentified bridge, probably near Anderson, ca. late 1870s. Photographed by M. D. Goodlander.
Note in the foreground the photography wagon with the names McKeown and Swan painted on it. McKeown and Swan
worked together in Anderson in the 1870s, a fact that helps identify the location and date of this image.

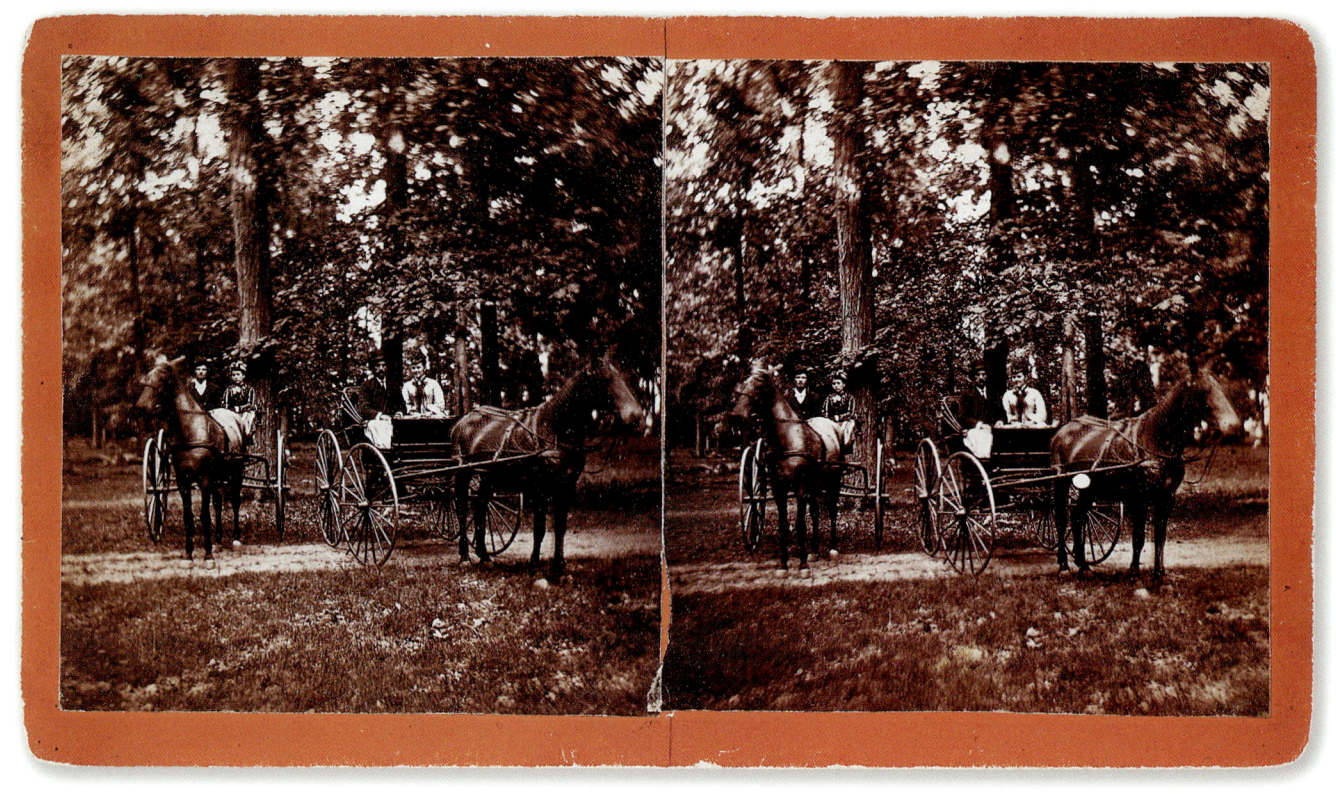

Couples in buggies at the mounds, near Anderson, ca. 1880s. Photographed by M. D. Goodlander.
The mounds, located east of Anderson, were used by the Adena and Hopewell peoples and are thought to predate Christ. They are now part of Mounds State Park.

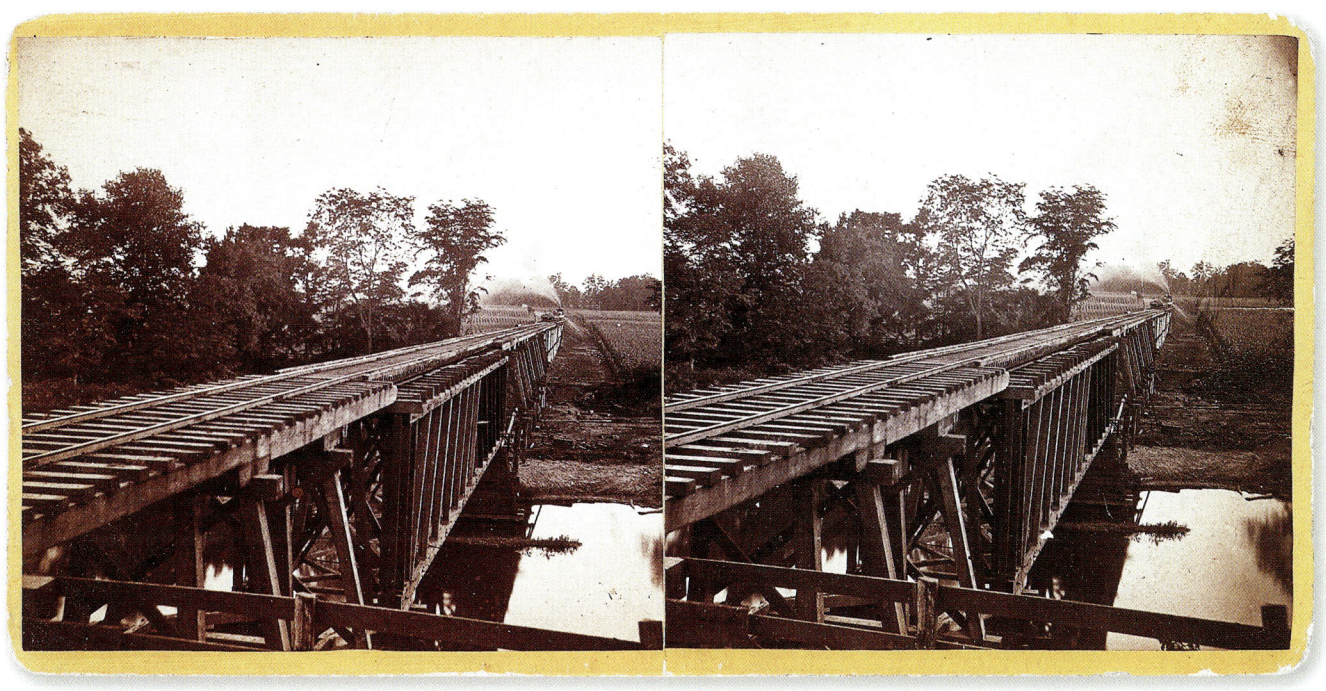

Unidentified railroad bridge, probably in the Anderson area, ca. 1880s. Photographed by M. D. Goodlander.

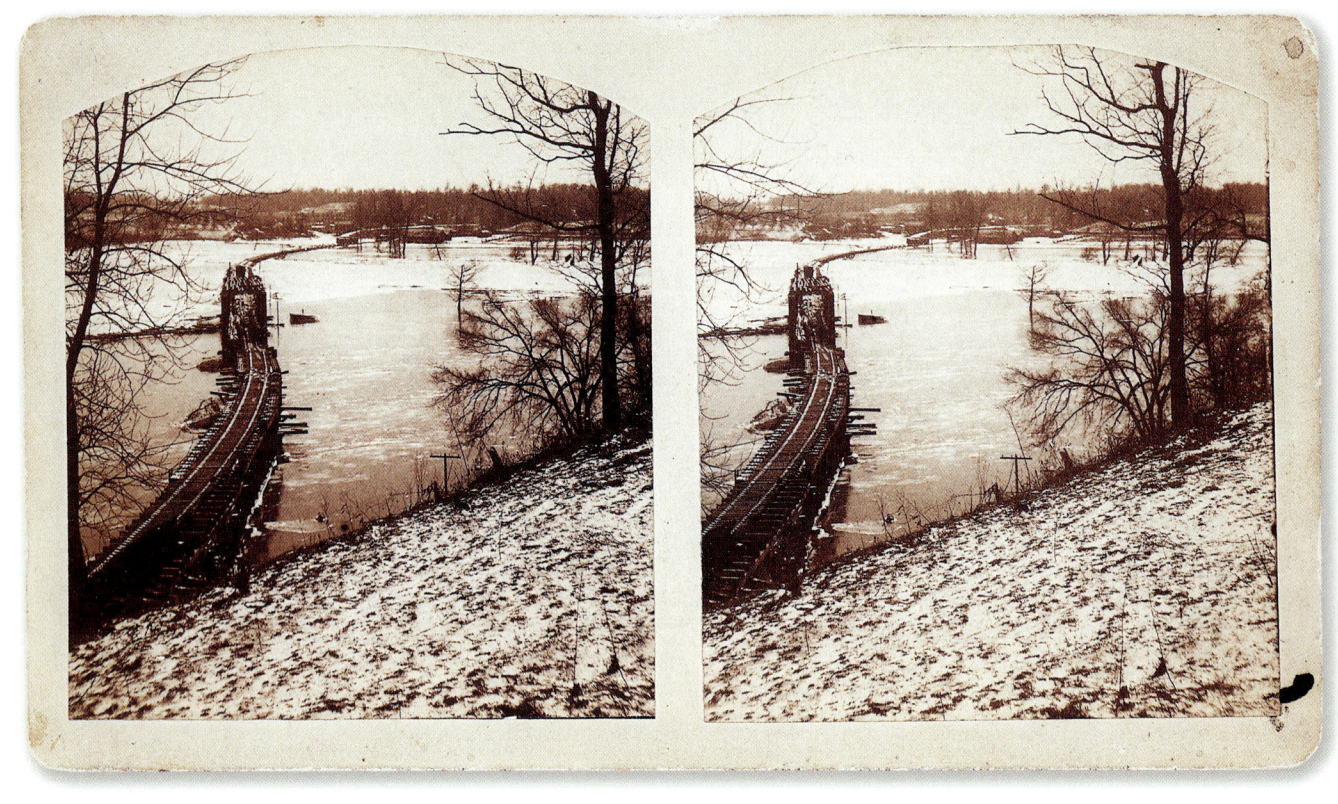

*Cincinnati, Wabash and Michigan Railway bridge, near Anderson, ca. 1880s. Photographed by M. D. Goodlander.
The caption on the back of the card says the view is looking south from Hanna Hill, presumably across
the White River toward town. The railway completed its line to Anderson in 1876.*

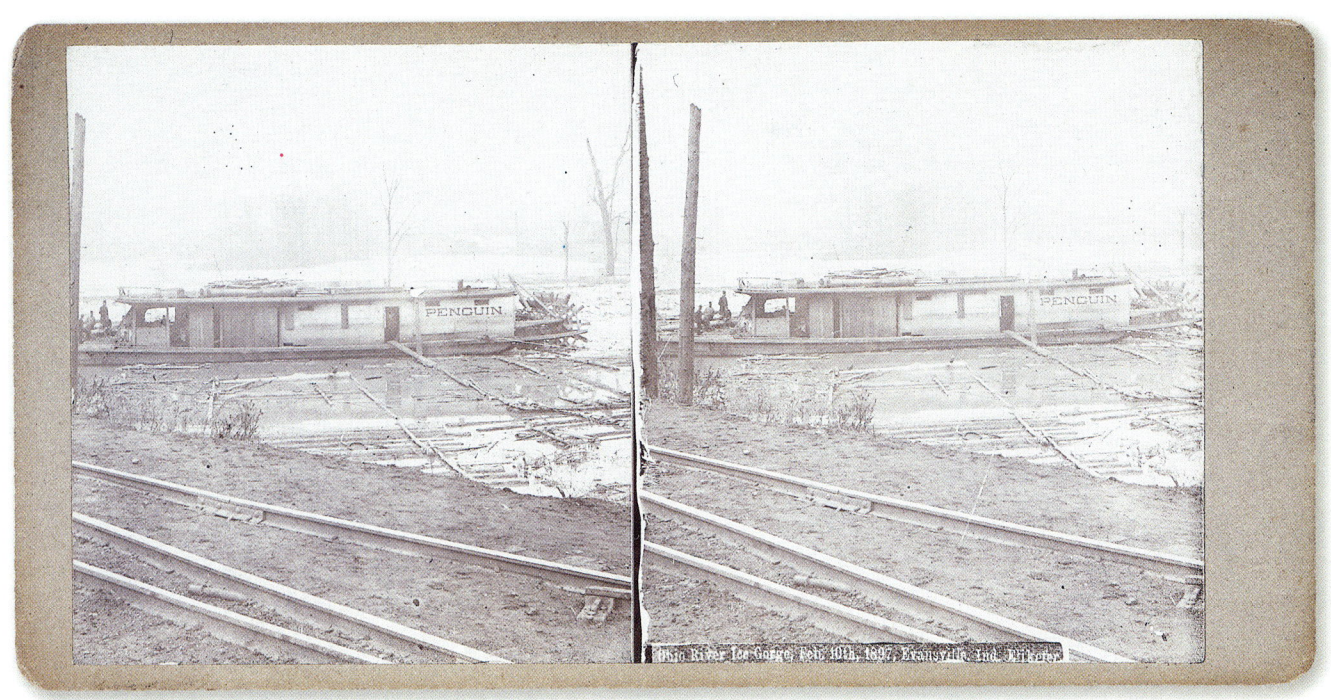

Ohio River Ice Gorge, Feb. 10th, 1897, Evansville, Ind. Elikofer.

The Penguin *towboat, Evansville, 1897. Photographed by Fred Elikofer.*
The Penguin *was on its way to Evansville from Cairo, Illinois, on the morning of 10 February when it was caught in an ice gorge. The captain tried*
but failed to steer the Penguin *up Pigeon Creek to escape the ice. The ice forced the* Penguin *into a railroad bridge and badly damaged it.*

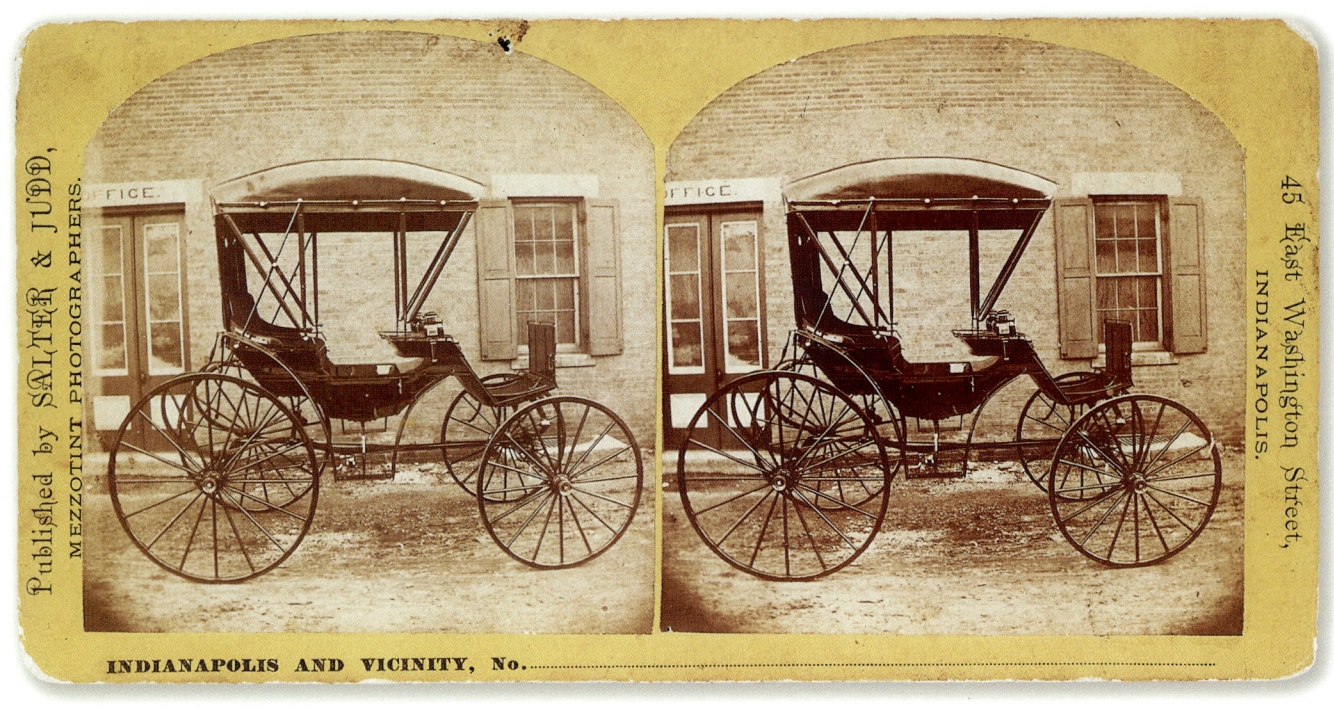

Within the stereo card:

Published by SALTER & JUDD,
MEZZOTINT PHOTOGRAPHERS.

OFFICE.

45 East Washington Street,
INDIANAPOLIS.

INDIANAPOLIS AND VICINITY, No.

Barouche manufactured by Wymond and Helfer, Indianapolis, ca. 1875. Published by Salter and Judd.
This card was apparently produced as advertising. The back of the card notes that the barouche sold for $550 to $650, "owing to material."

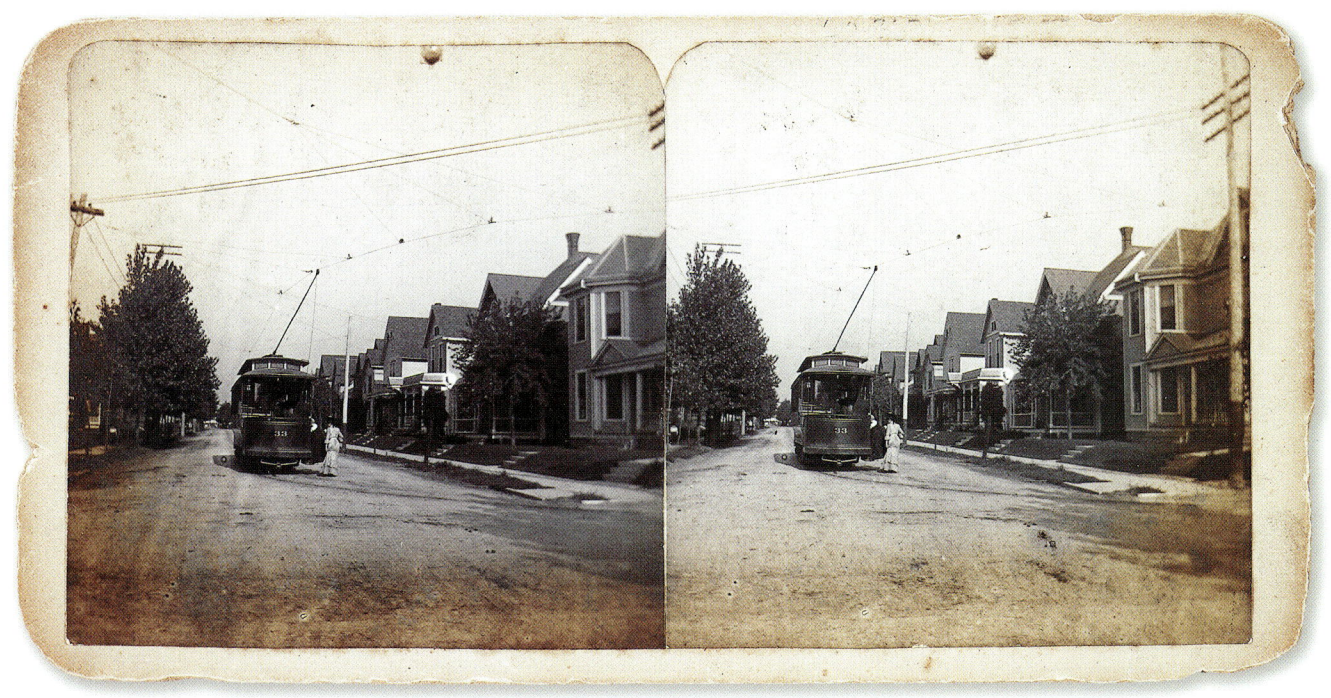

Streetcar in Muncie, ca. 1890s. Photographer unknown.

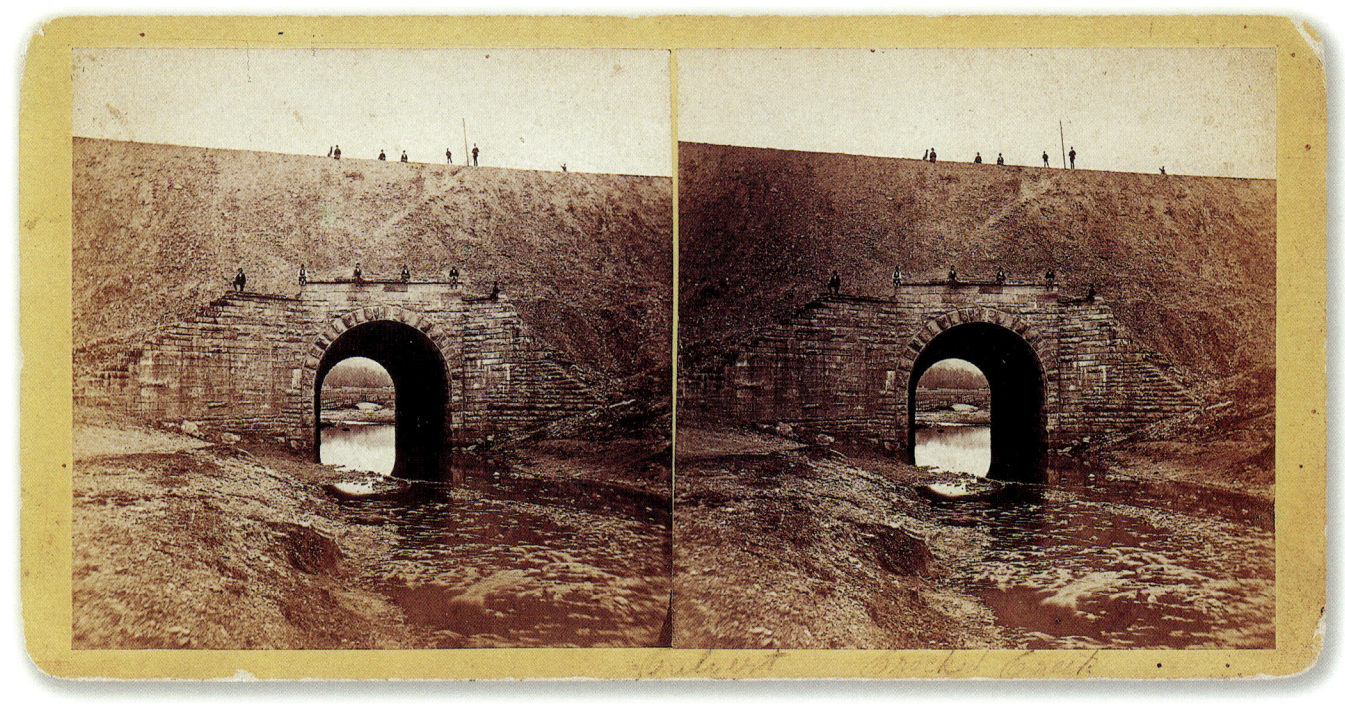

Jeffersonville, Madison and Indianapolis Railroad overpass at Crooked Creek, near Madison, ca. 1870s. Photographed by Joseph Gorgas.
Before a merger with the Jeffersonville Railroad in 1866, this line was known as the Madison and Indianapolis Railroad. Construction began in 1836,
and it was the state's first intercity railroad. It was known for its steep incline through the hills north of Madison.

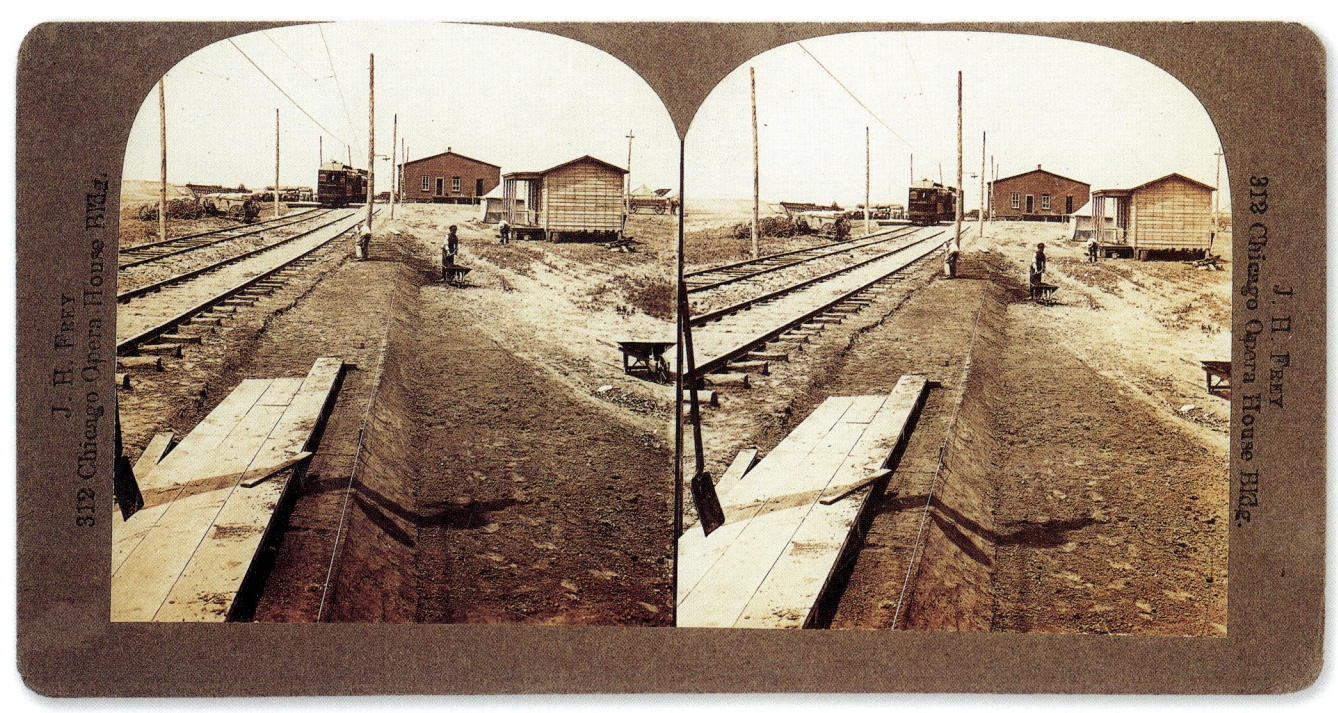

Chicago–New York Electric Air Line Railroad, South La Porte, ca. 1907. Photographed by J. H. Frey.
Developers of the Air Line (which was powered by electricity rather than steam) had ambitious plans to run it nearly 750 miles from Chicago to New York
and promised a one-way trip of only ten hours. They went bankrupt, however, and finished just under twenty miles of track, between Chesterton and La Porte.

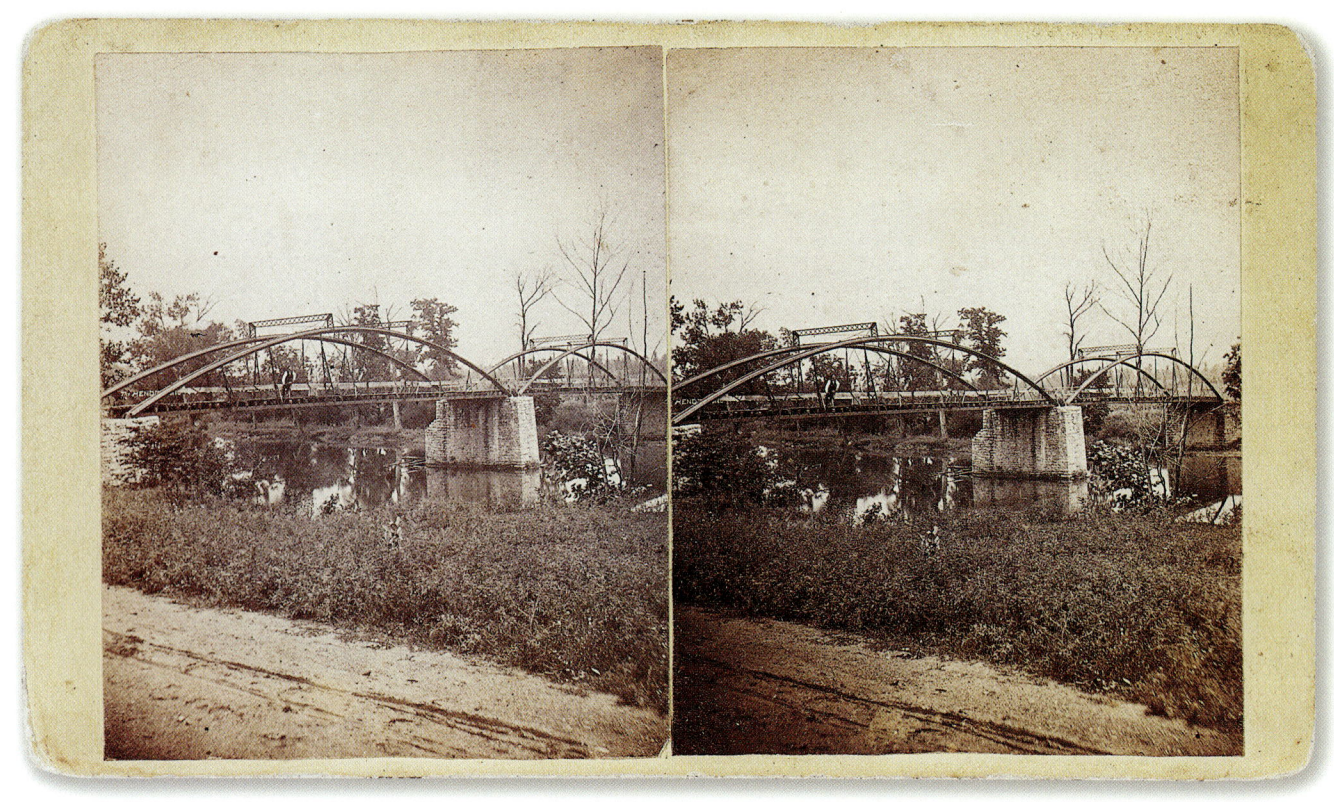

Bridge over the White River, west of Anderson, ca. 1880s. Photographed by M. D. Goodlander.

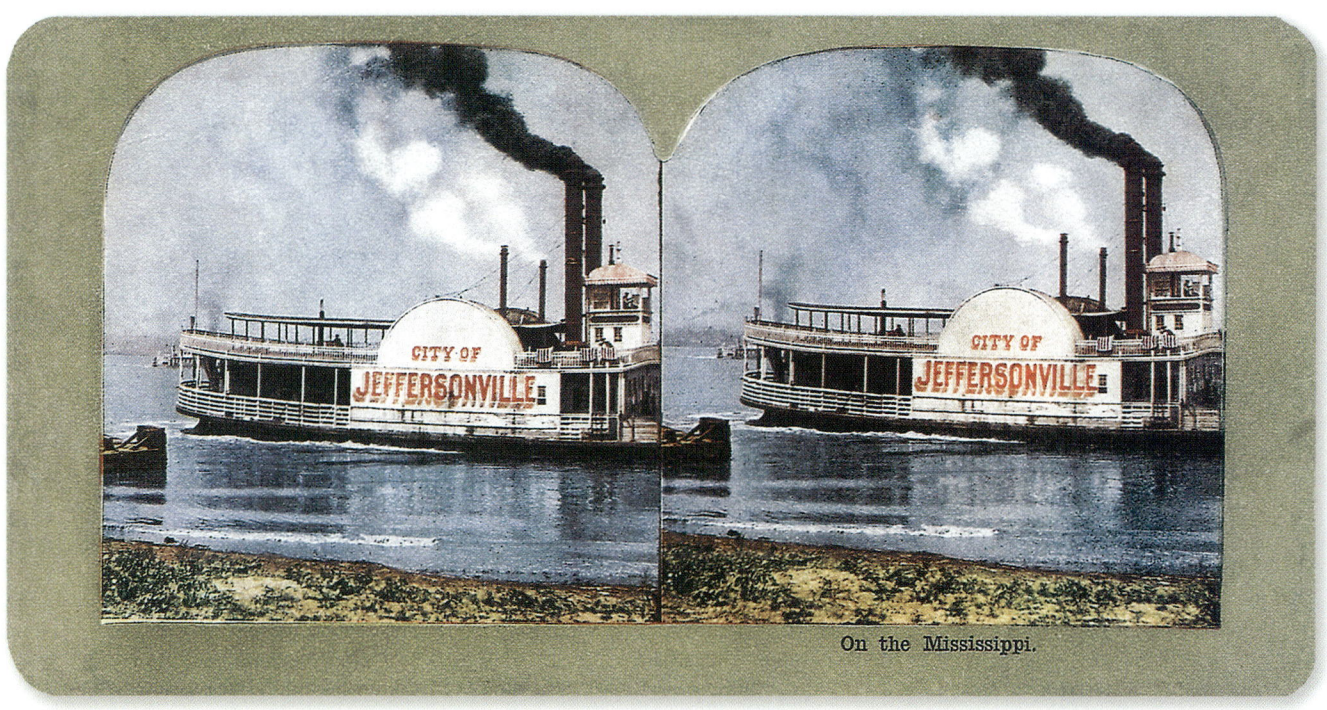

On the Mississippi.

City of Jeffersonville *steamboat, location unknown, ca. early 1900s. Photographer unknown.*
Workers at the Howard Shipyards in Jeffersonville built this ferry in 1891 and named it after their hometown. Though the caption indicates this view
was taken on the Mississippi River, it probably was not. The Louisville and Jeffersonville Ferry Company owned the City of Jeffersonville,
and the boat likely stayed on the Ohio River, transporting riders between Indiana and Kentucky.

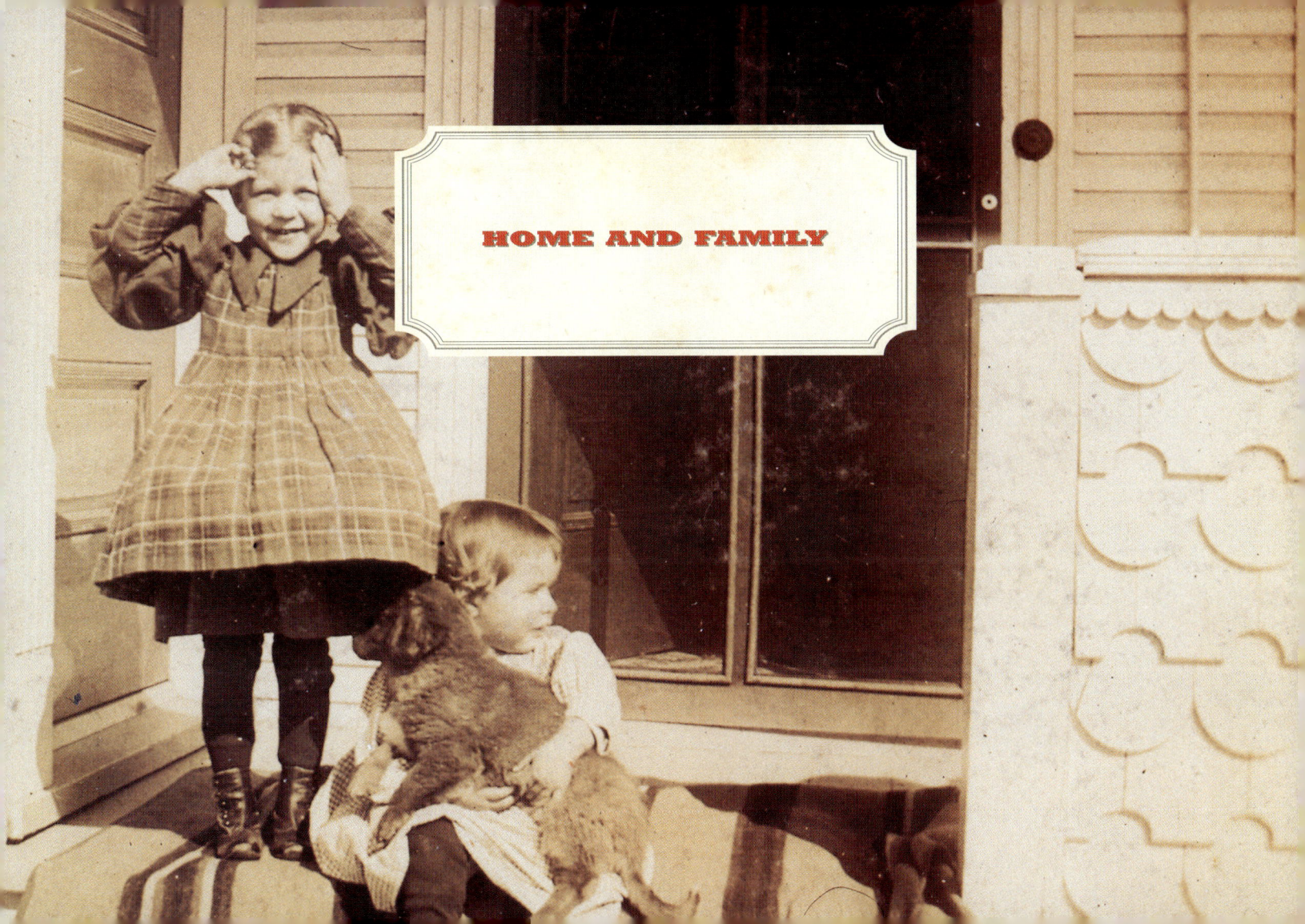

HOME AND FAMILY

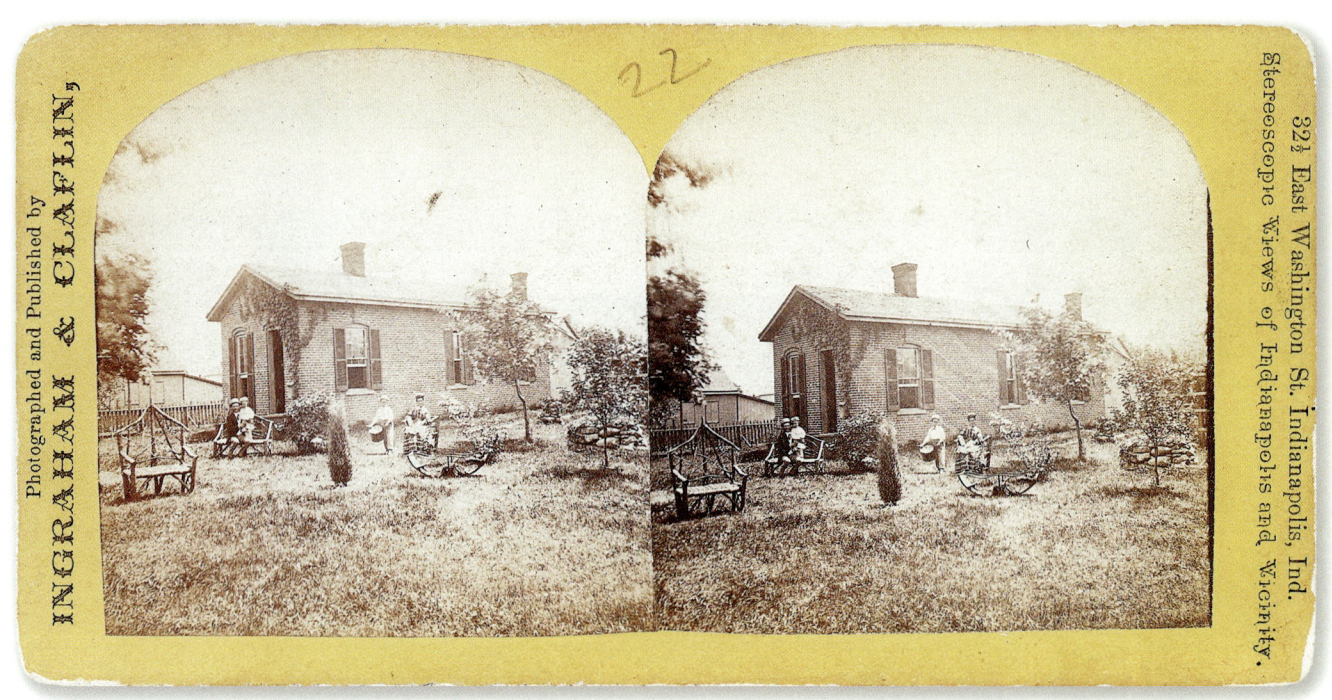

Photographed and Published by INGRAHAM & CLAFLIN,

32½ East Washington St. Indianapolis, Ind. Stereoscopic Views of Indianapolis and Vicinity.

Vail residence, Indianapolis, ca. 1870s. Published by Ingraham and Claflin.
Indianapolis city directories published in the 1870s (the period when Ingraham and Claflin were working together)
list a Sidney Vail living on East Washington Street, and perhaps this is his home.

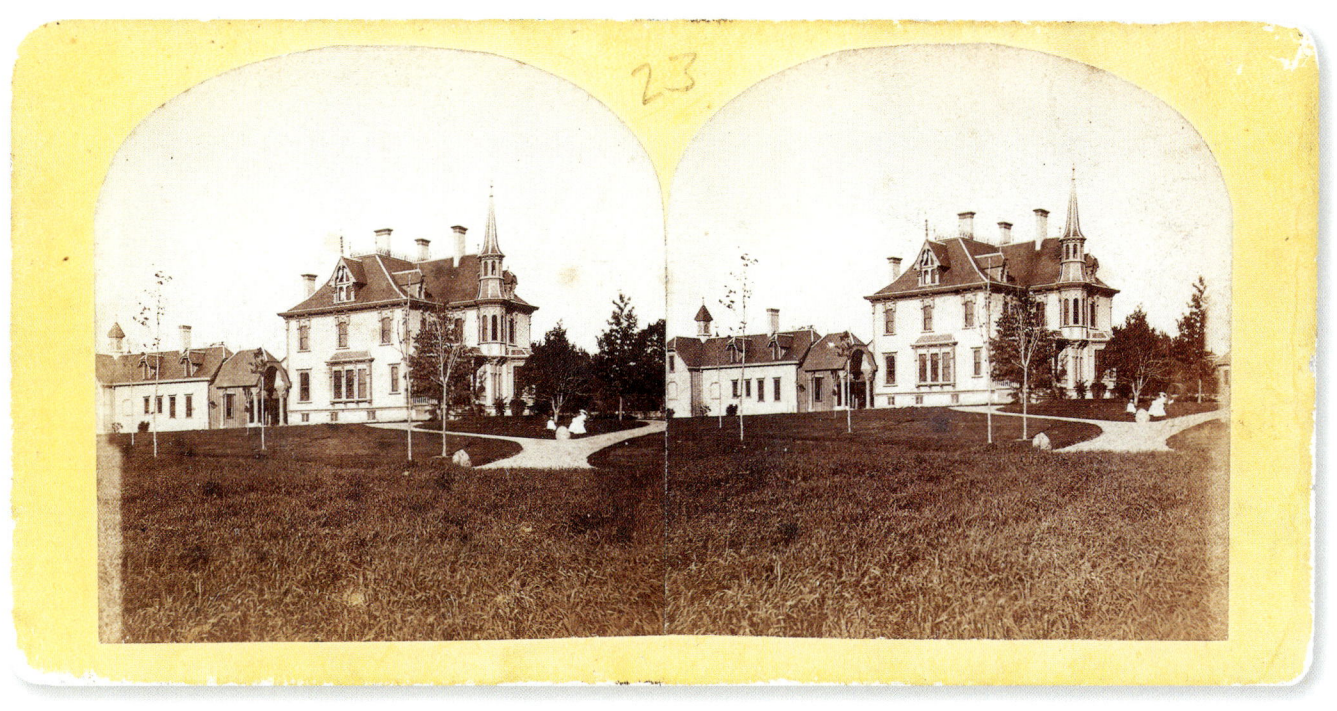

23

Stoughton Fletcher residence, Indianapolis, ca. 1870s. Published by Ingraham and Claflin.
Stoughton Fletcher was the son of Calvin Fletcher, an early settler of Indianapolis and one of its leading citizens.
This home stood on what is now Tenth Street, across from the Woodruff Place neighborhood.

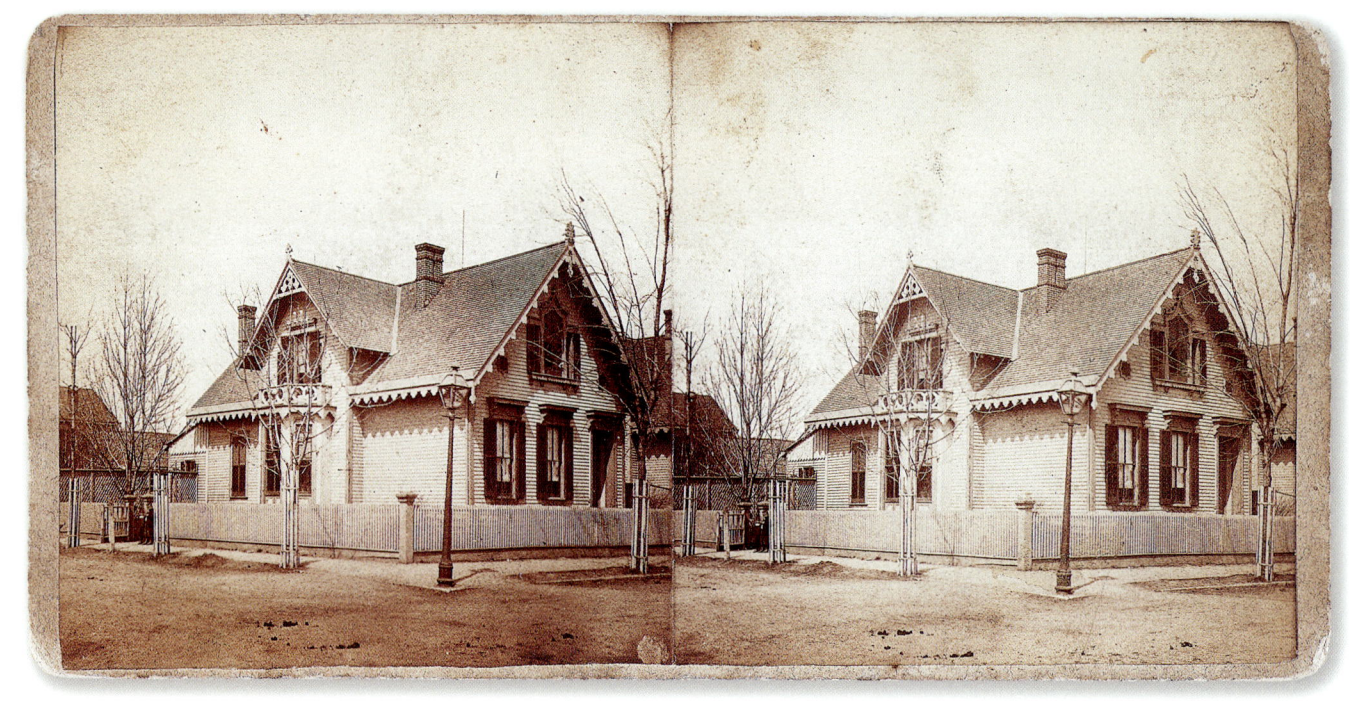

Herman Lieber residence, Indianapolis, ca. 1870s. Photographed by J. W. Pendergast.
Lieber owned a popular art emporium in the city and served as a patron for local artists, including T. C. Steele. This home was on North Delaware Street.

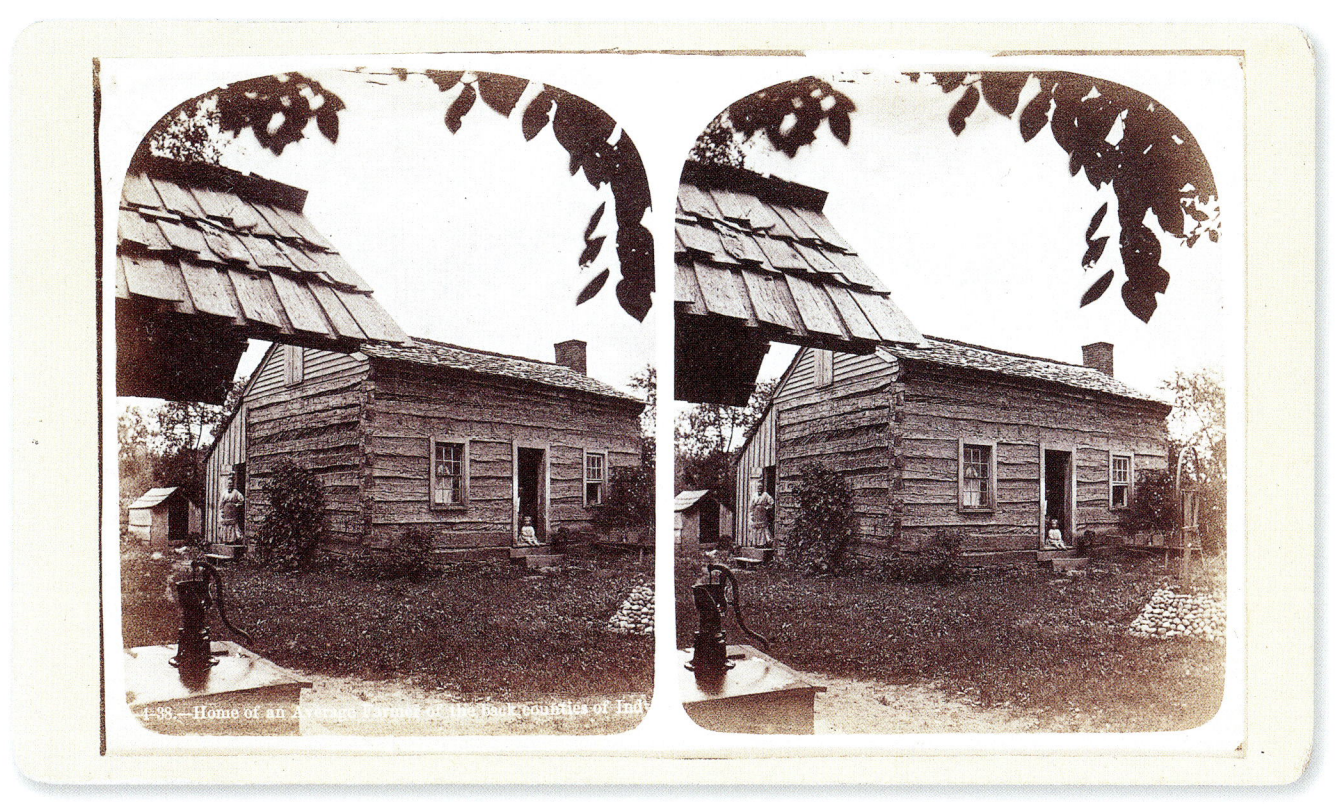

4-38.—Home of an Average Farmer of the Back counties of Ind.

Cabin, location unknown, ca. 1890s. Photographer unknown.
The caption on this scene indicates that it is the home of an average farmer of the back counties of Indiana.

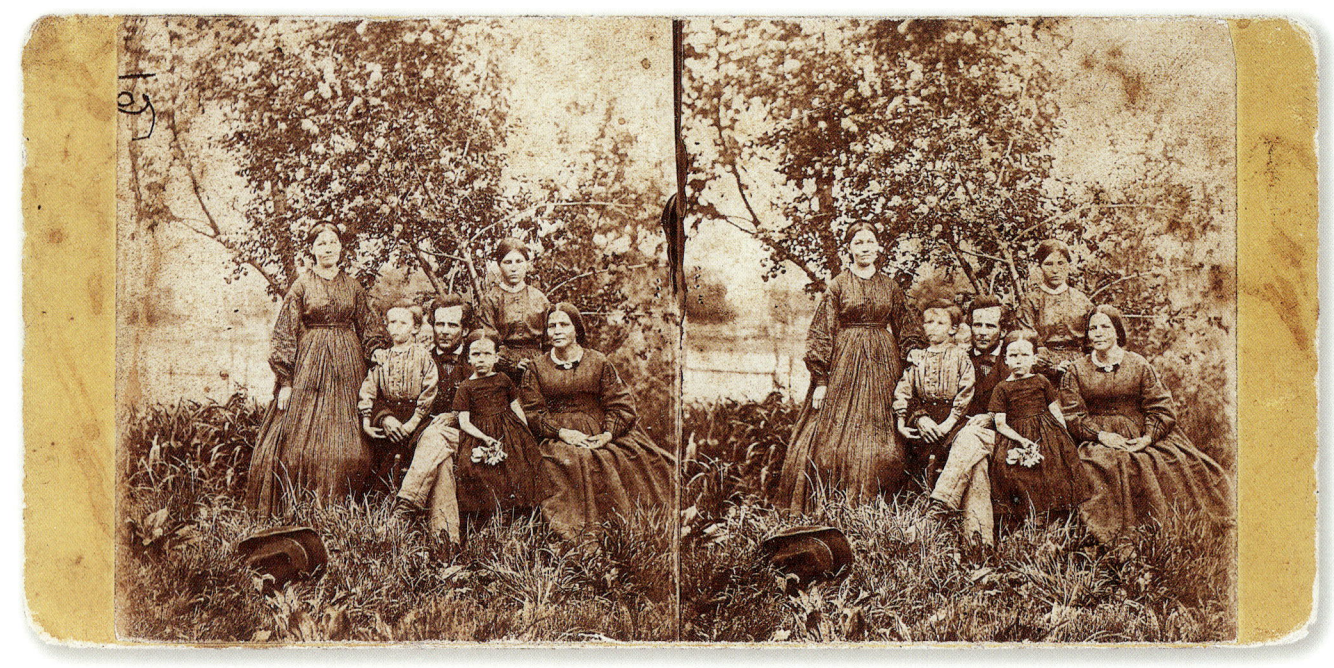

Joseph B. and Elizabeth Lewis and children, near Pendleton, 1865. Photographed by Ridgeway Glover.
The two women standing are identified as helpers.

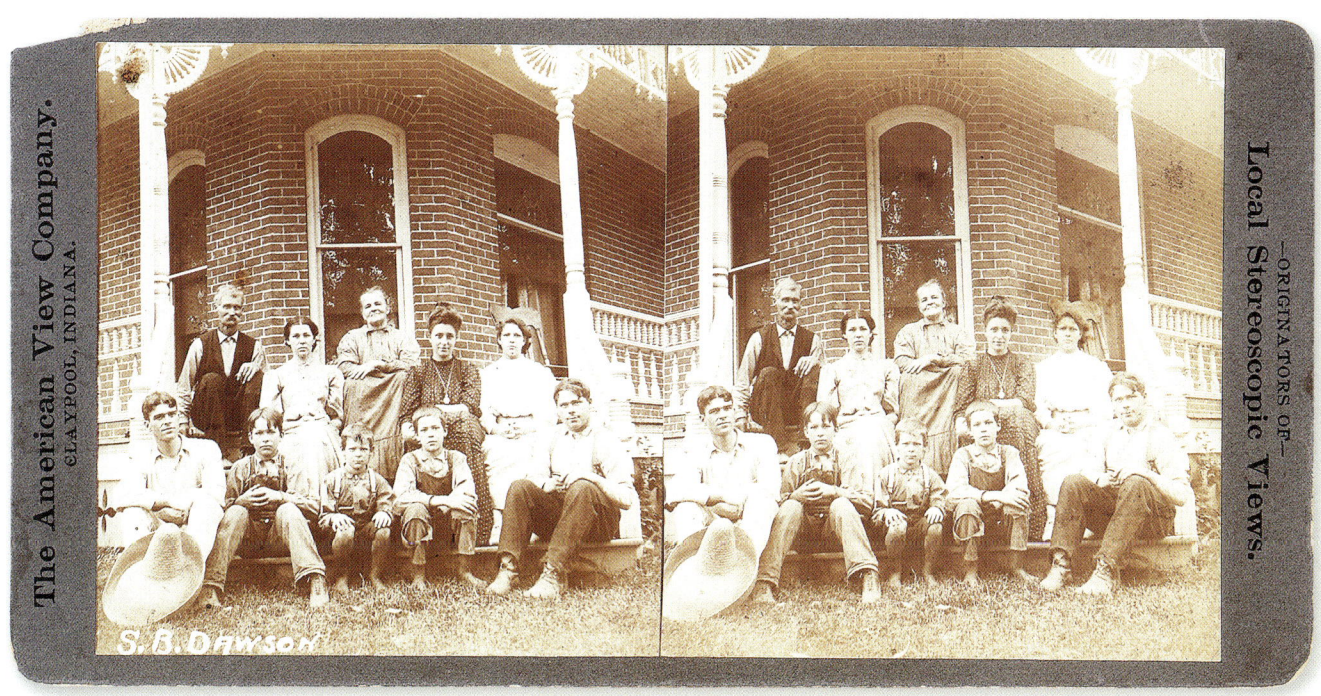

S. B. Dawson

S. B. Dawson family, Fulton County, ca. early 1900s. Published by the American View Company.
The 1900 census lists a Samuel B. Dawson and wife Martha living in Henry Township, Fulton County. According to the census,
the Dawsons had eight children—five sons and three daughters.

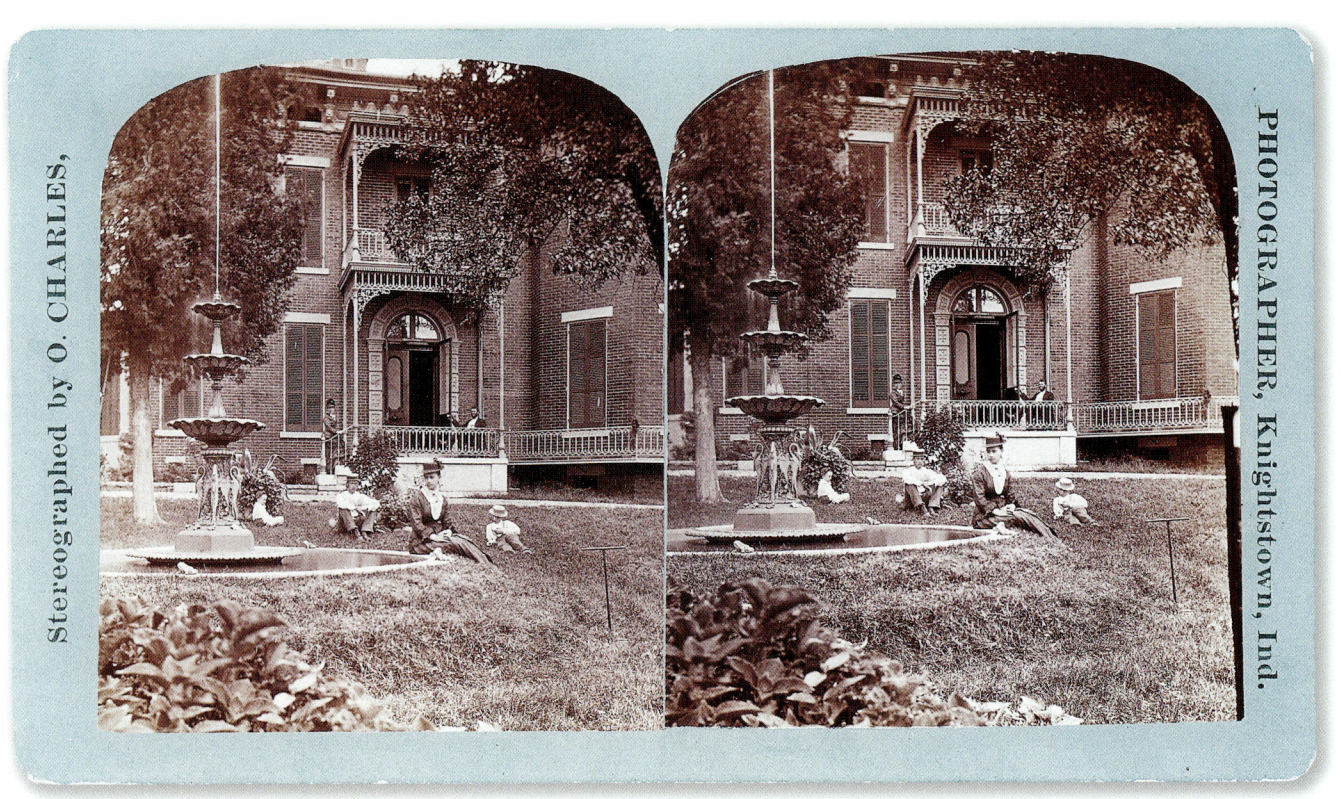

Stereographed by O. CHARLES,

PHOTOGRAPHER, Knightstown, Ind.

Unidentified family, probably near Knightstown, ca. 1880s. Photographed by Oliver Charles.
This is obviously a prosperous family, considering the size and style of the house, the fashionable clothes, and the fountain in the yard.

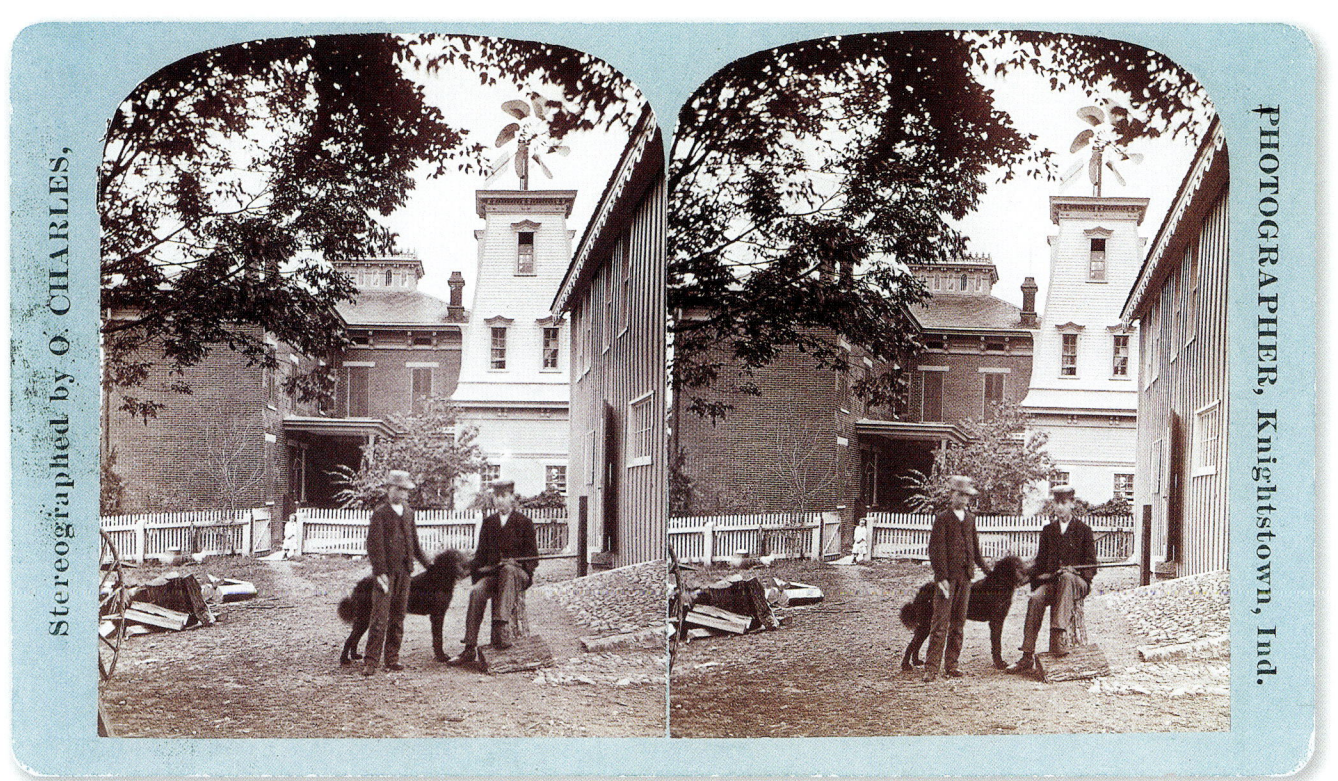

Boys with gun and dog, probably near Knightstown, ca. 1880s. Photographed by Oliver Charles.
The boys are in back of the house pictured on the opposite page.

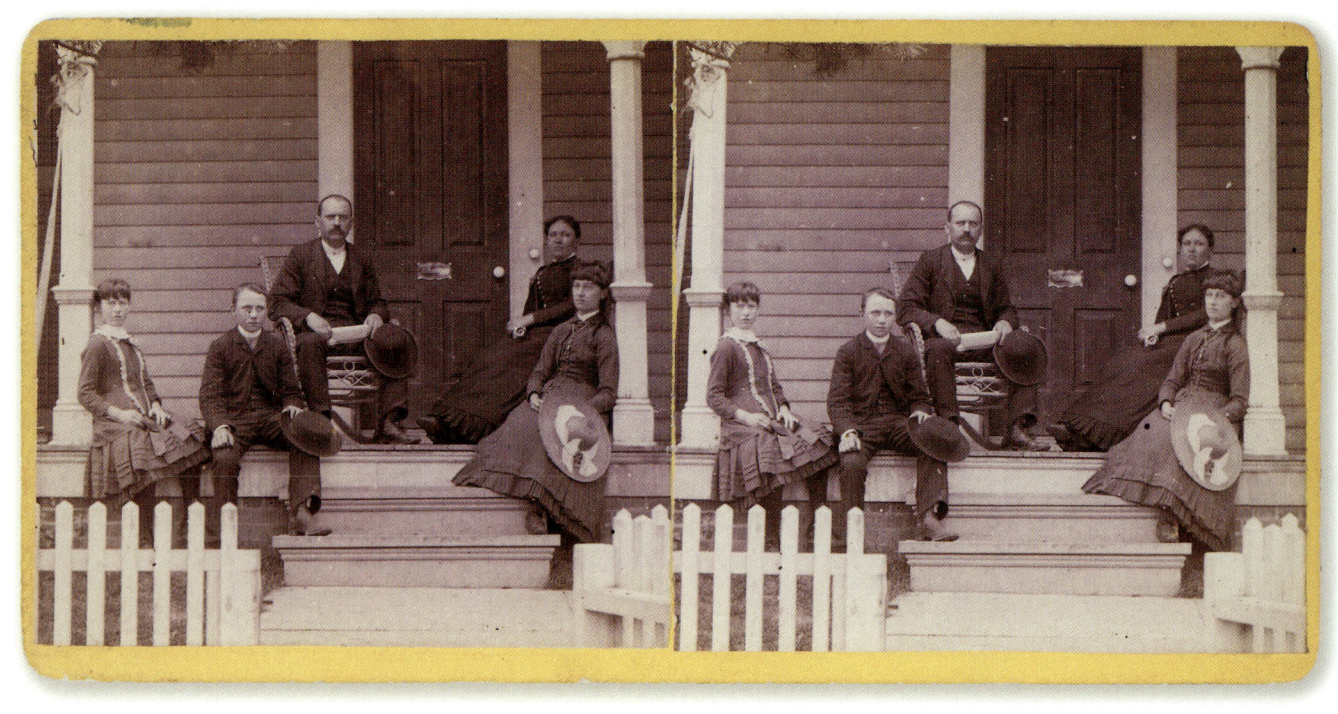

Unidentified family, location unknown, ca. 1880s. Photographed by M. D. Goodlander.
Because Goodlander's studio was in Muncie and he photographed around Delaware and Madison Counties, this family probably lived in that area.

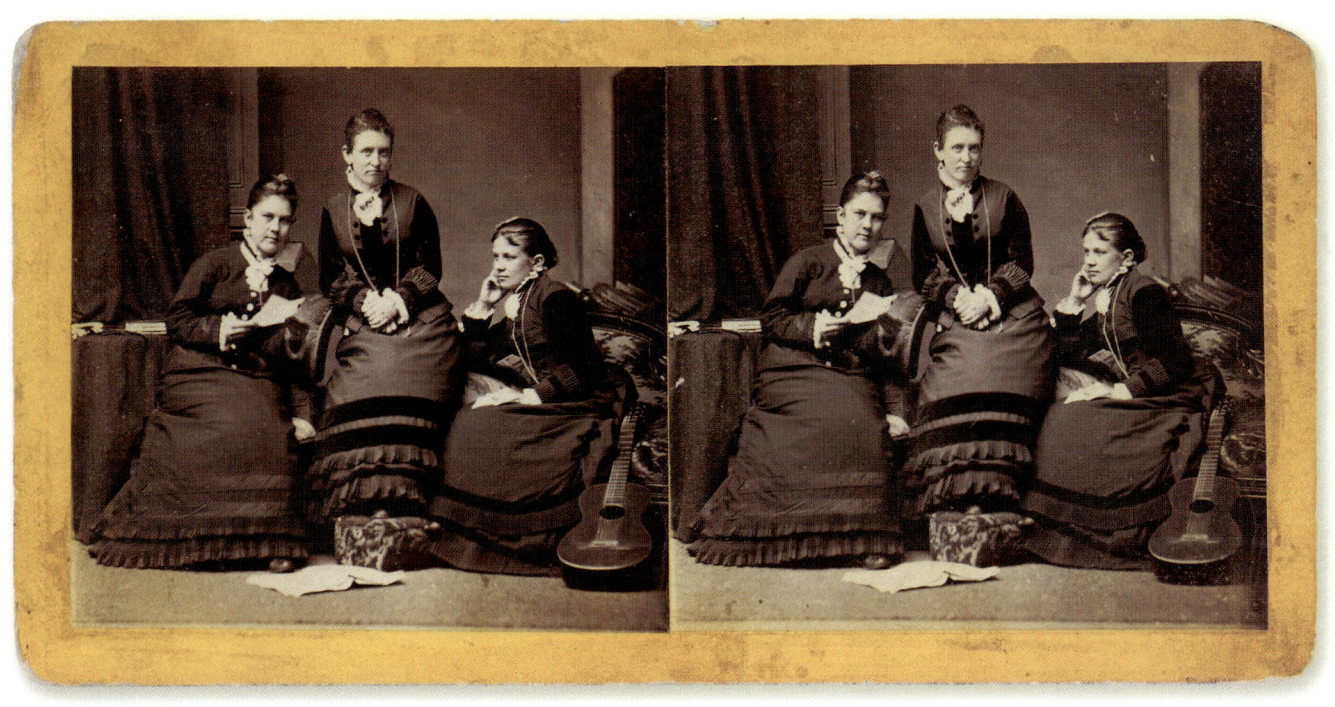

Unidentified women, location unknown, ca. 1880s. Photographed by M. D. Goodlander.
This photograph was probably taken in east-central Indiana, where Goodlander focused his business.

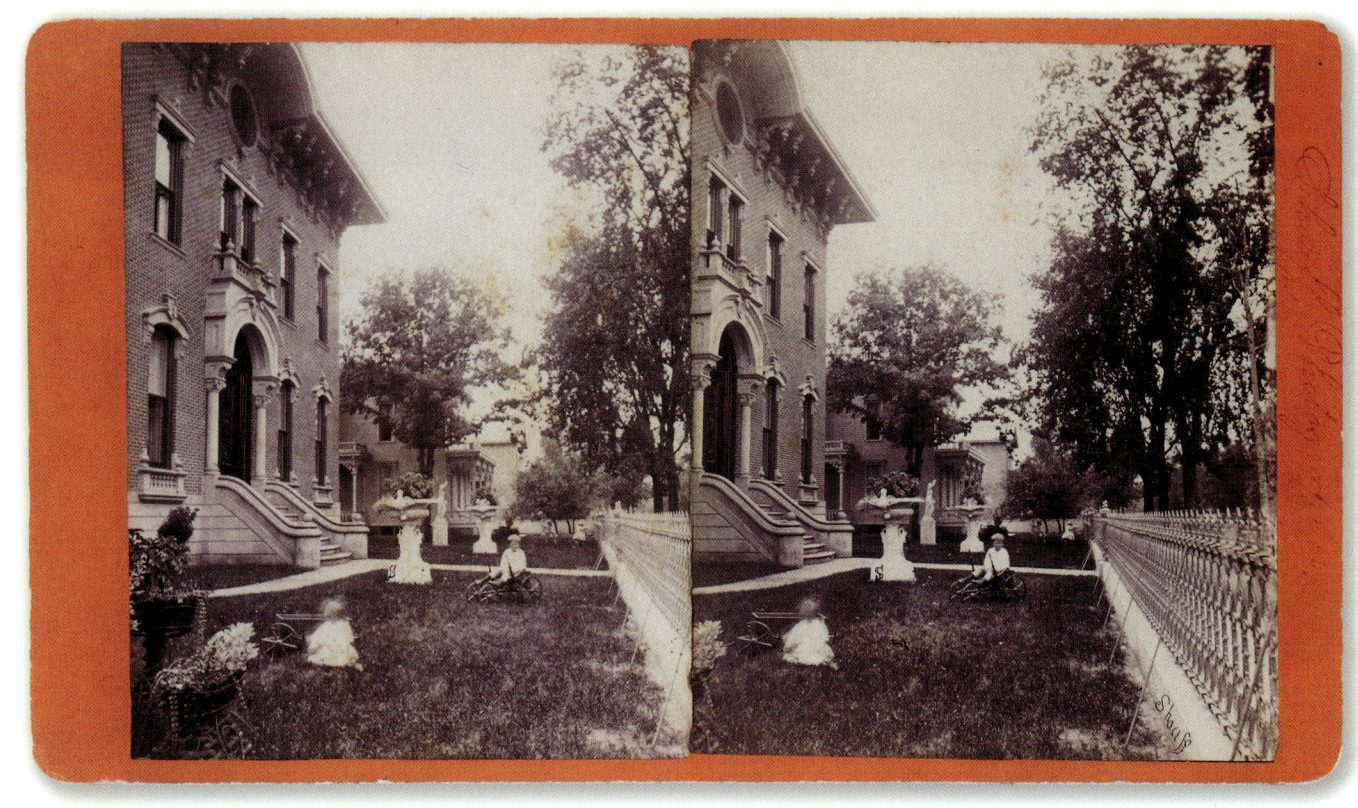

Olds family residence, Fort Wayne, ca. 1880s. Photographed by John A. Shoaff.
This home was built by Henry G. Olds, a prominent Fort Wayne manufacturer. It was located on West Berry Street. In later years it housed the Mizpah Shrine Temple.

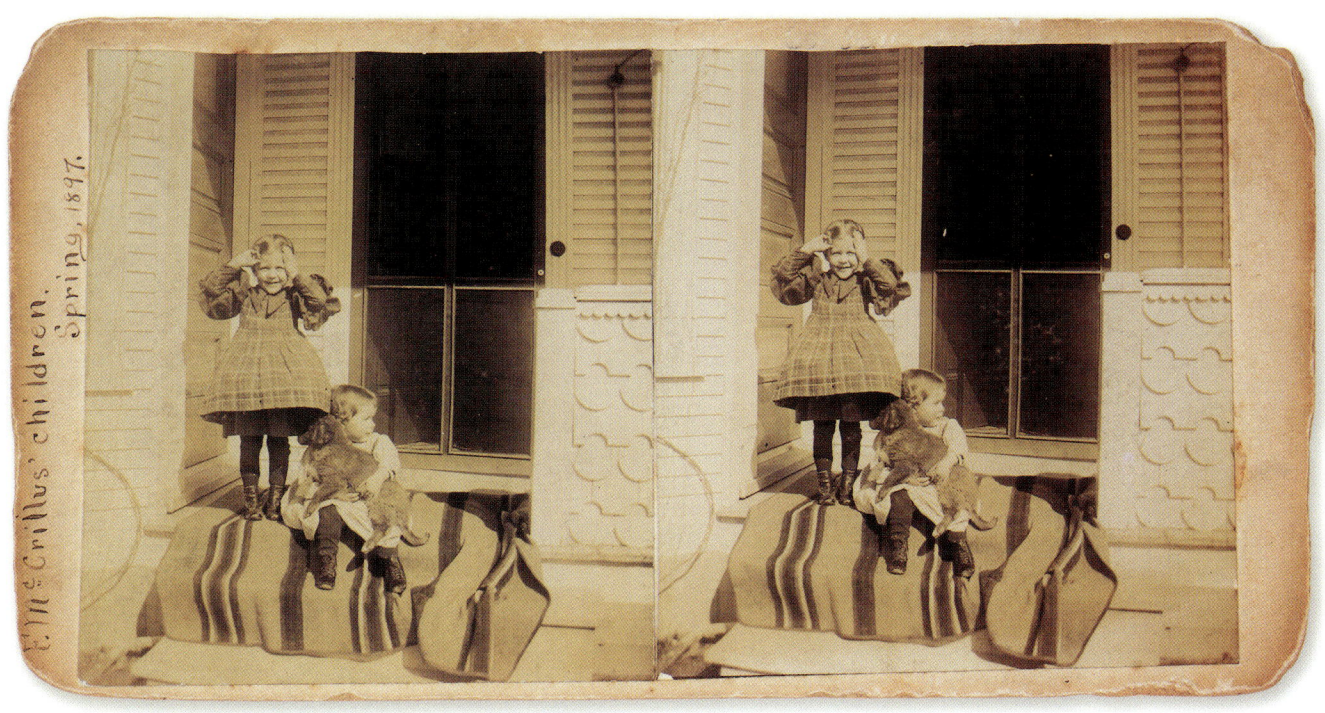

Frank McCrillus's children, Muncie, 1897. Photographer unknown.
The McCrilluses lived on Bethel Avenue.

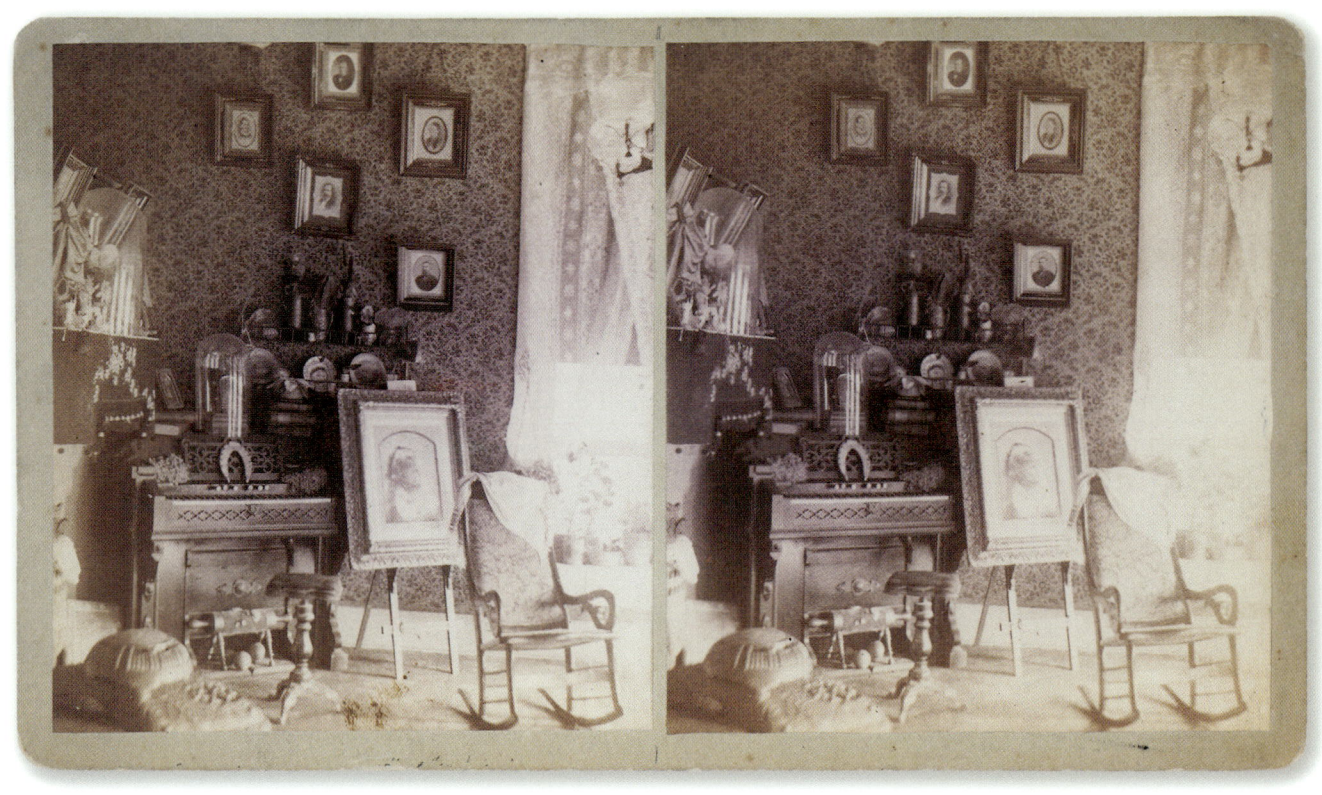

Parlor, location unknown, ca. 1880s. Photographed by M. D. Goodlander.
A customer might have hired Goodlander to take this photograph, or perhaps Goodlander took it in his own Muncie home.

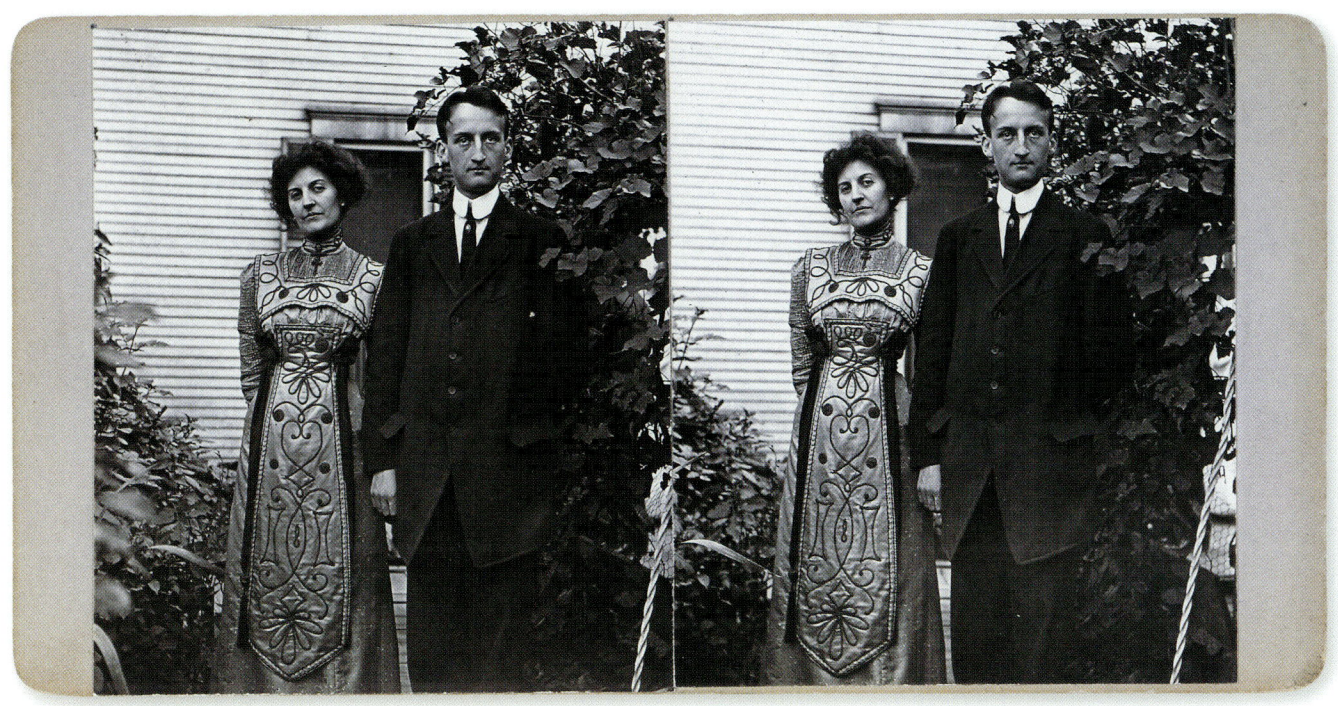

Cora Covault and Phil Thomas, Hartford City, 1909. Photographed by Clay H. Tuttle.
Covault married Tuttle in 1911.

165

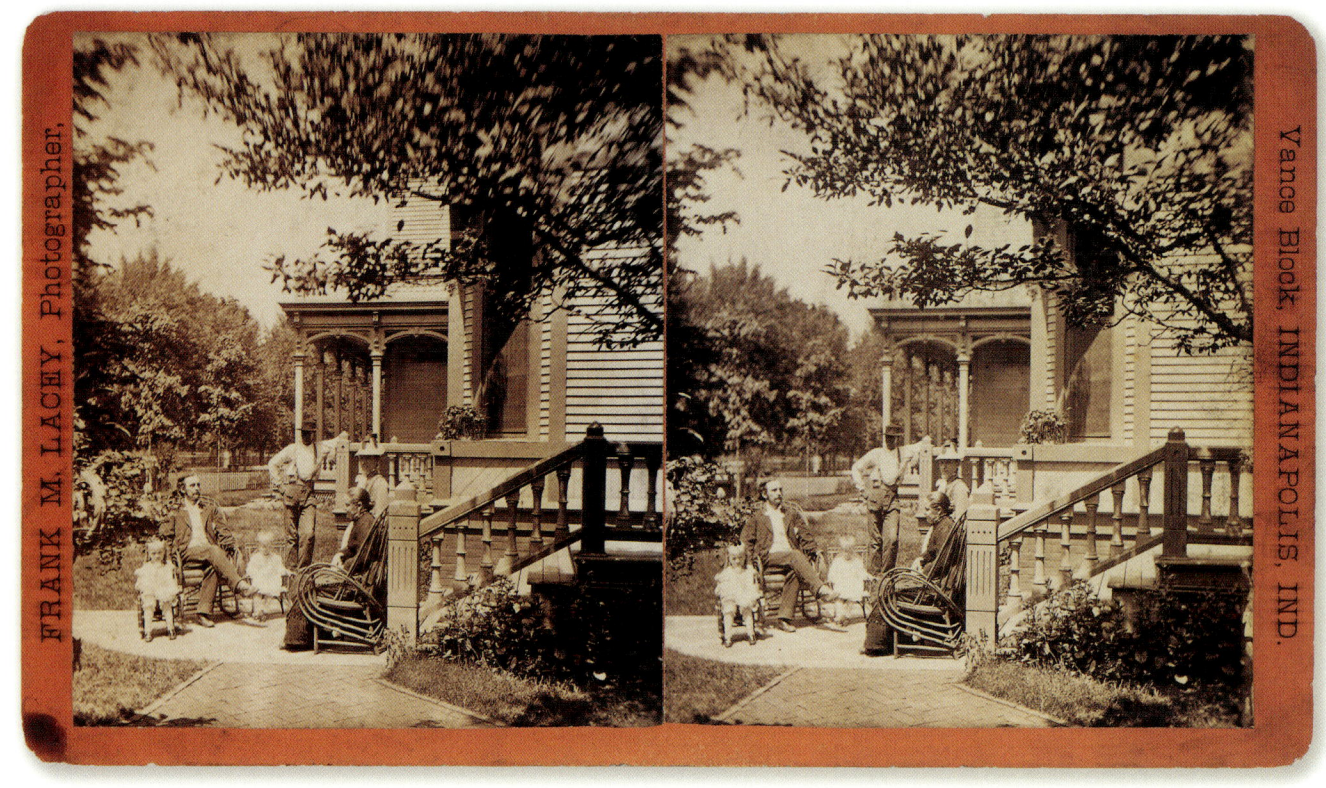

Henry and Elizabeth Pierce and family, Indianapolis, ca. late 1870s. Photographed by Frank M. Lacey.
Henry Pierce was a prominent lawyer, and this photo was taken at the first of at least two homes he and his family lived in on North Meridian Street.

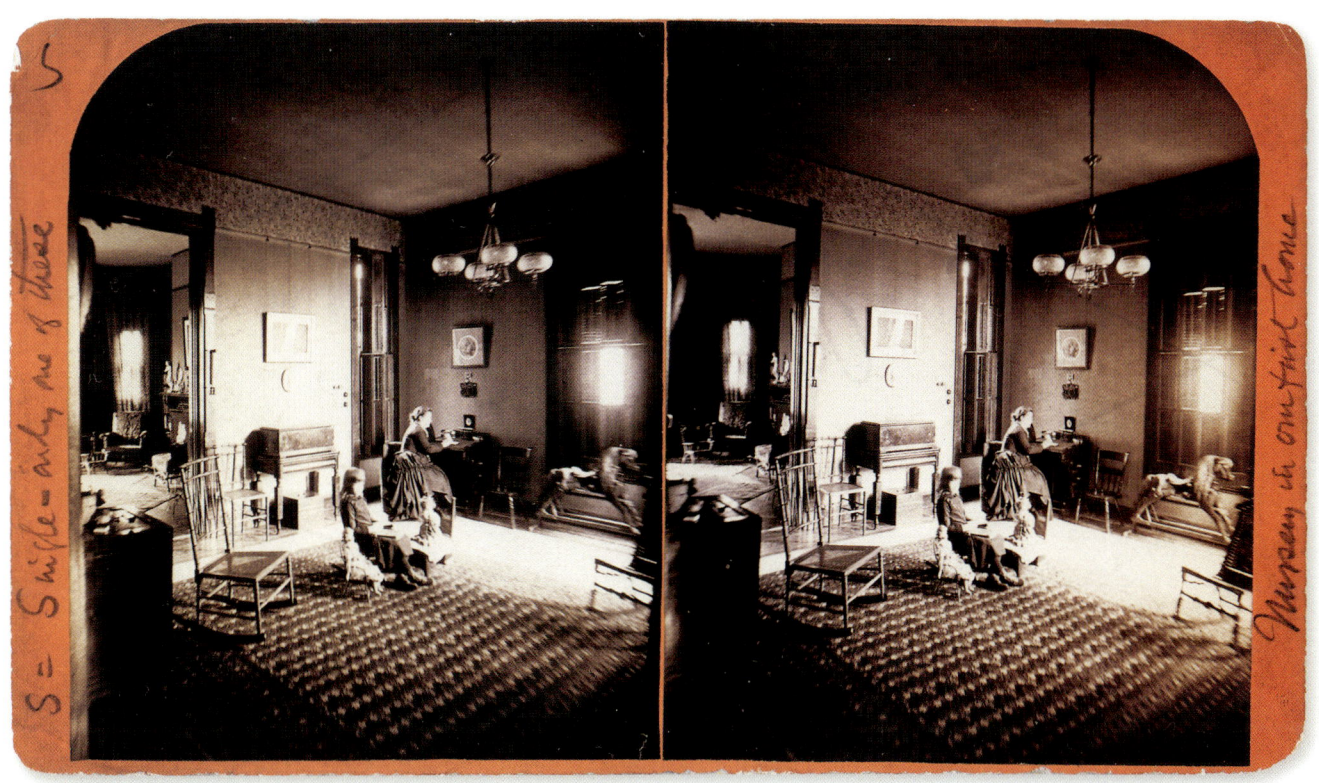

Nursery in Pierce residence, Indianapolis, ca. late 1870s. Photographer unknown.
The handwritten caption indicates this was the nursery in the family's first North Meridian Street home.

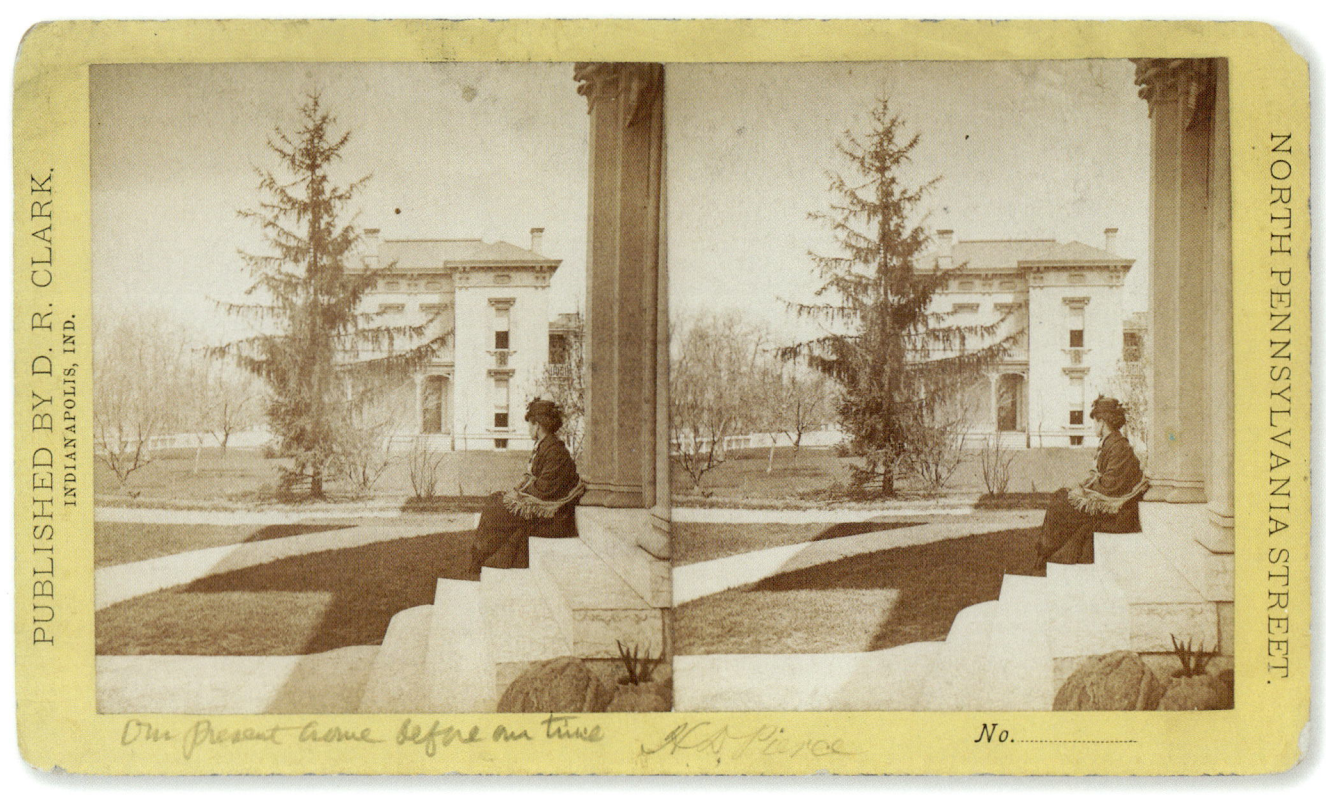

Our present home before our time *H. D. Pierce*   No.

Future Pierce residence, Indianapolis, ca. late 1870s. Photographed by D. R. Clark.
In the mid-1880s Henry Pierce and family moved to this house, which was located on North Meridian Street,
south of the house they had been living in. As the caption states, this view of the home was taken before the Pierces moved there.

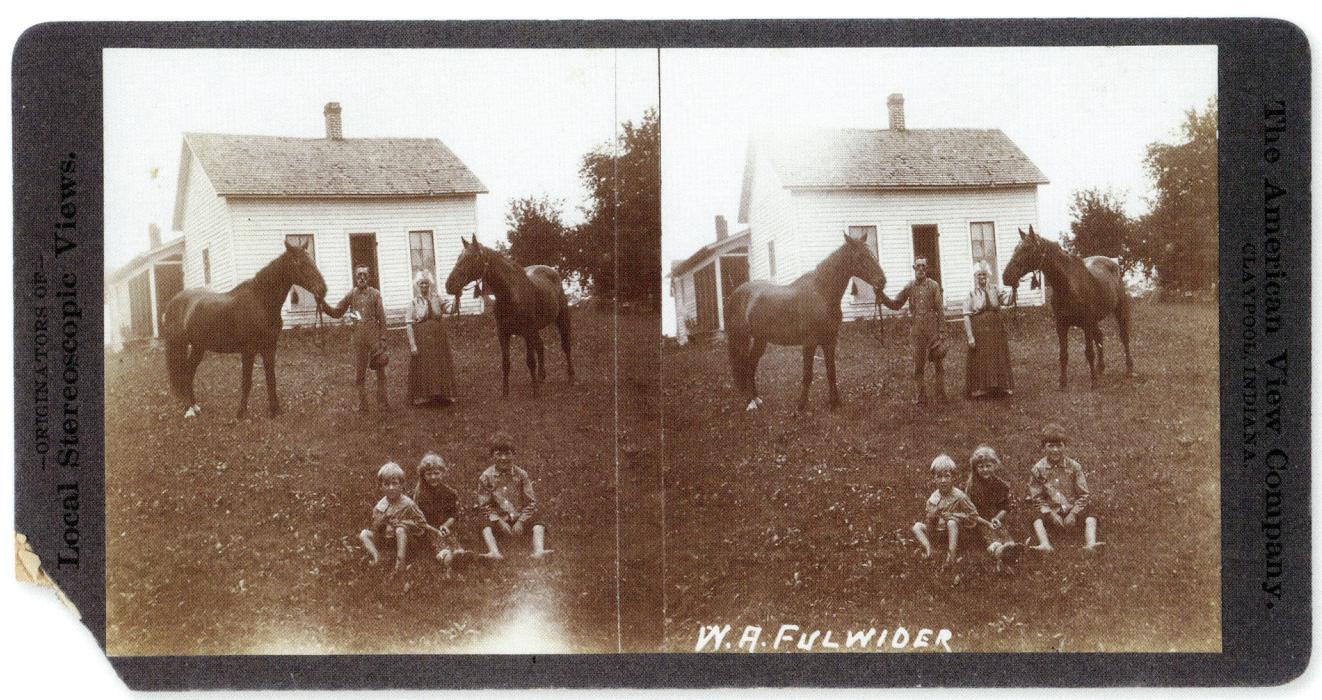

W. A. Fulwider, Kosciusko County, ca. early 1900s. Published by the American View Company.
The 1900 census lists a William A. Fulwider and wife Emily living in Prairie Township, Kosciusko County.
The children are too young to be the Fulwiders', but perhaps they are grandchildren.

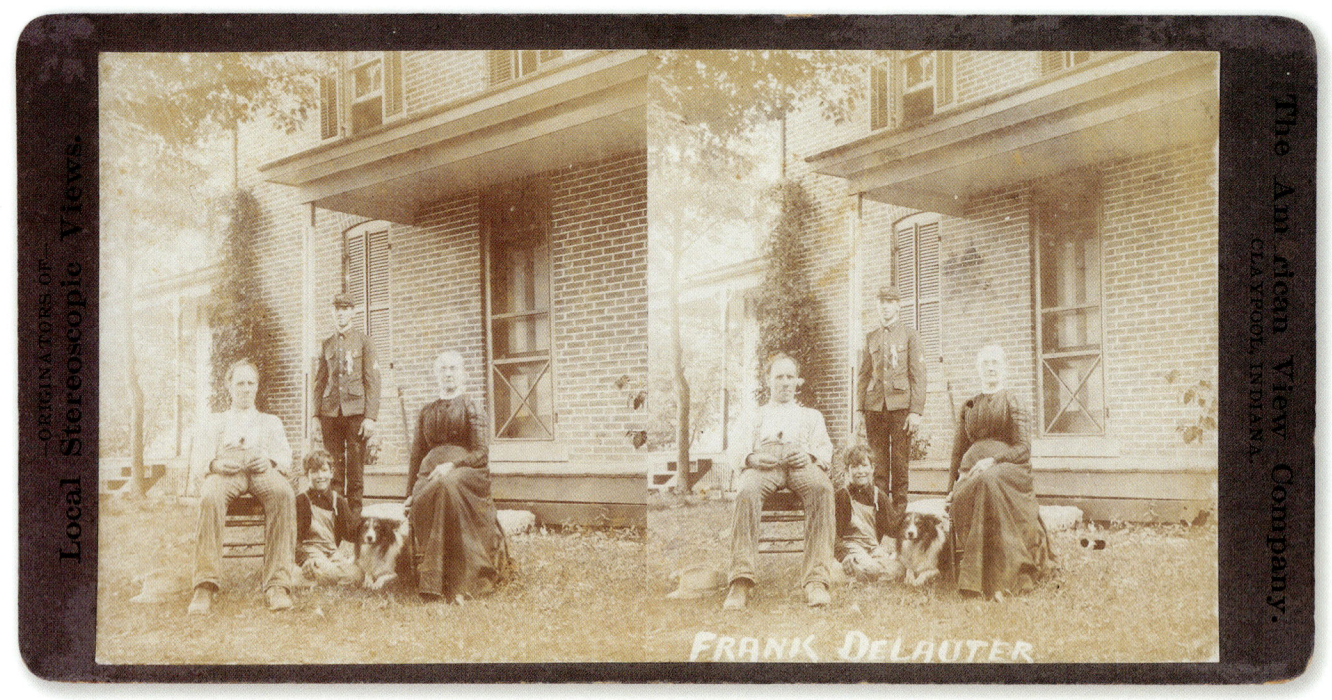

ORIGINATORS OF
Local Stereoscopic Views.

The American View Company.
CLAYPOOL, INDIANA.

FRANK DELAUTER

Frank Delauter and family, probably Wabash County, ca. early 1900s. Published by the American View Company.
The 1900 census lists a Frank Delauter and wife Sarah living in Pleasant Township, Wabash County. According to the census,
Sarah was twelve years older than her husband, information that seems compatible with this image. The census also indicates
the Delauters had two sons, but it lists years of birth that do not appear to match the ages of the boys seen here.

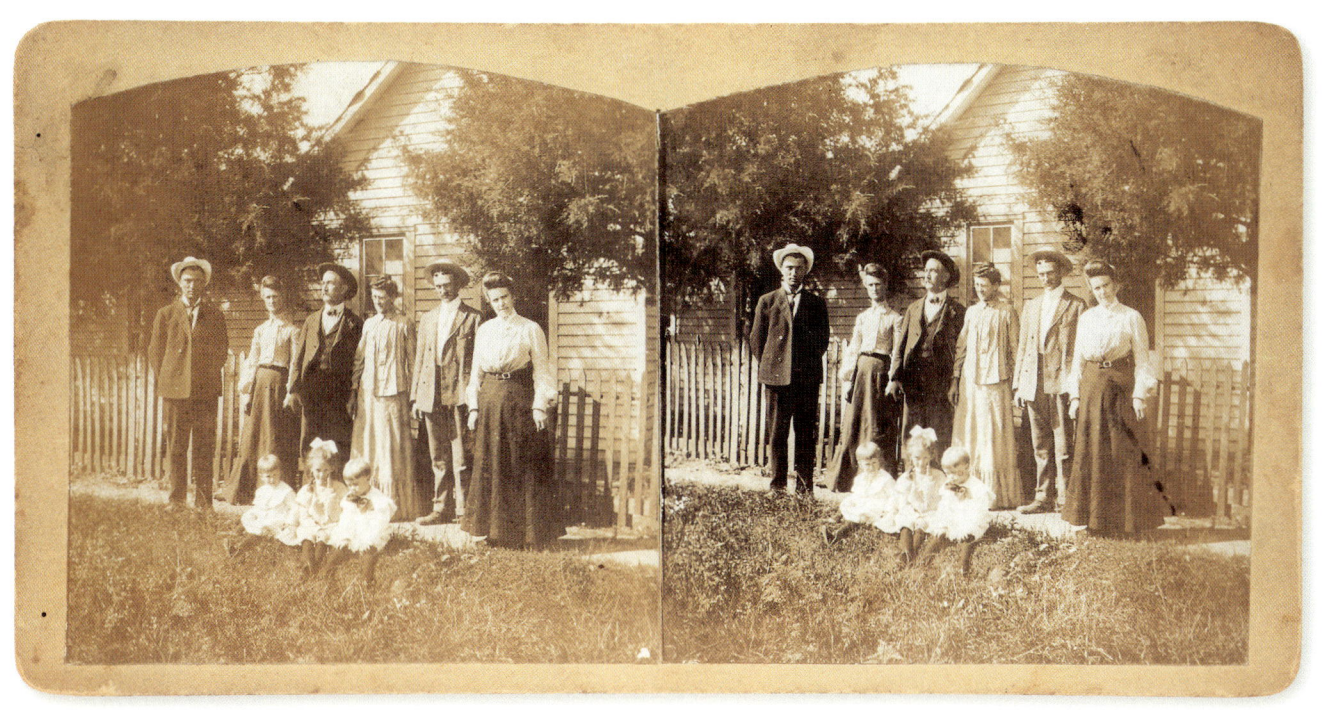

Unidentified family, possibly from Clinton County, ca. early 1900s. Photographer unknown.

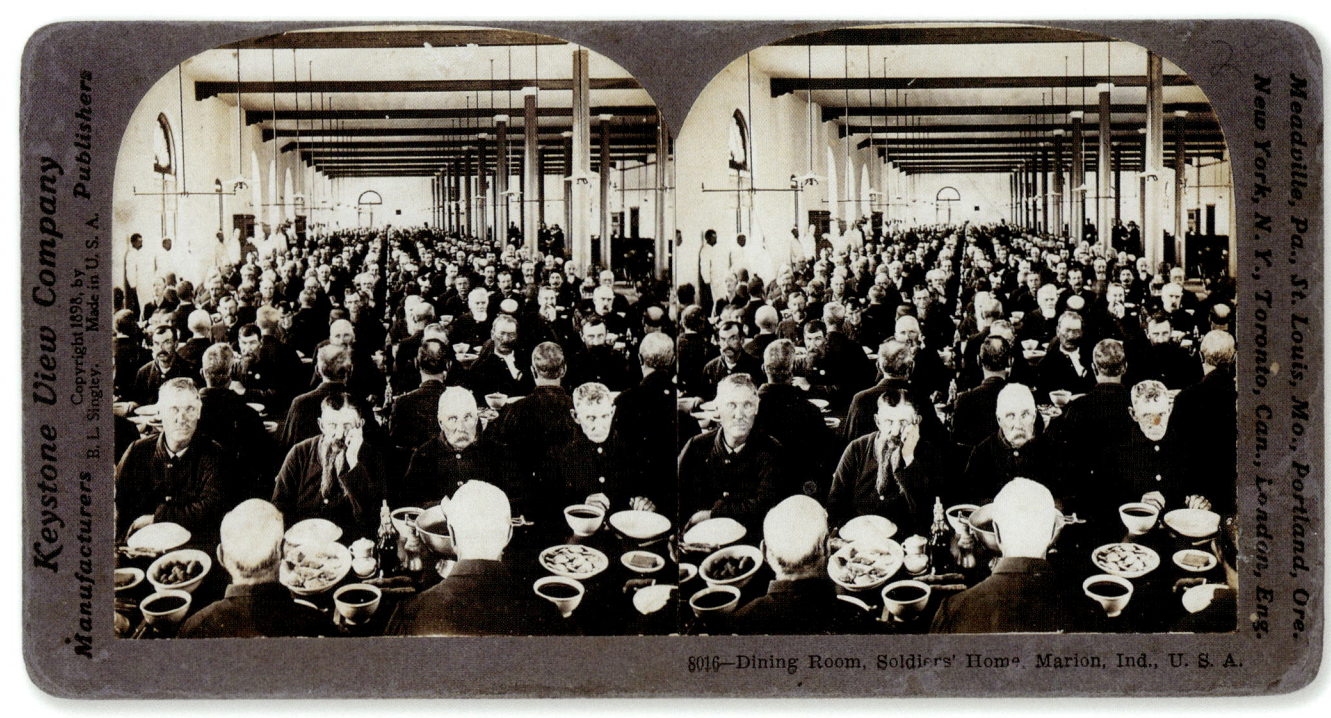

172

Residents of the National Home for Disabled Volunteer Soldiers gather for dinner, Marion, 1898. Published by the Keystone View Company.

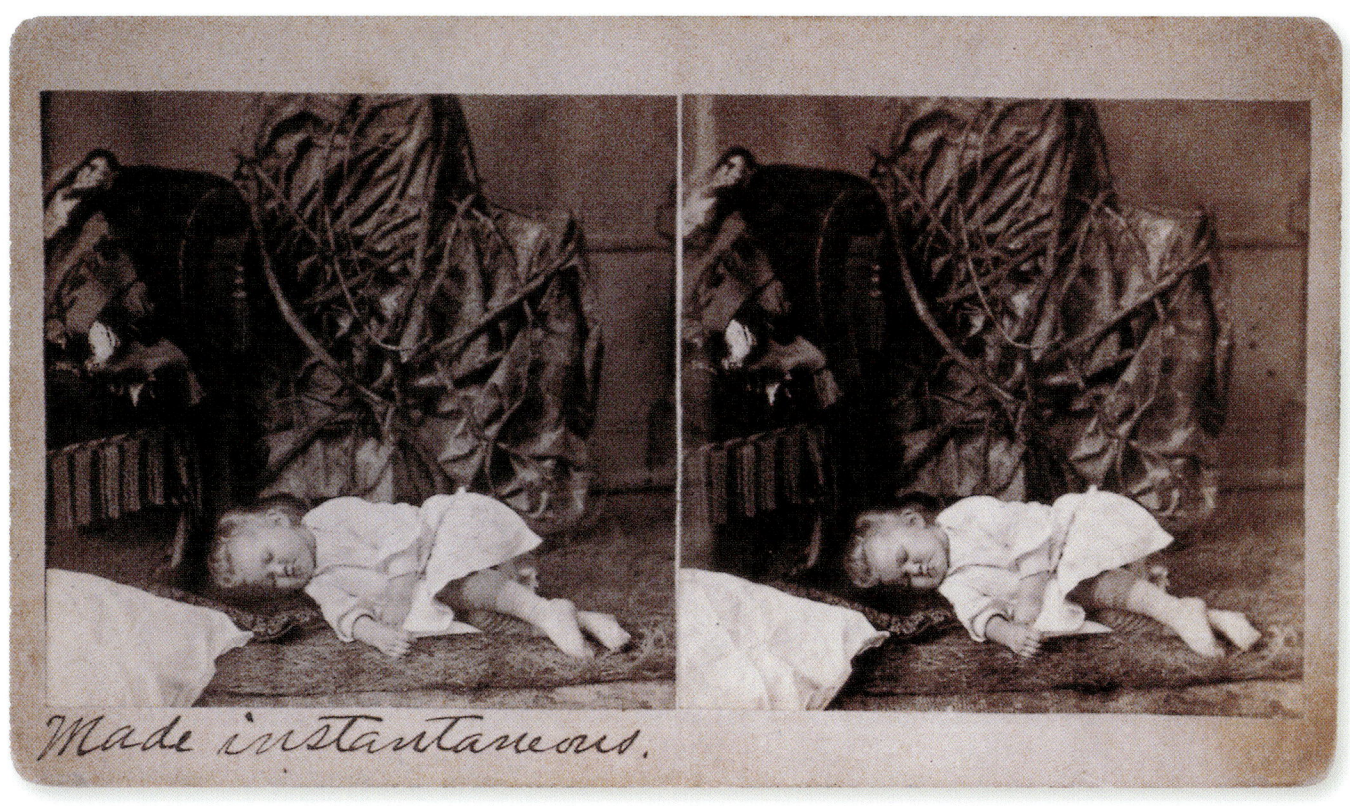

Made instantaneous.

Maude Goodlander in her noonday nap, Muncie, ca. early 1880s. Photographed by M. D. Goodlander.
Maude was M. D. Goodlander's daughter.

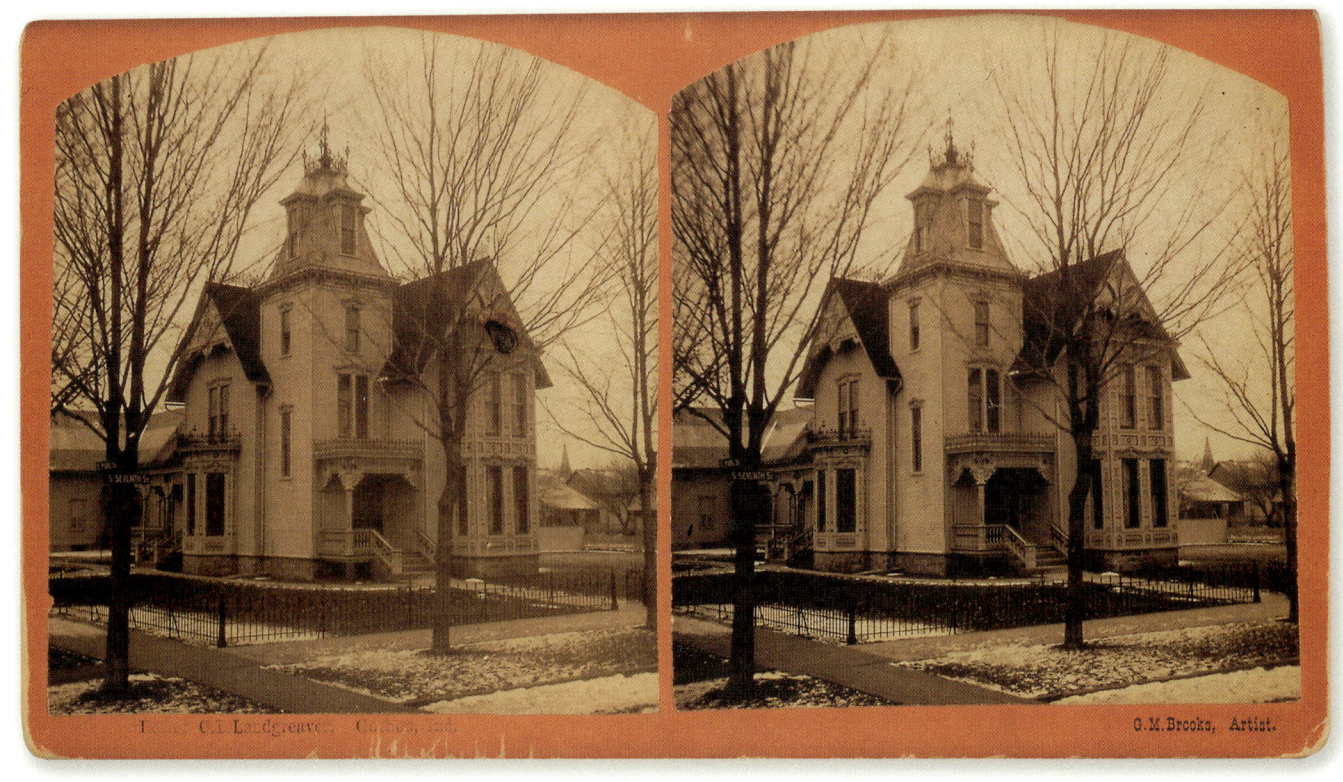

C. L. Landgreaver residence, Goshen, ca. 1880s. Photographed by G. M. Brooks.
This house stood on the corner of Seventh and Purl Streets.

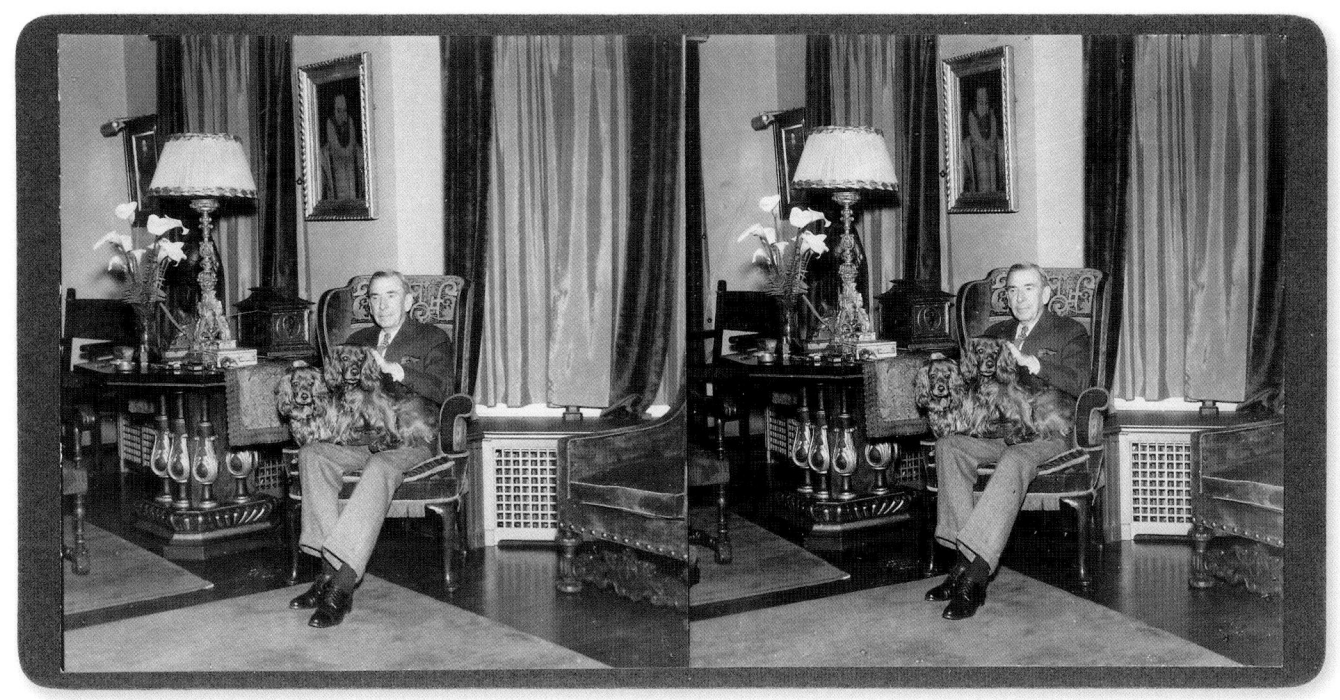

Booth Tarkington with dogs, Indianapolis, ca. late 1930s. Photographer unknown.
Tarkington, a well-known Hoosier author, wrote often about the people, places, and social customs of his native Midwest.
Two of his books, The Magnificent Ambersons *and* Alice Adams, *won Pulitzer Prizes for fiction.*

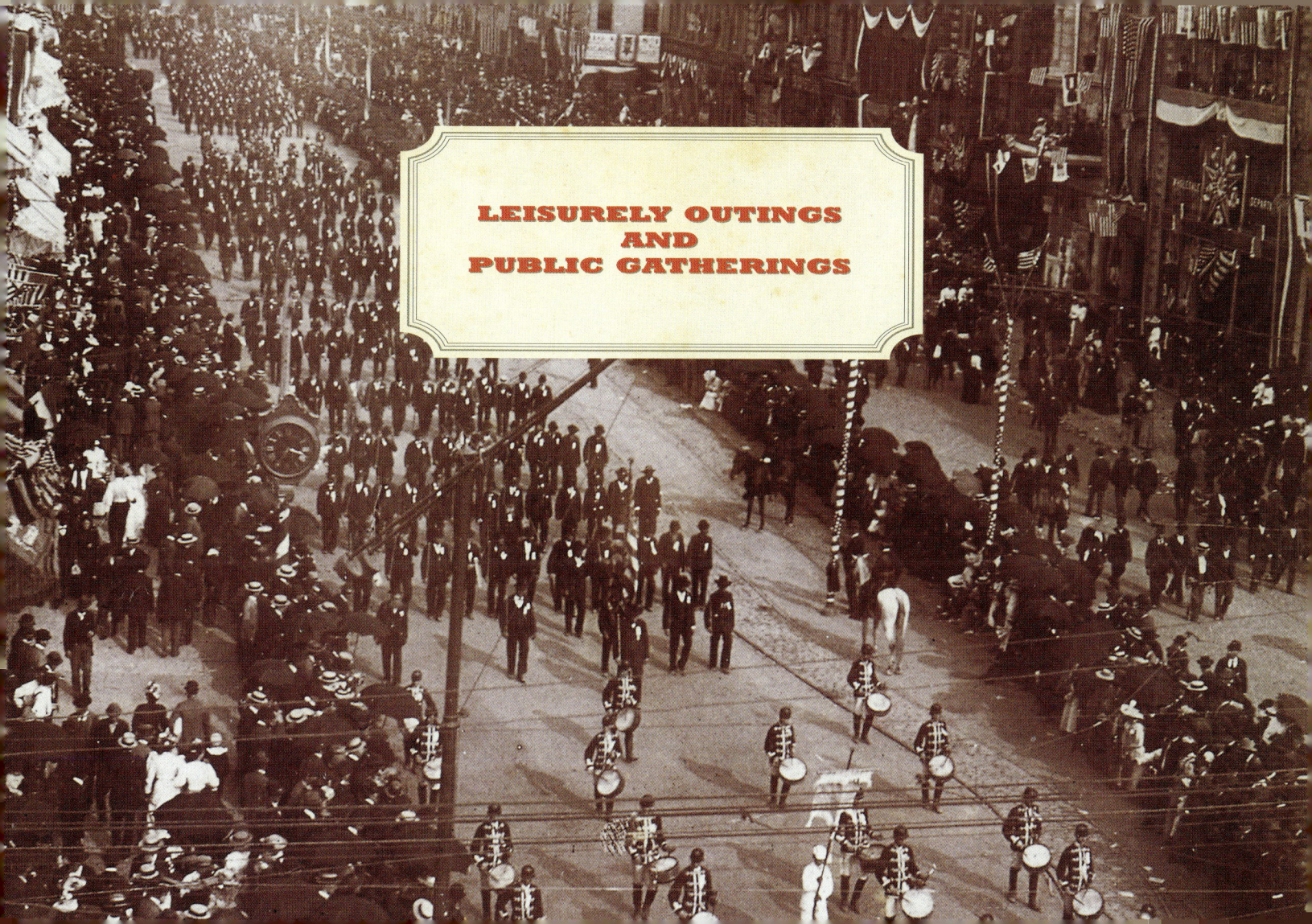

LEISURELY OUTINGS
AND
PUBLIC GATHERINGS

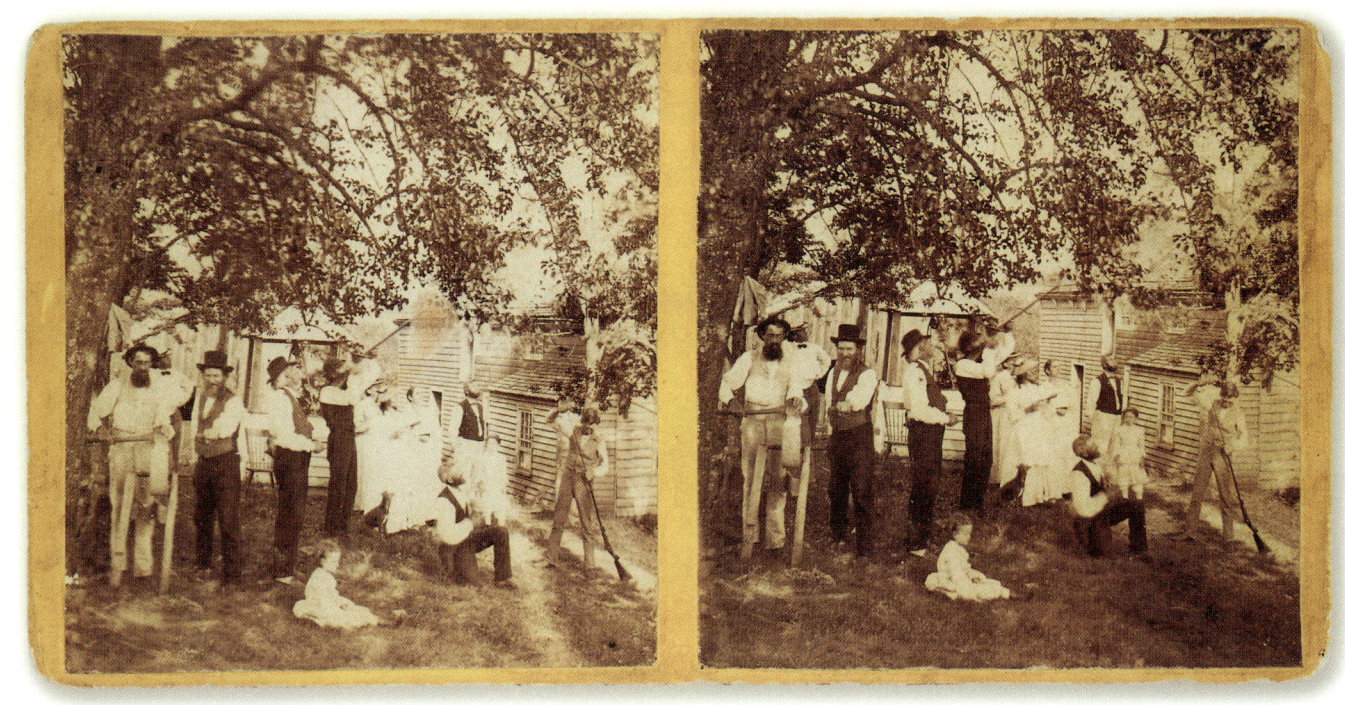

Shooting birds, Aurora, 1871. Photographed by P. Wheeler.

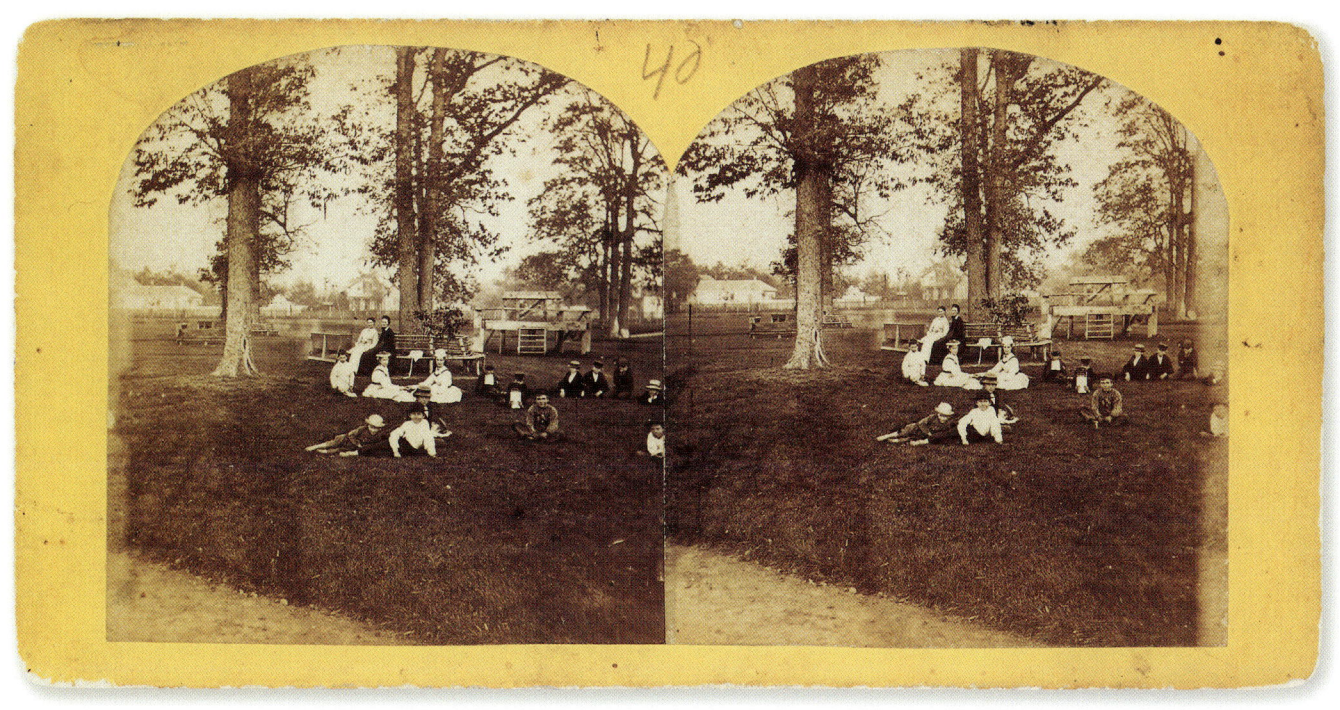

Women and children relaxing in Military Park, Indianapolis, ca. 1870s. Published by Ingraham and Claflin.
Military Park, Indianapolis's oldest park, was the site of Indiana's first state fair in 1852 and served as a military camp during the Civil War.
Today it is a popular venue for festivals and other public events.

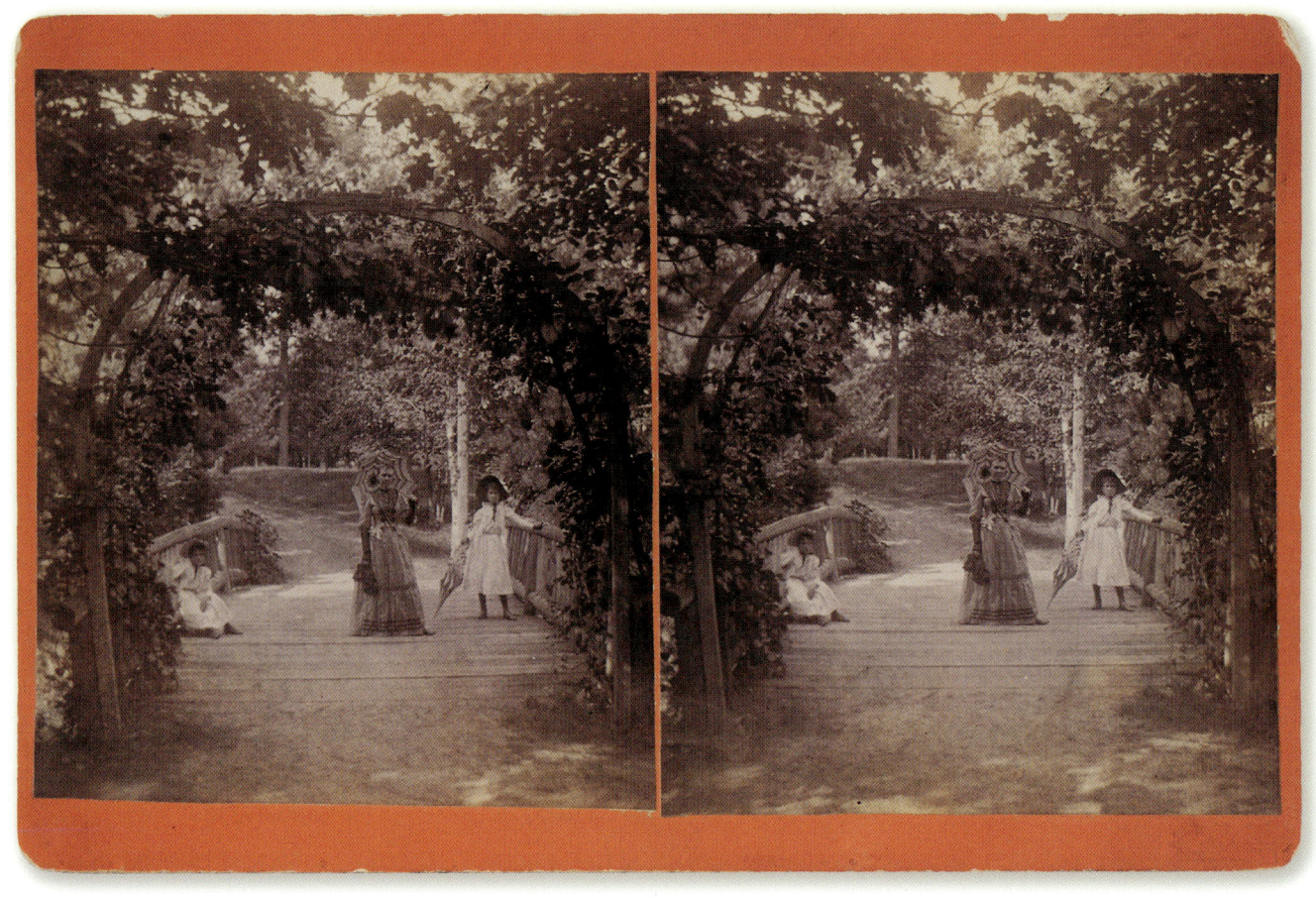

Woman and girls under an arbor in a park, location unknown, ca. 1880s. Photographed by M. D. Goodlander.
It is likely this view was taken in Muncie or Anderson, where Goodlander tended to photograph.

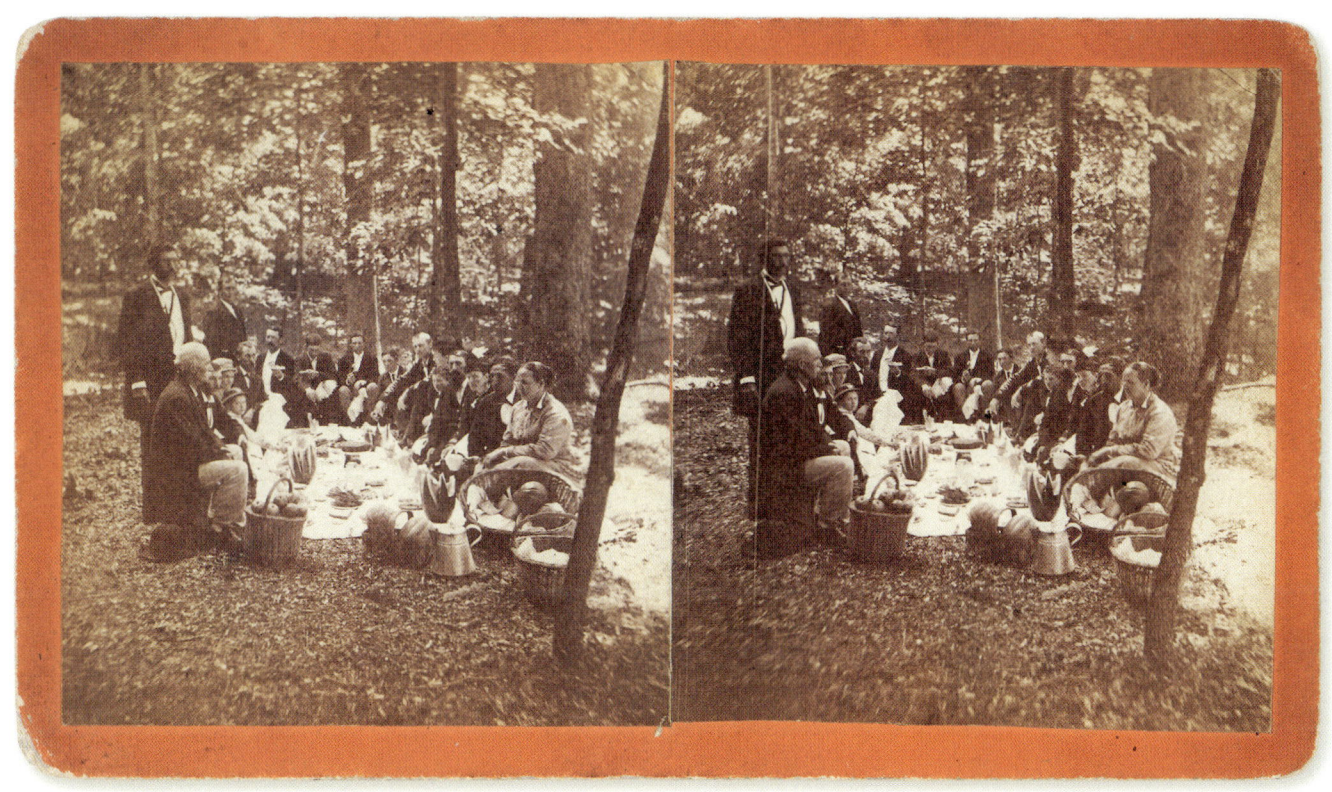

Picnic scene, location unknown, ca. 1880s. Published by M. D. Goodlander.
The man standing at left appears to be Goodlander, and the view was probably taken around Muncie or Anderson, perhaps by an assistant.

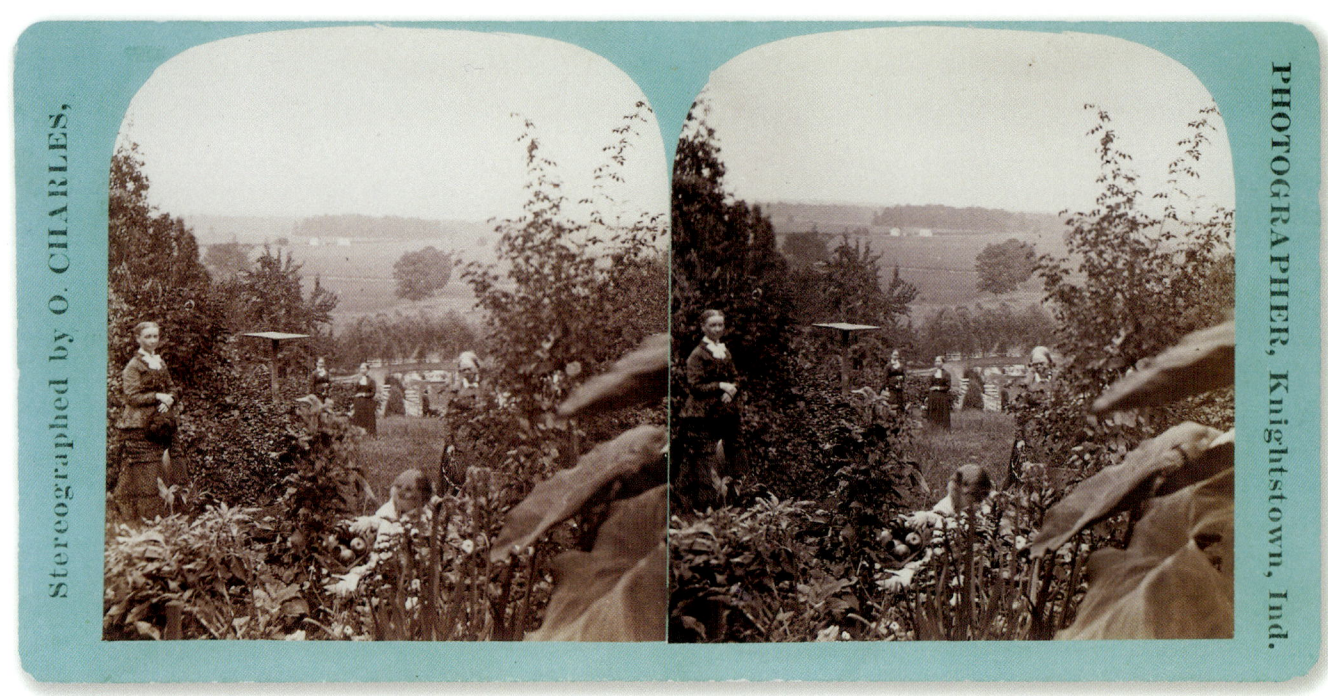

Stereographed by O. CHARLES,

PHOTOGRAPHER, Knightstown, Ind.

Family gathering in gardens, probably near Knightstown, ca. 1880s. Photographed by Oliver Charles.
The view on the opposite page was taken at the same estate, and other images of the house appear on pages 158 and 159.

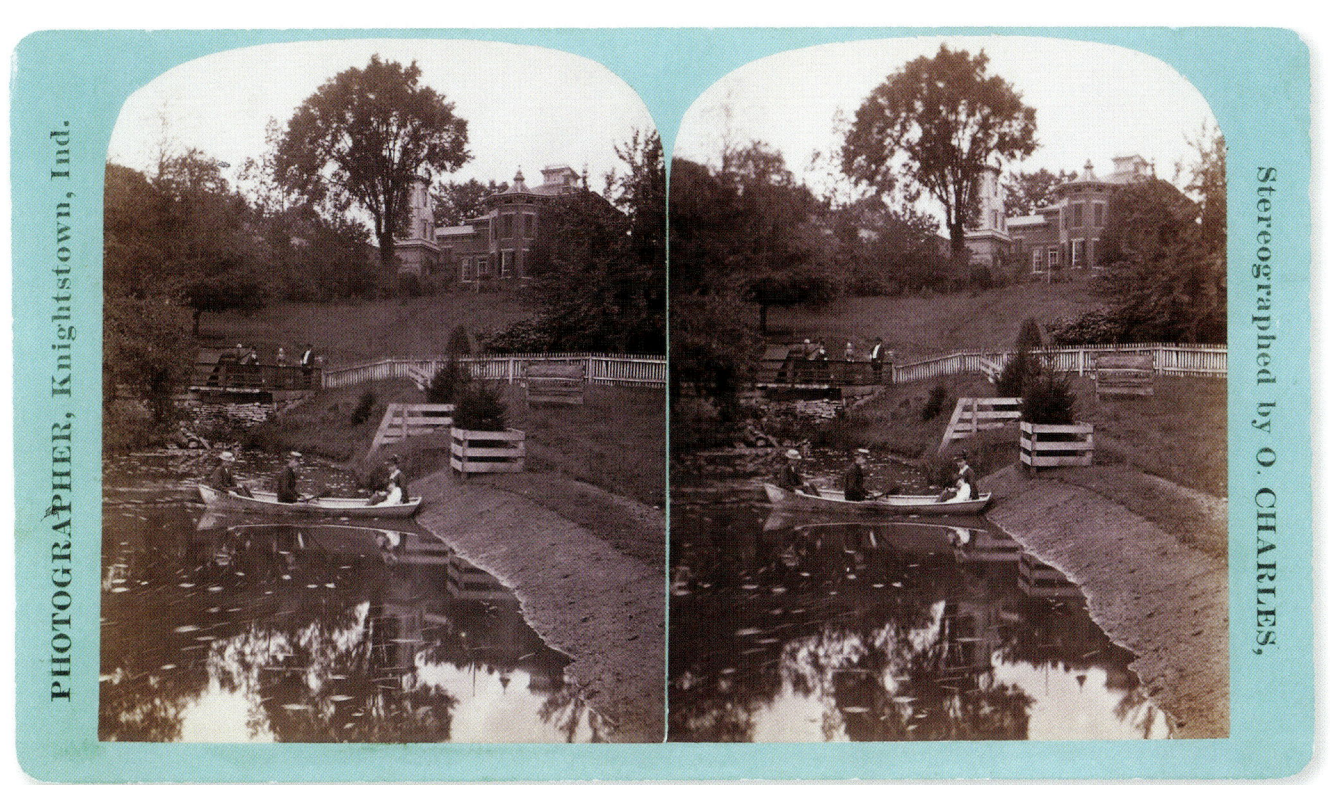

183

Boating on a pond, probably near Knightstown, ca. 1880s. Photographed by Oliver Charles.

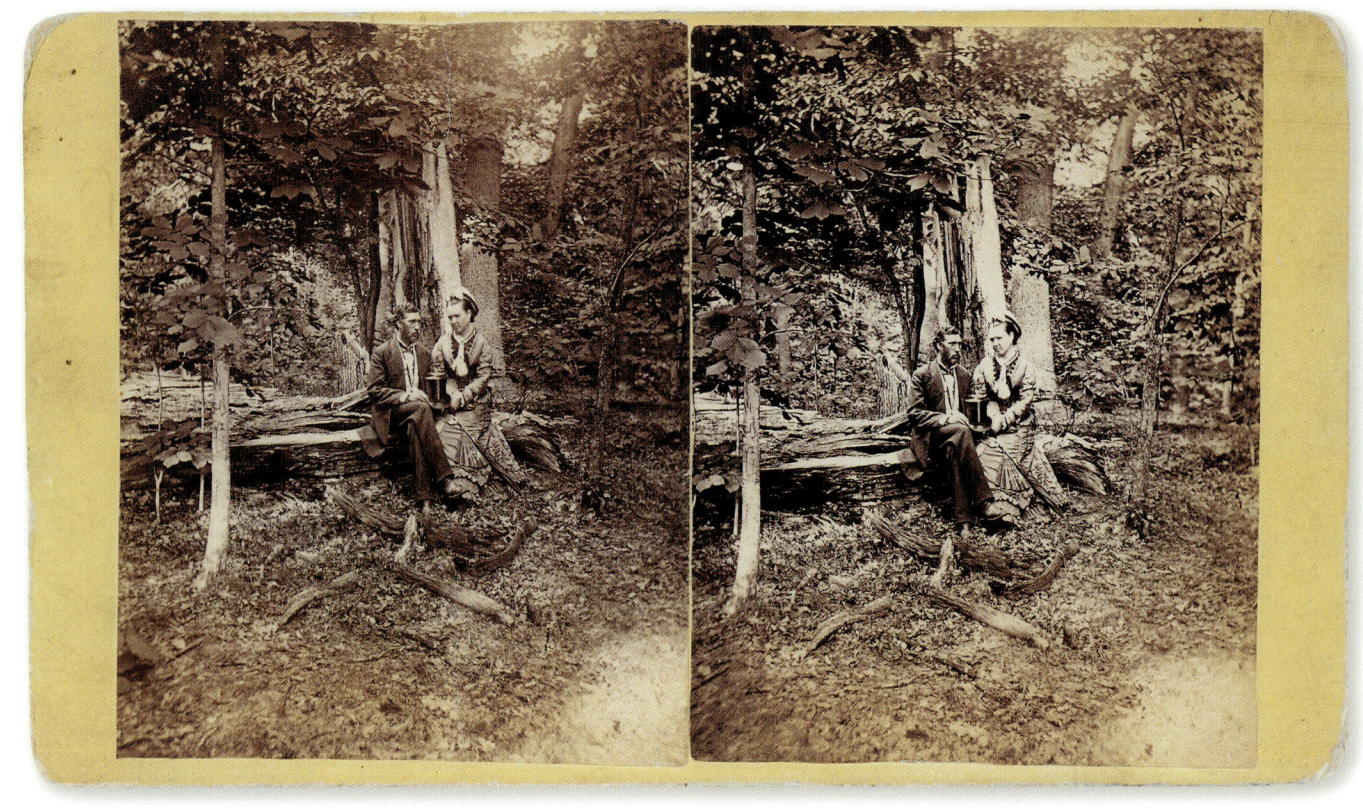

M. D. Goodlander and wife, location unknown, ca. 1880s. Published by Goodlander.
An assistant probably shot this somewhere in Delaware or Madison Counties. On the back of the card Goodlander wrote, "The Boss," no doubt a reference to his sitting mate.

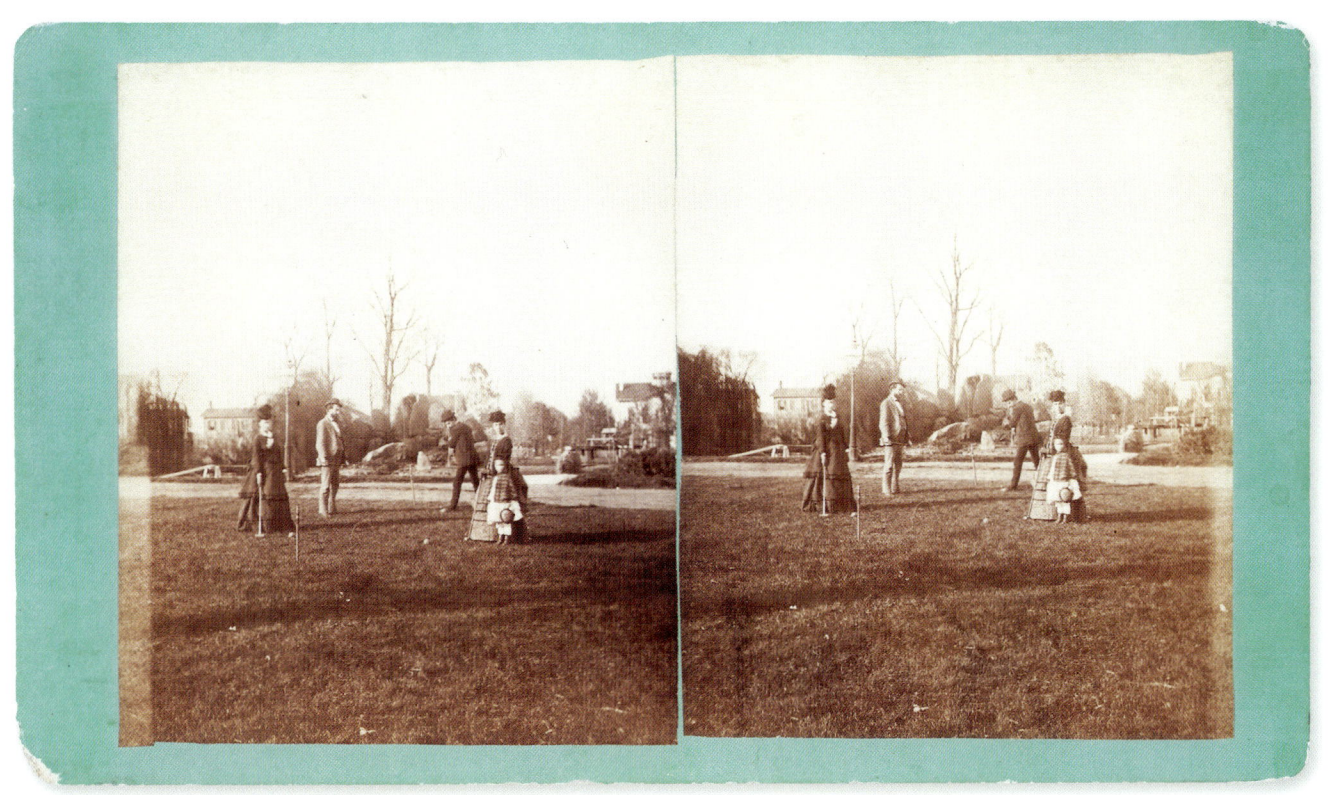

Couples playing croquet, Indianapolis, ca. 1880s. Photographed by C. N. Beamer.

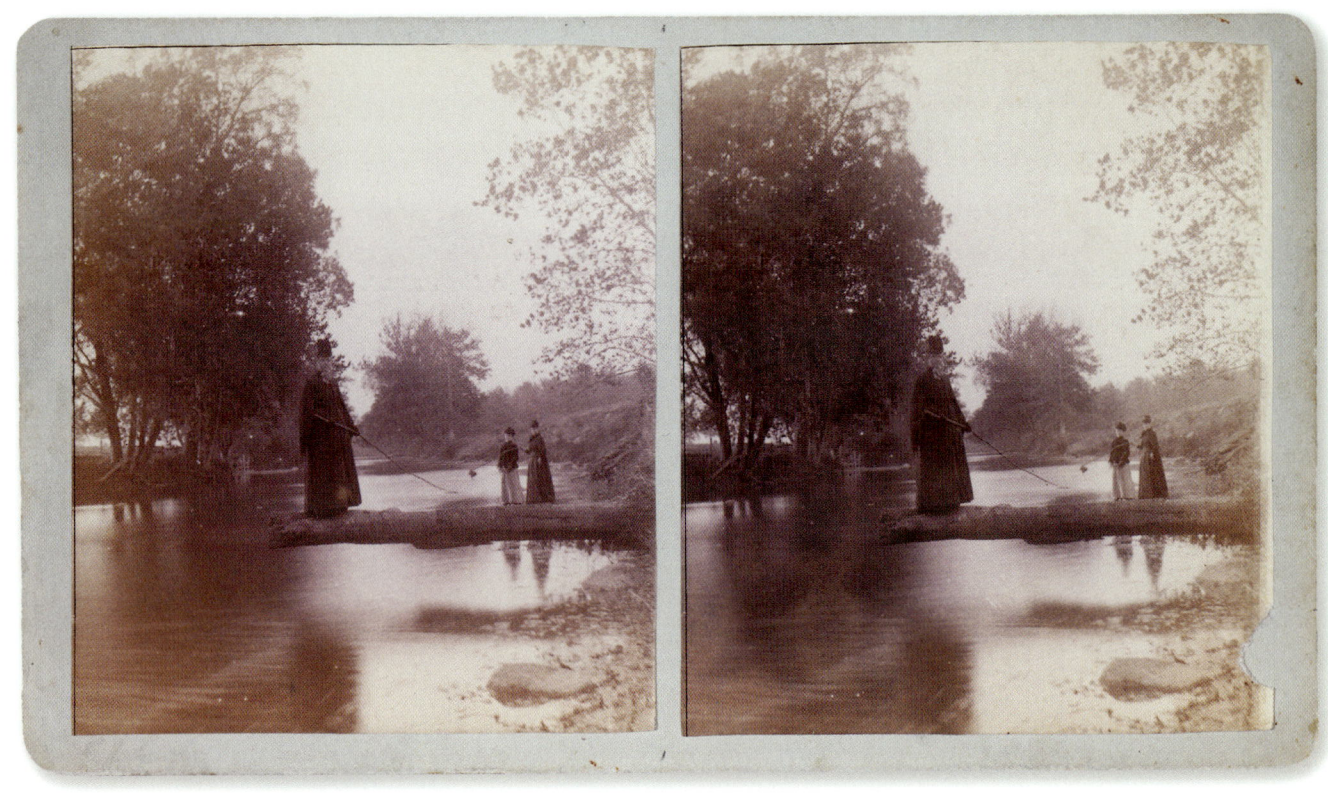

View along the White River, location unknown, ca. 1880s. Photographed by M. D. Goodlander.
The caption on the back of this view indicates it was taken at Parker Moors, which was probably in either Delaware or Madison County.

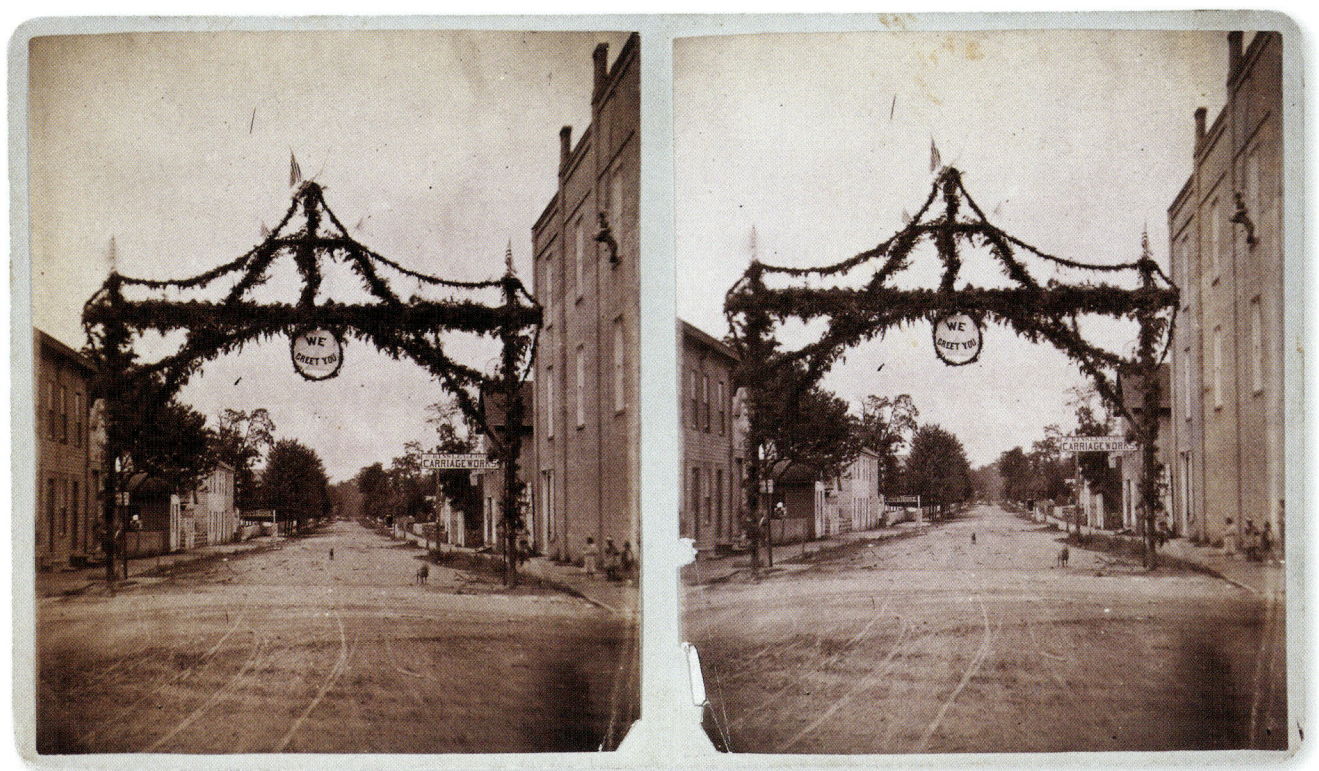

Decorations for a band tournament, Muncie, ca. 1880s. Photographed by M. D. Goodlander.

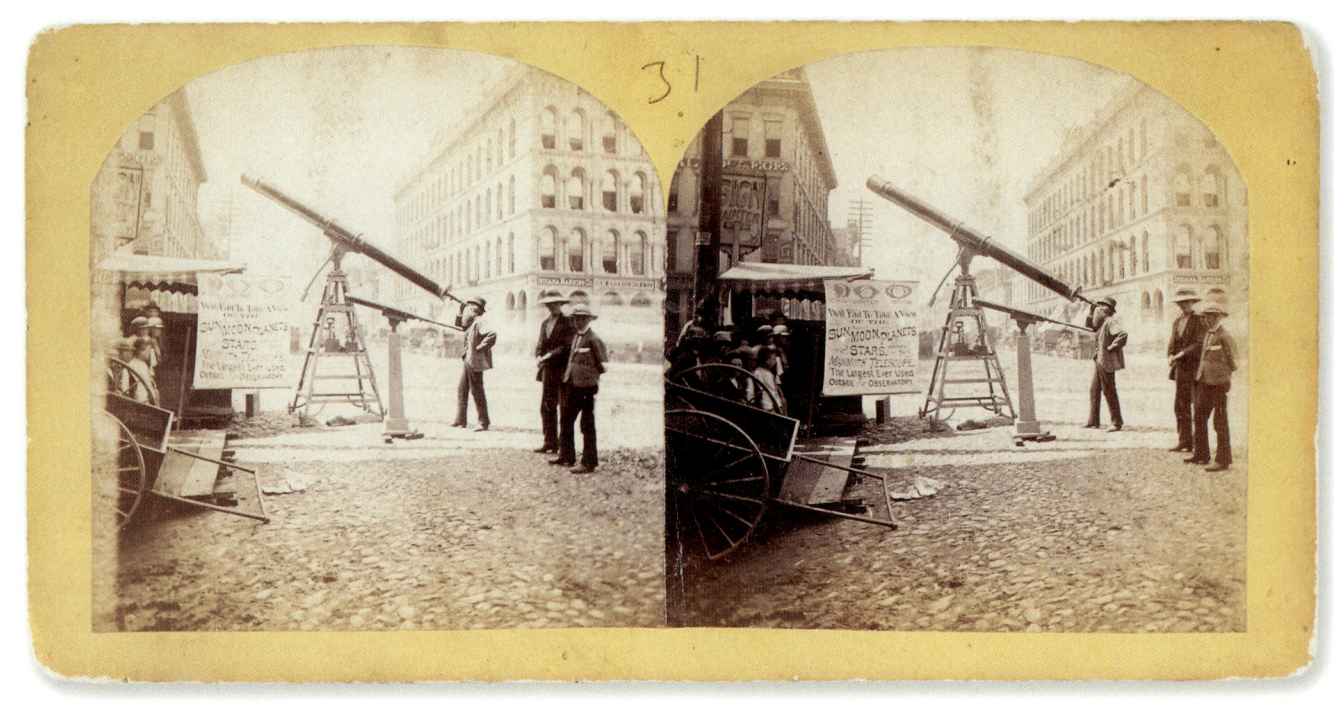

Giant telescope, Indianapolis, ca. 1870s. Photographed by Charles B. Ingraham.
The sign says this portable telescope was the largest ever used outside of an observatory. It may have been set up to view an eclipse or some other celestial event.

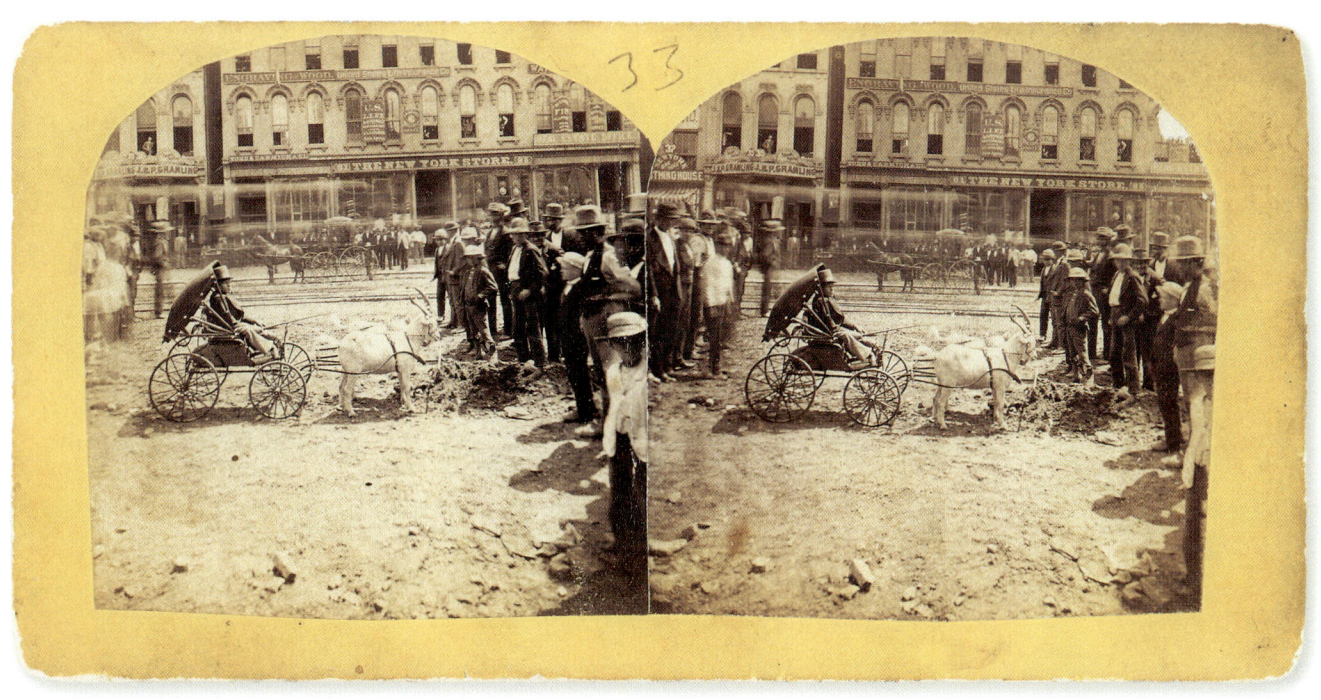

Man in a buggy, Indianapolis, ca. 1870s. Photographed by Charles B. Ingraham.
This scene was photographed along Washington Street. The man and his goats may have been part of a traveling entertainment show.

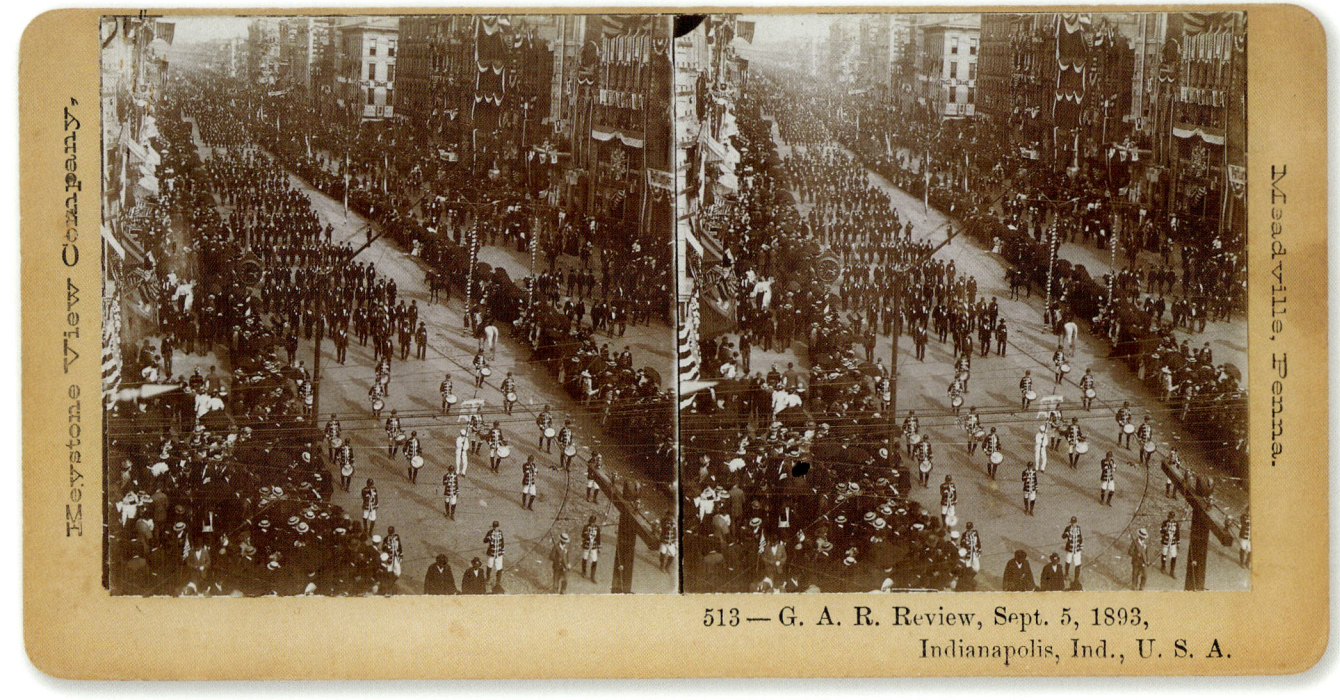

513 — G. A. R. Review, Sept. 5, 1893,
Indianapolis, Ind., U. S. A.

Grand Army of the Republic review, Indianapolis, 1893. Published by the Keystone View Company.
The G.A.R. was a Civil War veterans group that held many encampments in the Hoosier capital.
The 1893 encampment drew some 75,000 visitors to the city, and a highlight of the festivities was the review seen here.

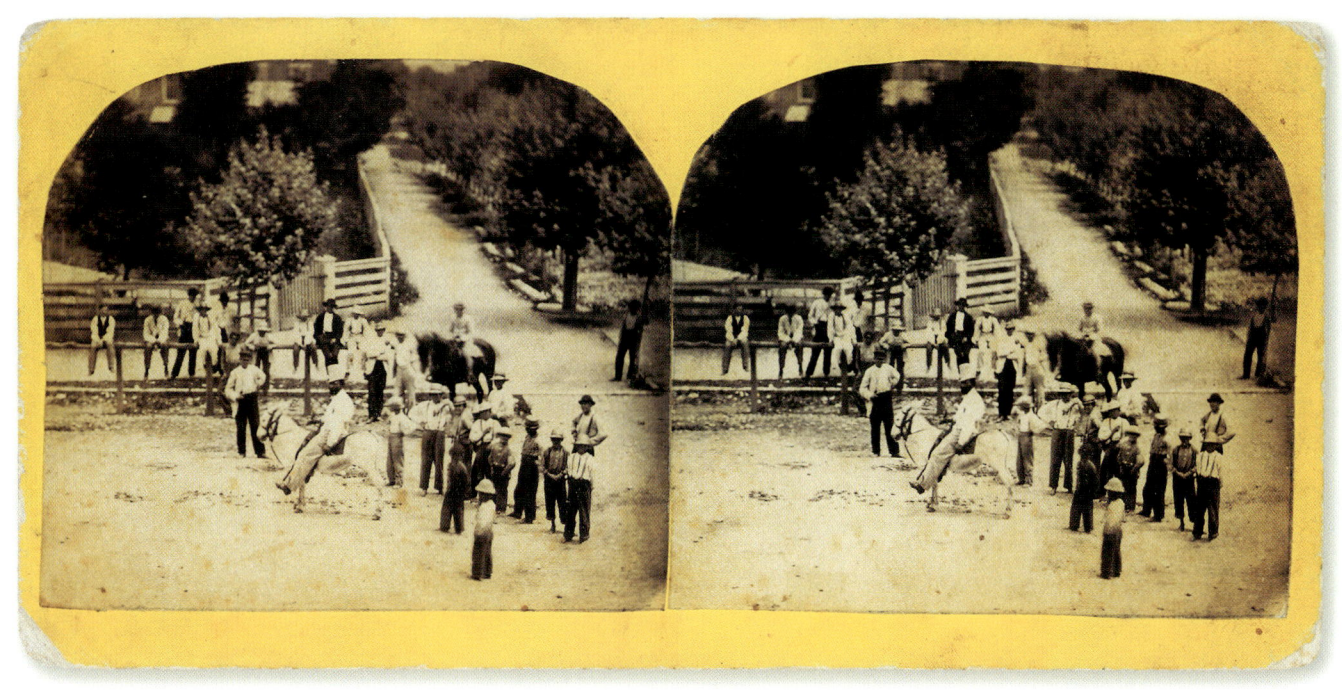

Gathering on the southwest corner of the courthouse square, Peru, ca. late 1860s. Published by Cain and Tracy.

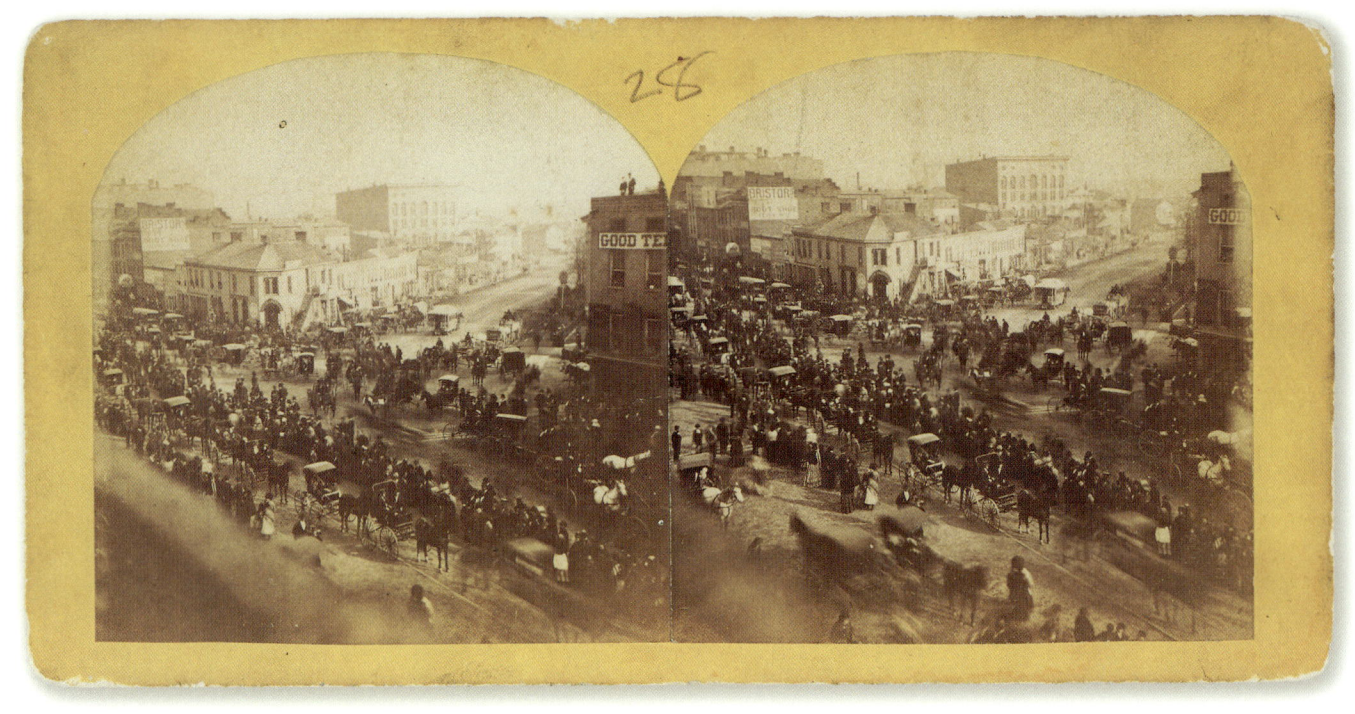

Funeral procession of Daniel Glazier, Indianapolis, 1873. Photographed by Charles B. Ingraham.
Glazier served as Indianapolis's fire chief and died fighting a blaze at the city's Woodburn Sarven Wheel Company on 11 March.
He was the first firefighter to die in the line of duty in the city, and at the time, his funeral was one of the largest the city had ever witnessed.

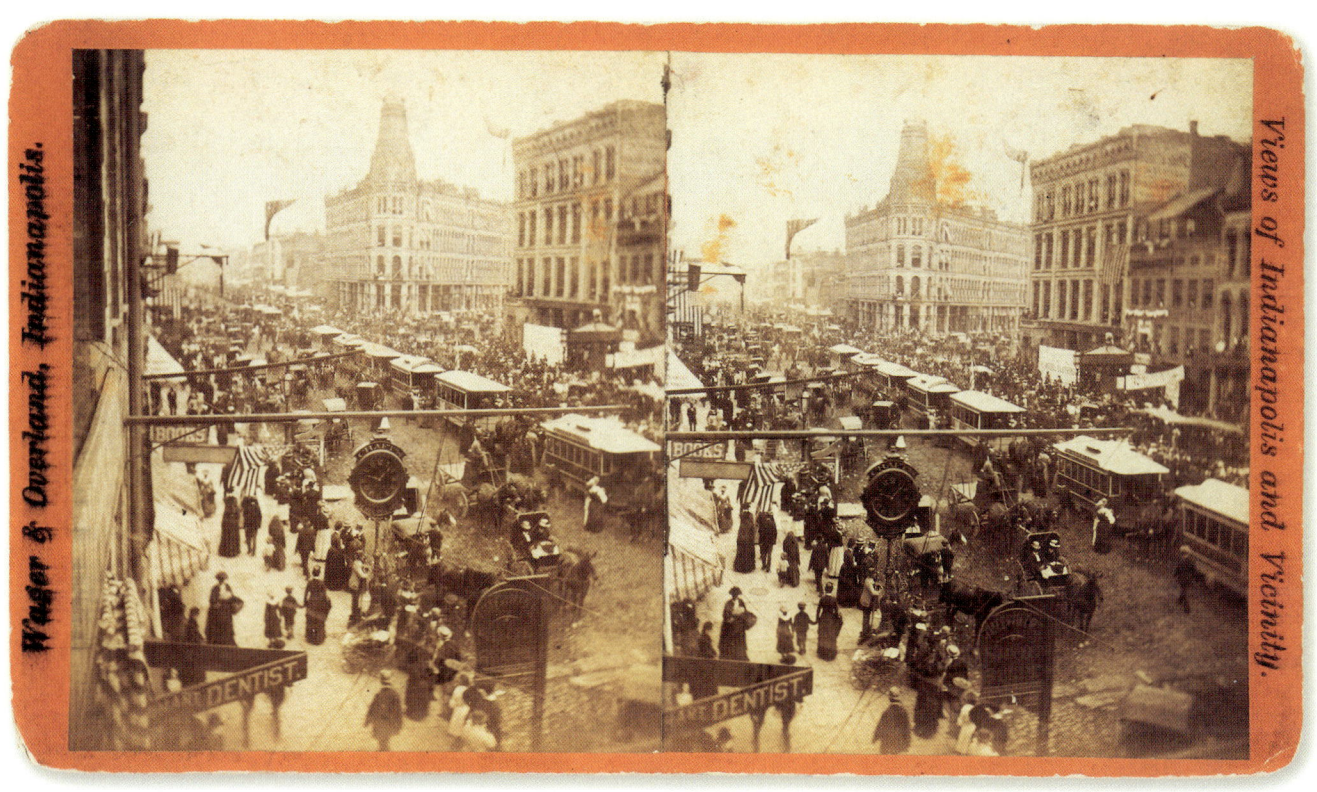

193

Washington Street, Indianapolis, ca. mid-1880s. Published by Wager and Overland.
The flags and long line of streetcars suggest the setting of a parade. The intersection is the same as the one shown in the stereograph on
the opposite page, and a comparison of the two views illustrates the rapid growth of Indianapolis at the end of the nineteenth century.

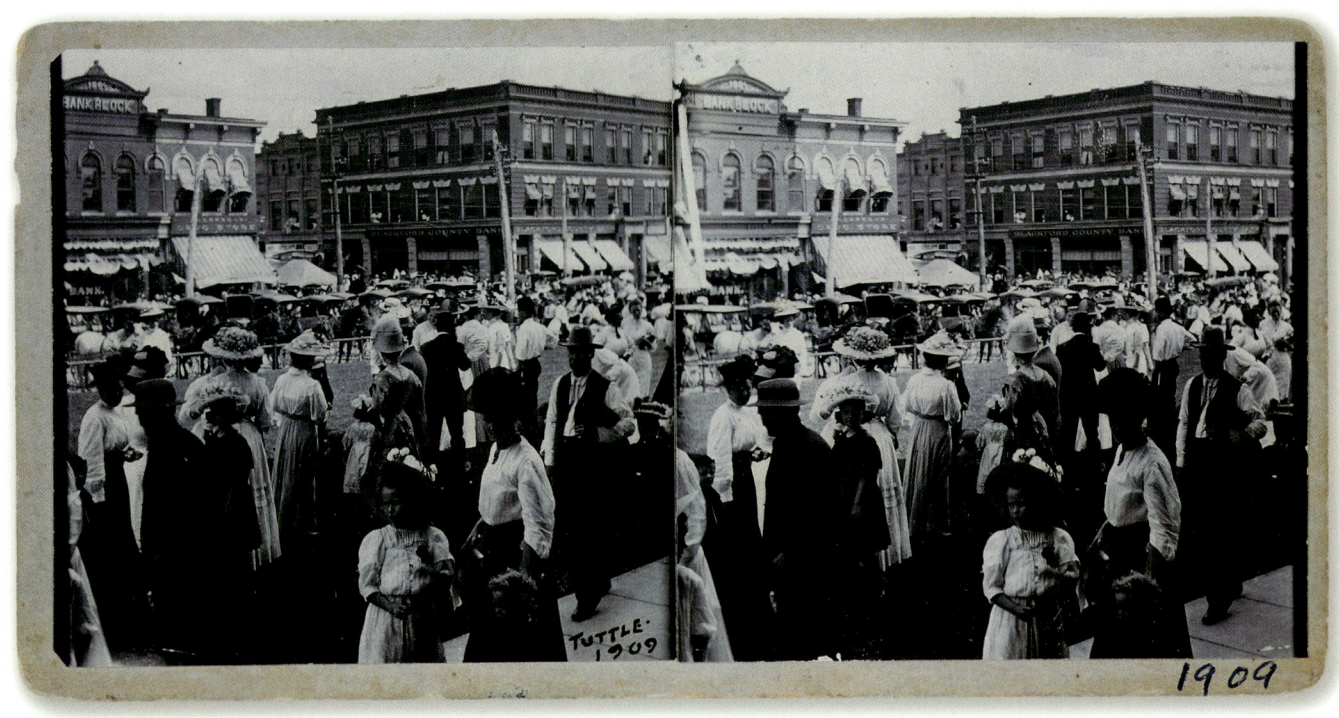

Crowds on the courthouse square, Hartford City, 1909. Photographed by Clay H. Tuttle.
These Blackford County residents were likely gathering for a parade, perhaps part of the carnival seen in the next two views.

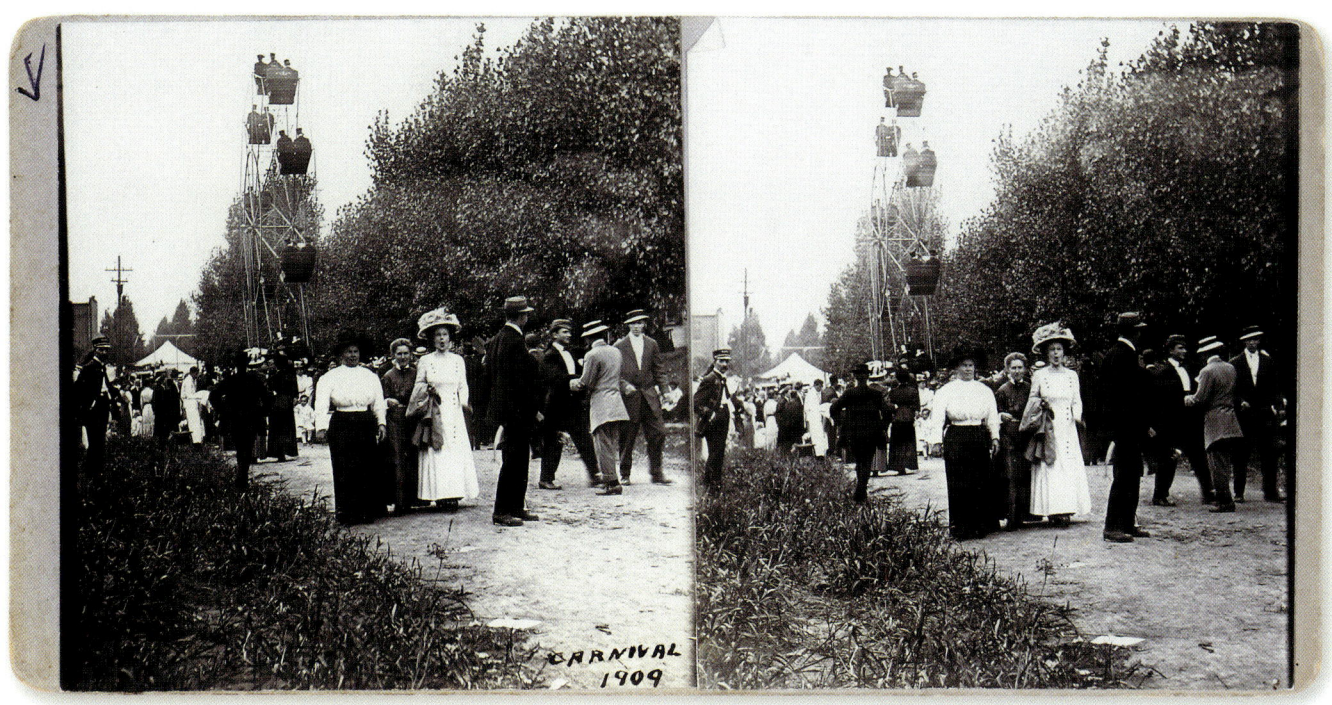

Carnival, Hartford City, 1909. Photographed by Clay H. Tuttle.

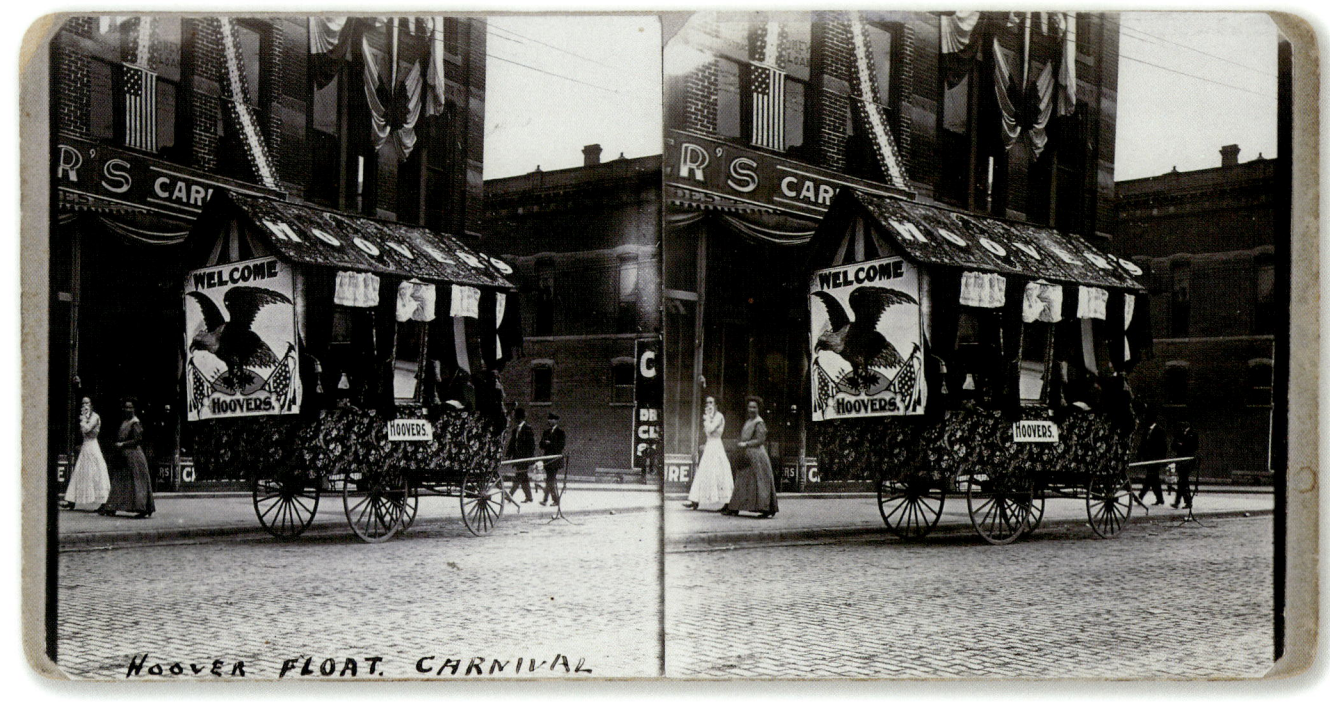

Carnival float, Hartford City, ca. 1909. Photographed by Clay H. Tuttle.

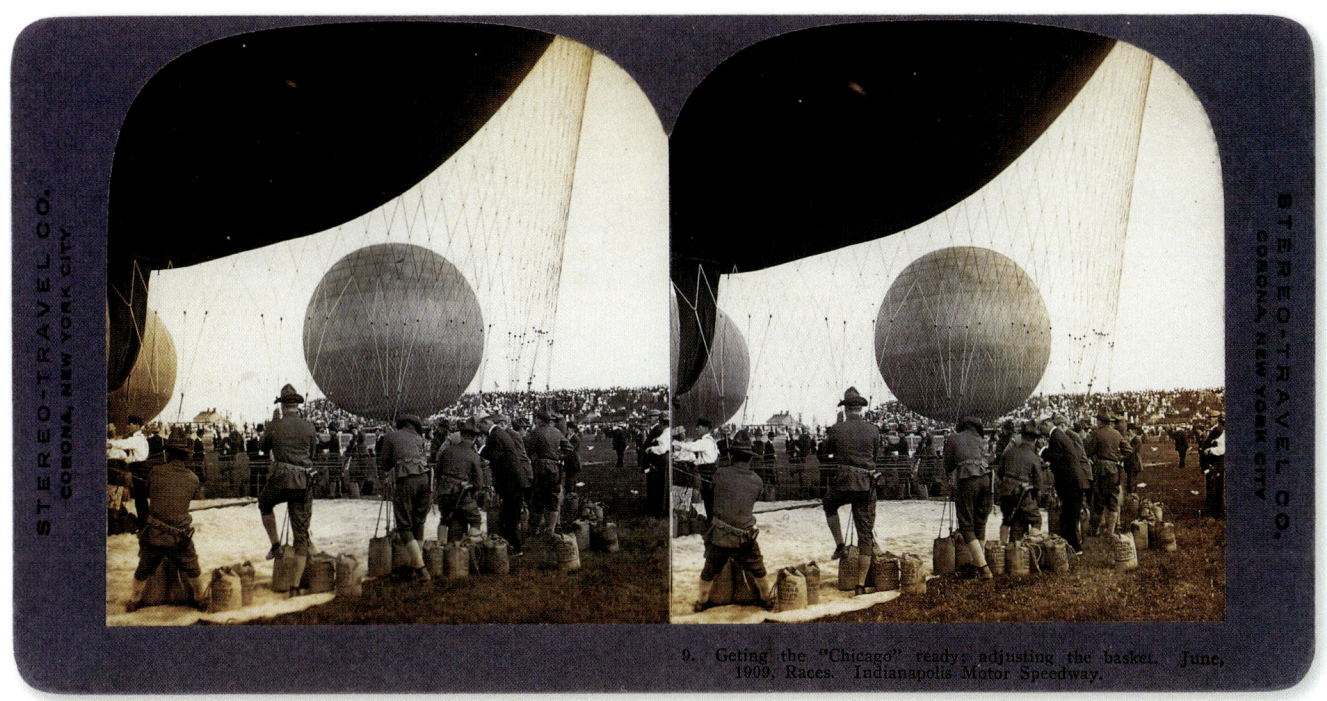

9. Geting the "Chicago" ready; adjusting the basket. June, 1909, Races. Indianapolis Motor Speedway.

197

Balloon races, Indianapolis Motor Speedway. 1909. Published by the Stereo-Travel Company.
The Speedway hosted the U.S. National Championship balloon-racing competition on 5 June. It was the first competitive event ever held at the track.

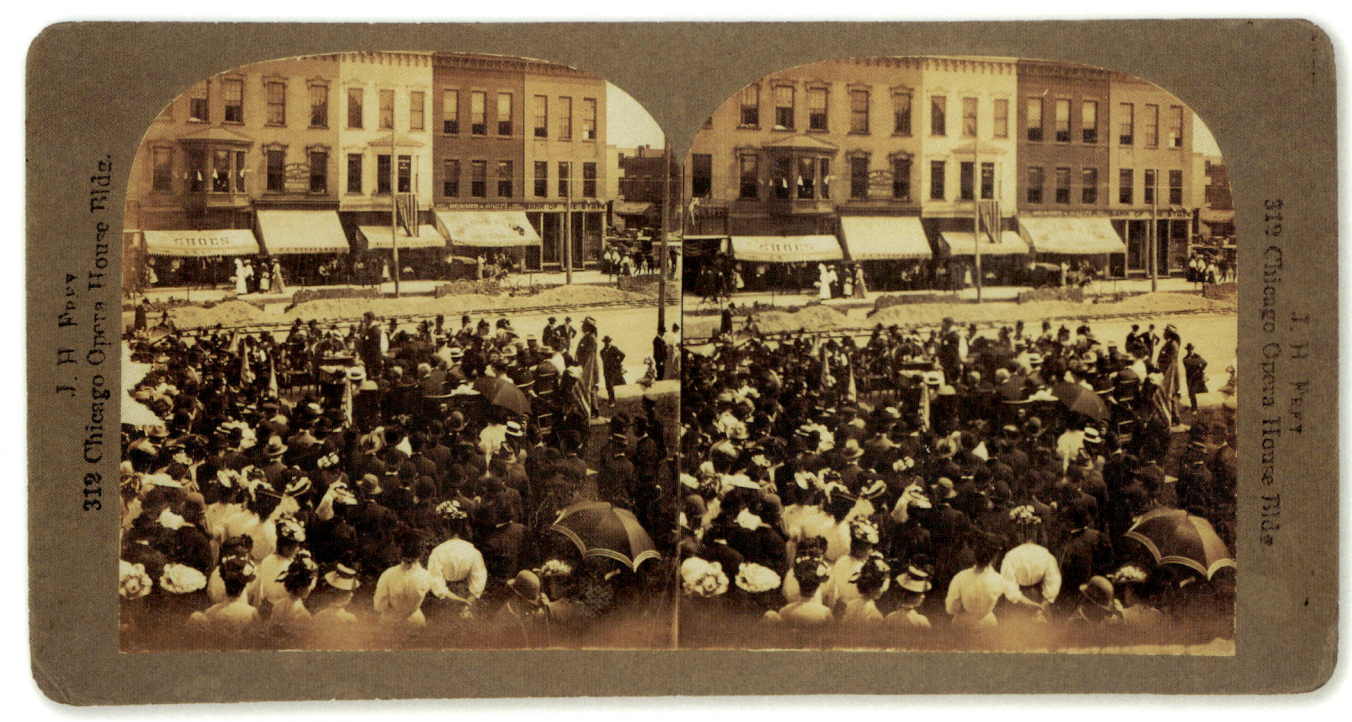

Ceremonies for the opening of the Chicago–New York Electric Air Line Railroad, La Porte, 1907. Photographed by J. H. Frey.
The ceremonies were held on 15 June in front of the La Porte County Courthouse, and in this photo the mayor of Mishawaka addresses the crowd.

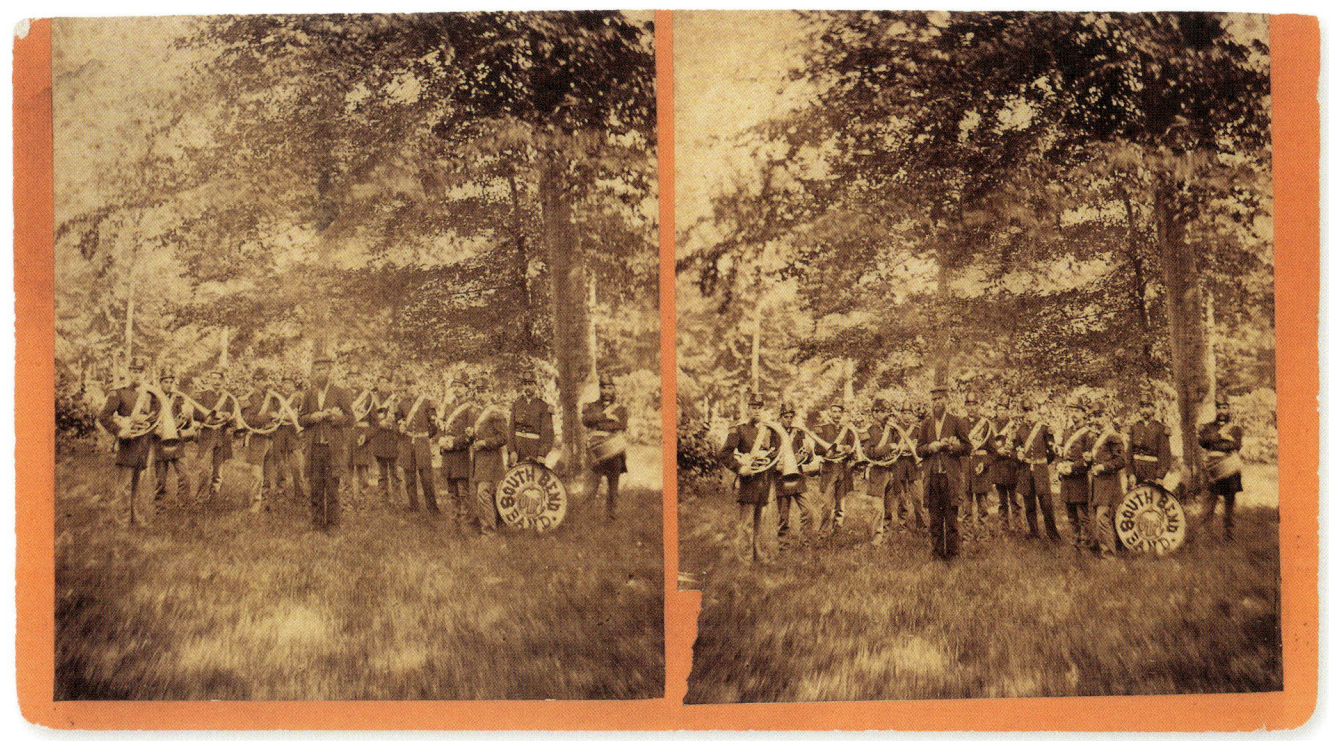

South Bend Band, location unknown, ca. 1870s. Photographed by James Bonney.

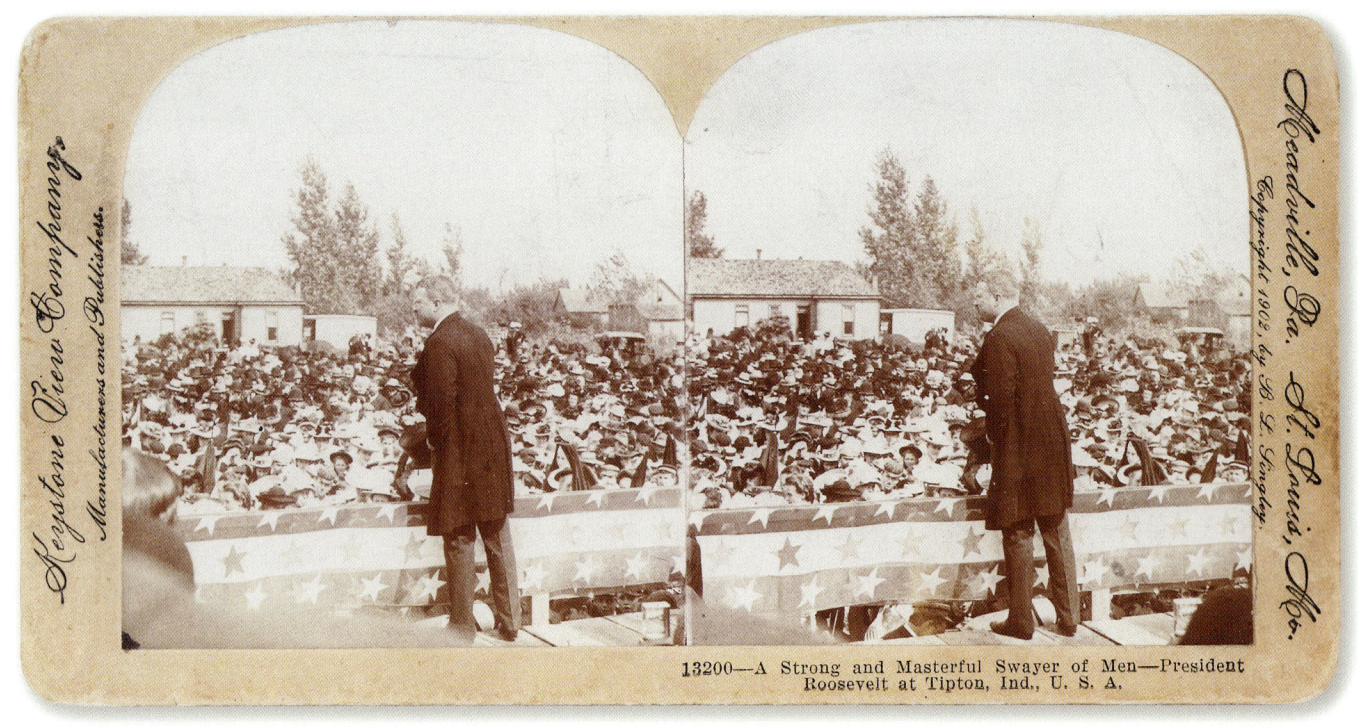

13200—A Strong and Masterful Swayer of Men—President Roosevelt at Tipton, Ind., U. S. A.

President Theodore Roosevelt speaking at Tipton, 1902. Published by the Keystone View Company.
Roosevelt visited Indiana on 23 September, making speeches at Logansport, Kokomo, Tipton, Noblesville, Indianapolis, Anderson, Muncie, and Fort Wayne.
The day began with rain, but the sun came out when he gave the speech at Tipton, and, according to the Indianapolis News,
"the official photographers became numerous and busy on the speakers' stand."

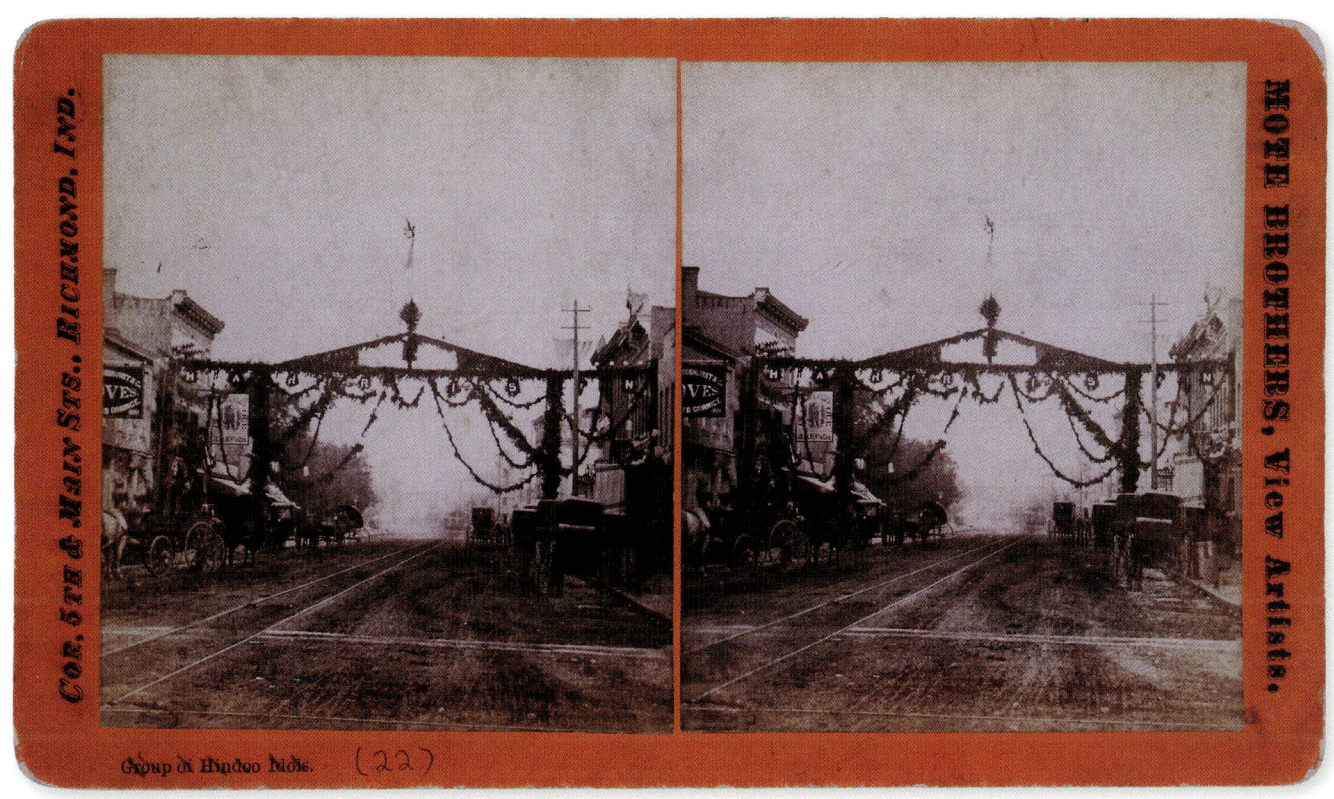

Group of Hindoo Idols. (22)

Political parade decorations, Richmond, ca. 1876. Published by Mote Brothers.
The decorations on the arch spell "Harrison." This view probably dates to 1876, when Benjamin Harrison ran for the Indiana governorship.

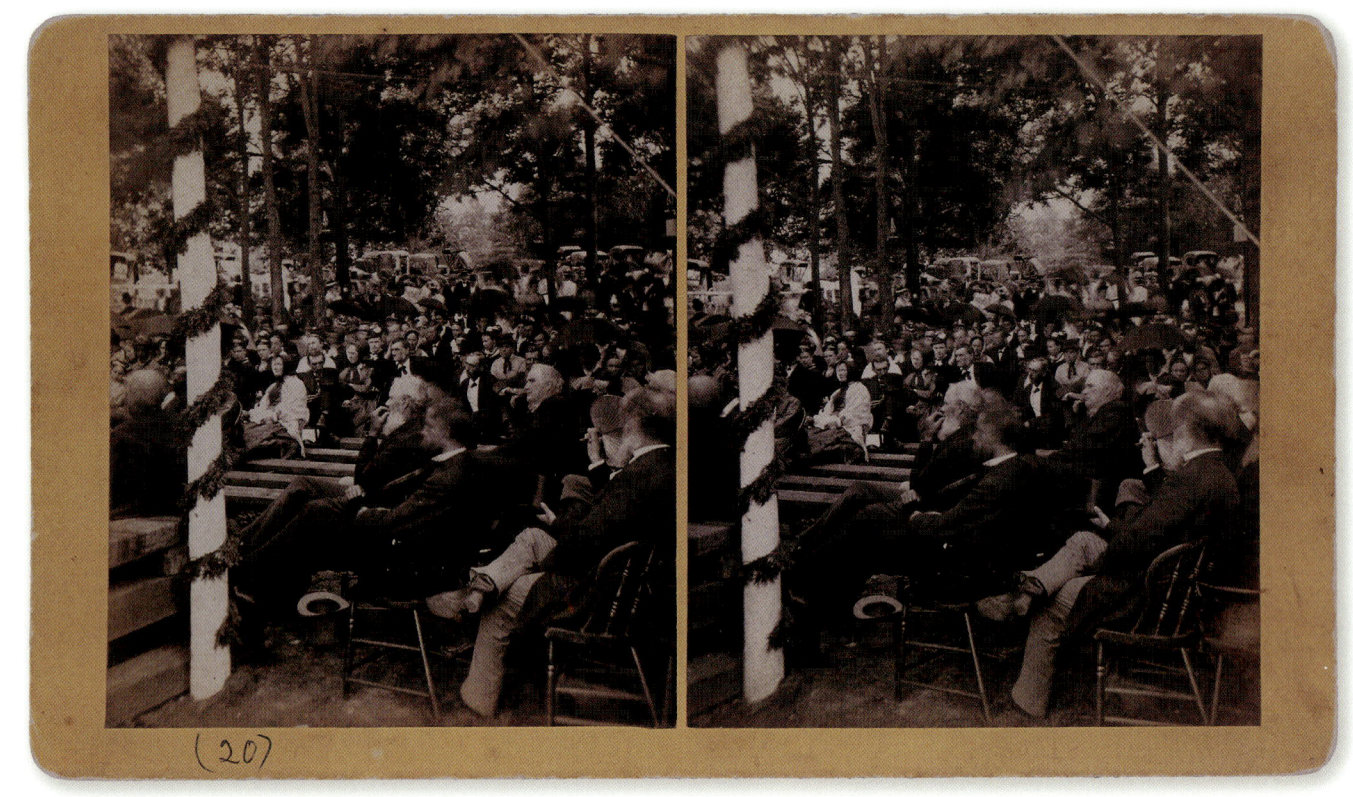

(20)

Indiana Yearly Meeting of Friends, Richmond, ca. 1880s. Photographer unknown.
The Society of Friends began holding yearly meetings in Richmond in 1821. At these meetings Society members discussed issues
relating to the group's discipline and doctrine and decided official Society policies and regulations.

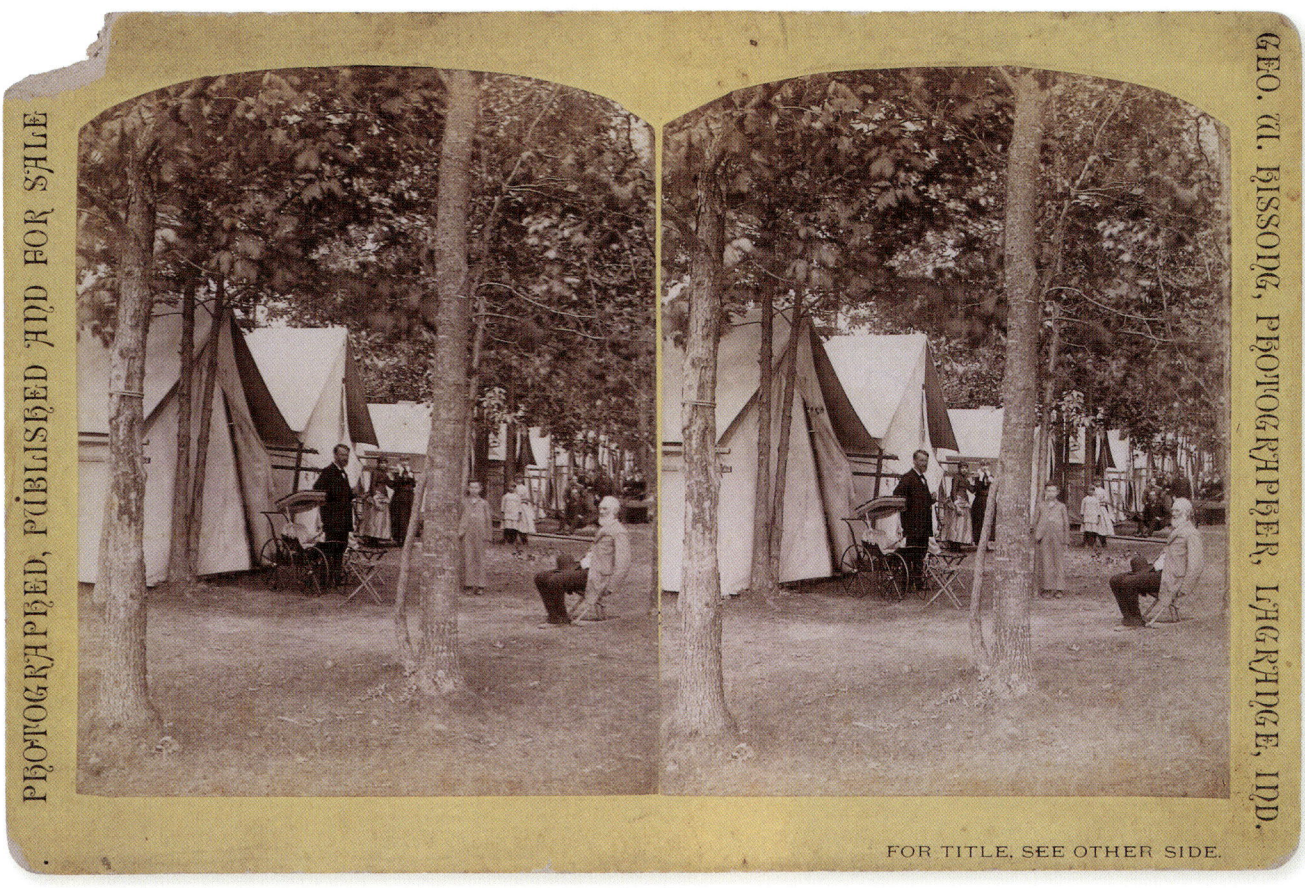

FOR TITLE, SEE OTHER SIDE.

Vacationers, Rome City, ca. 1880s. Photographed by George W. Hissong.
Rome City sits on the shores of Sylvan Lake, and the area was once the site of popular chautauquas. This view was taken on First Avenue.

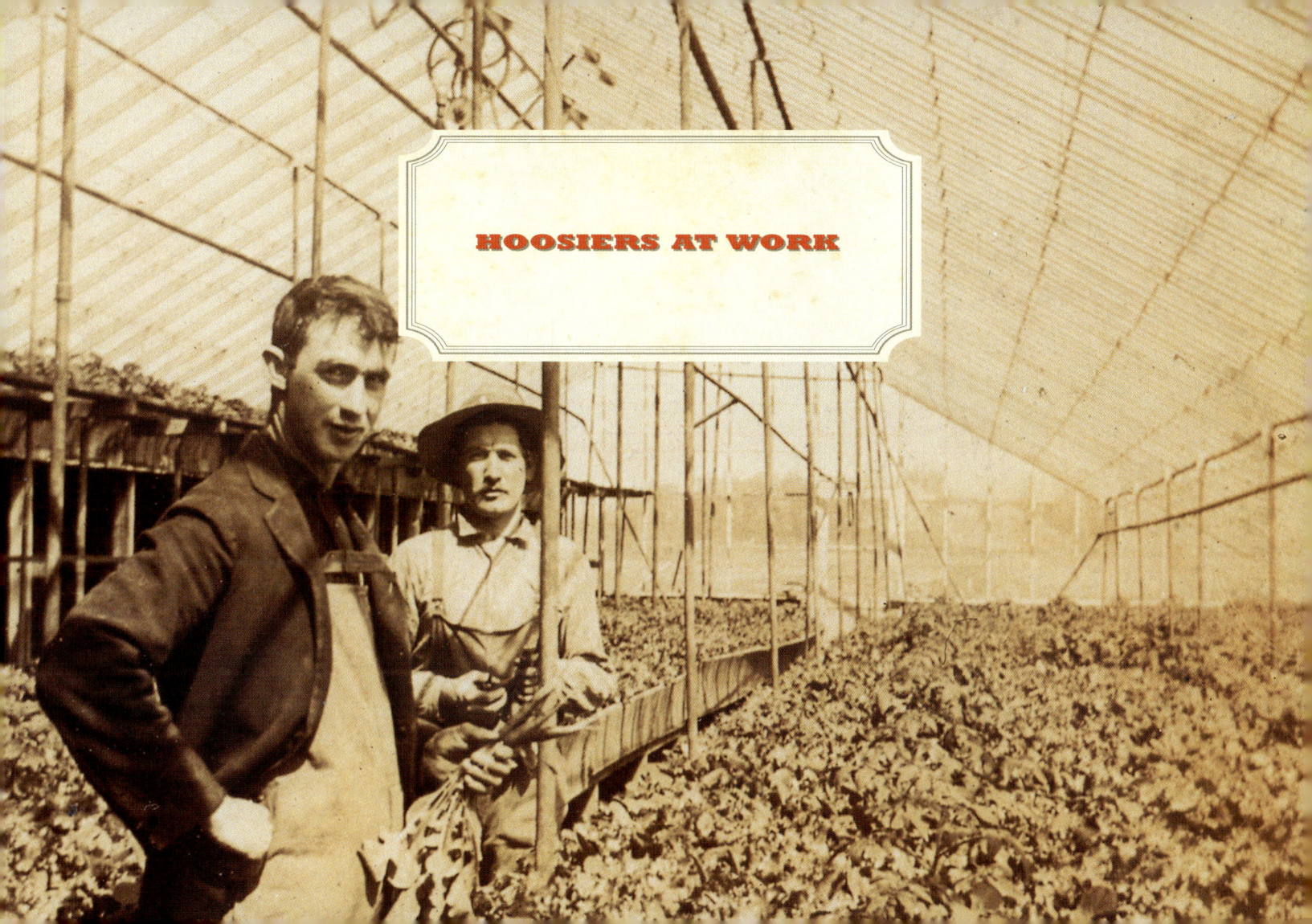

HOOSIERS AT WORK

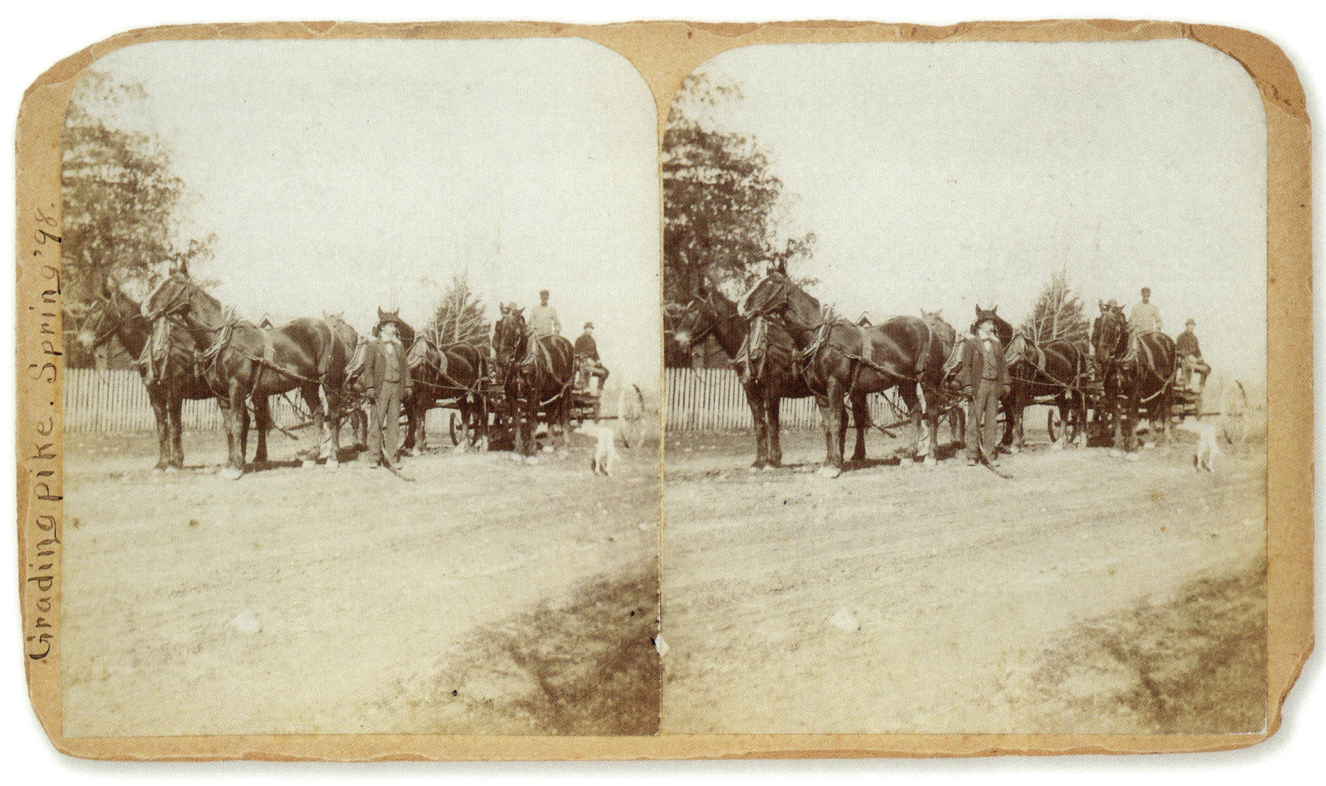

Grading the pike, Muncie, 1898. Photographer unknown.

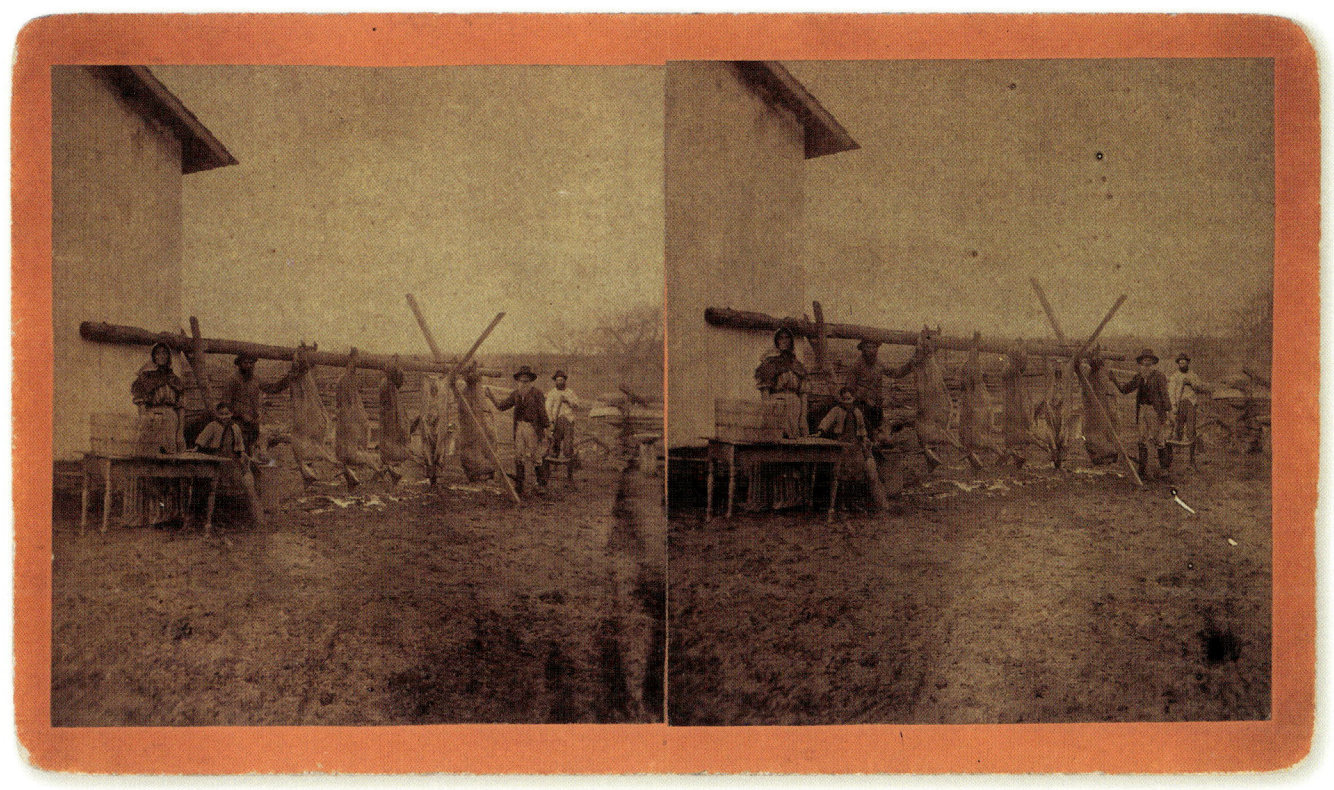

Butchering hogs, location unknown, ca. 1880s. Photographed by M. D. Goodlander.
These farmers probably lived in east-central Indiana, where Goodlander focused his work.

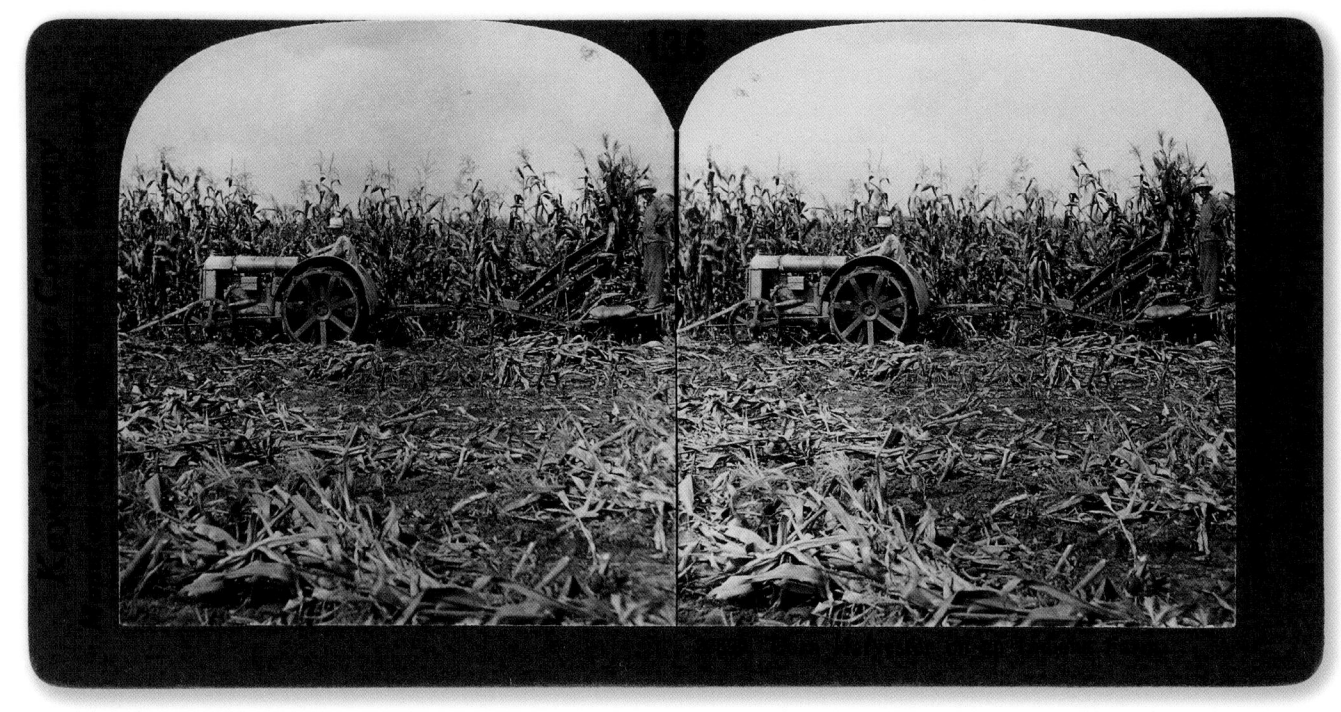

Harvesting corn, location unknown, ca. 1920s. Published by the Keystone View Company.

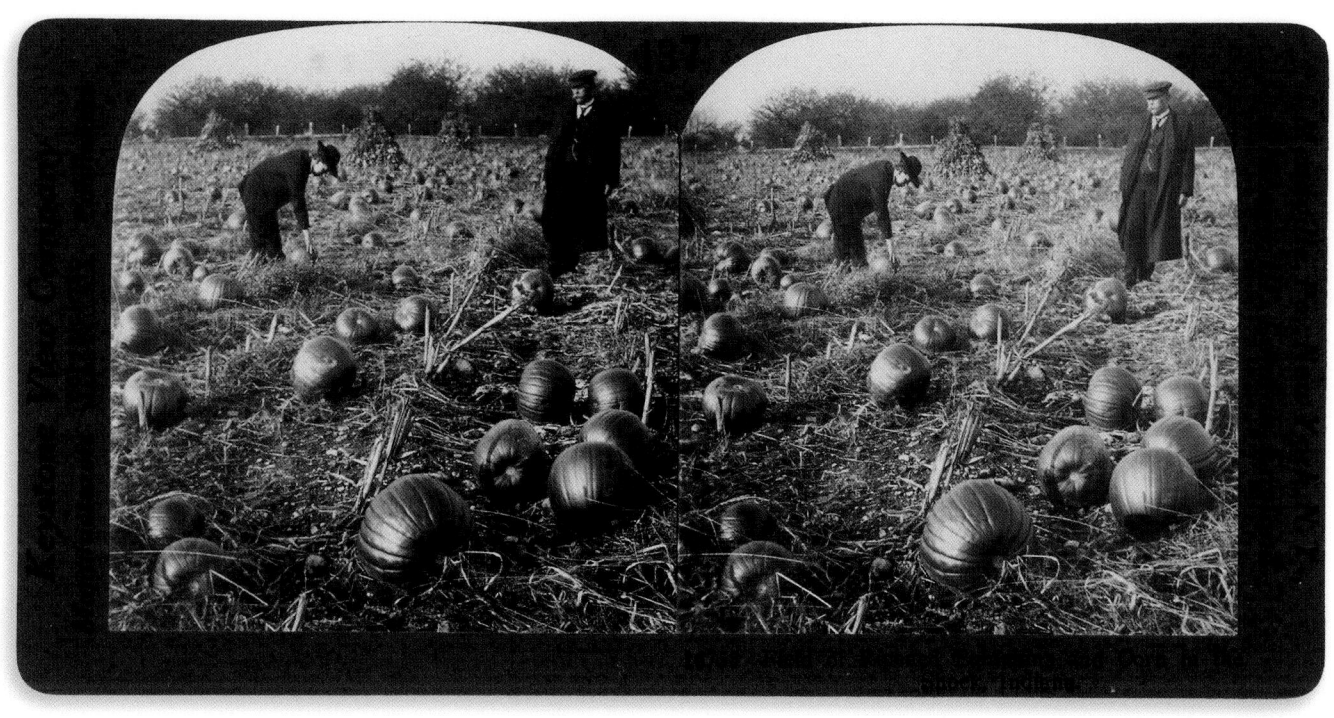

209

Picking pumpkins, location unknown, ca. 1920s. Published by the Keystone View Company.

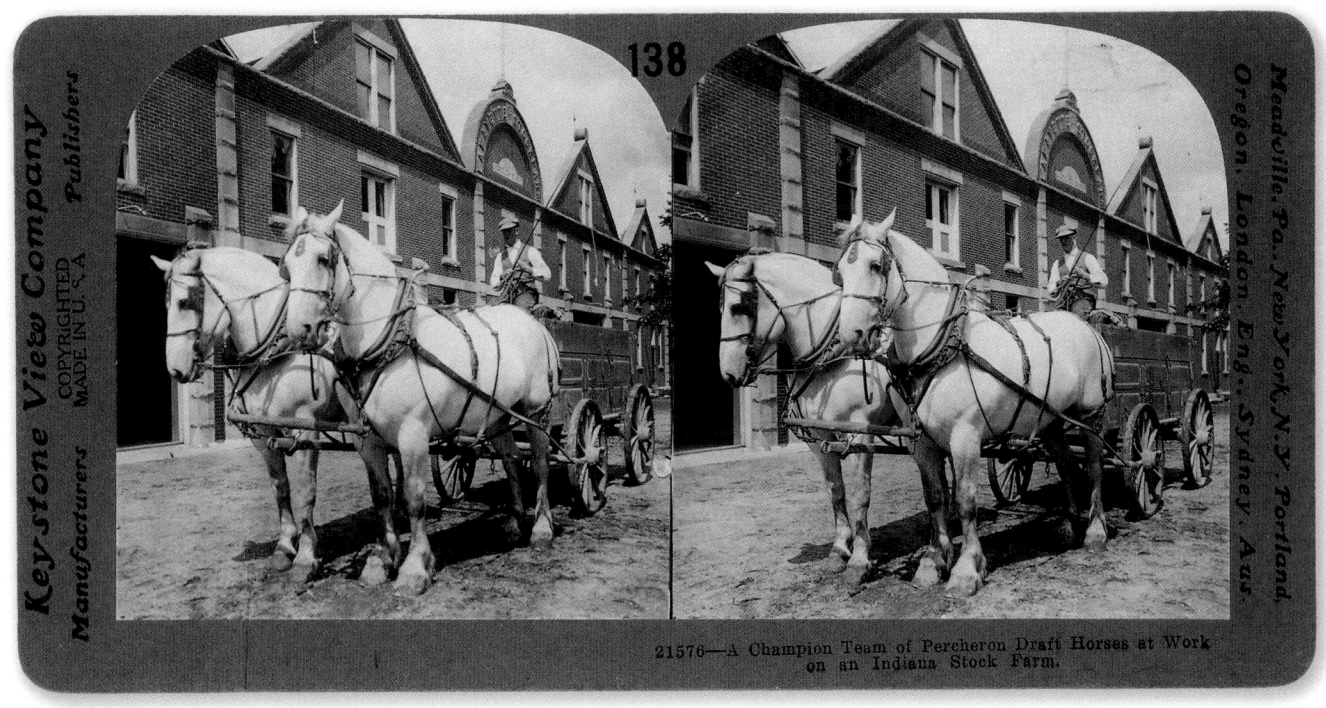

138

21576—A Champion Team of Percheron Draft Horses at Work
on an Indiana Stock Farm.

Team of Percherons, Lafayette, ca. 1920s. Published by the Keystone View Company.
The sign on the barn identifies this farm as the Lafayette Stock Farm. It was owned by Jeptha Crouch and family and was famous for the horses it bred.

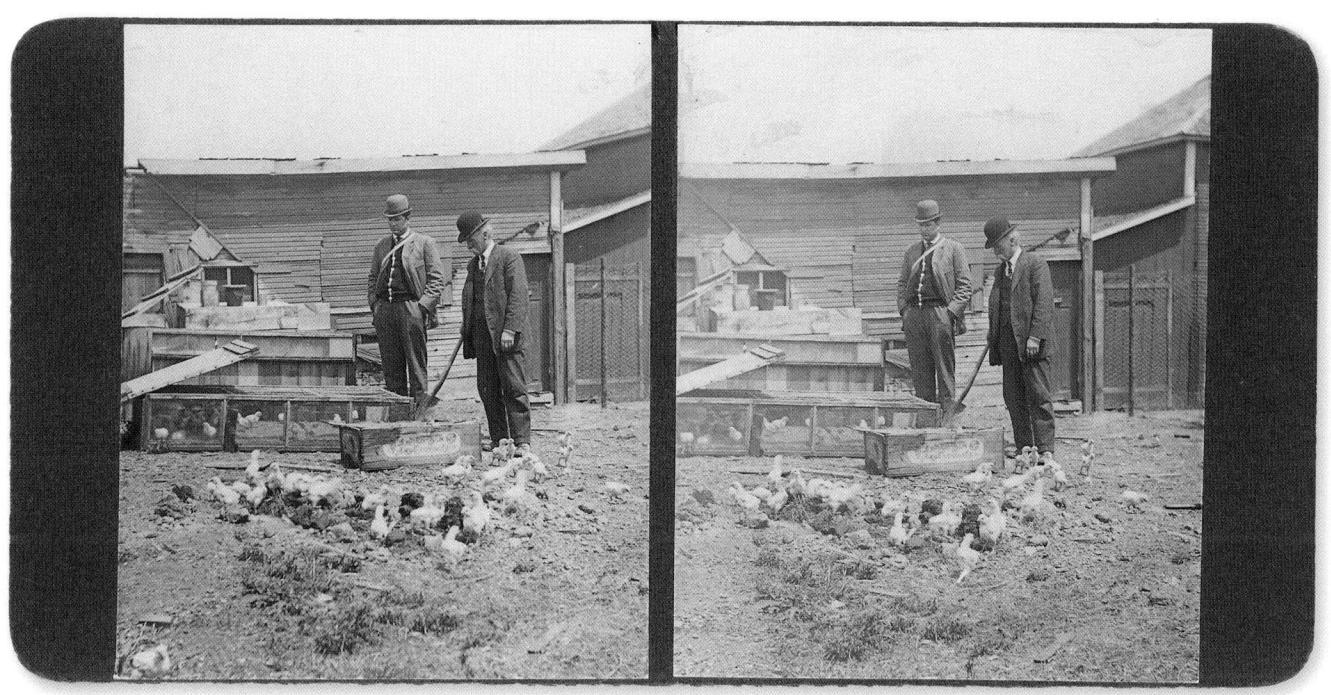

Men inspecting young chickens, Blackford County, 1910. Photographed by Clay H. Tuttle.

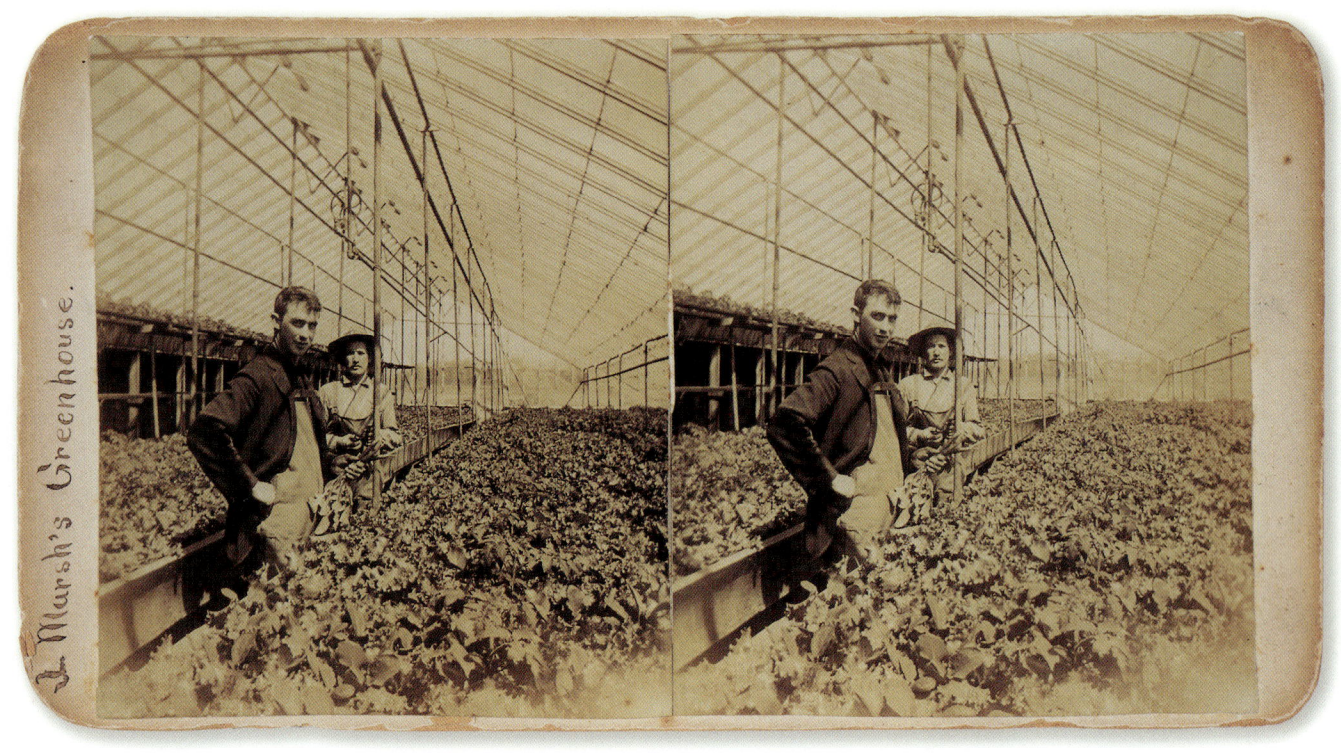

J. Marsh's greenhouse, probably near Muncie, ca. 1900. Photographer unknown.

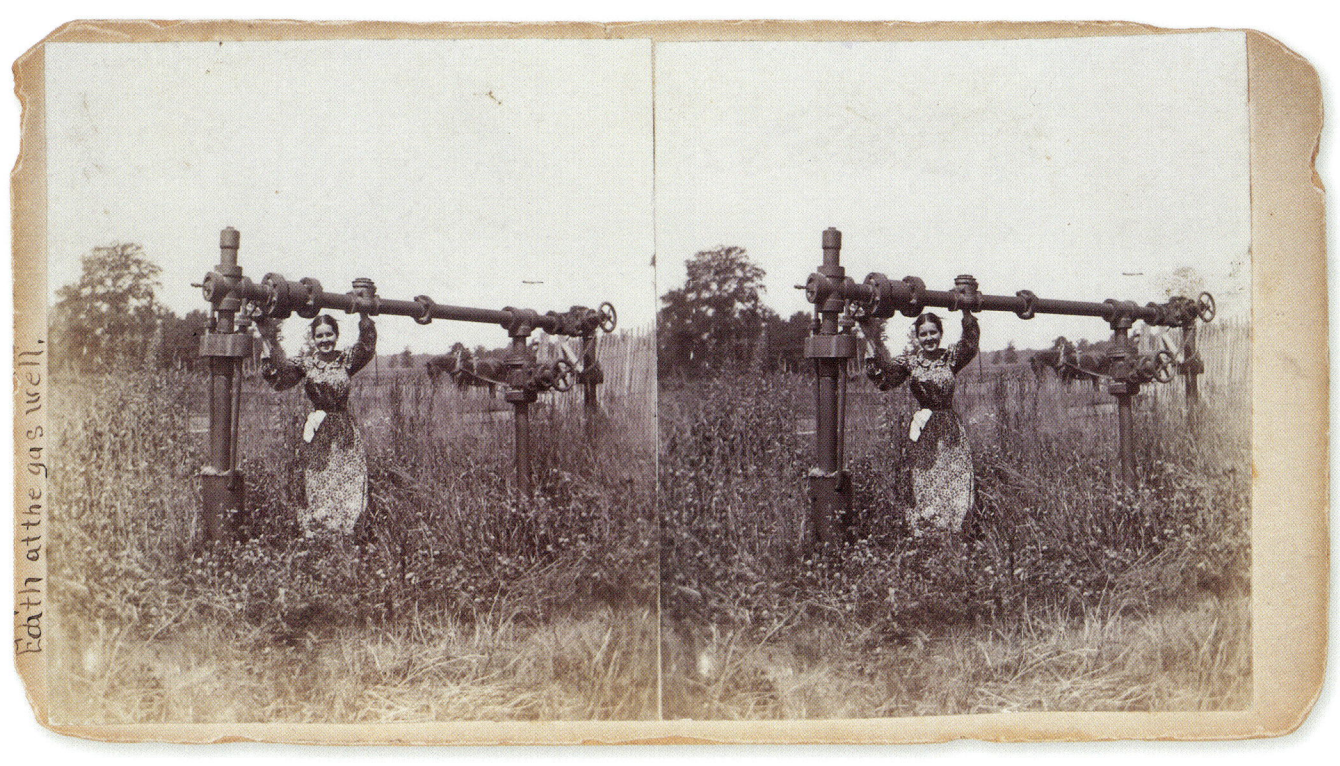

Edith at the gas well,

Edith at the gas well, probably near Muncie, ca. 1900. Photographer unknown.
The discovery of natural gas in east-central Indiana in 1886 led to rapid growth in the region. The opportunity for cheap energy
attracted manufacturers and other businesses, and cities in the area benefited from the influx of investors and workers. After a decade and a half of heavy use
and flagrant waste, however, the gas fields began to dry up, and by the early 1900s the Indiana gas boom had gone bust.

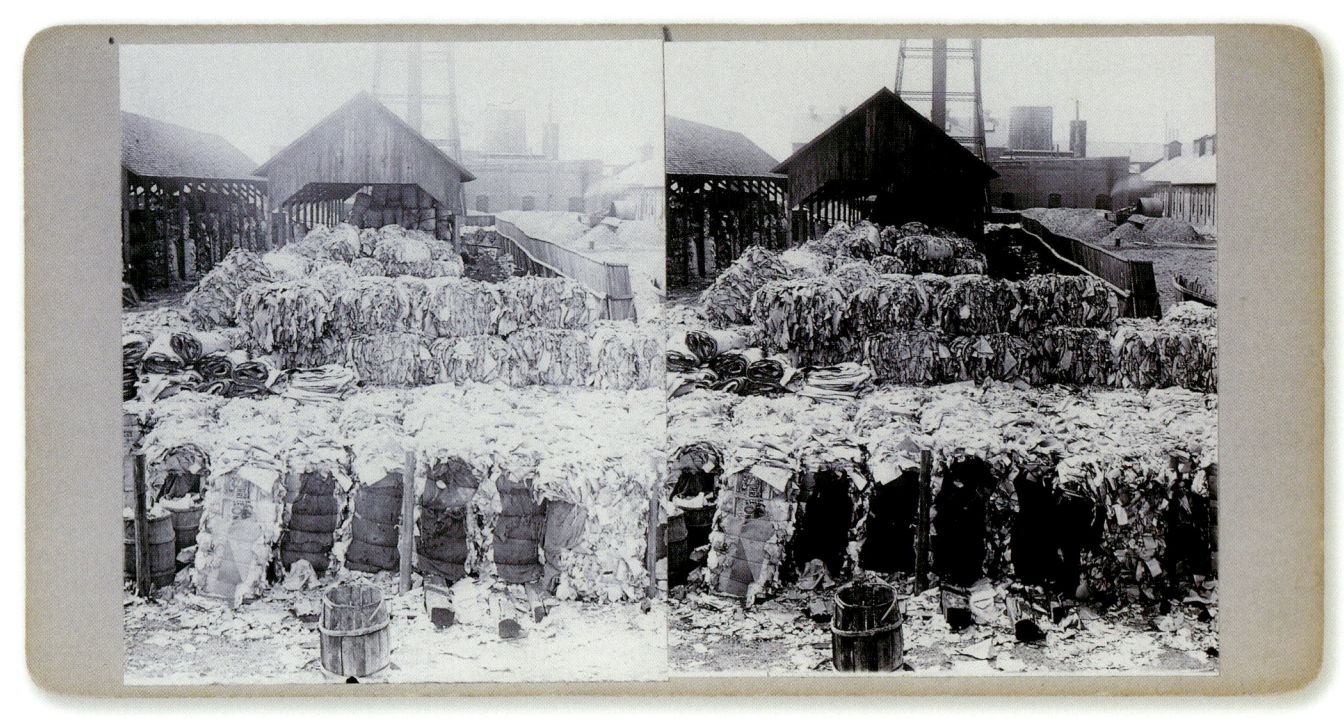

Wayne Paper Mill, Hartford City, 1910. Photographed by Clay H. Tuttle.

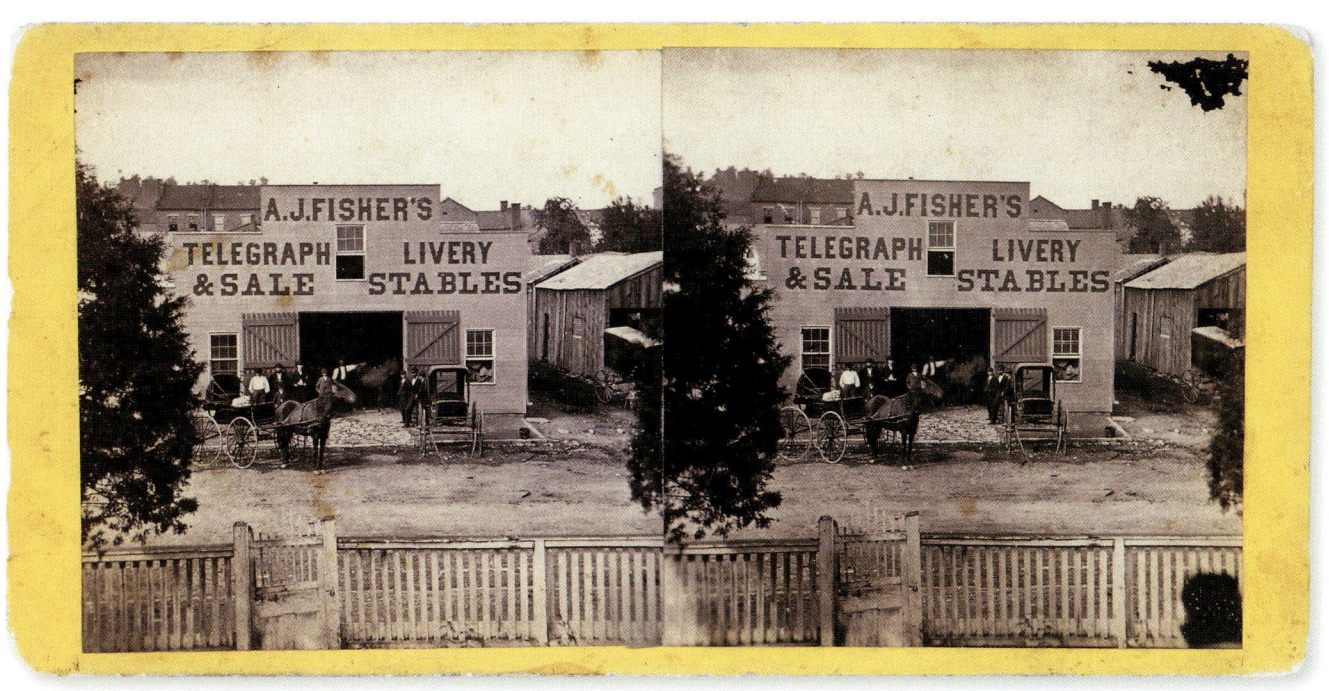

A. J. Fisher's livery stables, Madison, ca. 1870s. Photographed by J. R. Thorne.

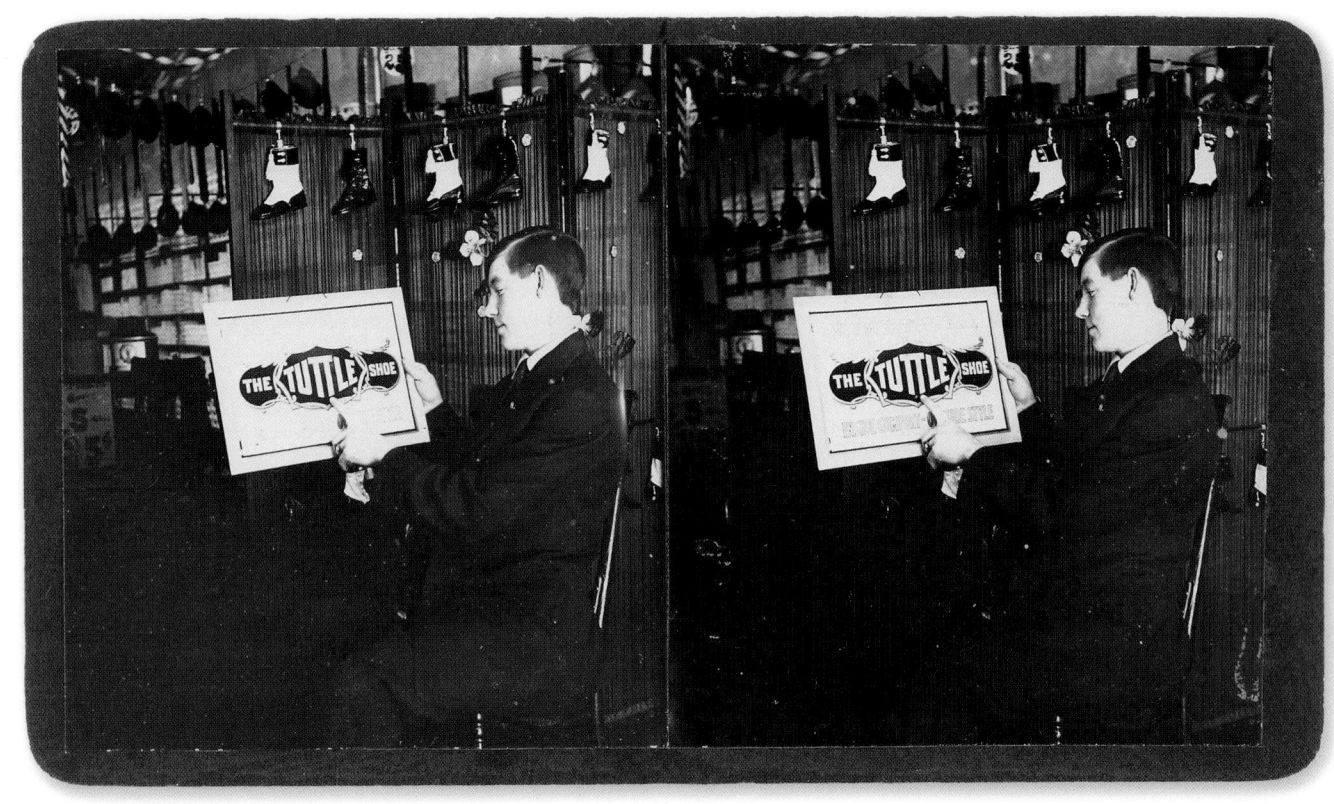

Tuttle shoe store clerk Marcell Parker, Hartford City, 1910. Photographed by Clay H. Tuttle.

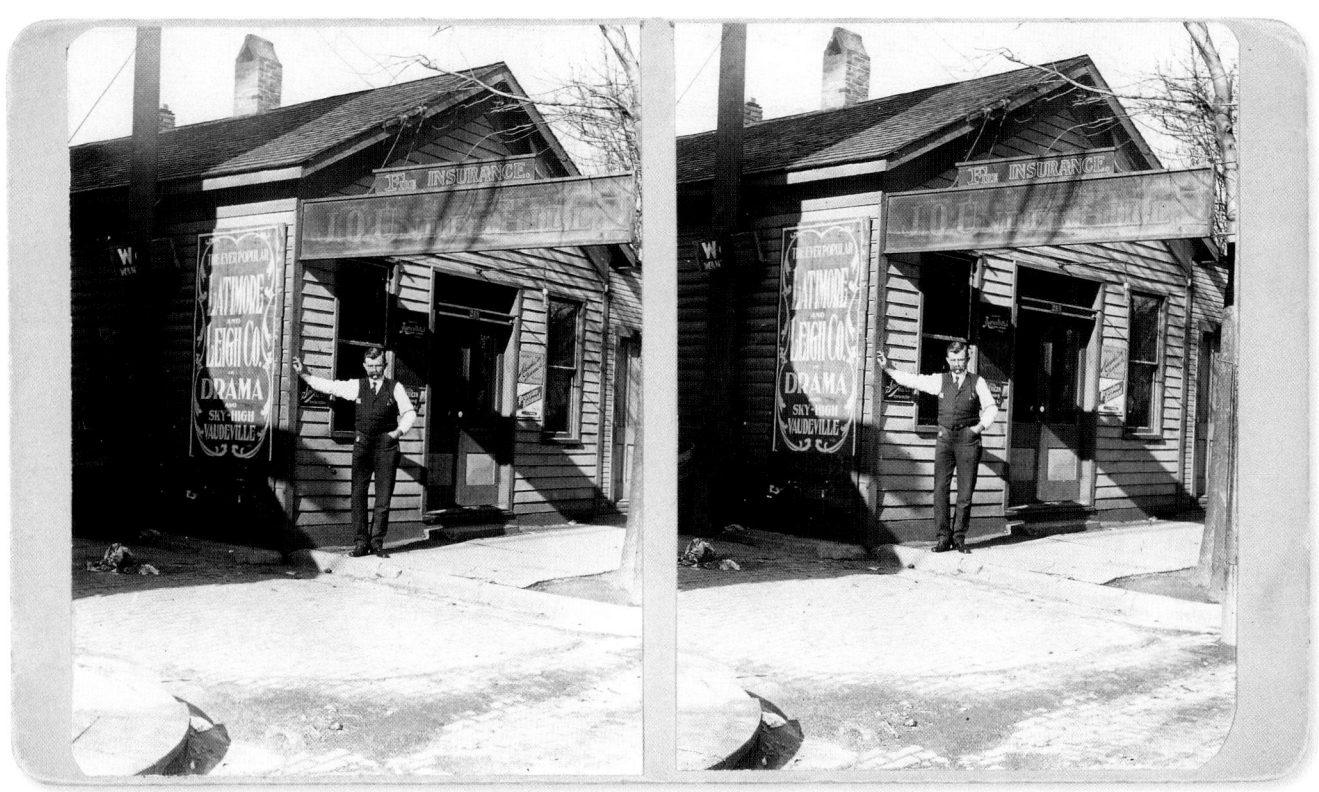

J. O. Underhill insurance agency, Hartford City, 1909. Photographed by Clay H. Tuttle.

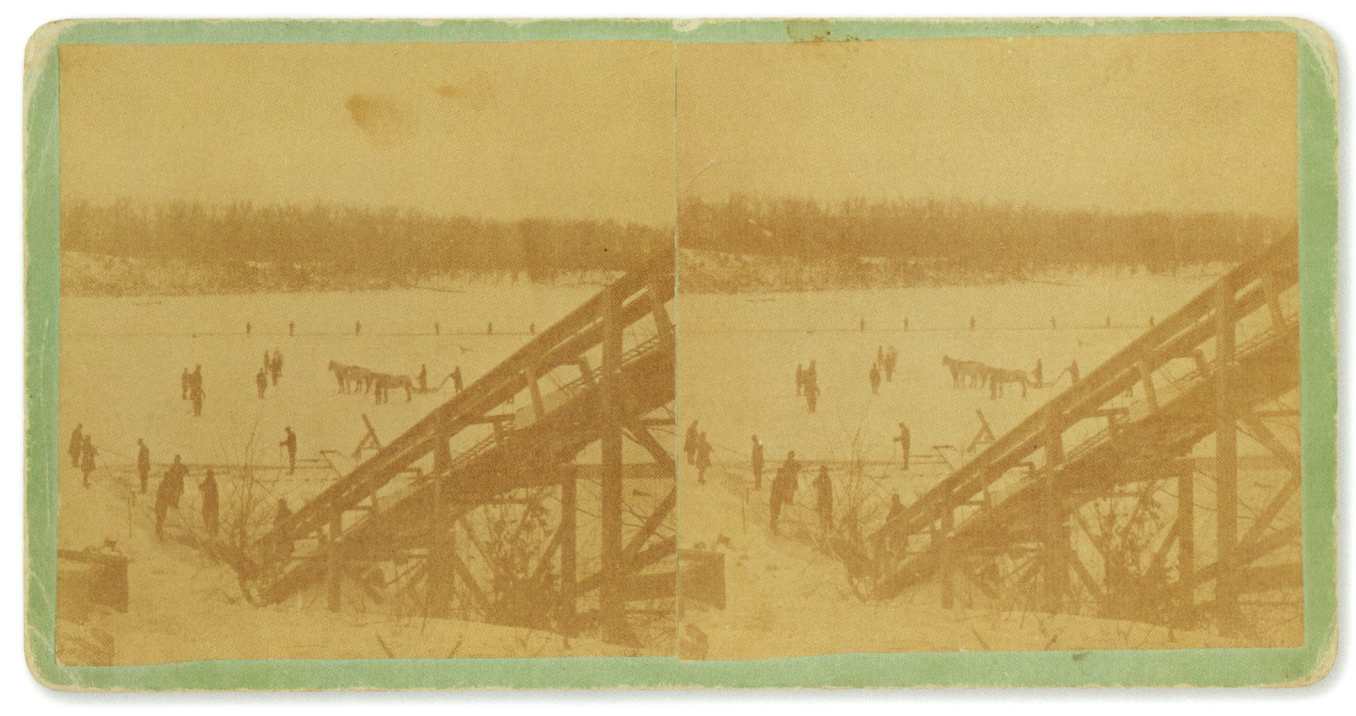

Knickerbocker Ice Company harvesting ice on Stone Lake, La Porte, ca. 1870s. Photographer unknown.
According to local historians, more ice was shipped from La Porte in the 1870s than from anywhere else west of the Hudson River.

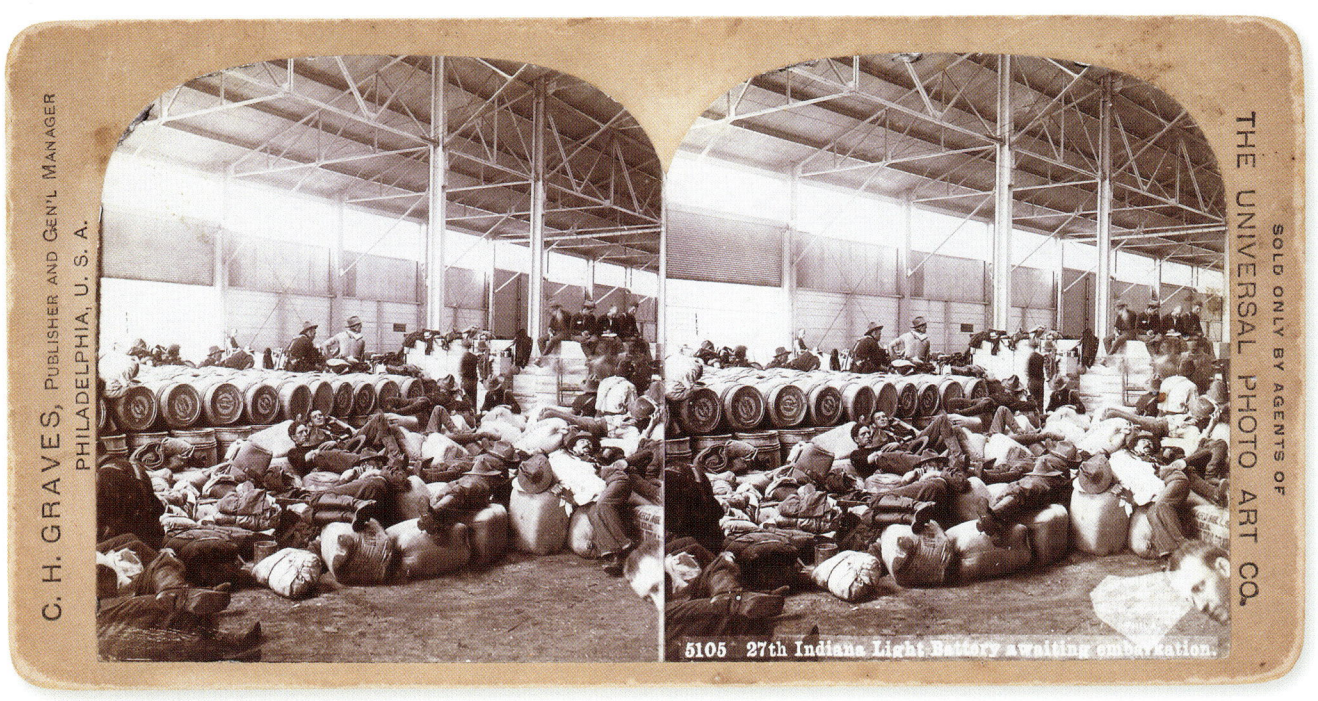

5105   27th Indiana Light Battery awaiting embarkation.

Troops from the Twenty-seventh Indiana Artillery Battery await embarkment during the Spanish-American War, location unknown, 1898.
Published by the Universal Photo Art Company. The soldiers left the state fairgrounds in Indianapolis for Chickamauga Park, Georgia, in the spring of 1898.
They landed in Puerto Rico in August and made it to the lines at San Juan, but peace came before they saw action.

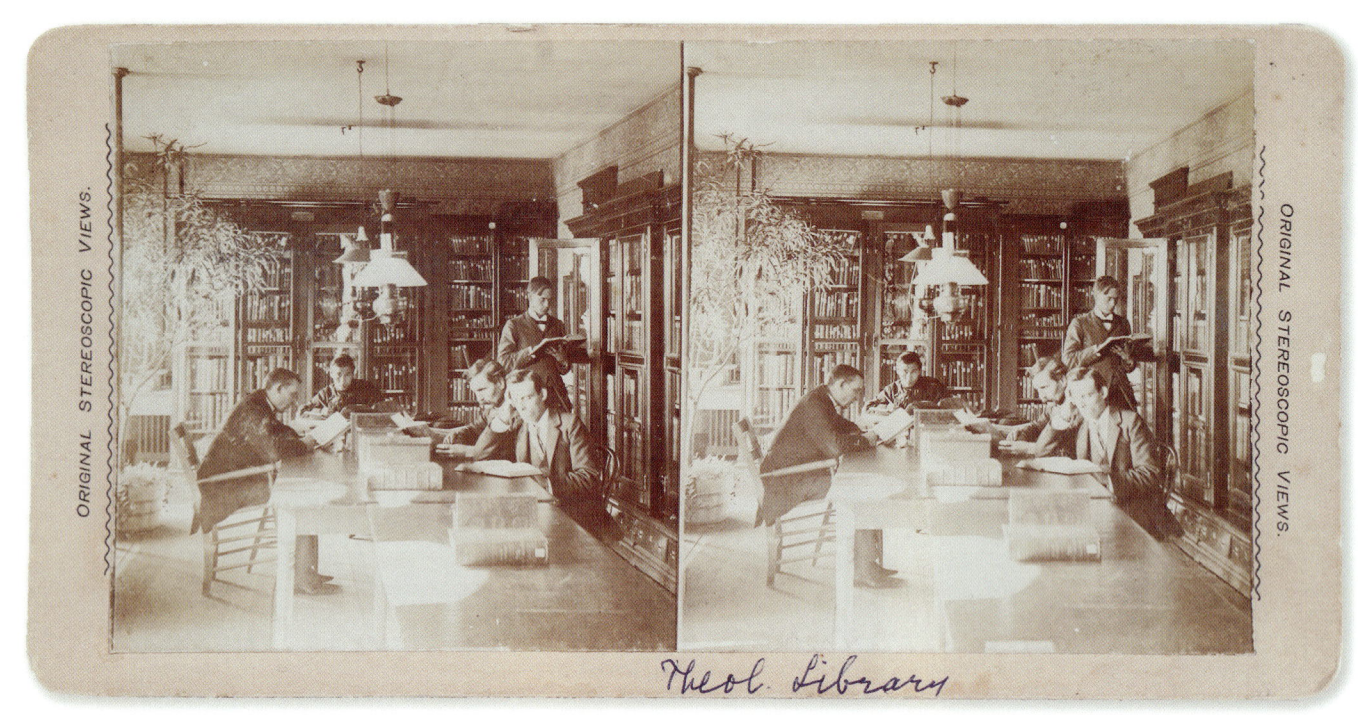

ORIGINAL STEREOSCOPIC VIEWS.

ORIGINAL STEREOSCOPIC VIEWS.

Theol. Library

Young men studying in DePauw University's theology library, Greencastle, ca. late 1890s. Photographed by W. D. Fairchild.

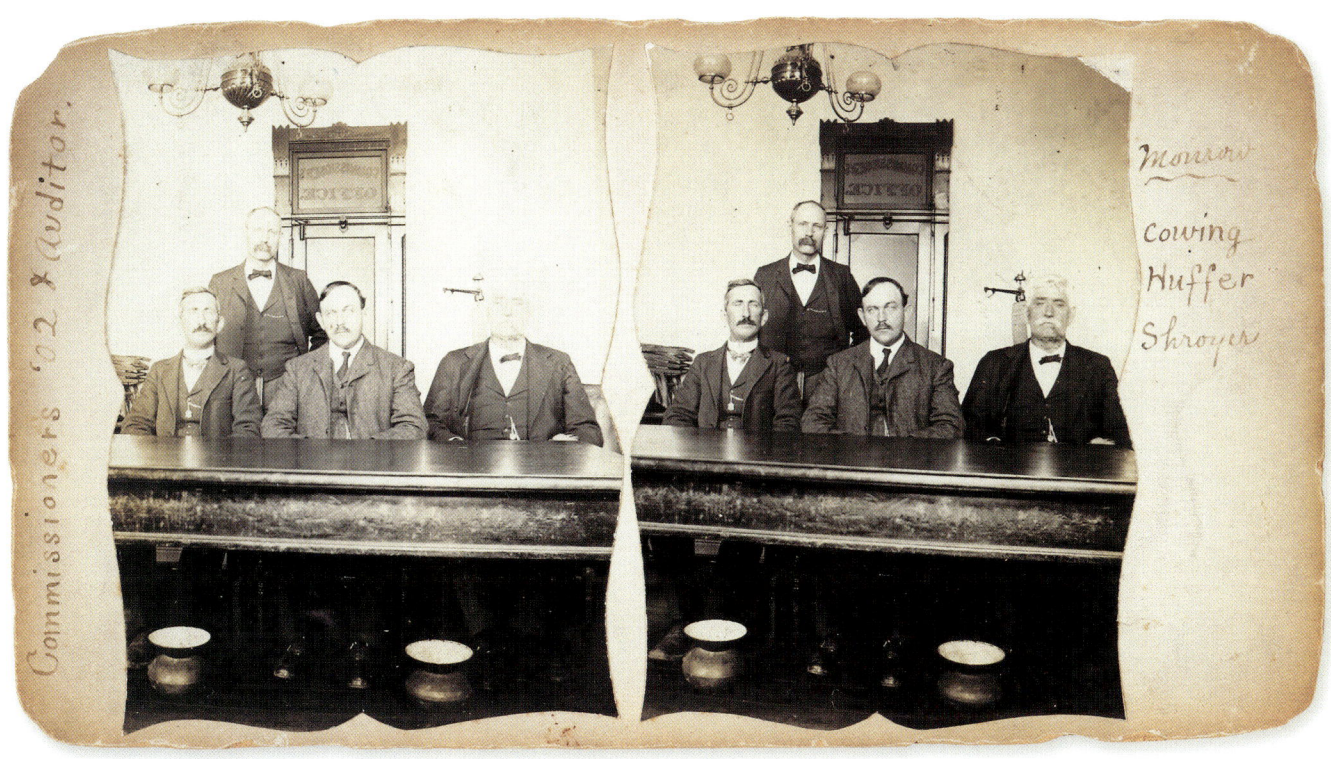

Delaware County commissioners and auditor, Muncie, 1902. Photographer unknown.

221

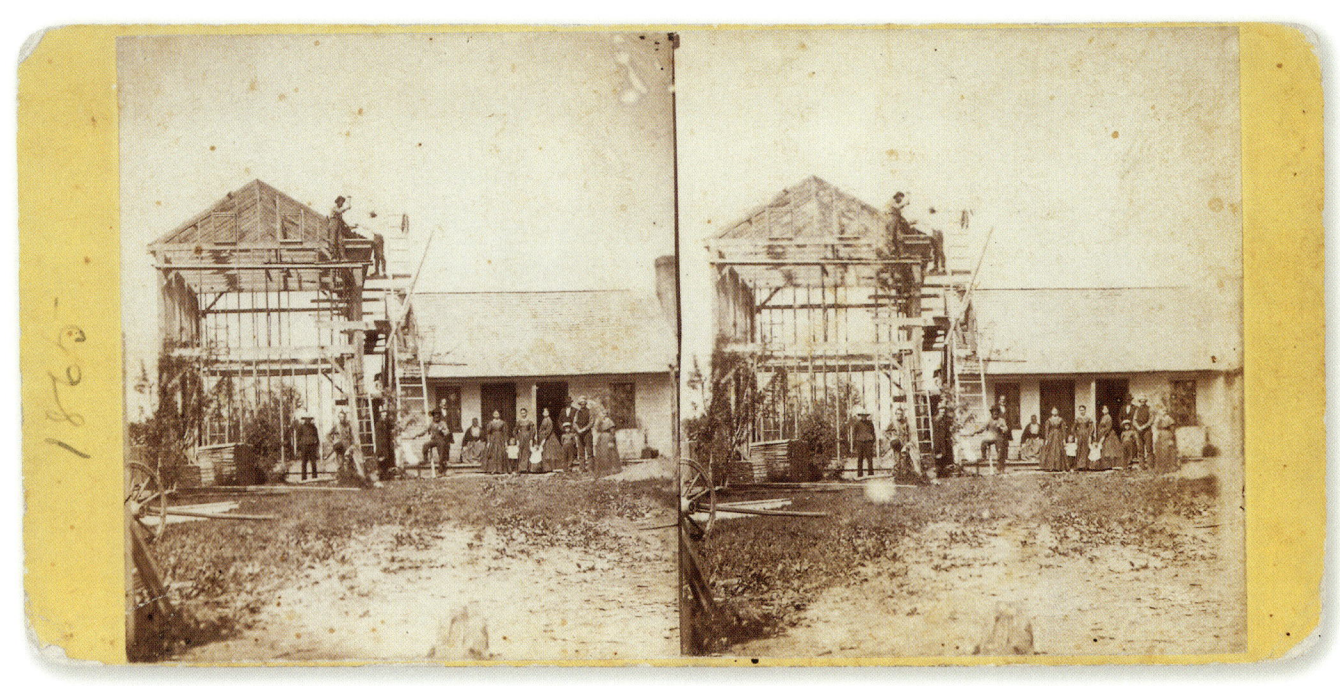

Lewis family building an addition to its home, near Pendleton, 1865. Photographed by Ridgeway Glover.

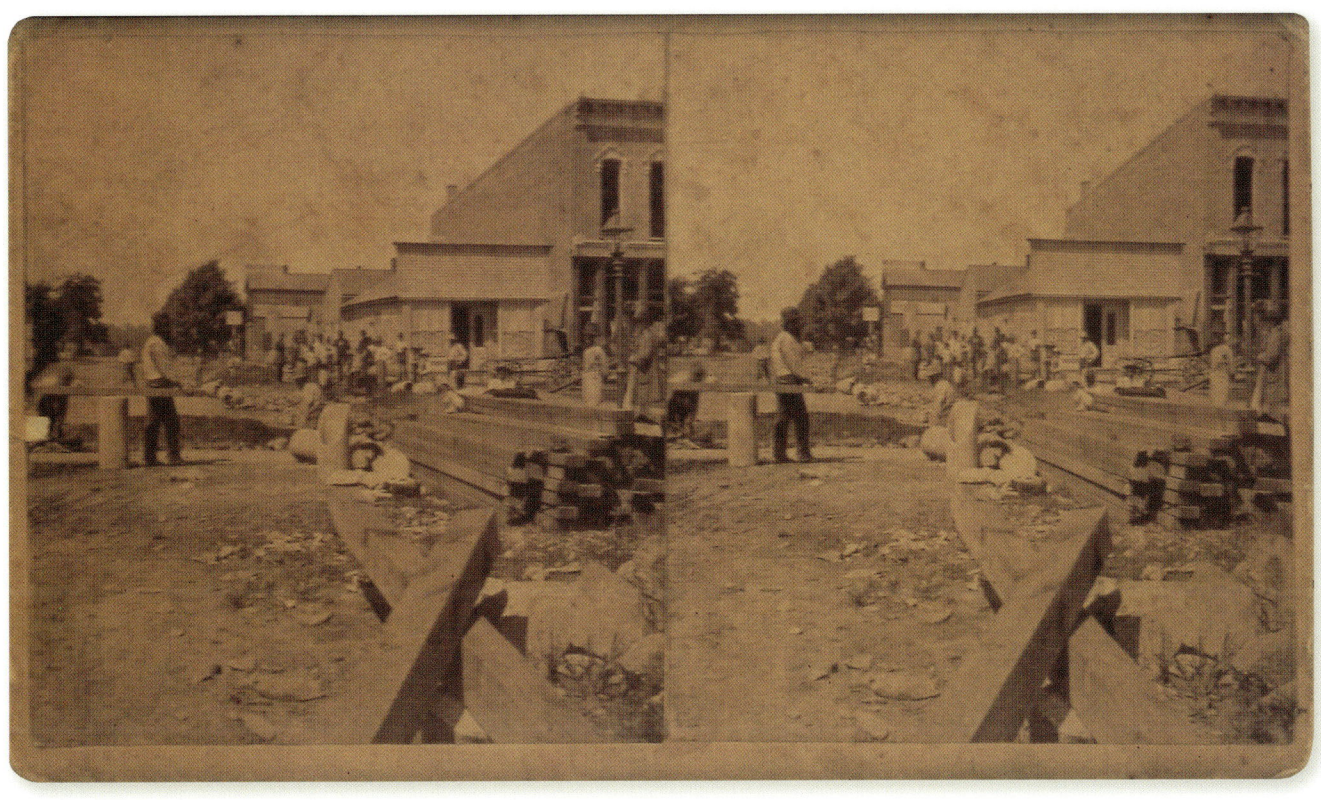

Installing new waterworks, Goshen, ca. 1870s. Photographer unknown. This photograph was taken on Market Street.

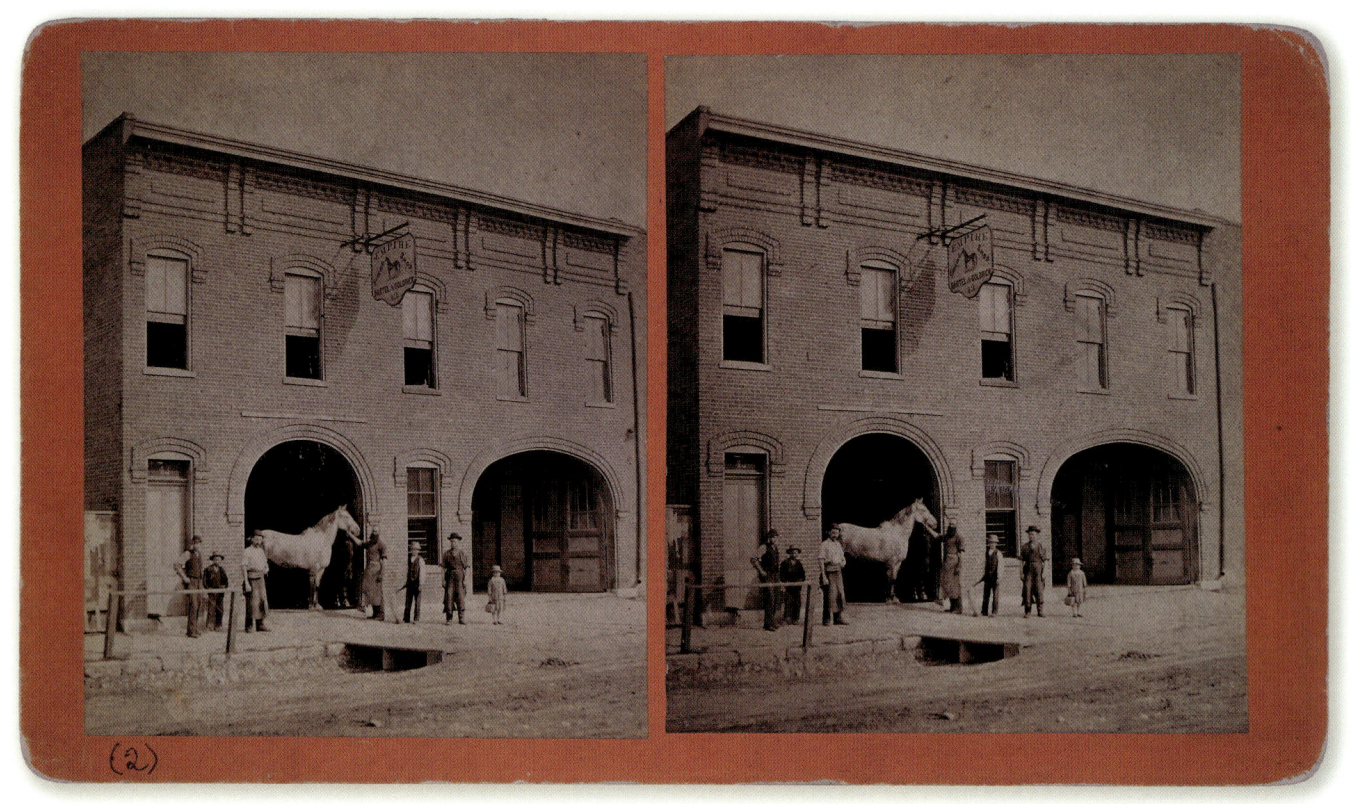

(2)

Empire Shoeing Shop, Richmond, ca. early 1880s. Photographer unknown.
The shop stood on South Sixth Street.

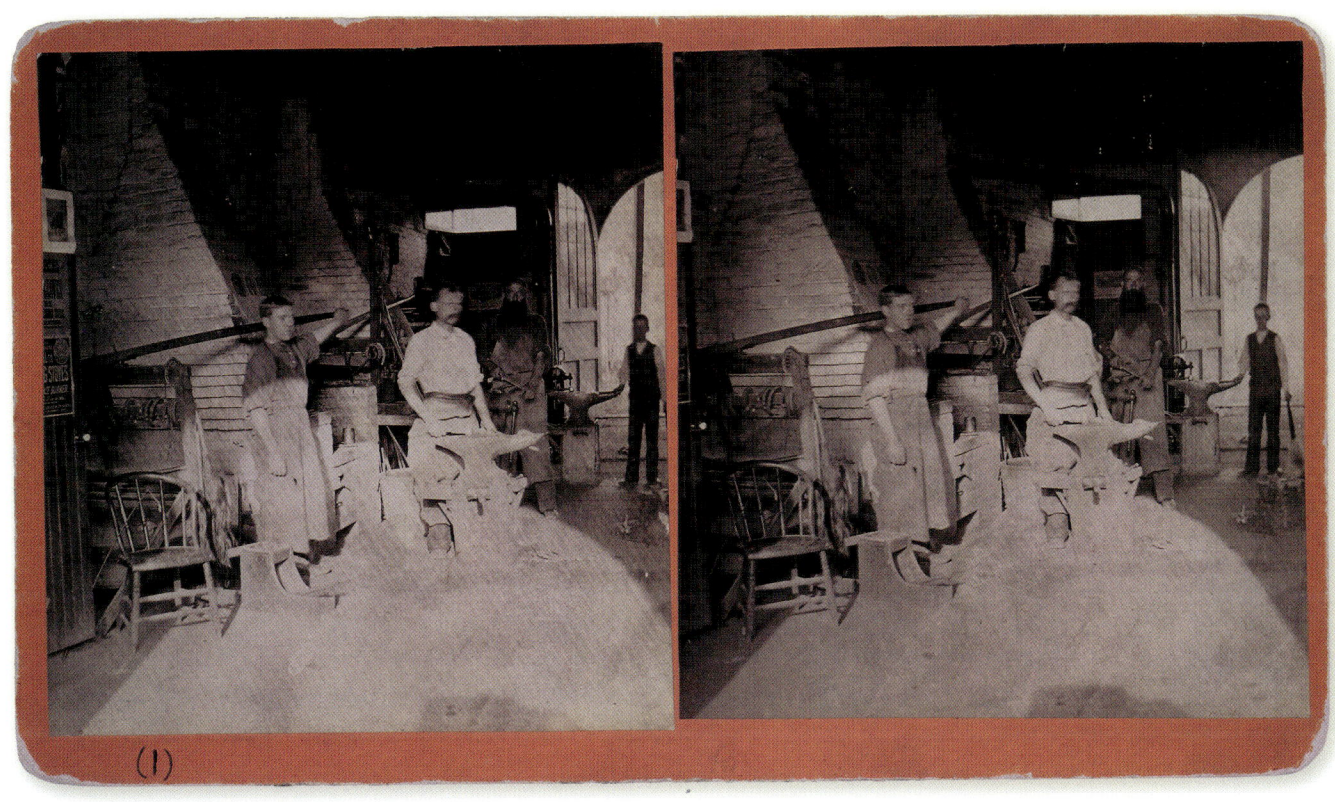

(1)

Interior view of the Empire Shoeing Shop, Richmond, ca. early 1880s. Photographer unknown.

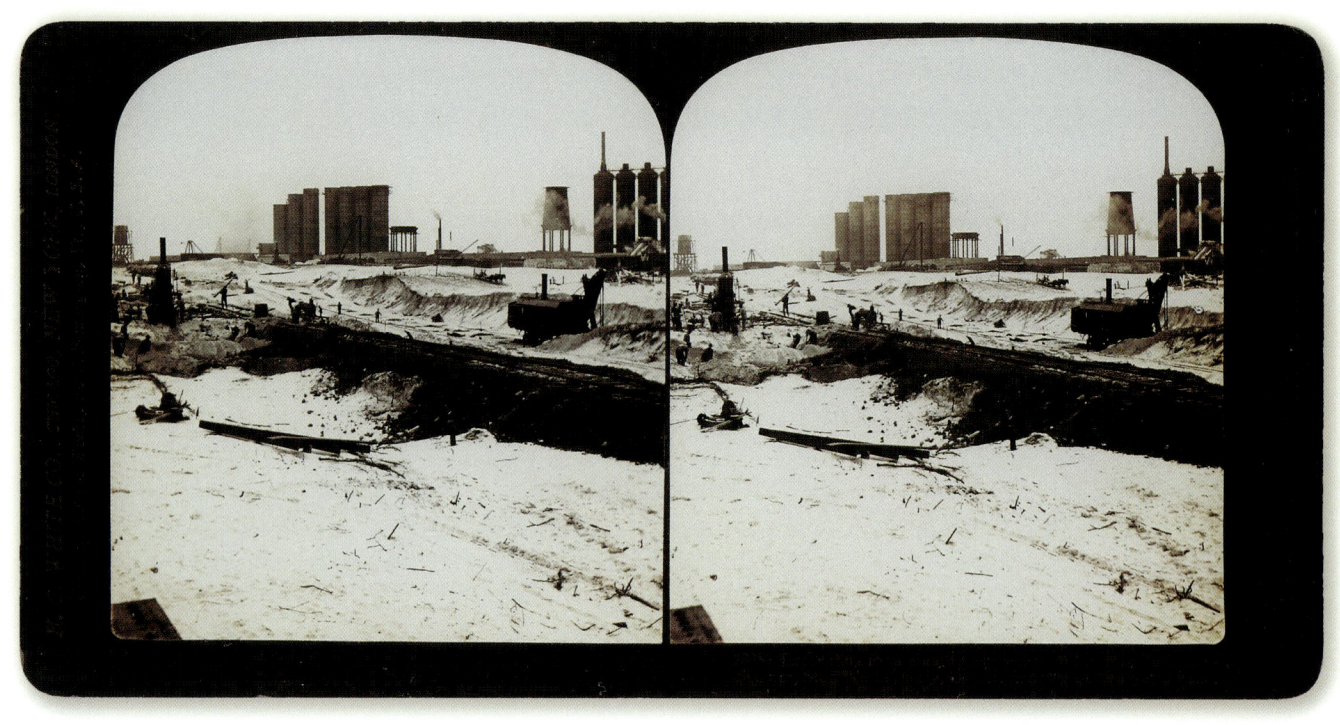

Excavation work for an open-hearth mill at the U.S. Steel Corporation's Gary Works, ca. 1907. Published by the H. C. White Company.
U.S. Steel built the world's largest steel facility on the shores of Lake Michigan in the early 1900s and developed the city of Gary to accommodate its workers.

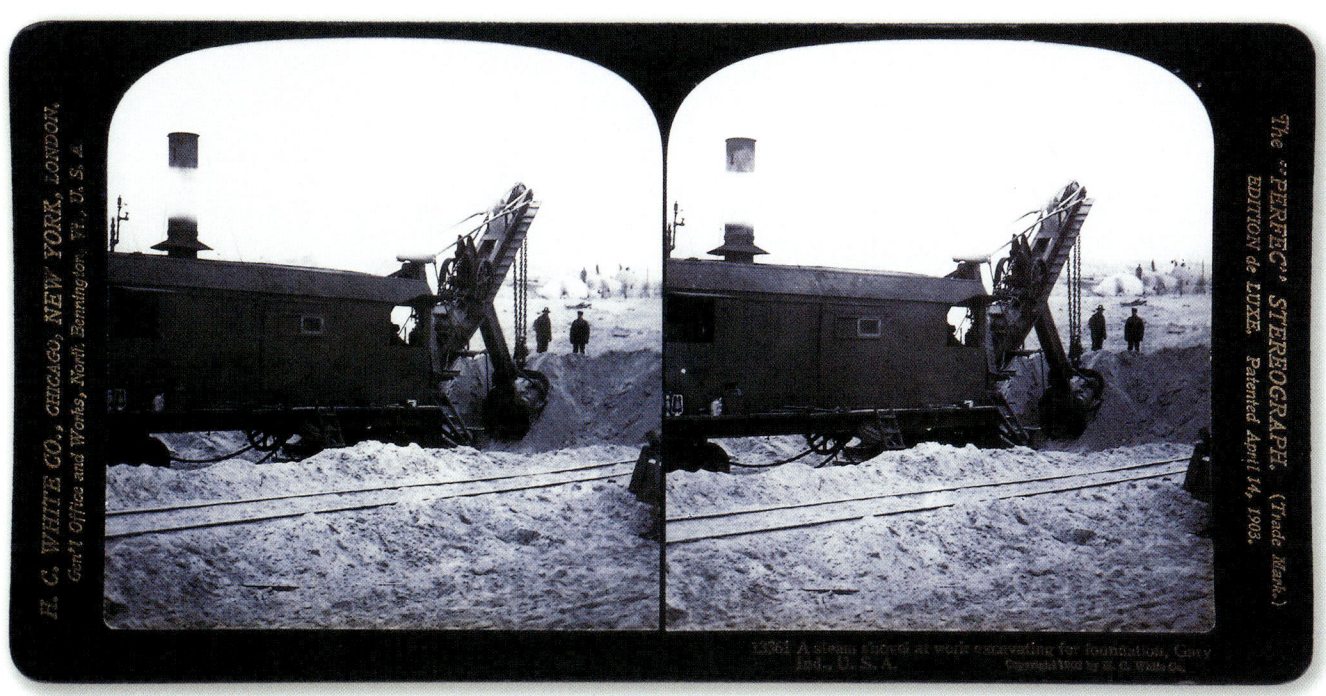

13361 A steam shovel at work excavating for foundation, Gary, Ind., U.S.A.
Copyright 1907 by H. C. White Co.

Steam shovel digging for foundations at the U.S. Steel Corporation's Gary Works, ca. 1907. Published by the H. C. White Company.

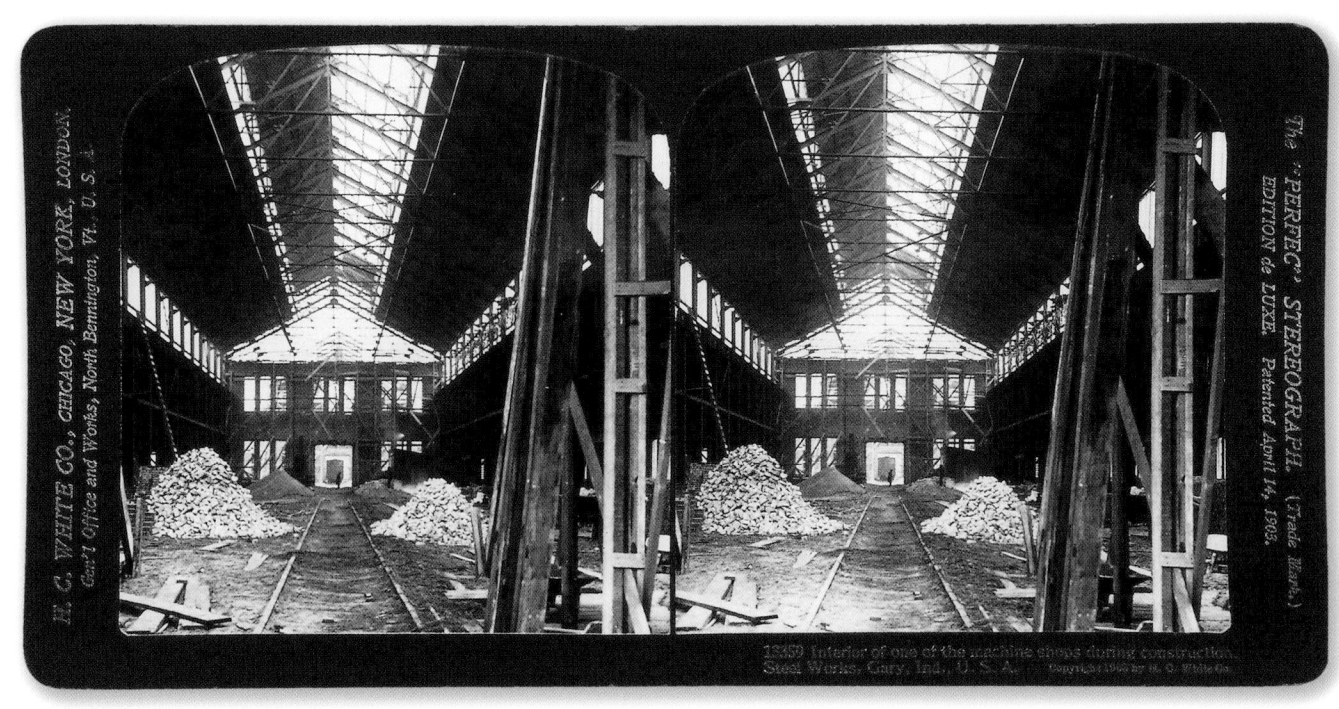

Interior of a machine shop under construction at the U.S Steel Corporation's Gary Works, ca. 1907. Published by the H. C. White Company.

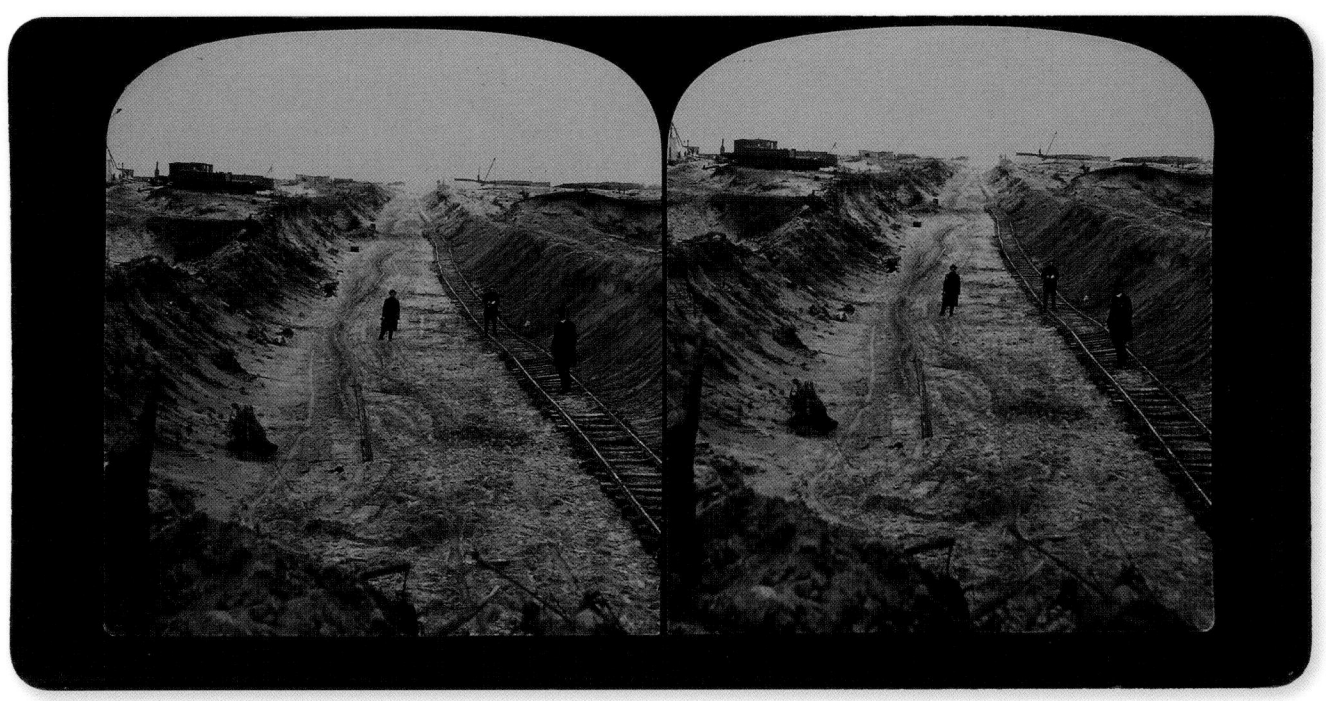

Street construction, Gary, ca. 1907. Published by the H. C. White Company.
According to the caption, this was one of sixteen cuttings, each a mile long, made for building the new city's streets.

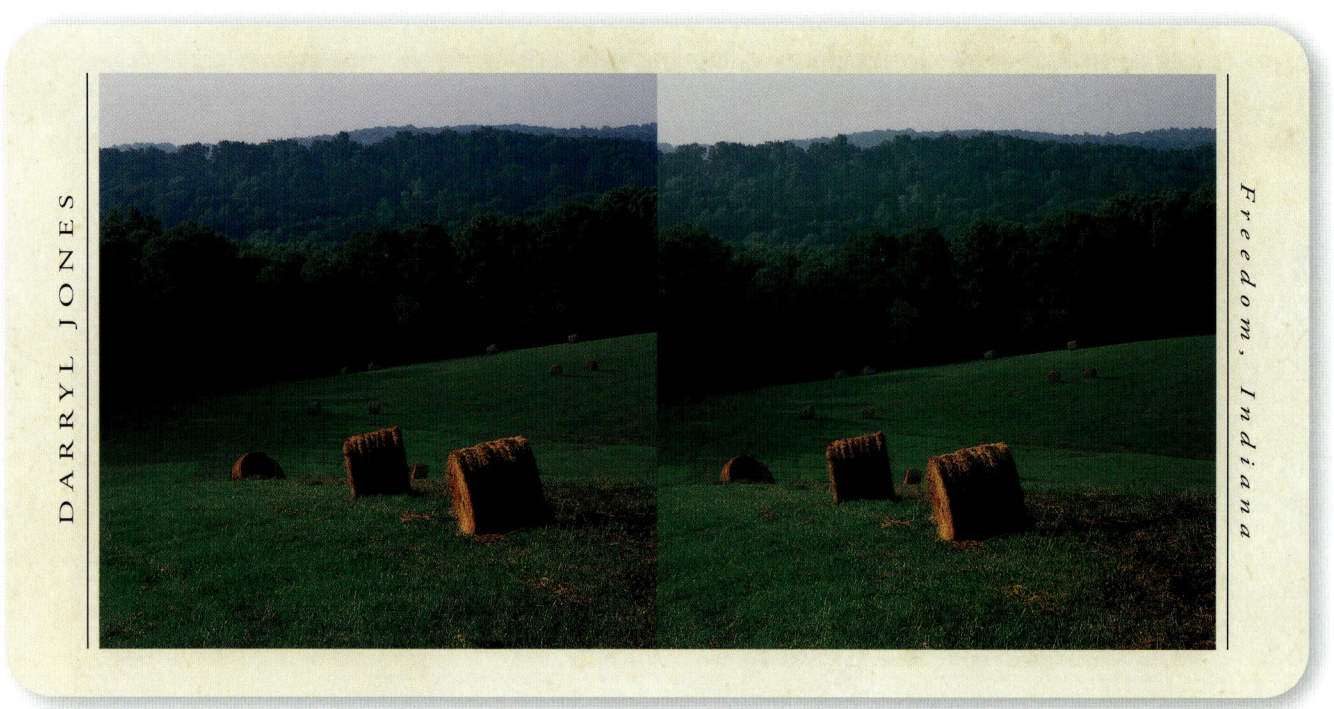

DARRYL JONES

Freedom, Indiana

Kelley Hill, Brown County, 1998.

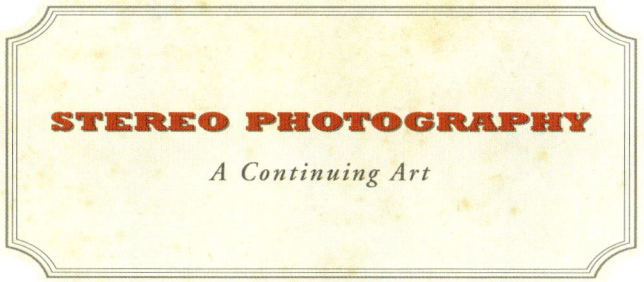

STEREO PHOTOGRAPHY

A Continuing Art

AS WITH MANY WHO GREW UP IN THE 1950S, MY FIRST ENCOUNTER WITH STEREOSCOPIC IMAGES CAME FROM a View-Master—a handheld plastic stereo viewer with two eyepieces. Users inserted into the viewer a disk (also called a reel) with seven sets of stereo slides. Pushing a lever made the disk rotate, advancing the images. Thousands of reels were available on nearly any subject, including national and state parks, historic homes, movie stars, and even cartoon characters. When holding the viewer toward light and looking into the eyepieces, the user was confronted with an amazing three-dimensional color image. It was like being in a darkened cave and looking out at the world. The image was somewhat small and surrounded by blackness, but it provided a magical look into a lifelike three-dimensional environment. Because only one person could view at a time, users would have to take turns and let others share in the enjoyment (or fight to prevent a brother or sister from looking). My parents often bought View-Master reels at tourist stops during family trips, and my sister and I spent many hours looking at the stereo images.

In my youth it never occurred to me that I, too, could make three-dimensional images like those I saw through the View-Master. It seemed too complicated for me to do myself; surely it would require a large amount of resources to produce such images. Later, as a young man studying photography, I further dismissed the idea of stereo photography. From 1967 to 1969 I worked part-time at Sunny Schick's Camera Shop in Fort Wayne while attending Indiana University. I used to see Stereo Realist cameras in the display case, but I never used

DARRYL JONES

one. The "old-timers" would come in and talk about their stereo cameras and projectors from the early 1950s, but 8 mm motion-picture cameras and television had replaced the interest in stereo. The whole topic of 3-D was something of the past, and it was a dying practice. I was twenty years old and actively shooting with 35 mm and 120 roll film, developing my film, making enlargements in my basement darkroom, and exhibiting mounted photographs. I had no time or interest in learning about stereo photography.

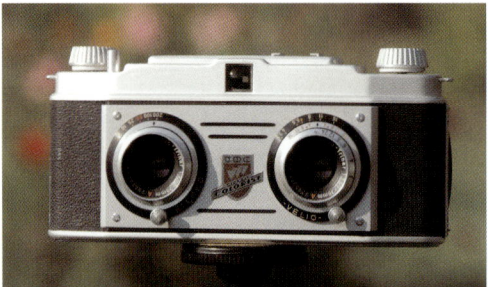

TDC Stereo Colorist camera, manufactured ca. 1954.

Now, though, I am one of the old-timers, and I have a renewed respect for all those who pioneered the art of photographing in three dimensions. For the past ten years I have studied the craft, learning all I can about the history and practices of making stereo photographs. My first attempts to make my own stereo images, I admit, were unsuccessful. I purchased a Nimslo stereo camera in 1993 and took one roll of film during a family trip out West. The Nimslo company had to print the photographs at its own lab, but it went bankrupt before I had the film processed. I was not off to a good start.

Then in 1994 Fred Jungclaus lent me his father's Stereo Realist 35 mm camera and asked me to take photographs of the Indianapolis 500 race. Fred was in charge of designing the race program and was exploring the possibility of publishing stereo images in it. Using the Realist was a delight for me, and for the first time I had great success in actually making true three-dimensional images. Fred and I sent the film to Kodak for processing and had the slides specially mounted onto cards. Fred had a viewer, so we could see the images in depth! I was amazed by them, but the camera and viewer belonged to Fred, so I still did not actively pursue stereo photography.

In 1997 I took architectural photographs of the Hendricks County Historical Museum, housed in the former county jail and sheriff's residence in Danville, Indiana. The director showed me all the rooms, and in the parlor on a table was an antique stereoscope from the 1870s. In the stereoscope was a card with contemporary color images of the front of the building. While I had seen that type of viewer in museums, I had never seen a card showing a modern-day view. I asked how the images were produced, and I learned that they were taken with

232

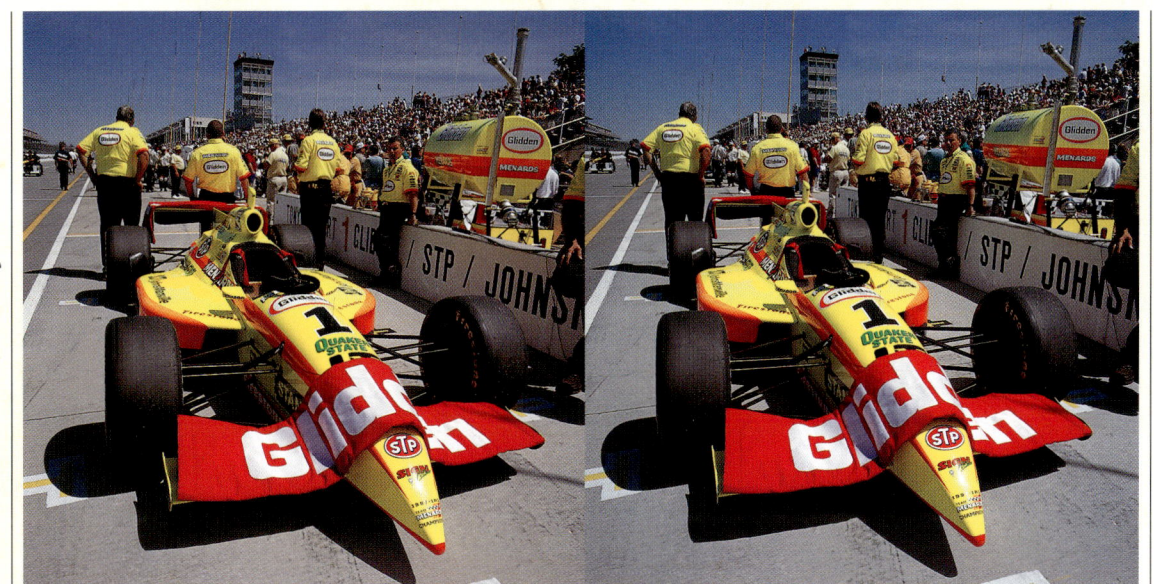

Indianapolis Motor Speedway, 1998. Tony Stewart's team awaits the start of the Indianapolis 500.

a simple disposable 35 mm camera, printed at a local one-hour lab, and taped to the card. The photographer created the stereo effect by taking two separate photographs, moving the camera about three inches between exposures and thus replicating the distance between human eyes. Though the photographer's method was elementary, it worked. The stereoscope allowed the user to see the two photographs on the card as one three-dimensional image. For the first time, I knew I could carry out the entire process of creating stereoscopic photos myself. I left the museum and embarked on a new adventure.

While driving from Danville to Indianapolis I stopped at several antique malls. At one of them I purchased an 1870s stereoscope and a small collection of stereo cards. Then I called Jack's Camera Shop in Muncie to inquire about used stereo cameras. The shop had a 1950 Kodak 35 mm stereo camera for sale, so I drove to Muncie to buy it. Now that I had both a camera and viewer, I began taking my

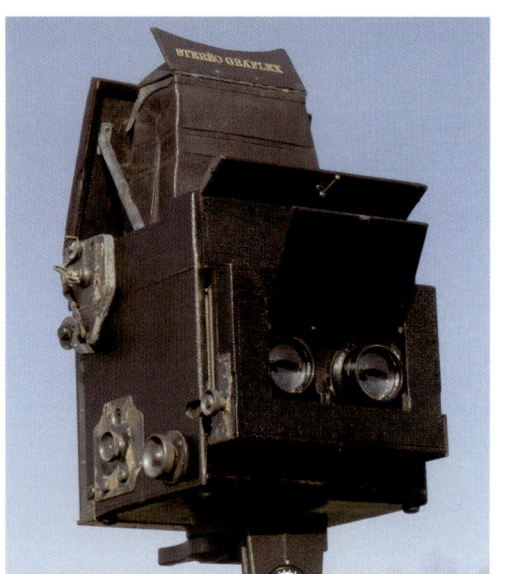

Graflex stereo camera, manufactured ca. 1907.

own stereo photographs. The next morning I shot two rolls of film and sent them out for processing and printing. Then I cut black mounting board to the $3^1/2$-by-7-inch card size required for the viewer. By that evening I was trimming the color photographs and mounting them to the cards. By trial and error I determined which were the right and left photographs. (With the images reversed, the background appeared in front of the foreground, causing some dizziness, so I quickly caught on to the correct arrangement.) Now I was actively engaged in producing stereo images, and I knew it was just the beginning.

The history of stereoscopy fascinated me, and I began to utilize the techniques of the earliest stereo photographers. With the rising popularity of stereographs in the mid–nineteenth century, camera manufacturers had introduced a slider bar, so that after a photographer took one image he could slide the camera several inches and shoot another. This had allowed the photographer to take both a left and a right image successively, exactly as the eyes saw the object. As I explored the field of stereo photography, I attempted to re-create this same setup. I made a slider bar and placed a Polaroid camera on it; then I mounted the slider bar and camera on a tripod. Next I carried out a series of experiments by taking several sets of photographs, varying the distance between each exposure. The images developed in a minute, and I taped them to a mount board and placed the board in the antique stereoscope. Instantly I could see the three-dimensional effects, and I could determine what distances were most successful. I had the exciting sense of replicating history.

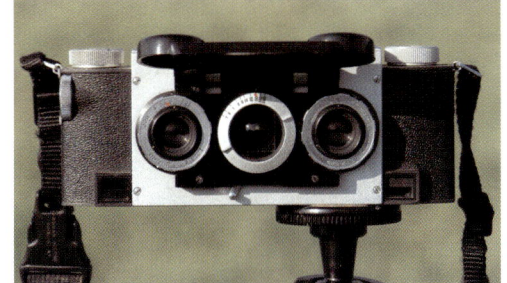

Stereo Realist camera, manufactured ca. 1950.

I also tried to duplicate some of the early viewing techniques, particularly those introduced by Sir Charles Wheatstone, inventor of the stereoscope. Wheatstone's stereoscope consisted of two mirrors placed at ninety-degree angles to each other so that each mirror reflected a drawing directly in front of it. By placing the nose near where the mirrors met, the user saw the two drawings as one solid three-dimensional image. I bought two mirrors, placed them at right angles to each other, and studied the Wheatstone principles. I enlarged the Polaroid images on a color copier and began to work with other viewing designs.

Rick Ropkey of Indianapolis's Ropkey Graphics encouraged me with this and helped by enlarging a pair of my Polaroid images on a thirty-by-sixty-inch sheet of paper. I taped this to the wall and began trying out different distances from which to view the stereo pair.

I discussed these new projects with Seldon Bradley, who quickly searched the Internet and found two commercially available viewers for multiple-size stereo prints. Both viewers used mirrors in the manner of a periscope. One viewer was designed for the standard side-by-side mounting technique, and the mirrors were placed horizontally in opposite directions. The other viewer had the mirrors placed vertically and required the prints to be placed one above the other. As with traditional stereoscopes, these viewers forced the eyes to see one three-dimensional image, but their unique designs did give me ideas for new methods of presenting stereo photos.

I began to experiment with every camera I owned because I wanted to see how different film formats appeared in three dimen-

235

sions. I placed each camera on a slider bar and varied the distance I moved the camera after the first exposure. In stereo photography, there is a relationship between the foreground and background and the angle of the camera lens. If an object is close (four or five feet away), and the background is infinity, then the separation of the camera between exposures should be about the distance between the human eyes—two and a half to three inches. If the foreground object is some distance away (perhaps a building across the street), and the background is again infinity, the separation could be twelve to nineteen inches. If the foreground object is even farther away (a hill two hundred yards in the distance, for example), and the background is infinity, the separation might be thirty-six to forty-eight inches. I used a slider bar up to sixty inches long in order to experiment with these distances.

Because the subject matter might change in the short time required to move the camera, though, I added a second camera to the slider bar. The cameras I used were a Nikon 35 mm and a Hasselblad ELM 120, both motorized. I attached an electric cable release to each, and when I tripped it, both cameras fired. Sometimes the camera separation needed to be greater than the length of my slider bar, so I mounted each camera on a separate tripod (perhaps thirty to one hundred feet apart). In place of a cable release I utilized remote radio receivers mounted on each camera. With the radio transmitter in my hand I could stand one hundred yards away and still fire both cameras at the same time with the push of a single button.

The Hasselblad ELM cameras have the smallest base width of any 120-format camera, and when two cameras are mounted side by side, the distance between the centers of the two lenses is three and a half inches, close enough to the distance between human eyes. As long as the foreground is no closer than six feet, the stereo effect is accurate. To experiment with this setup, I mounted two of these cameras onto a tripod and went into the woods to take photos at various distances. Using a tape measure, I was sure to maintain a distance of six feet from the lens to the foreground. The resulting images convinced me that this was a flexible camera system, for I could change lenses from wide angle to telephoto according to the scene I wanted to photograph.

On an early excursion with this new setup, I drove through Brown County on State Road 46 and came upon freshly cut hay on Kelley Hill. I experimented with one camera and determined that a 250 mm telephoto lens was just right to photograph a round bale against the distant rolling hills. The bale was about forty yards away, and the hills focused at infinity. Figuring the relationship between the foreground and background and factoring in the telephoto effect, I calculated that the base separation of

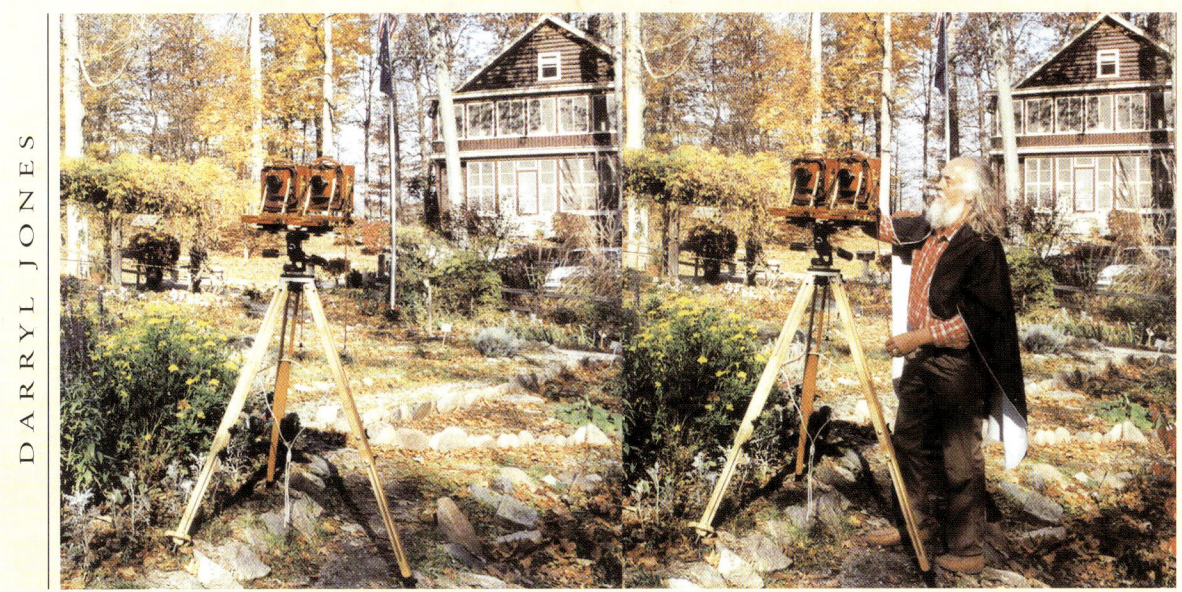

Darryl Jones with his four-by-five-inch view cameras at the Gene Stratton-Porter State Historic Site in Rome City.

the two cameras from center of lens to center of lens should be nineteen inches. I set up both cameras and took the stereo image. The result was just what I had hoped for.

On another occasion I stopped to take photographs from a hill near Vandalia in western Owen County. I used the same camera system with the 250 mm lenses, only now the foreground was approximately three hundred yards away and the background hills were about six hundred yards away. I used a range finder to help me calculate these distances. Because of the extreme distance of the subject from the camera, I had to separate the cameras and place them on individual tripods with thirty feet between the lenses. I composed the image in the viewfinder of the first camera then proceeded to set up the second camera according to the distance required. I purchased a 360-degree circular level to help me learn the film-plane angle of the first camera, for the second camera needed to have the same angle. I also had to purchase a good compass in order to place the second camera in such a way that its film plane formed a straight line with the first camera. In order to ensure that the height of each camera was the same, I used a surveyor's

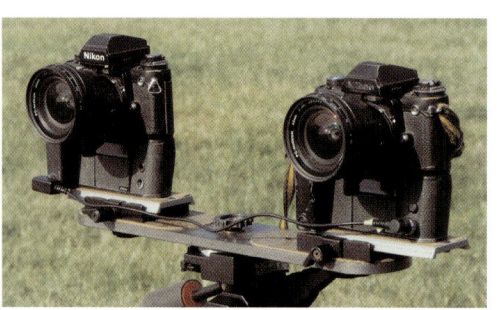

Two Nikon F3 cameras on a sliding bar.

transit attached to the second tripod and raised or lowered the tripod head until it lined up with the first camera. Then I attached a radio receiver to both cameras and stood in the middle with the transmitter. I took a light-meter reading and set the shutter speed and f-stop to get the correct exposure, then I pushed the button on the radio transmitter, firing the shutters of both cameras simultaneously.

No matter what camera systems are used, from 35 mm to eight-by-ten-inch, I have to use the same procedure to produce an accurate stereo effect. Two 35 mm cameras mounted side by side on a slider bar gives a base separation of seven inches between the lenses; therefore, I have to be careful how close the foreground is in relation to the lenses. If 28 mm lenses are used, I have to make sure that the subject is no closer than twelve feet. A 50 mm normal lens requires a distance of thirty feet from the closest object. The longer the lens, the farther away must be the foreground.

Even if only one camera is used, the distance I move the camera on the slider bar varies according to the relation between the foreground, the background, and the focal length of the lens. I

238

like to use a single Hasselblad six-by-six-centimeter square-format camera for many interior stereo photographs because it most approximates what the lens's circular image provides. (All lenses, when focused, project a circular image onto the film plane; the format of the camera dictates how much of that circular image will appear on the film.) For most interiors I use a 40 mm wide-angle lens and stop the lens down to a setting of f/22, which gives me the best depth of field possible—from three feet to infinity. I mount the camera

Two Hasselblad panoramic cameras on a sliding bar.

and slider bar on the tripod and compose the image in the viewfinder. Then I check my depth of field to make sure that the closest and farthest objects are in focus. Afterward, I determine how far I should move the camera on the slider bar for the second exposure. By keeping the lens set to f/22, my only adjustment for the correct exposure is the length of time that the shutter should remain open. Interiors are generally somewhat dark, so my shutter times are in the range of fifteen to ninety seconds. After the first exposure I move the camera and make a second exposure.

When the subject matter is an architectural exterior, I prefer to use two four-by-five-inch view cameras. These are the classic wooden cameras with leather bellows. The image on the ground glass is upside down and backward, and the photographer must place a dark cloth over his or her head and the camera in order to see and focus. The camera-lens plane and focus plane are adjustable, and the photographer can raise or lower the lens or slide and tilt the back. Each of these movements is indispensable for obtaining a correct image of the building. If the camera back is parallel with the wall of a building, the image on the focusing screen will appear straight and clear, but if the camera is tilted and the back is at an angle to the wall, the image will appear distorted. The photographer can either raise the lens or tilt both the camera back and the lens so they are parallel with the wall. I always focus and compose with one camera first, and then I set up the second camera according to all the stereo requirements. Because the building often is between thirty to seventy-five feet away, the separation between the cameras is usually between twelve and nineteen inches.

Exhibiting stereo images is a challenge, and at each of my shows I have attempted to demonstrate all the various methods of viewing them. In May 1998 I exhibited some of my stereo photography at the Christian Theological Seminary in Indianapolis. The show was titled *Nature as Theophany*, and in it I presented my stereo views of nature. To exhibit small prints, I used my 1870s stereoscope and my viewer with the vertically placed mirrors. What excited me was the opportunity to experiment with a type of display I had never seen before. I had six pairs of stereo images enlarged to forty-eight by forty-eight inches and mounted and framed. The seminary provided movable panels, and I arranged them in such a way to display three sets of prints using the Wheatstone technique of viewing. For each of these sets, I separated the two images and placed them so they faced each other at a distance of six feet. Then the gallery staff and I put a pedestal between them and placed two mirrors at right angles to each other on top of the pedestal, reflecting toward the images. Many visitors walking by wondered why two identical prints were facing each other, until they looked at the corner of the two mirrors. Then they were amazed at the three-dimensional world appearing as if real in front of them. The images were of a creek bed in the woods during early spring, and the visitors felt as if they could almost put their hands under fallen branches or even pick up rocks. Because the prints were forty-eight by forty-eight inches and viewed from a dis-

tance of thirty-six inches, visitors had the illusion that they were actually in the woods. This was a replication of Wheatstone's original demonstration, and everyone involved learned from it as had the early scientists.

My next stereo exhibition also occurred in Indianapolis in October 1998 at the Photography Gallery, owned by Robert and June Green. I mounted and framed about forty pairs of stereo prints, each individual print enlarged to eight by eight inches; with the two prints placed beside each other, the finished stereo view was eight by sixteen inches. In addition to the display techniques used in the first exhibition, I made available my side-by-side handheld mirror viewer. I attempted to instruct each person who came to the gallery how to use the viewer. Once visitors caught on to the technique, they could walk around the gallery and see all the images in three dimensions.

An area of stereoscopy that I have not worked with involves the use of digital cameras and computers, but I do hope to work with them soon. There are new methods for viewing three-dimensional images on monitors and HDTV screens using liquid-crystal shutter glasses. These look like sunglasses, but each lens contains a liquid crystal that can be turned on and off and synchronized to the refresh rate of the screen. As the left stereo image appears on the screen, the liquid

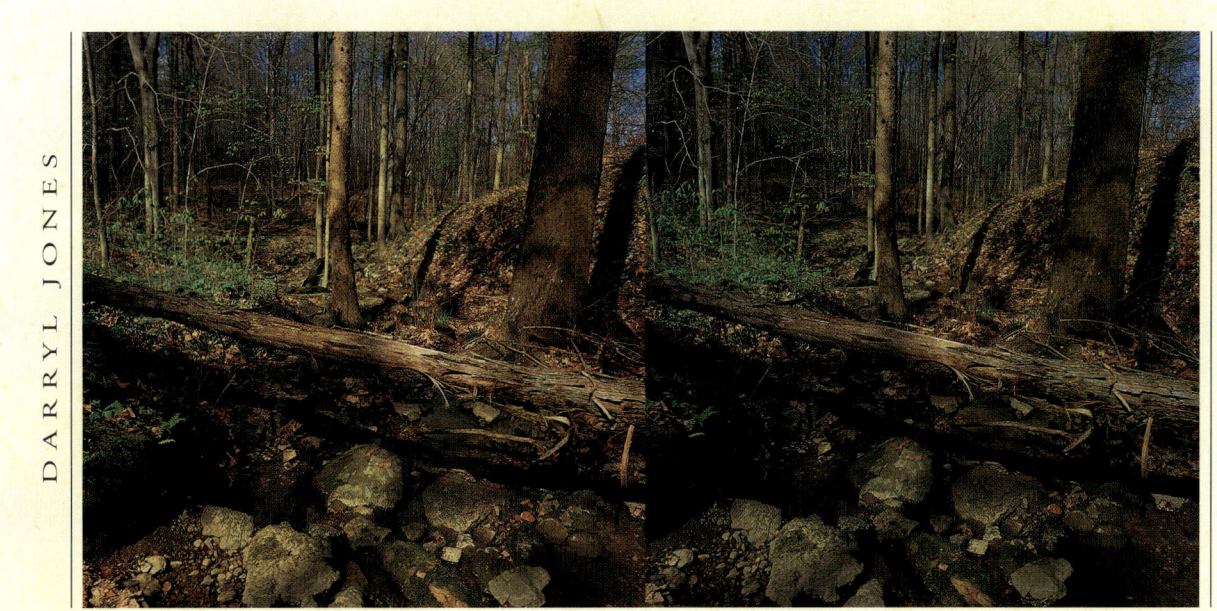

DARRYL JONES

Freedom, Indiana

Owen County woods, 1998.

crystal closes in the right-eye lens so that the left eye sees only the left image. One-sixtieth of a second later the screen changes to the right stereo image, and the liquid crystal in the left-eye lens closes so that the right eye sees only the right image. When this happens sixty times per second, the brain does not detect the two separate images but sees them as one three-dimensional image.

Stereo photography is as old as the history of photography itself, but as demonstrated above, it remains a viable process with the adoption of modern technologies. I encourage all contemporary photographers to experiment with both old and new techniques for taking stereo images. All of us—even amateur photographers—can create the types of scenes we loved so much when we were children looking through the View-Master, and by exploring and enhancing the art of stereoscopy, we can continue to add depth and dimension to our life experience.

DARRYL JONES *is known for photographing the people and places of his native Indiana. He provided images for* Destination Indiana: Travels through Hoosier History *and* A Simple and Vital Design: The Story of the Indiana Post Office Murals, *both published by the Indiana Historical Society. His photographs have also been featured in the books* Indiana, Indiana II, Indianapolis, *and* The Spirit of the Place: Indiana Hill Country.

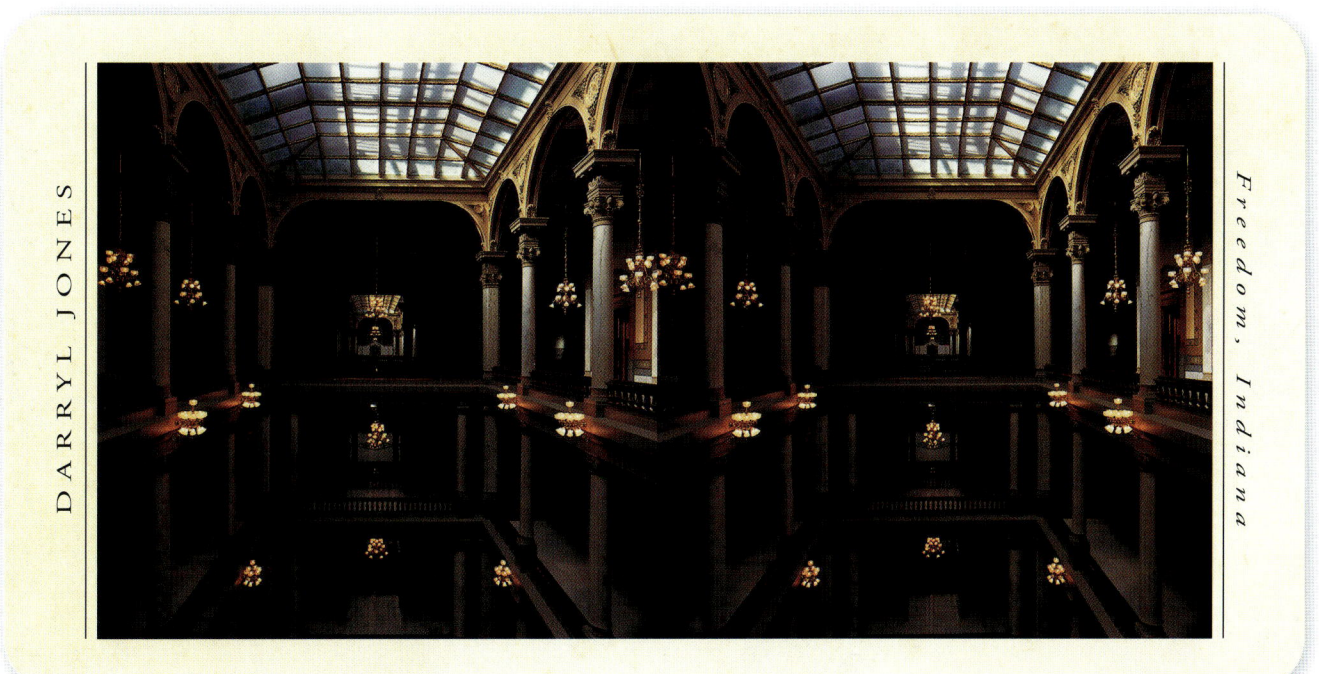

Indiana State Capitol, Indianapolis, 1999. Indiana's statehouse was completed in 1888, and in the ensuing decades it saw much redecoration and renovation. In the late 1980s the state legislature authorized a restoration to return the structure to its original appearance in time for its centennial. A historical view of the exterior is found on page 85.

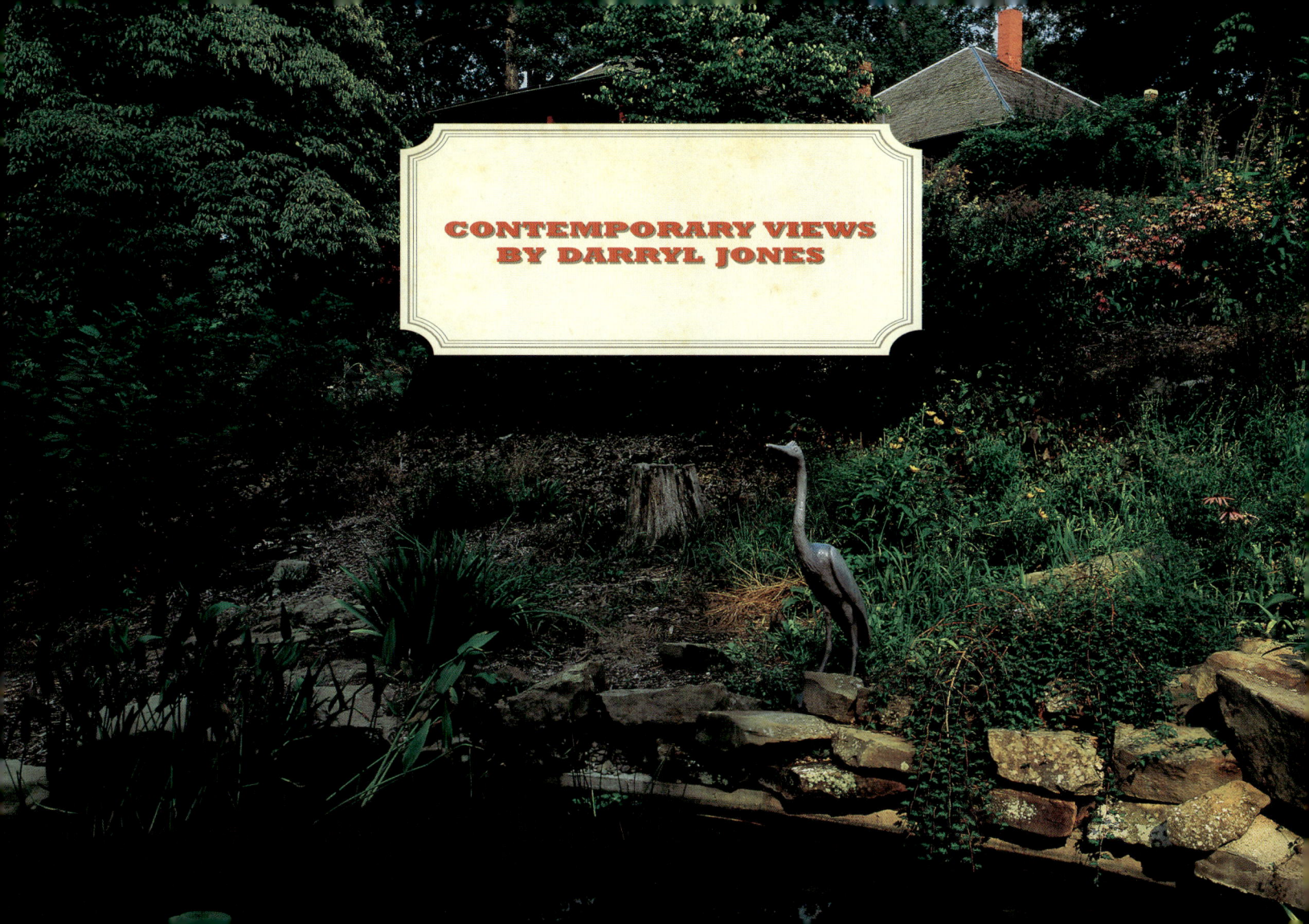

CONTEMPORARY VIEWS
BY DARRYL JONES

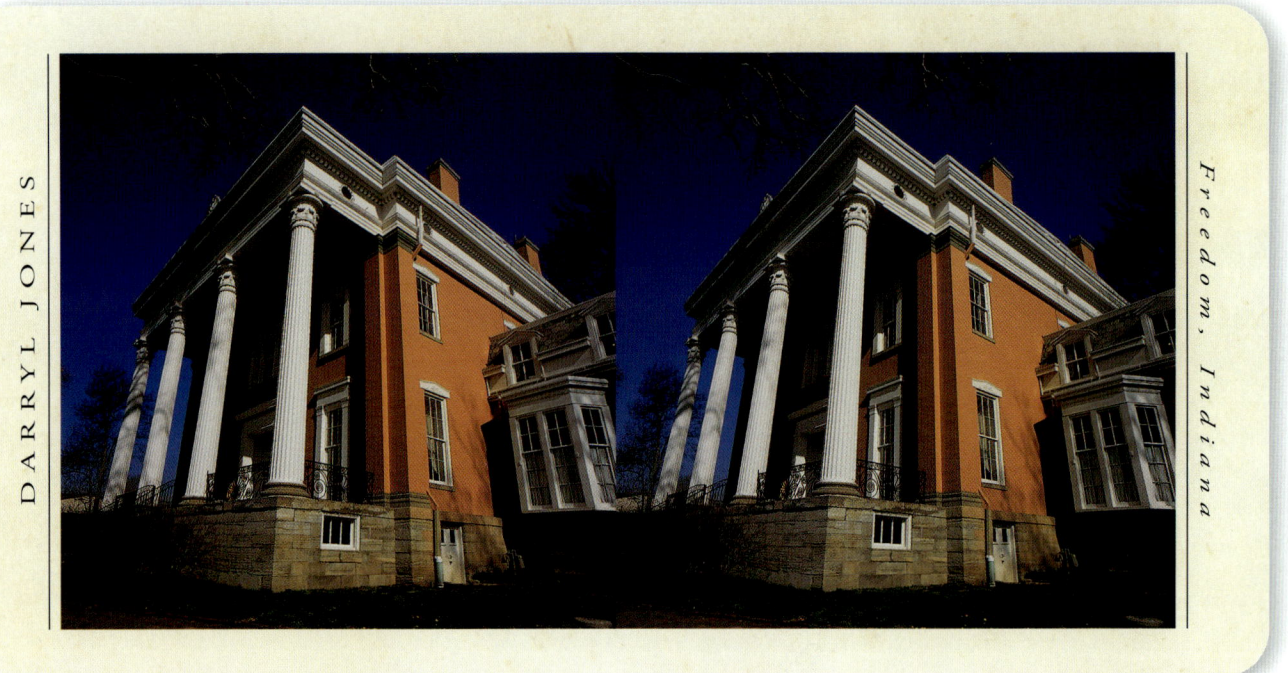

DARRYL JONES

Freedom, Indiana

*Lanier Mansion, Madison, 1999. James F. D. Lanier, a prominent banker, built this home in the early 1840s. Though he lived in it
for only seven years, family members continued to own it until 1925, when they turned it over to the state as a memorial.
Visitors to the home are rewarded with majestic views of the Ohio River.*

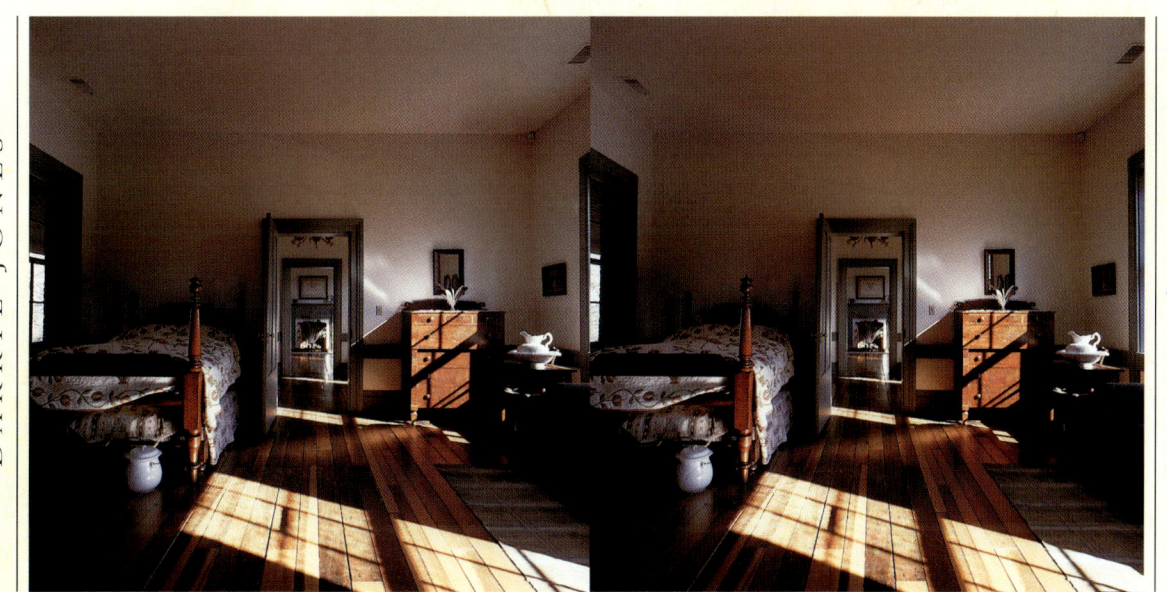

Colonel William Jones State Historic Site, Gentryville, 1999.
Jones, a Spencer County storekeeper, employed Abraham Lincoln when the latter was a young man in Indiana. After he became
an Illinois attorney, Lincoln returned to Spencer County for a visit and stayed in this home, which Jones built around 1834.

DARRYL JONES

Freedom, Indiana

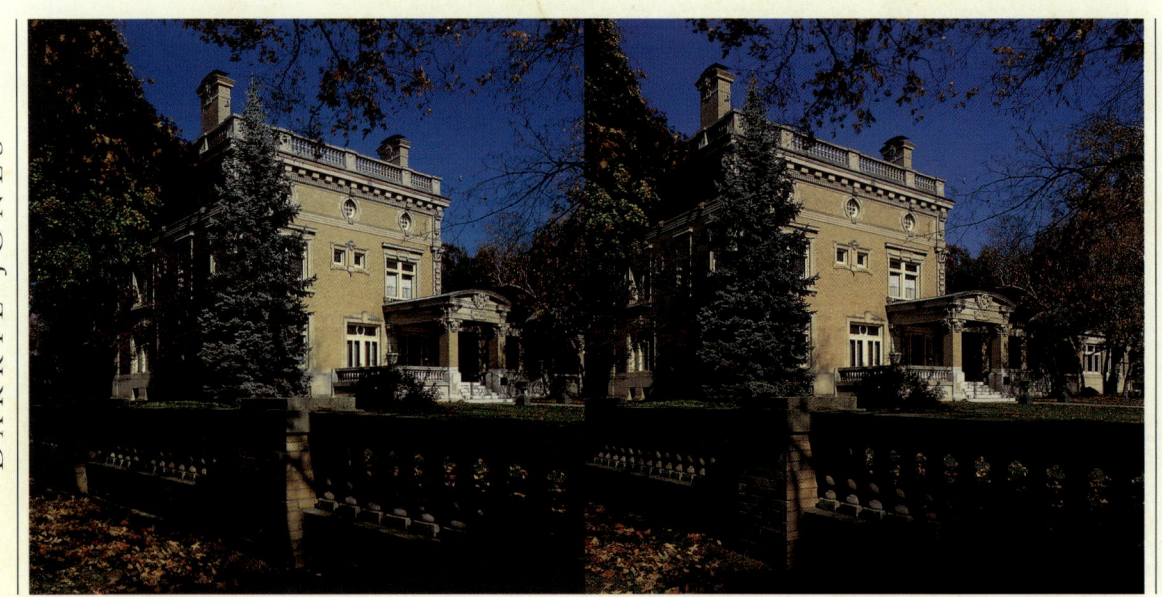

Ruthmere, Elkhart, 1999. Ruthmere was the home of A. R. and Elizabeth Beardsley. A. R. Beardsley, the general manager of the Miles Medical Company, ordered the three-story Beaux Arts–style mansion built with as many local materials as possible. He and his wife lived in the home from 1910 until their deaths in 1924.

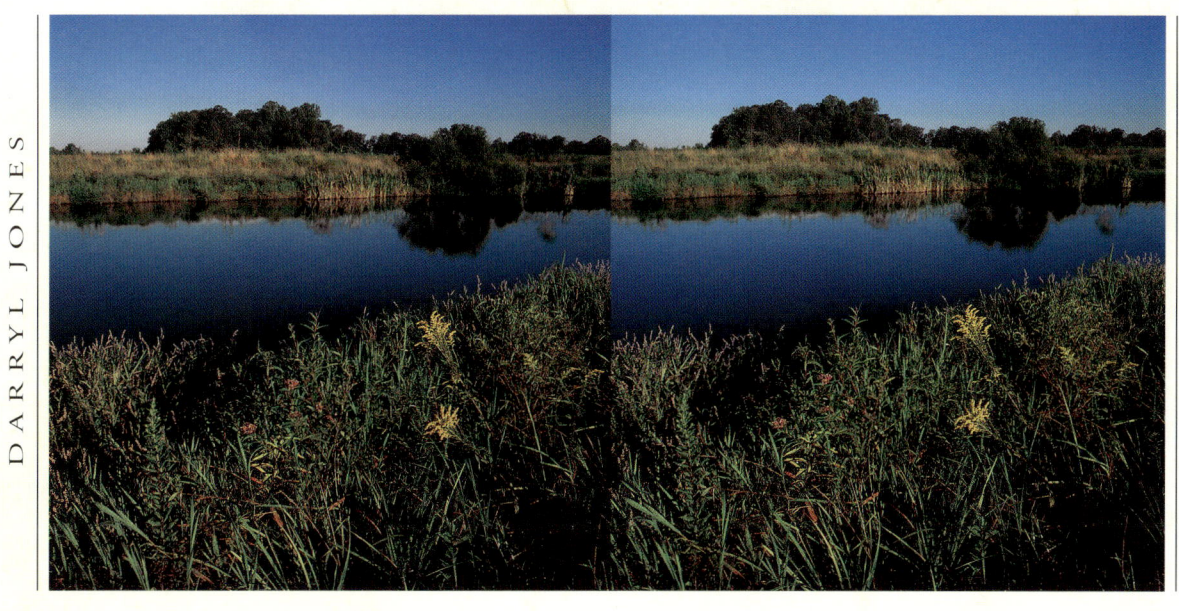

Owen County pond, 1998.

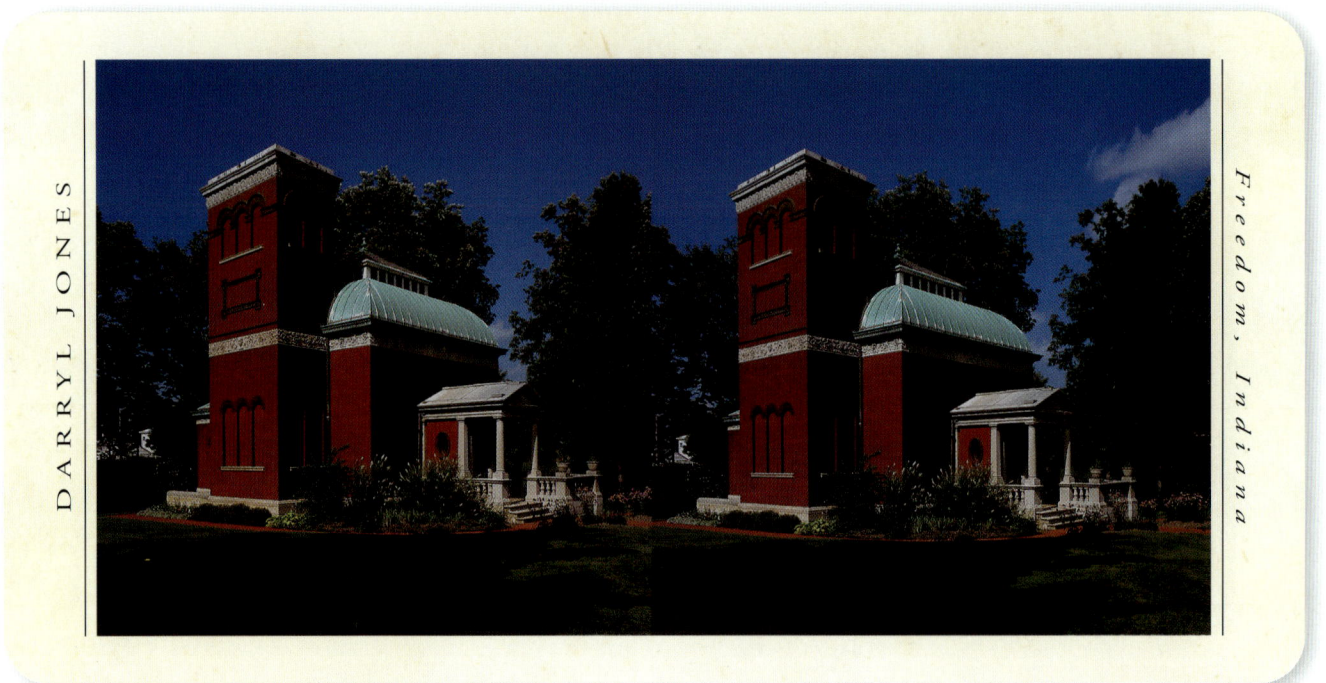

General Lew Wallace Study and Ben-Hur Museum, Crawfordsville, 1999. Wallace served as a general in the Civil War, as a governor of the New Mexico Territory, and as an ambassador to Turkey, but he is best known for his novel Ben-Hur *and other books. He worked out of this one-room study in Crawfordsville.*

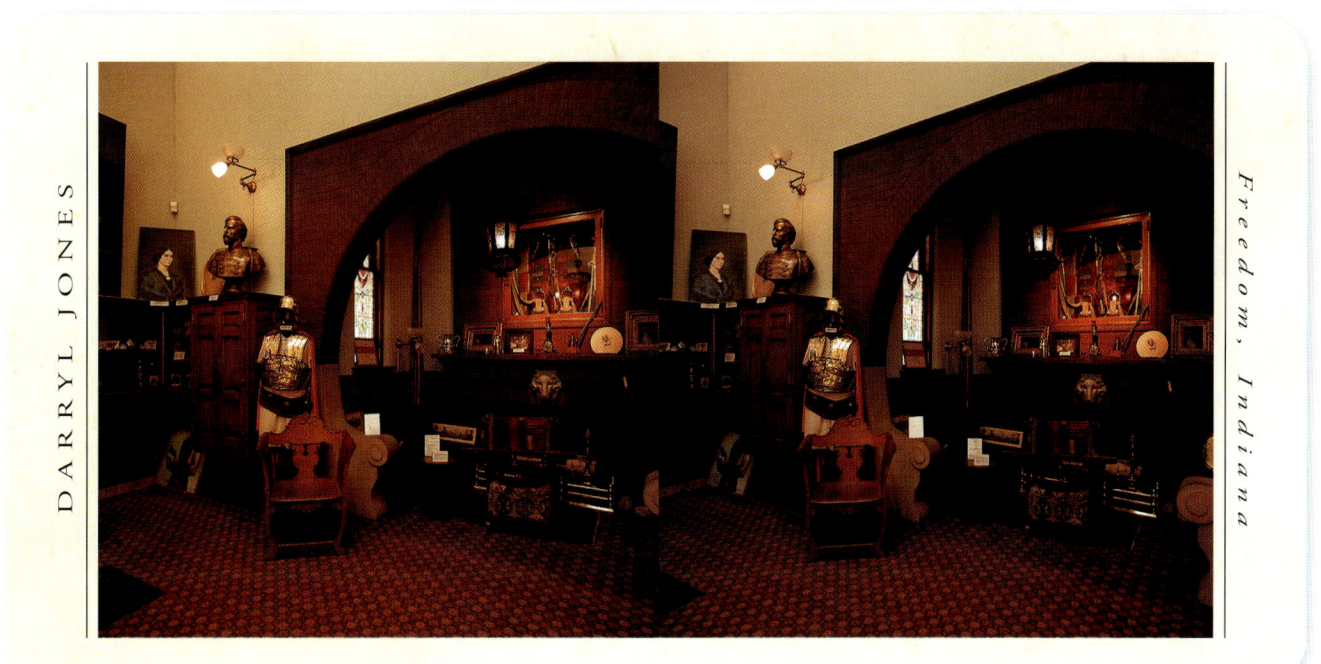

DARRYL JONES

Freedom, Indiana

General Lew Wallace Study and Ben-Hur Museum, Crawfordsville, 1999.

DARRYL JONES

Freedom, Indiana

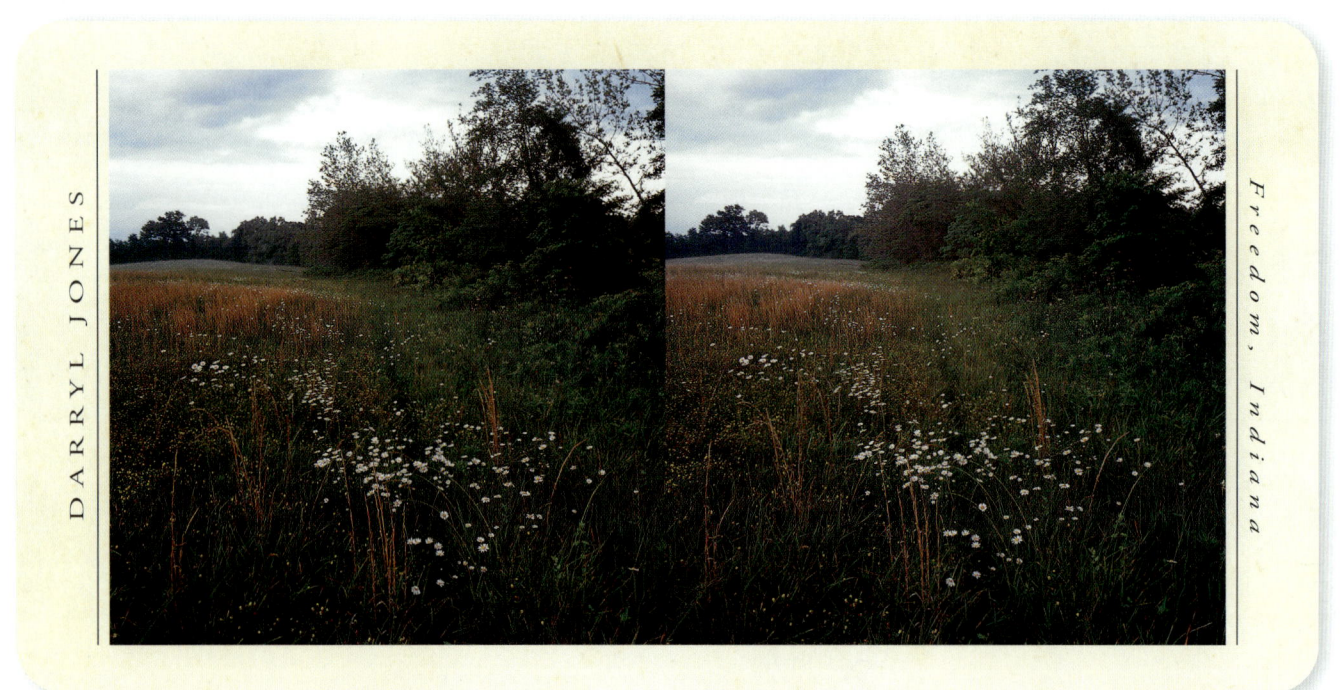

Owen County field, 1998.

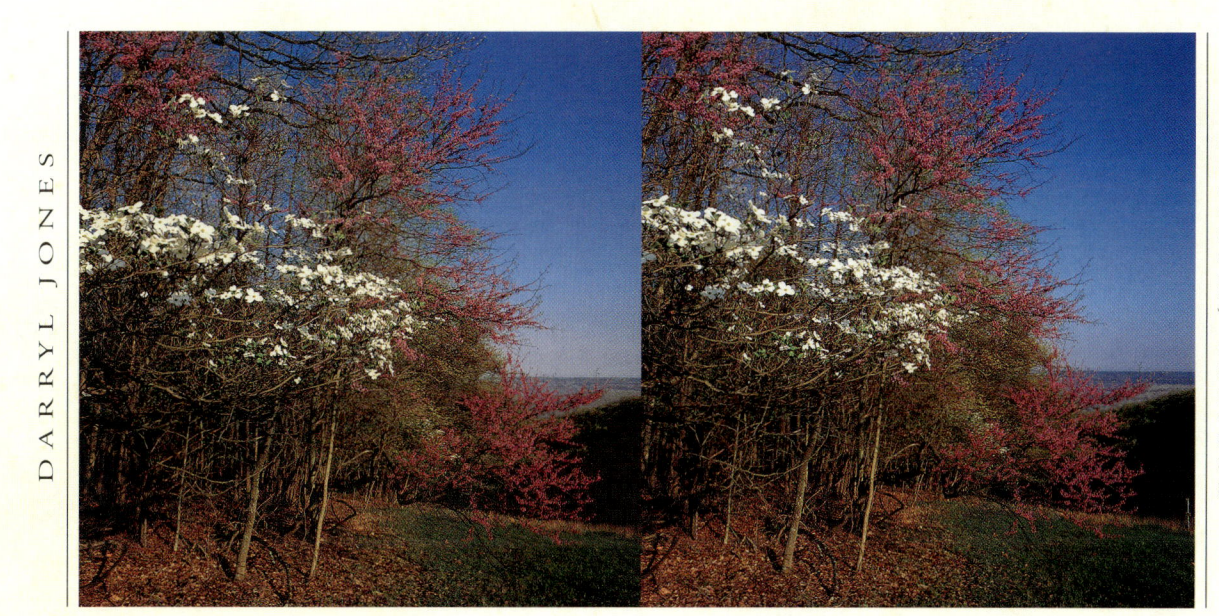

Owen County woods, 1998.

DARRYL JONES

Freedom, Indiana

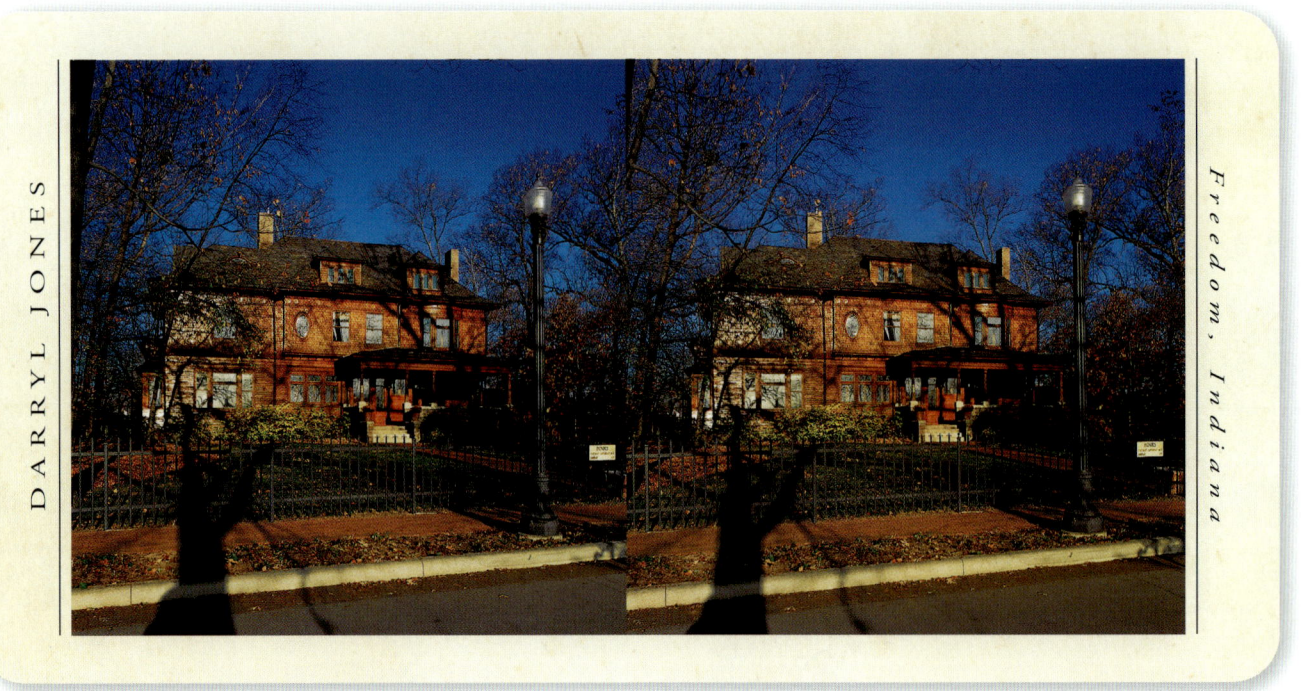

Oakhurst, Muncie, 1999. George A. Ball, one of five brothers who founded the Ball Brothers Glass Manufacturing Company, built this home in the 1890s. Today it is noted for its attractive gardens, which are open to the public.

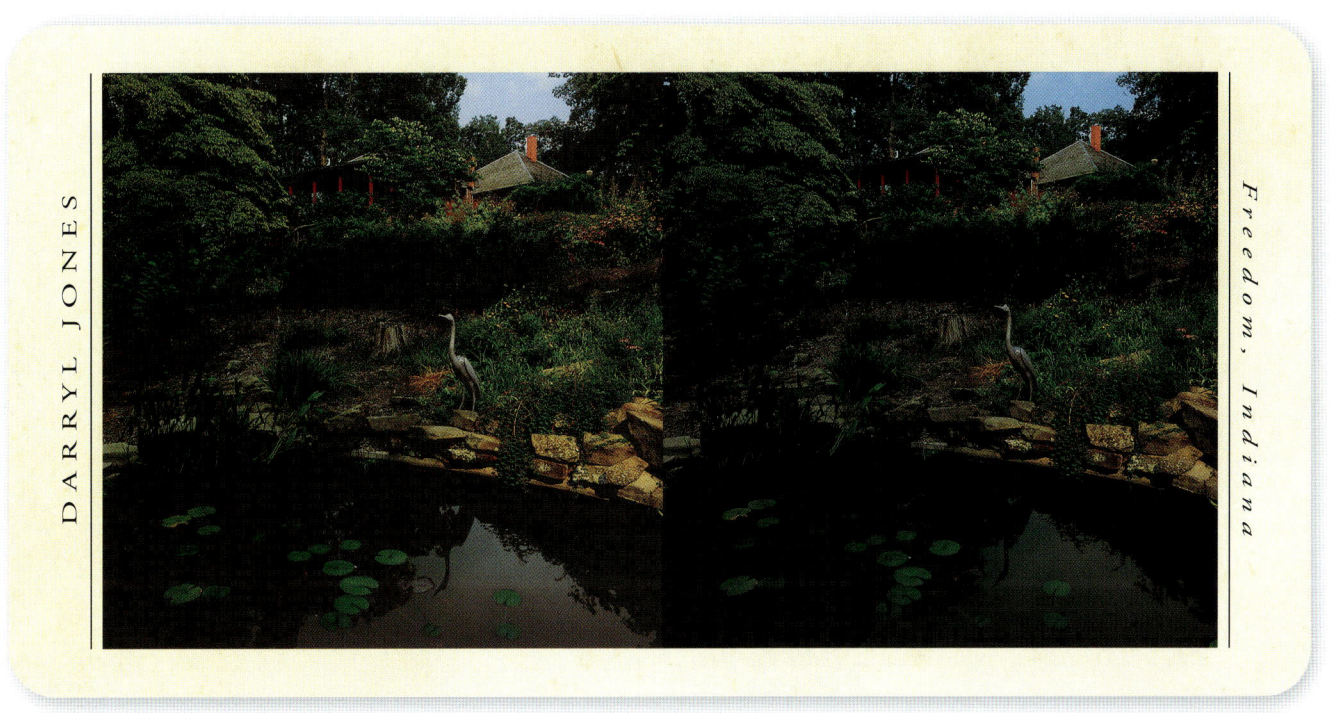

255

T. C. Steele State Historic Site, Belmont, 1999. Steele, a celebrated member of the Hoosier Group artists, built this Brown County home in 1907. He featured the surrounding landscape in many of his paintings.

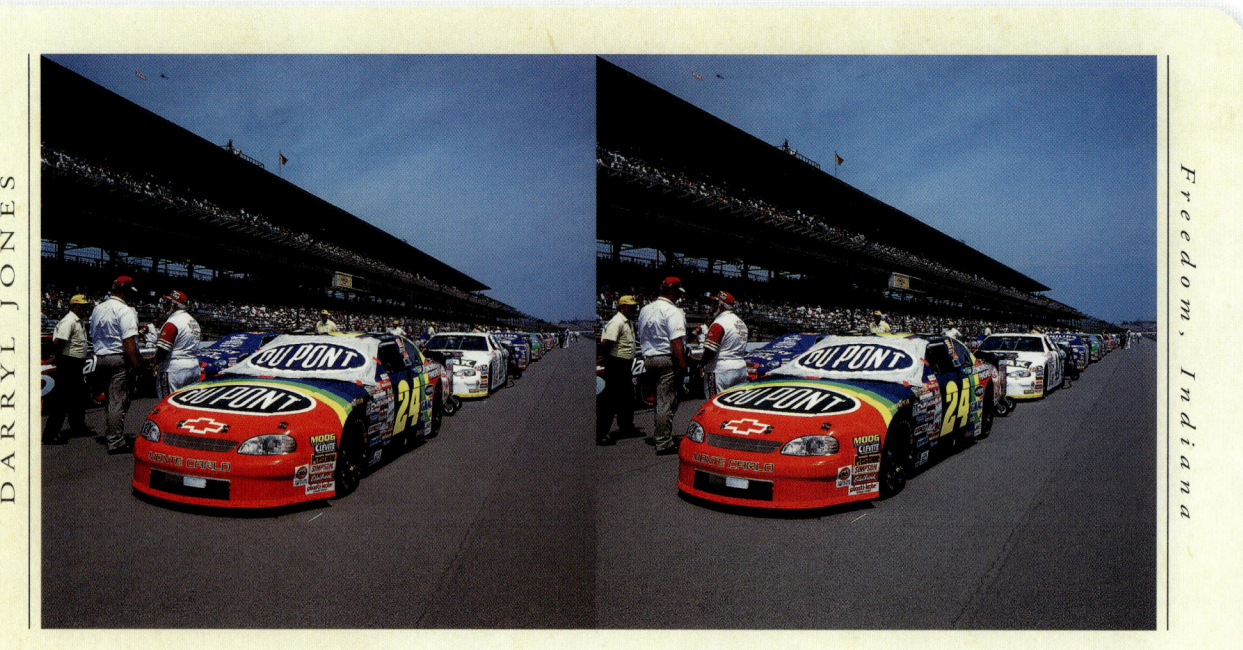

Indianapolis Motor Speedway, 1999. Jeff Gordon's car is at the start of the lineup for the Brickyard 400.

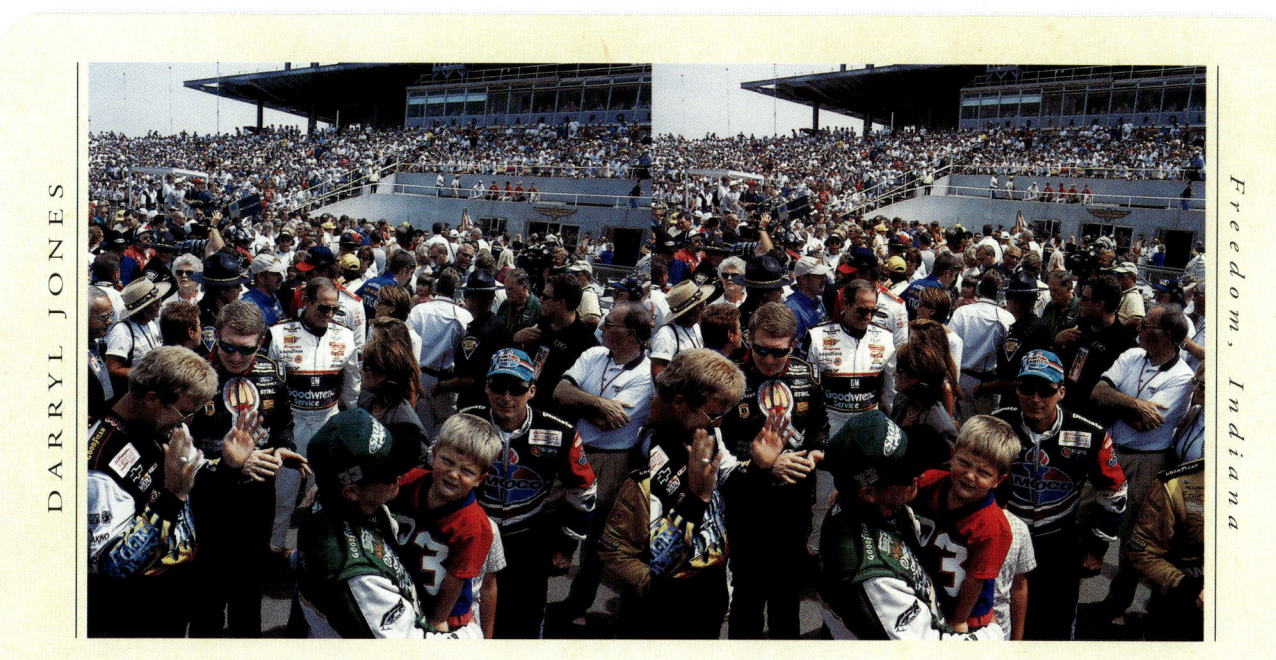

Indianapolis Motor Speedway, 1999. This view, taken at the Brickyard 400, features Dale Earnhardt, left of center in the white racing suit, and other popular drivers.

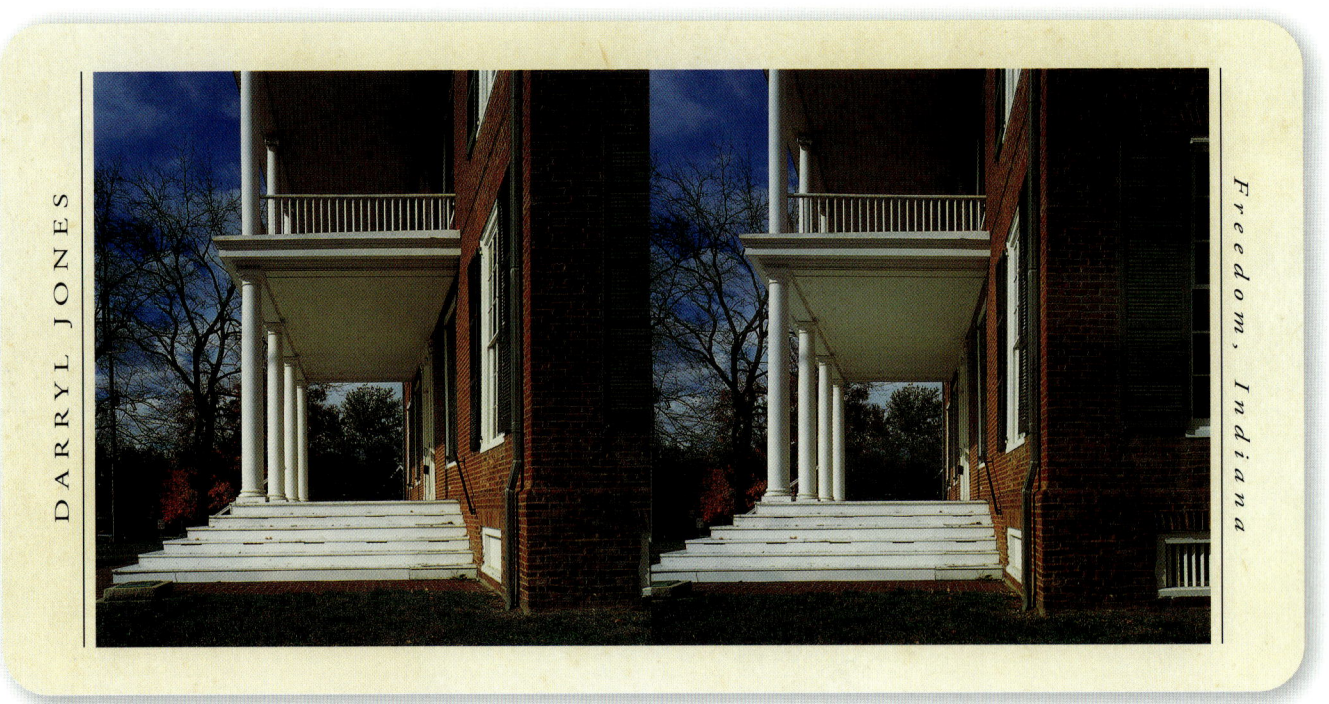

DARRYL JONES

Freedom, Indiana

Grouseland, Vincennes, 1999. William Henry Harrison built Grouseland in 1803–1804 while serving as governor of the Indiana Territory and lived there until his term ended in 1812. Some claim the house was the first brick structure built in the territory.

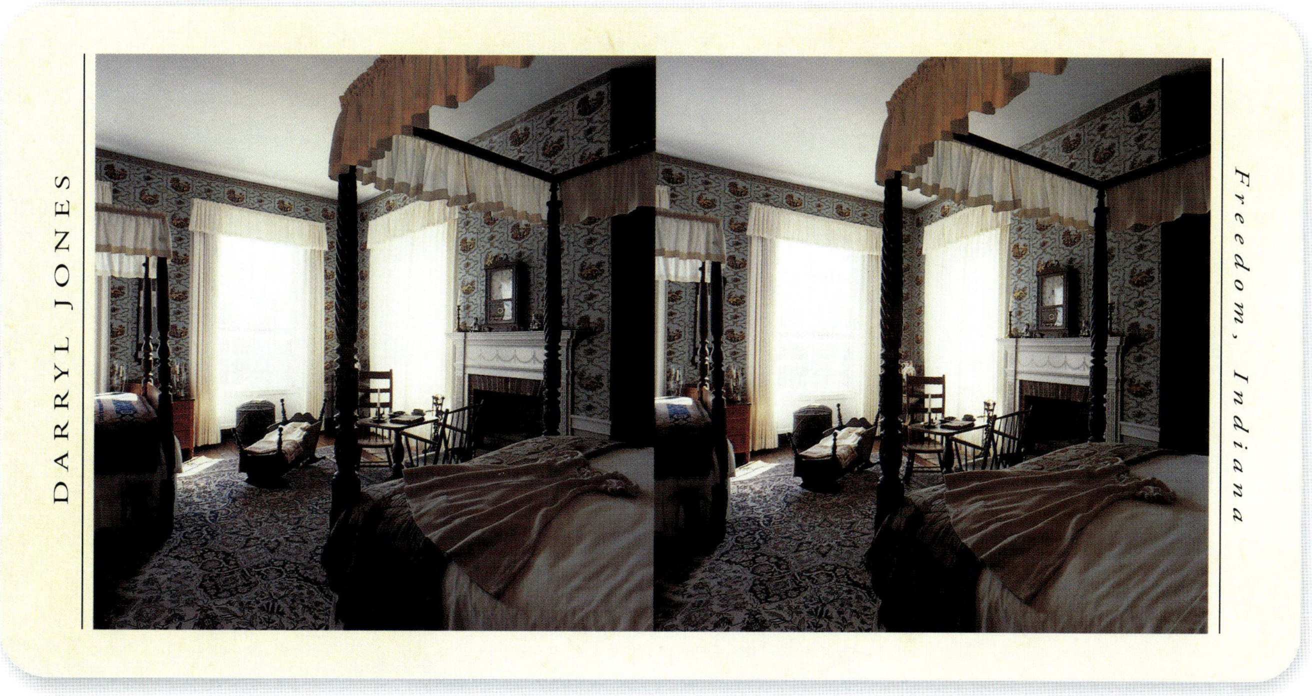

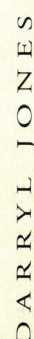

DARRYL JONES

Freedom, Indiana

Grouseland, Vincennes, 1999.

DARRYL JONES

Freedom, Indiana

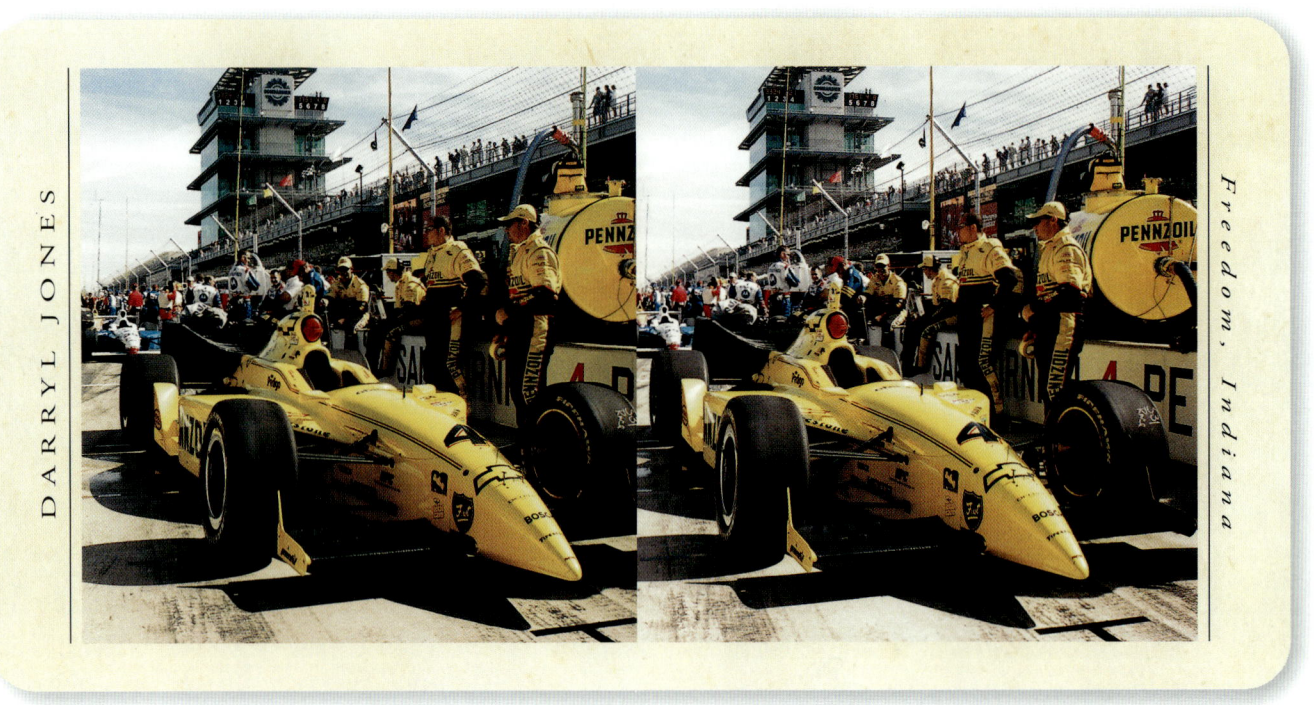

Indianapolis Motor Speedway, 2002. Sam Hornish's pit crew takes a break before the start of the Indianapolis 500. A comparison of this view with the similar one on page 233 shows many changes at the Speedway, including a new pagoda-style scoring tower and luxury suites.

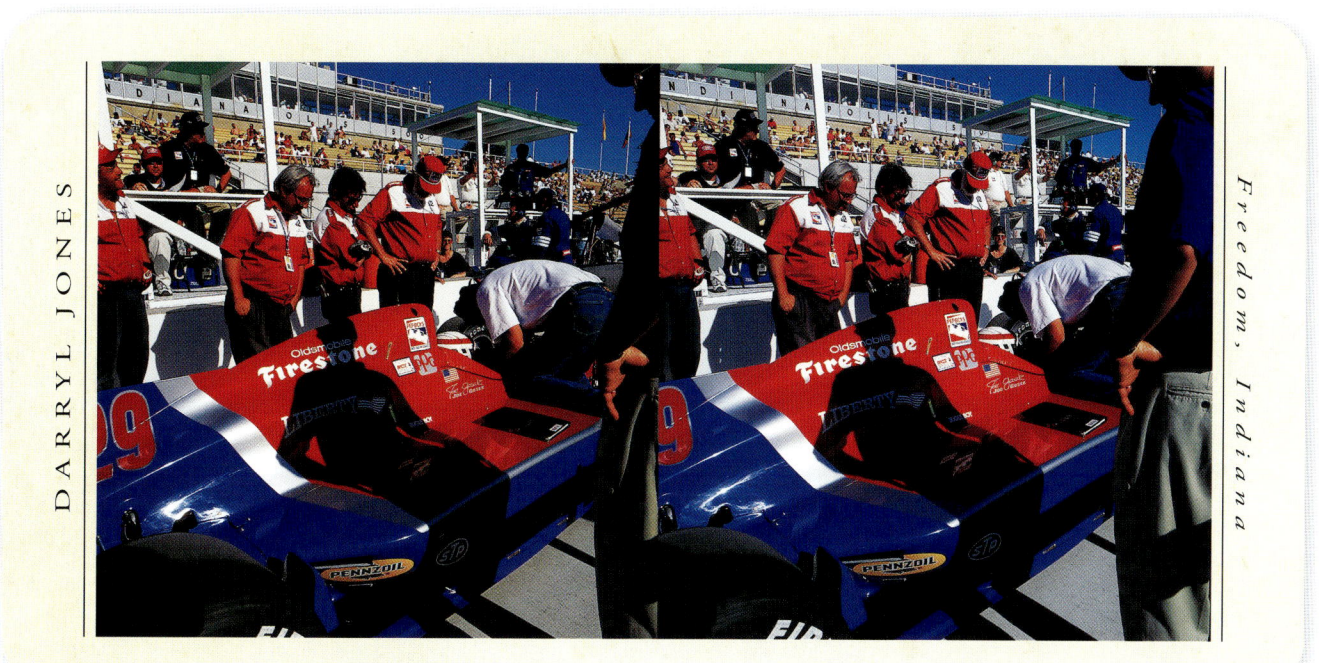

DARRYL JONES

Freedom, Indiana

Indianapolis Motor Speedway, 1998. A pit crew examines a car during time trials for the Indianapolis 500.

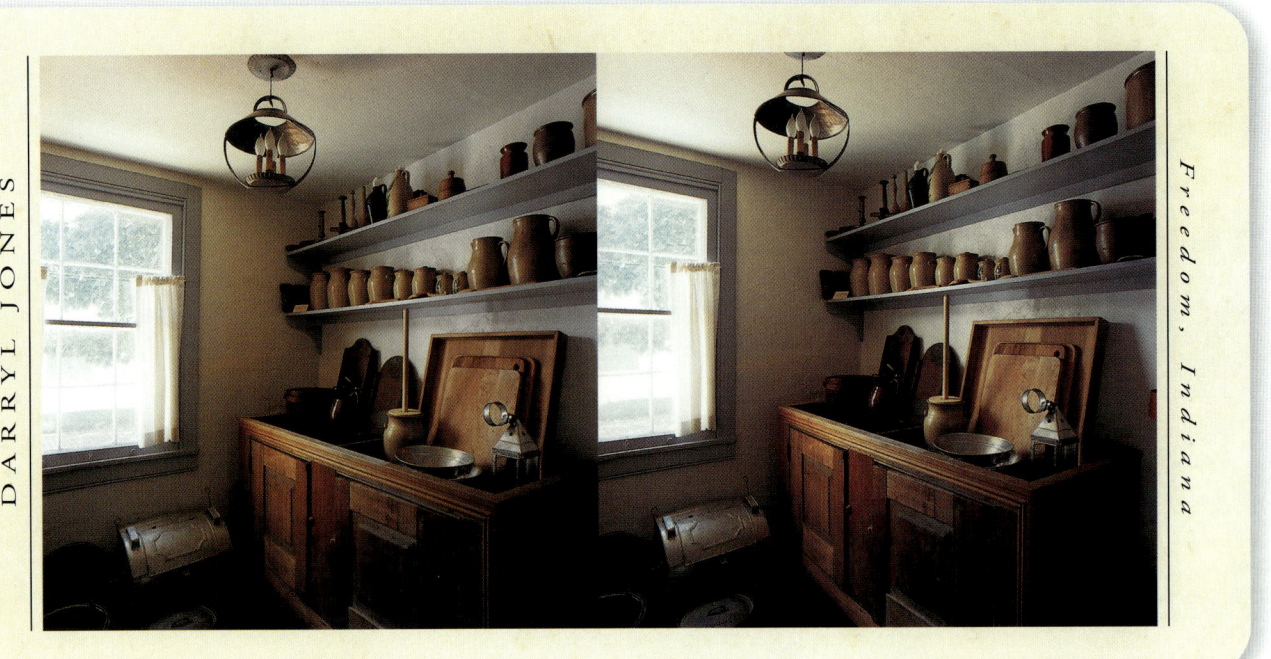

DARRYL JONES

Freedom, Indiana

Huddleston Farmhouse Inn Museum, near Cambridge City, 1999. John and Susannah Huddleston built this home along the National Road in the early 1840s. It was a popular resting place for weary nineteenth-century travelers.

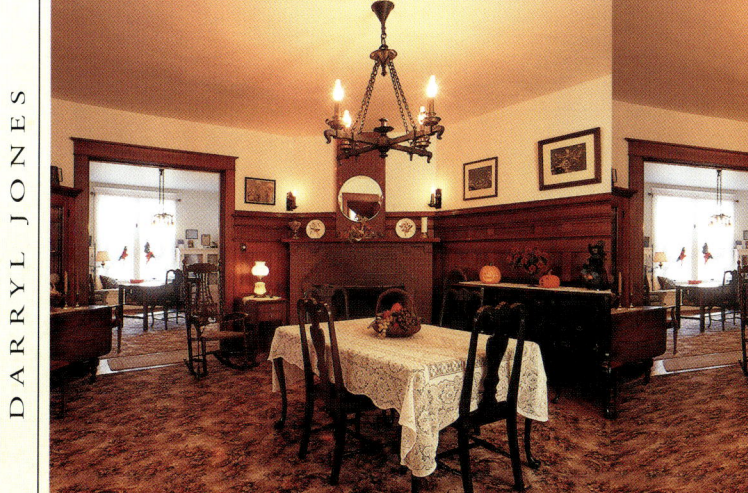

Gene Stratton-Porter State Historic Site, Rome City, 1999. Stratton-Porter, a popular author in the early 1900s, was an avid naturalist. She built this home on the shores of Sylvan Lake in 1913.

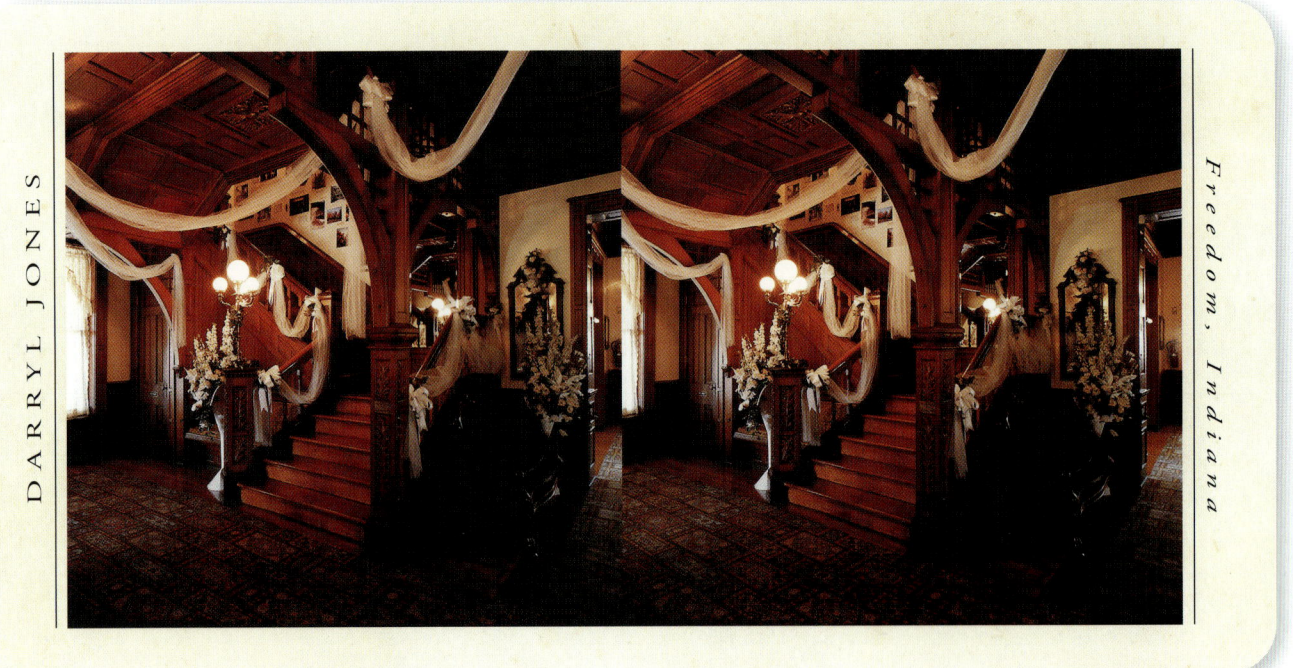

DARRYL JONES

Freedom, Indiana

Seiberling Mansion, Kokomo, 1999. Monroe Seiberling owned a glass company in Kokomo in the late 1880s and early 1890s and during that time constructed this stately home for his family.

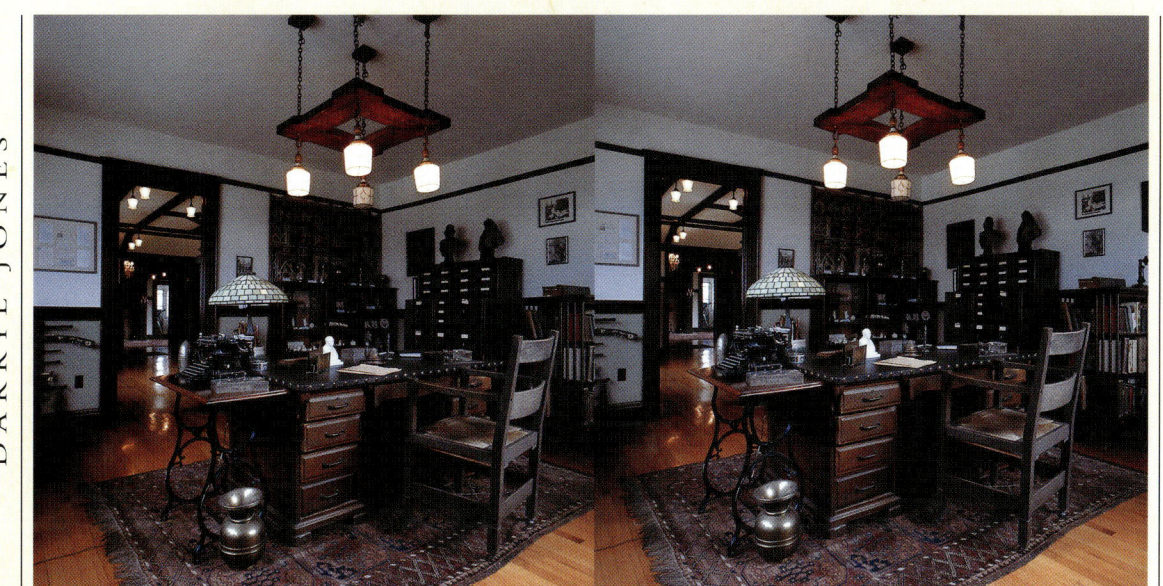

Hazelden, Brook, 1999. Hazelden was the home of George Ade, a popular essayist and playwright at the turn of the twentieth century, and was noted for the parties and celebrations its owner hosted.

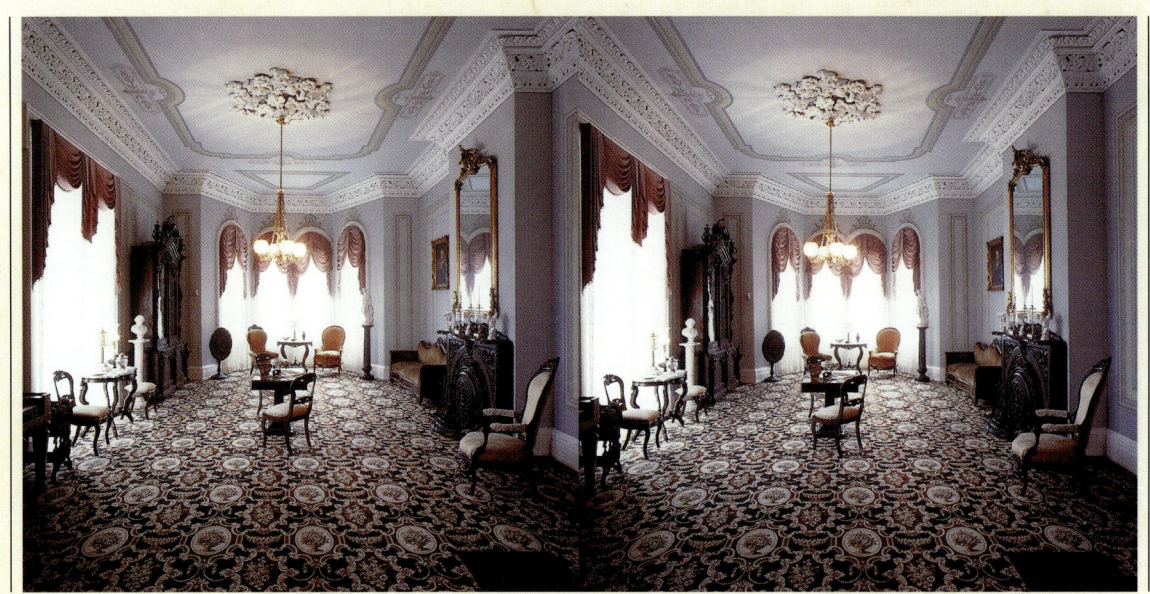

Hillforest, Aurora, 1999. Thomas Gaff, a brewer and distiller in the Ohio River town of Aurora,
built this home in 1855. It features a porch and balcony reminiscent of a steamboat deck.

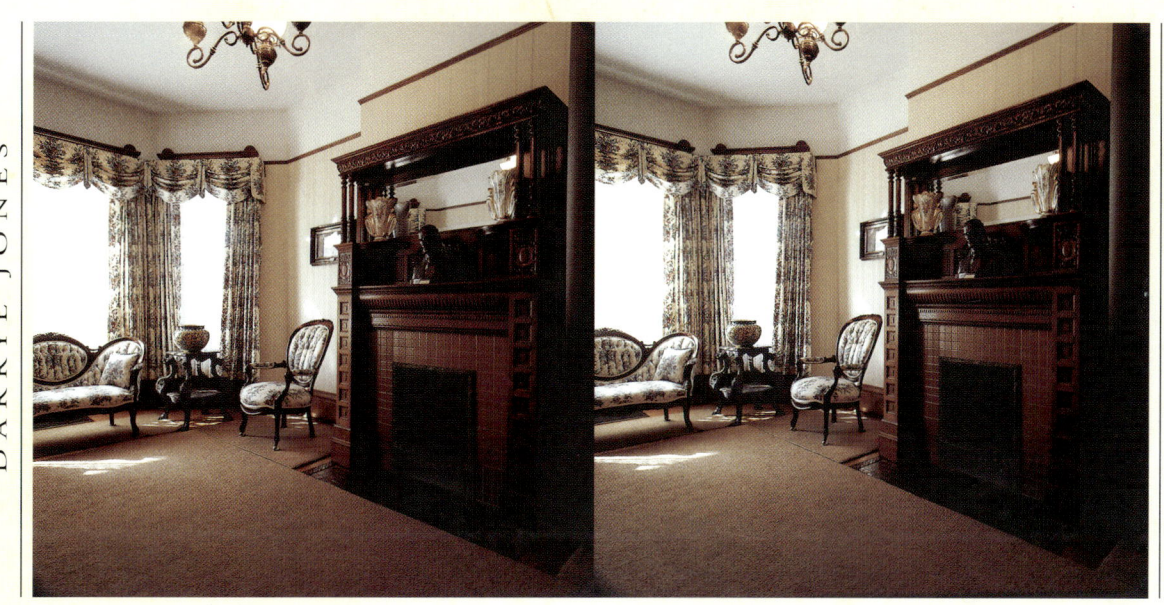

Eugene V. Debs Home, Terre Haute, 1999. Debs, the well-known union activist and five-time presidential candidate, lived in this house from 1890 until 1926.

DARRYL JONES

Freedom, Indiana

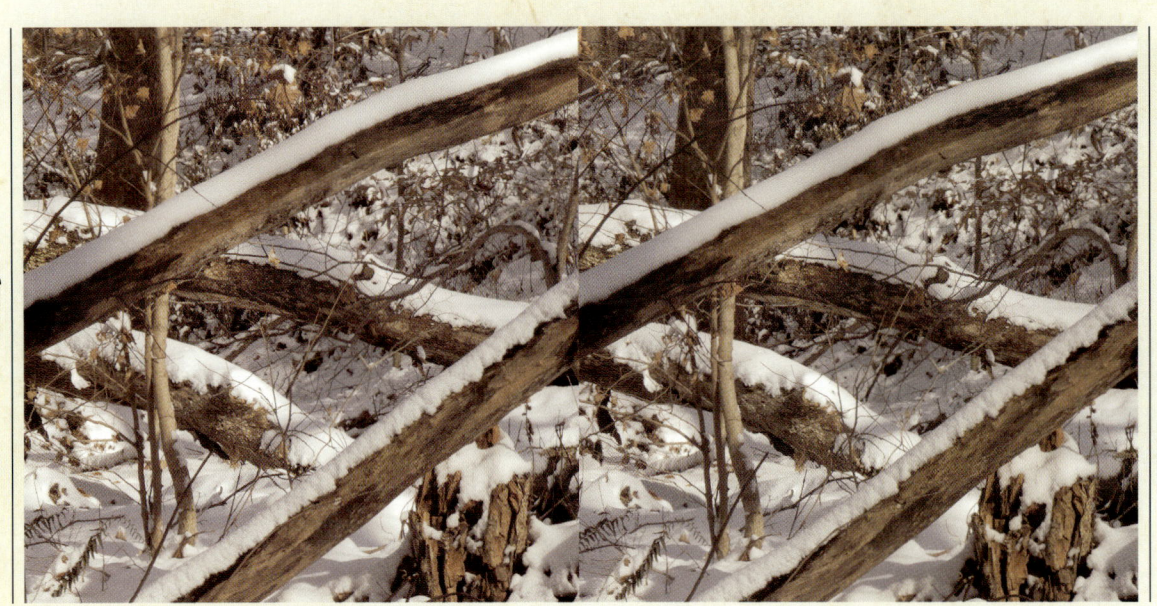

Owen County woods, 2002.

DARRYL JONES

Freedom, Indiana

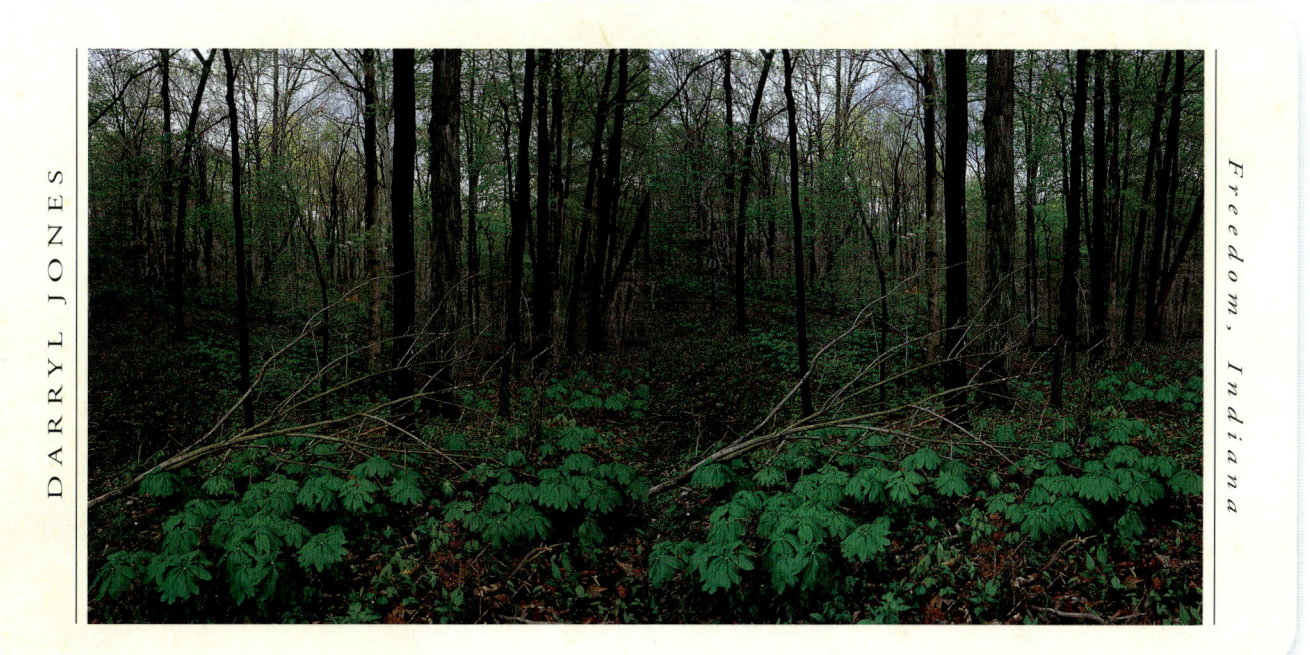

Owen County woods, 1998.

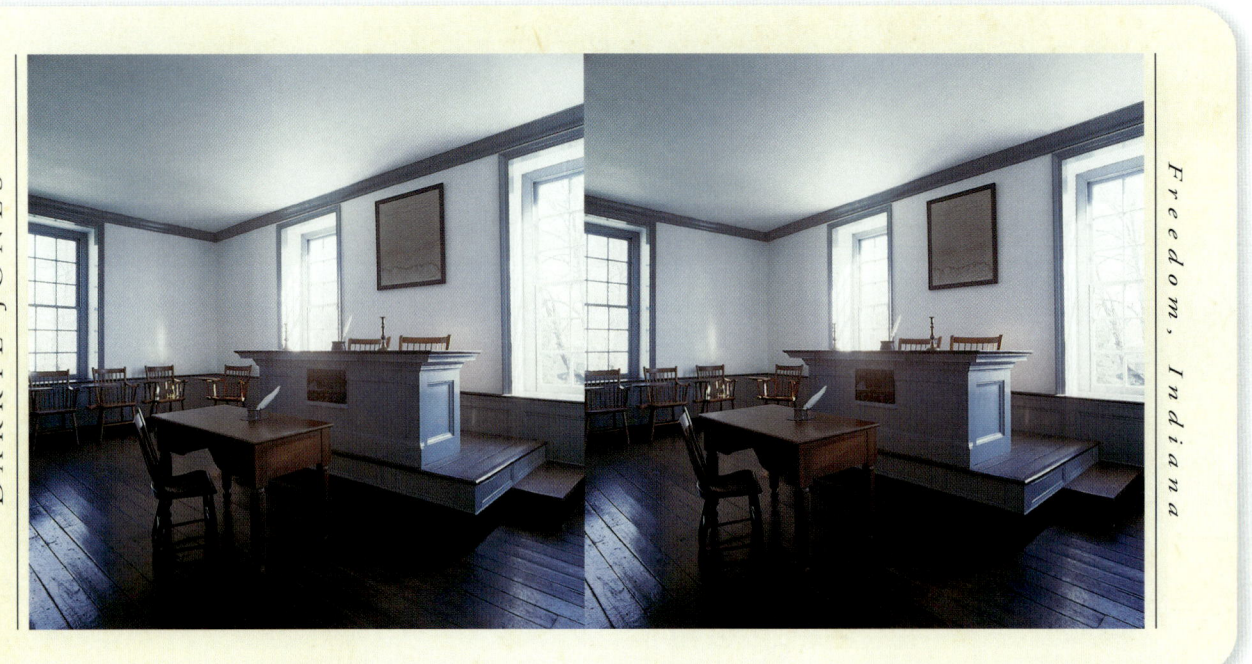

DARRYL JONES

Freedom, Indiana

*Corydon Capitol State Historic Site, Corydon, 1999. This building served
as Indiana's capitol from 1816 to 1825.*

DARRYL JONES

Freedom, Indiana

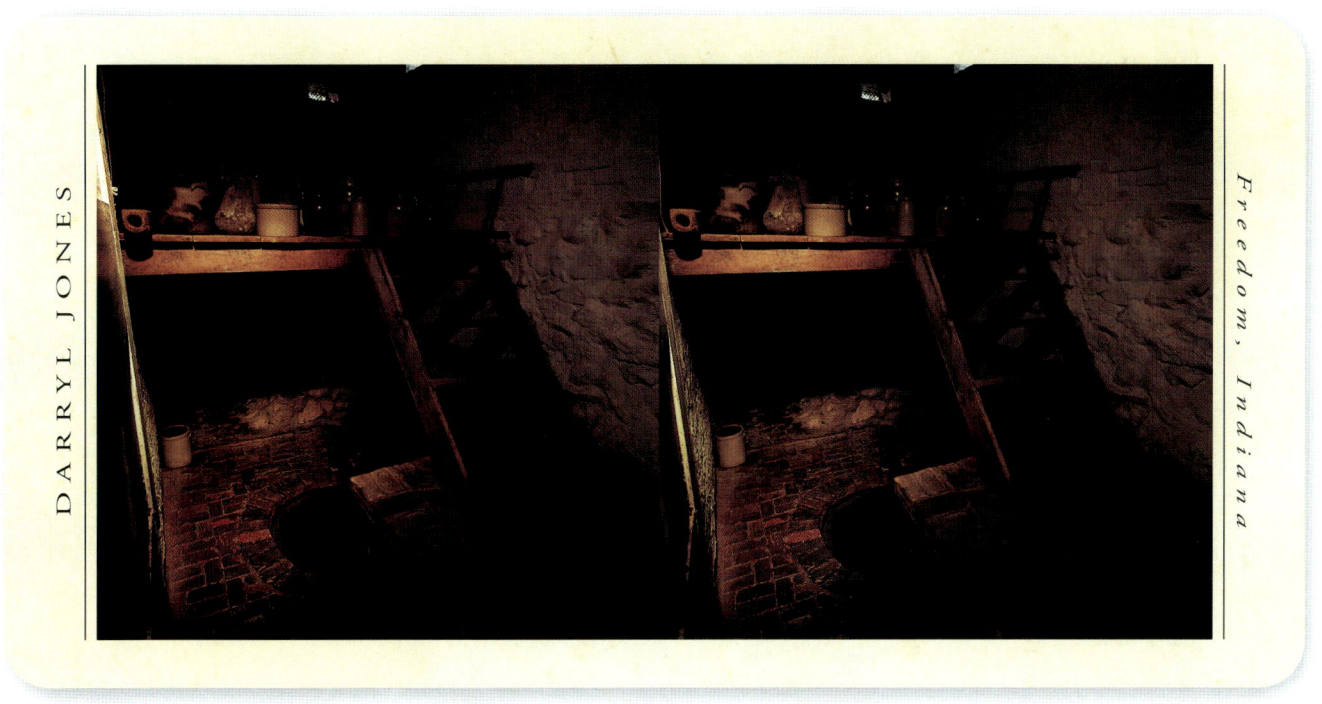

Levi Coffin State Historic Site, Fountain City, 1999.
Coffin and his wife, Catharine, lived in this home from 1839 to 1847 and during that time helped thousands of African Americans flee slavery.
They sheltered so many runaway slaves in their home that it became known as the Grand Central Station of the Underground Railroad.

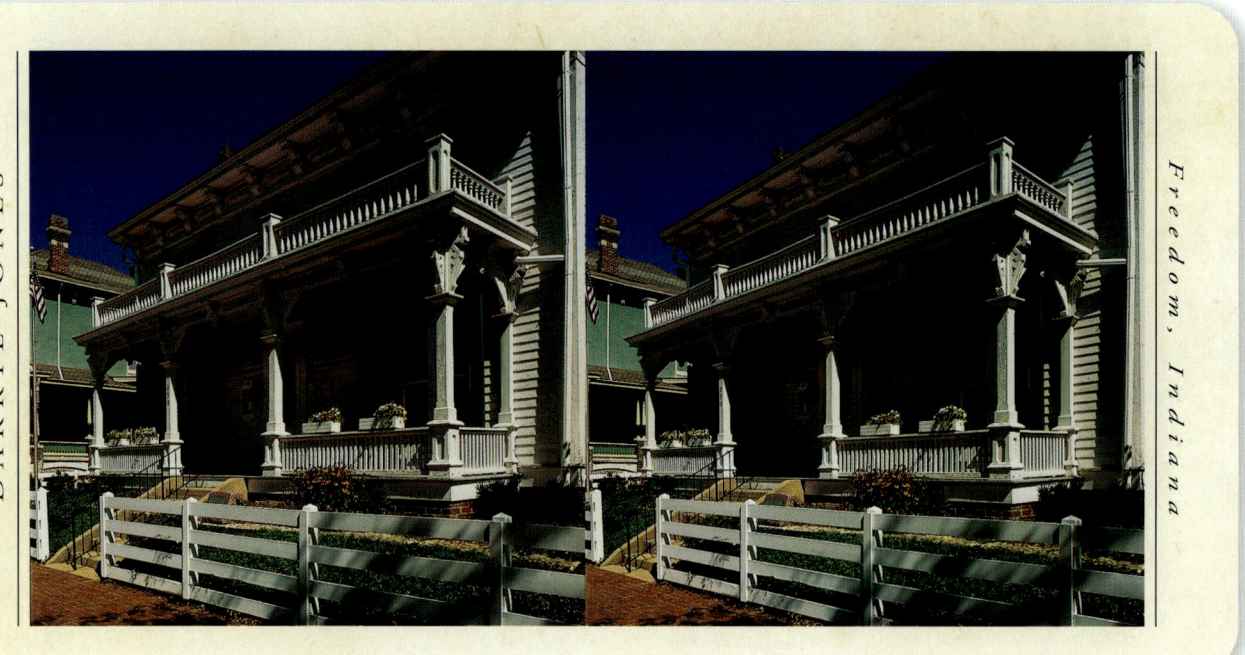

272

DARRYL JONES

Freedom, Indiana

James Whitcomb Riley Old Home and Museum, Greenfield, 1999.
Riley, popular in the late nineteenth and early twentieth centuries for his homespun verse, grew up in this house.
His father built it in 1850, and today the city of Greenfield operates it as a museum.

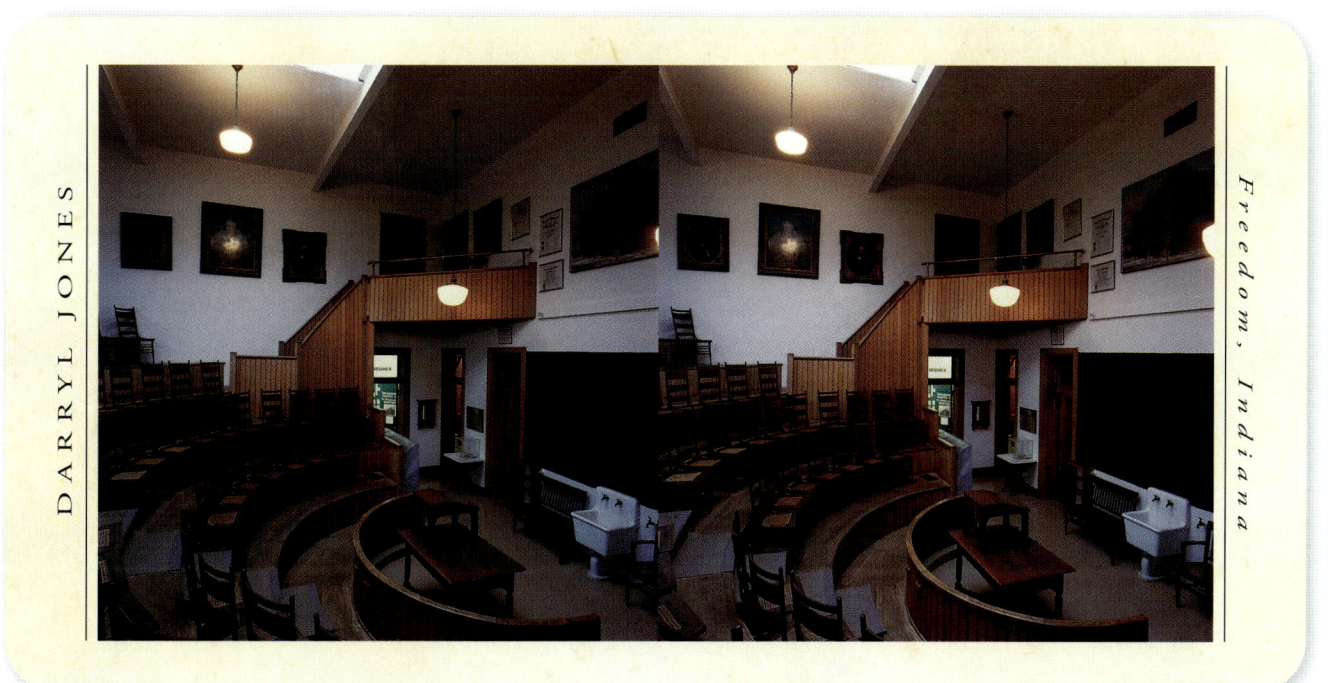

DARRYL JONES

Freedom, Indiana

Indiana Medical History Museum, Indianapolis, 1999.
The museum operates out of the old Pathology Building at the former Central Indiana Hospital for the Insane. The building opened in the 1890s
with state-of-the-art research facilities, and it served as a laboratory and classroom until the 1950s.

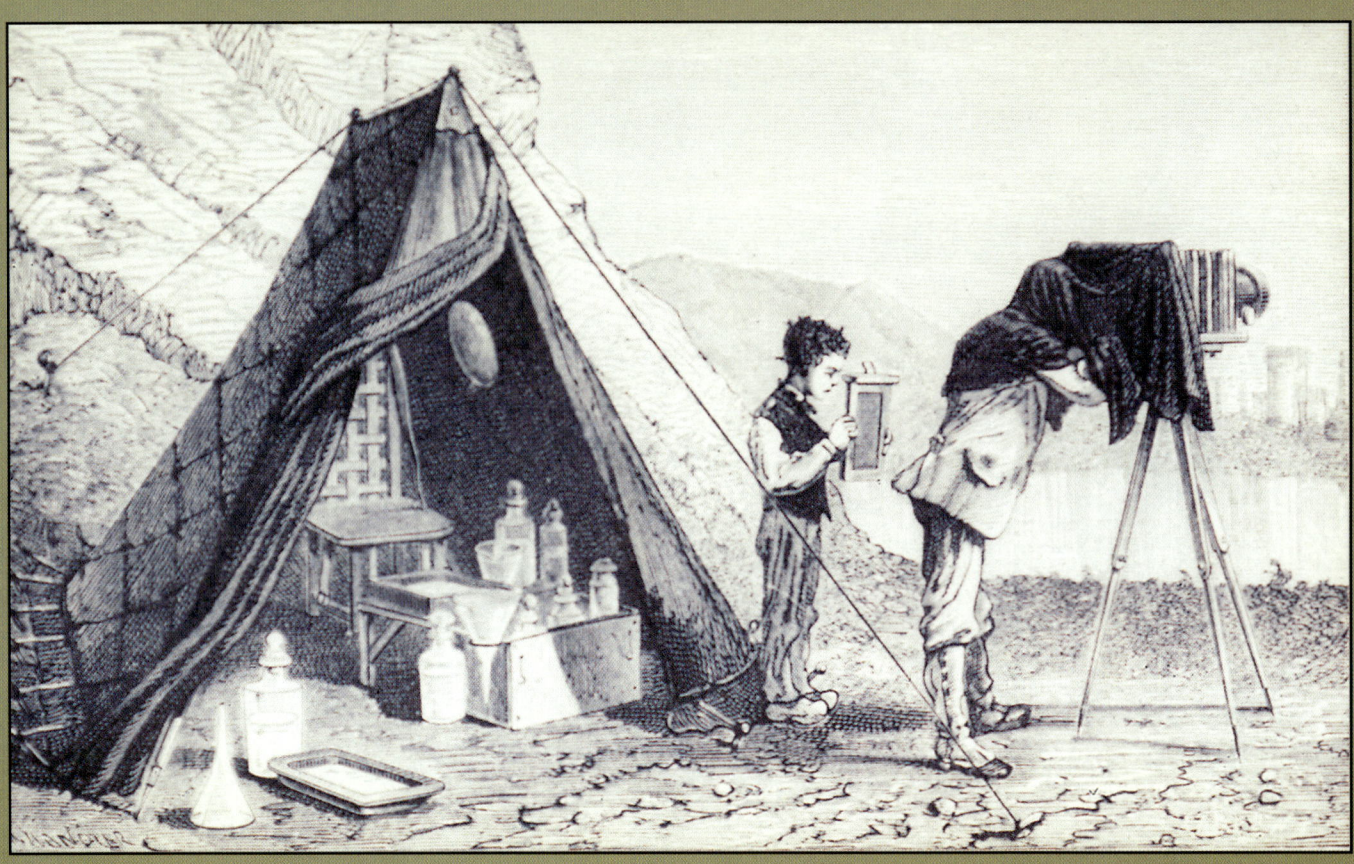

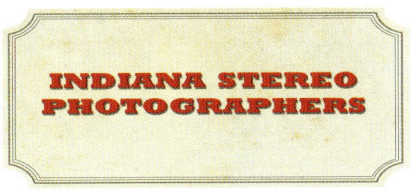

INDIANA STEREO PHOTOGRAPHERS

THIS DIRECTORY LISTS PHOTOGRAPHERS WHOSE STEREOGRAPHS OR ADVERTISEMENTS FOR STEREO IMAGES were viewed by the authors during the research for this book. The list includes, when known, the photographer's name and birth and death dates, the gallery name and location, and the dates the photographer was known to have worked at that location. The dates are often approximate based on the content within the stereograph or when a photographer or gallery was known to have been in operation. No attempt has been made to include assistants or employees who worked for these photographers.

More complete biographical and studio information is available on many of these photographers in the Indiana Photographers Project database compiled by Joan E. Hostetler. To date she has documented more than five thousand photographers who worked in the state from 1841 though 1940. Although sources are not included in this list, most of the information came from imprints on the stereographs, newspaper advertisements, city and state directory listings, period photography magazines, county histories, and census records.

A directory of this type is ongoing and never complete. Please contact the editors at the Indiana Historical Society Press to provide further details or to contribute information about additional photographers.

Photographer	Birth Date	Death Date	Gallery	Location	Dates of Activity
———			American View Company	Claypool	1900s
———			Indiana College of Fine Arts & Photography	Wabash	1874–ca. 1880
G. W. Apple	1828		National Photograph Establishment	Indianapolis	1860s
C. N. Beamer				Indianapolis	1880s
James Bonney	7 Nov. 1831	18 Apr. 1910		South Bend	1860s–1890s
W. R. Brooke				Bristol	
G. M. Brooks				Goshen	ca. 1880s
John W. Bryant	ca. 1845			La Porte	1870s–1890s
Cornelius Theodore Cain	1842	1906	Cain & Tracy	Peru	1860s
Jarvis Calvert	17 June 1842	1917		Mooresville	1867–1890s
William A. Cauldwell				Indianapolis	ca. 1890
Oliver Charles	ca. 1834		Charles & Hart O. Charles	Knightstown Knightstown	1860s–1870s 1870s–1890s
David Brainard Claflin	9 Feb. 1837	1895	Ingraham & Claflin	Indianapolis	ca. 1872–ca. 1874
Daniel R. Clark	1831	Apr. 1895		Lafayette Indianapolis	1860s ca. 1870–1887
Matthias B. Collins	18 Feb. 1842			Martinsville	1879–1890s
A. A. Cooke				Gas City	1890s
William T. Cowey		18 Feb. 1874		Brookville	1870s
Aaron B. Craycraft	ca. 1846			Vincennes	ca. 1880
Charles P. Curtis	12 Apr. 1877	5 Feb. 1939		Argos	1900s–1936
——— Donner			Friedgen & Donner	Columbus	1870s–1880s
Frederick A. Elikofer				Evansville	1880s–1920s
John W. Ennis	ca. 1843		Ennis & Haller	Attica	

Photographer	Birth Date	Death Date	Gallery	Location	Dates of Activity
———— Estell	ca. 1830		Maxwell & Estell	Richmond	1860s
W. D. Fairchild				Greencastle	1890s–1900s
George W. Finley				Madison Jeffersonville	1870s 1870s–1900s
William G. Flanders				[South Bend?]	ca. 1880s
Frank P. Ford	ca. 1846			Kendallville	1870s–1880s
George H. Friedgen	ca. 1851		Friedgen & Donner	Columbus	1870s–1880s
Ridgeway Glover	29 May 1831	14 Sept. 1866		Spring Valley/Pendleton	1865
Marquis D. Goodlander	ca. 1845	1934		Anderson Muncie	1870s 1880s–1900s
Robert Gordon				Indianapolis	1860s–1880s
Joseph Gorgas	7 Feb. 1829	6 Apr. 1903	Gorgas Gorgas & Mulvey	Madison Madison	1850s–1890s 1860s
Ben Hains	ca. 1865	18 Oct. 1904		New Albany	
———— Haller			Ennis & Haller	Attica	
———— Hart			Charles & Hart	Knightstown	1860s–1870s
———— Hartwell			Wright & Hartwell	Lafayette	1870s
John Heddon	ca. 1808			Elkhart	
H. Oscar Heichert	ca. 1821			Frankfort	1860s–1880s
George W. Hissong	9 Mar. 1840	1 Apr. 1923	Hissong & Son	Lagrange	1870s–1900s
J. Hodges				Newburgh	
William L. Hoff				Lagrange	1870s
A. E. Hoover			Tuttle & Hoover	Plymouth	early 1880s
Jacob W. Husher	ca. 1823	6 Apr. 1879		Terre Haute Greencastle	1860s–ca. 1873 ca. 1873–1879

Photographer	Birth Date	Death Date	Gallery	Location	Dates of Activity
Charles B. Ingraham	Sept. 1820	6 July 1898	Ingraham's Photographic Rooms Ingraham & Claflin	Indianapolis Indianapolis	ca. 1867–ca. 1872 ca. 1872–ca. 1874
Charles S. Judd	ca. 1845		Salter & Judd	Indianapolis	1874–1875
——— Keen			Keen Brothers	Culver	1890s–1910s
Wiley Kenyon		14 Mar. 1900		Crawfordsville	1860s–1870s
Frank M. Lacey				Indianapolis	1870s–1910s
Theodore C. Lawrence	19 Mar. 1838	12 May 1912		Ladoga	1870s–1890s
James McKeown	ca. 1841		McKeown McKeown & Swan	Anderson Anderson	1860s–1890s 1870s
Byron W. McLain	ca. 1843		Indiana College of Fine Arts & Photography	Wabash	1874–ca. 1880
——— Maxwell			Maxwell & Estell	Richmond	1860s
Henry C. Milice	ca. 1843	25 Dec. 1908		Warsaw	1856–ca. 1908
H. Miller				Indianapolis	
G. Mitchell				Greenfield	
Elisha J. Mote	1837	23 Apr. 1911	Mote & Swaine Mote Brothers	Richmond Richmond	1868–1874 1874–early 1880s
William Alden Mote	27 Aug. 1840	13 Jan. 1917	Mote Brothers	Richmond	1874–early 1880s
Oliver Mulvey	1837		Gorgas & Mulvey	Madison	1860s
Leonidas (Lon) M. Neely	ca. 1847			Muncie	1870s
——— Overland			Wager & Overland	Indianapolis	1883–1884
W. V. Overman				Elwood	ca. early 1900s
J. M. Paxson			Paxson Photograph Car	Plymouth	1875
A. J. Pearson				Spiceland	1880s
Charles H. Pease				Goshen	1870s

Photographer	Birth Date	Death Date	Gallery	Location	Dates of Activity
Henry K. Pendergast	1853	1 Mar. 1888	Pendergast Brothers Art Pavilion	Indianapolis	1870s–1880s
John W. Pendergast	1851	13 Oct. 1928	Pendergast Brothers Art Pavilion	Indianapolis	1870s–1880s
Elisha W. Poston	ca. 1833			Fort Wayne	1870s–1880s
Harvey M. Pound	28 Nov. 1831			Terre Haute	1860s
J. S. Reid				Orange	1860s
B. H. Roberts				Pendleton	1860s
W. P. Robins				Newtown	1900s
Thomas Harrie (Harvey) Rose	ca. 1852		Eureka Photographic Company	New Castle	1870s
C. W. Rugg				Lawrenceburg	1870s
William H. Salter	ca. 1835	23 Dec. 1882	W. H. Salter Salter & Judd	Indianapolis Indianapolis	1860s–1882 1874–1875
A. J. Savage				Vincennes	1860s
Julius T. Schaub	1842	14 Oct. 1934		Hope	1860s–1910s
J. M. Scott				Vincennes	
John A. Shoaff	ca. 1837			Fort Wayne	1860s–1892
Jacob H. Swaine	ca. 1839		Mote & Swaine	Richmond	1868–1874
———— Swan			McKeown & Swan Weatherford & Swan	Anderson West Baden Springs	1870s ca. 1880s
J. R. Thorne				Madison	1870s
Moses H. Tomlinson	3 Dec. 1836	30 Jan. 1927		Plainfield	1859–1910
William Townsend				Richmond	1870s
———— Tracy			Cain & Tracy	Peru	1860s
Clay H. Tuttle	5 Apr. 1869	9 Nov. 1939		Hartford City	1908–1917
Washington Tuttle	19 Apr. 1829	2 Dec. 1912	Tuttle & Hoover	Plymouth	early 1880s

Photographer	Birth Date	Death Date	Gallery	Location	Dates of Activity
Stephen D. Wager			Wager & Overland	Indianapolis	1883–1884
Charles E. Wallin				Fort Wayne	1870s
W. Blanch Ward			Union View Company	[Itinerant]	1870s
——— Weatherford			Weatherford & Swan	West Baden Springs	ca. 1880s
Edward Z. Webster	1821				
George Weingarth	1851			Shelbyville	1870s–1880s
P. Wheeler				Aurora	1870s
Andrew W. Wolever	12 Aug. 1852	28 Sept. 1936		Delphi	1874–1933
M. Wolfe				Richmond	1870s
Charles C. Wright	ca. 1839	ca. 1886	Wright & Hartwell	Lafayette	1870s
David H. Wright		Nov. 1908		Terre Haute	1870s–1890s
Sarah Ann (Judkins) Wright	ca. 1833		Wright & Hartwell	Lafayette	1870s

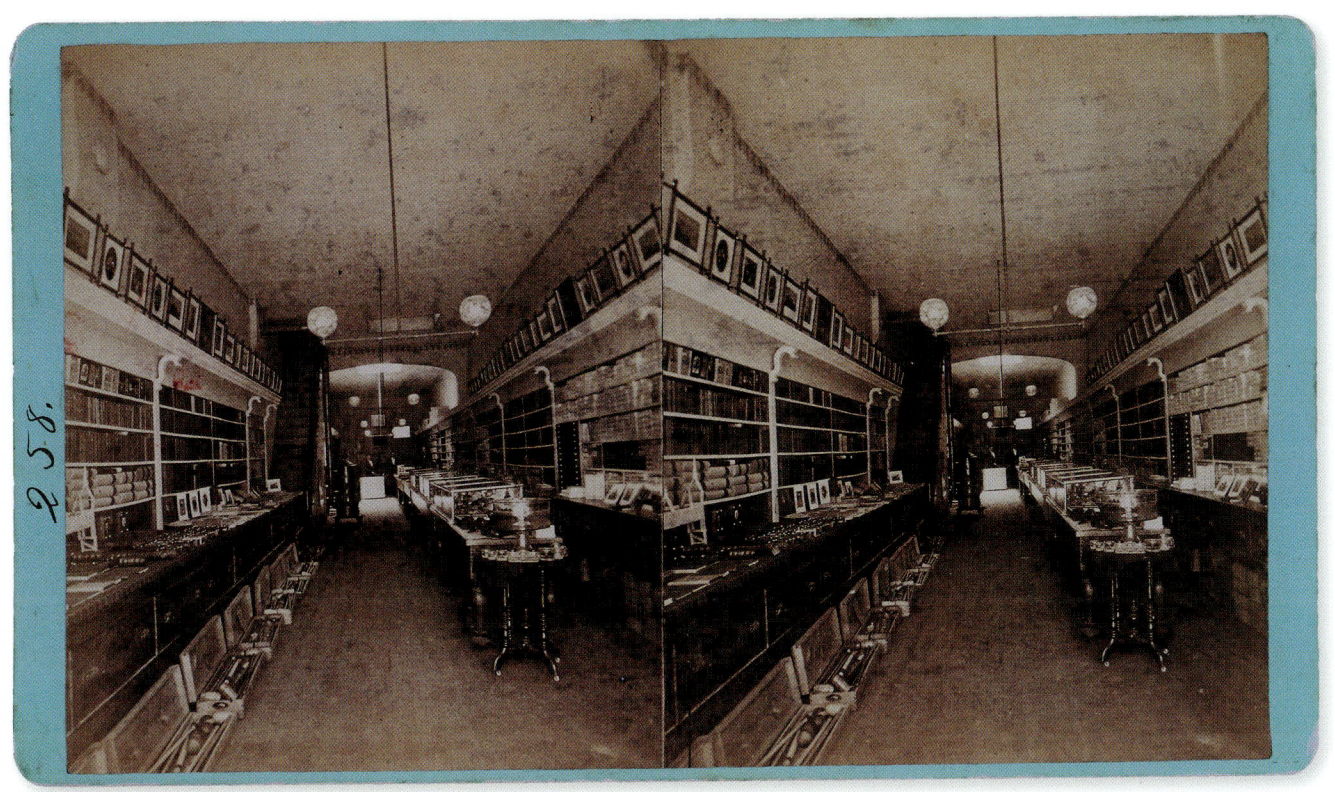

Store interior, Lafayette, ca. 1870s. Published by Wright and Hartwell.
Note the croquet sets along the front of the cabinets.

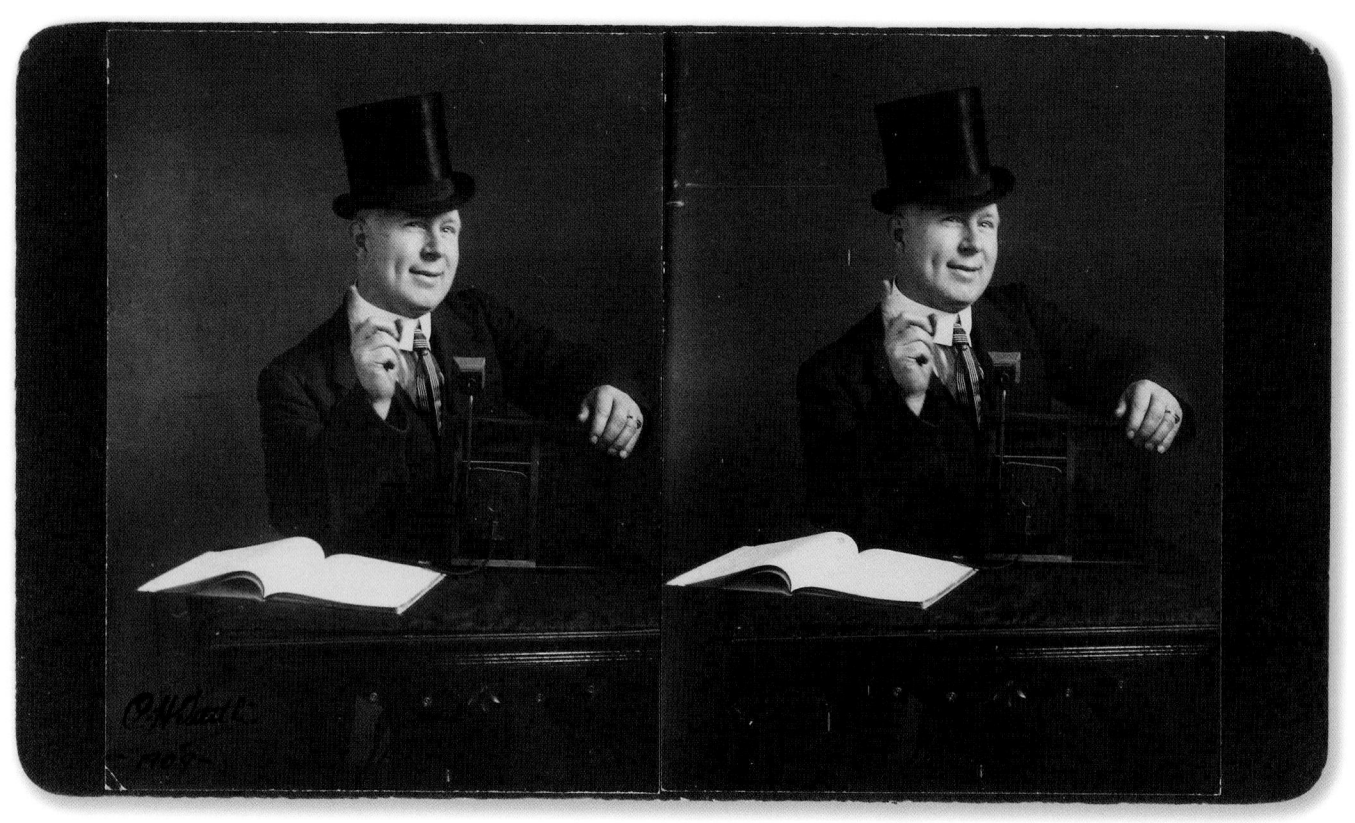

Clay H. Tuttle with camera, Hartford City, 1909. Self-portrait.
Tuttle made his living as a shoe salesman and practiced photography only as a hobby. His surviving work displays a fair amount of talent,
nevertheless, and plays an important role in documenting life in and around Hartford City.

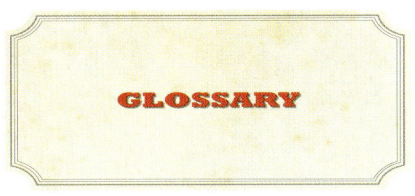

GLOSSARY

ALBUMEN SILVER PRINT Introduced by Frenchman Louis Désiré Blanquart-Evrard in 1850, this was the most popular photographic paper print for about forty years. To create albumen silver prints, photographers coated thin paper with egg whites and sensitized it with silver salts. They then made a contact print by placing the sensitized paper against a negative and exposing it to light. Although the prints were originally brighter, today they range from pale yellow to deep brown and often show fine cracks on the surface when viewed from an angle. Early stereographs, cartes de visite, and cabinet photographs usually were albumen silver prints.

ARTISTIC OR CABINET CARD An oversize stereograph mount measuring from about four by seven inches to five by seven inches. The term cabinet card is also used to describe a portrait mount popular from the 1880s well into the 1900s.

CALOTYPE OR TALBOTYPE Invented by William Henry Fox Talbot, the calotype process became available in 1840. It was a paper-negative print process similar to the negative processes we have today. Because of Talbot's restrictive patents and the grainy quality of the prints, calotypes did not gain great popularity, especially outside of England.

CARD OR MOUNT The stiff support made of laminated paper onto which stereo pairs were glued. It usually measured three and a half by seven inches.

CARTE DE VISITE A portrait format the size of a calling card. Cartes de visite were popular from the 1860s to the 1880s and were often exchanged among friends and displayed in albums.

COPY OR PIRATED PRINT A photographic copy of a stereo

view (not made from an original negative), usually mounted on a thin, poor-quality card. A copy print contains little information about the view, and the card usually includes a generic moniker such as "American Scenery" rather than the name of the photographer or publisher.

CURVED MOUNT A deliberately warped mount popular after about 1890, thought to enhance the stereo effect when viewed through the stereoscope.

DAGUERREOTYPE The first viable photographic process, invented by Frenchman Louis-Jacques-Mandé Daguerre and made available to the public in 1839. Popular from its inception through the 1850s, the daguerreotype was most often used for portraits and also for early stereographs. It was a direct-positive process (no negative was used) that resulted in a single, unique image on a sensitized copper plate. One of a kind, daguerreotypes were distinguished by their mirrorlike surface and unequaled image detail.

DOMED PRINT A stereo image with a deliberately cropped top. The domed croppings on stereo pairs removed any imperfections around the outer edges of the prints and improved the appearance of the card. Although domed prints began to be used in the late 1850s, uncropped views were made into the 1870s.

GELATIN DRY-PLATE NEGATIVE A commercially made glass-plate negative purchased already sensitized. Dry plates, which could be stored for long periods of time, quickly replaced the difficult wet-plate collodion process.

LITHOPRINT OR LITHOGRAPHIC PRINT An inexpensive, photomechanically produced stereograph made not with actual photographs but by a series of colored dots printed on the mount.

STEREOGRAPH, STEREOGRAM, STEREO VIEW, OR STEREO A card on which two almost identical images are mounted. When a stereograph is viewed through a stereoscope, its two images appear as one three-dimensional scene.

STEREOPTICON A lantern used to project glass slides onto a wall or screen. Unfortunately, this term is often confused with the stereoscope and stereograph, although there is no relationship.

STEREOSCOPE A device used to view stereographs, making the two images on the card appear as one three-dimensional view.

STEREOSCOPY The study of stereographs and three-dimensional image making.

WET-PLATE OR COLLODION NEGATIVE The most prevalent type of photographic negative from the mid-1850s to 1880.

The glass-negative support had to be sensitized in a darkroom immediately before exposure and then quickly developed. The process was time consuming and cumbersome but produced negatives of great clarity.

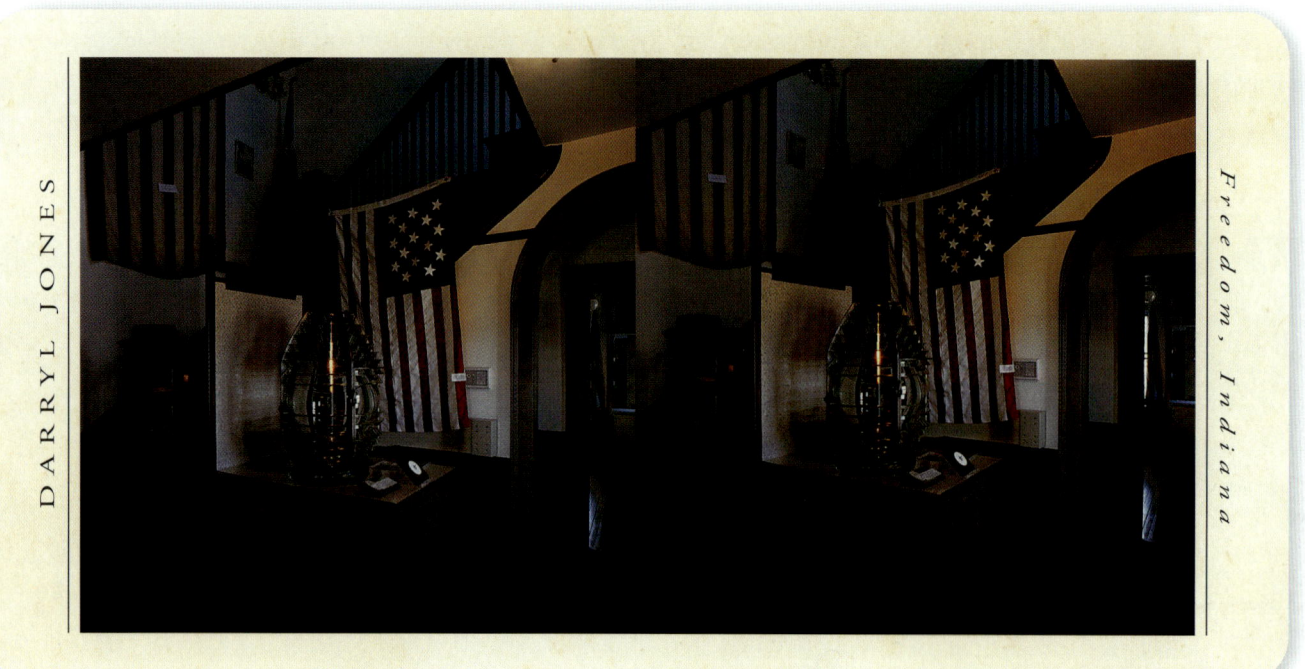

Old Lighthouse Museum, Michigan City, 1999.
The federal government constructed this lighthouse in 1858 and extensively remodeled it in 1904, moving its lantern to a new fog-signal lighthouse
at the entrance to Michigan City's harbor. The keeper continued to live in the old lighthouse until the late 1930s.

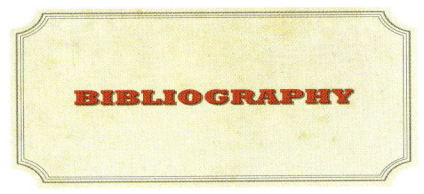

BIBLIOGRAPHY

Bennett, Mary, and Paul C. Juhl. *Iowa Stereographs: Three-Dimensional Visions of the Past*. Iowa City: University of Iowa Press, 1997.

Brewster, David. *The Stereoscope: Its History, Theory, and Construction*. 1856. Reprint, with an introduction by Rudolf Kingslake, Hastings-on-Hudson, N.Y.: Morgan and Morgan; London: Fountain Press, 1971.

Crain, Jim. *California in Depth: A Stereoscopic History*. San Francisco: Chronicle Books, 1994.

Darrah, William C. *The World of Stereographs*. Gettysburg, Pa.: Darrah, 1977.

Drouin, Félix. *The Stereoscope and Stereoscopic Photography*. Translated by Matthew Surface. 1894. Reprint, with a new introduction by Susan Pinsky and David Starkman, Culver City, Calif.: Reel 3-D Enterprises, 1995.

Earle, Edward W., ed. *Points of View: The Stereograph in America—A Cultural History*. Rochester, N.Y.: Visual Studies Workshop Press, in collaboration with the Gallery Association of New York State, 1979.

Gernsheim, Helmut. *The Origins of Photography*. New York: Thames and Hudson, 1982.

Jenkins, Harold F. *Two Points of View: The History of the Parlor Stereoscope*. Uniontown, Pa.: E. G. Warman Publishing, 1973.

Newhall, Beaumont. *The History of Photography: From 1839 to the Present*. 5th ed. New York: Museum of Modern Art, 1982.

Reynaud, Françoise, Catherine Tambran, and Kim Timby, eds. *Paris in 3D: From Stereoscopy to Virtual Reality, 1850–2000*. London: Booth-Clibborn Editions; n.p.: Paris-Musées, 2000.

Rinhart, Floyd, and Marion Rinhart. *The American Daguerreotype*. Athens: University of Georgia Press, 1981.

Rosenblum, Naomi. *A World History of Photography*. 3d ed. New York: Abbeville Press, 1997.

Sandweiss, Martha A., ed. *Photography in Nineteenth-Century America*. Fort Worth, Tex.: Amon Carter Museum; New York: H. N. Abrams, 1991.

Taft, Robert. *Photography and the American Scene: A Social History, 1839–1889*. New York: Dover Publications, 1938.

Tissandier, Gaston. *A History and Handbook of Photography*. Translated and edited by James Thomson. 2d ed. London: Sampson, Low, Marston, Low, and Searle, 1876; New York: Scovill Manufacturing Co., 1877.

Treadwell, T. K., and William C. Darrah. *Stereographers of the World*. [Columbus, Ohio]: National Stereoscopic Association, 1994.

Waldsmith, John S. *Stereo Views: An Illustrated History and Price Guide*. Radnor, Pa.: Wallace-Homestead Book Co., 1991.

Wing, Paul. *Stereoscopes: The First One Hundred Years*. Nashua, N.H.: Transition Publishing, 1996.

Zeller, Bob. *The Civil War in Depth: History in 3-D*. San Francisco: Chronicle Books, 1997.

STEREOGRAPH COLLECTIONS

Stereograph collections can be found in almost every historical society in the United States. Most of the historical stereographs reproduced in this book are held in the collections of the Indiana Historical Society's William Henry Smith Memorial Library, and much of the rest were borrowed from local historical societies across Indiana. Libraries, archives, and museums also serve as common repositories for stereograph collections.

Two of the largest collections of stereographs available to the public are the Keystone-Mast Collection and the Underwood and Underwood Glass Stereograph Collection. The Keystone-Mast Collection is located at the California Museum of Photography, affiliated with the University of California, Riverside. The museum also has collections of stereographs from the smaller firms that the Keystone View Company acquired. The Underwood and Underwood Glass Stereograph Collection is at the Archives Center in the Smithsonian Institution's National Museum of American History in Washington, D.C. Both collections are open to the public and available for use.

NATIONAL STEREOSCOPIC ASSOCIATION

Enthusiasts wanting to learn more about historical and contemporary stereographs can join the National Stereoscopic Association, P.O. Box 86708, Portland, Oregon 97286. The NSA has national and regional meetings and publishes a bimonthly magazine, *Stereo World*.

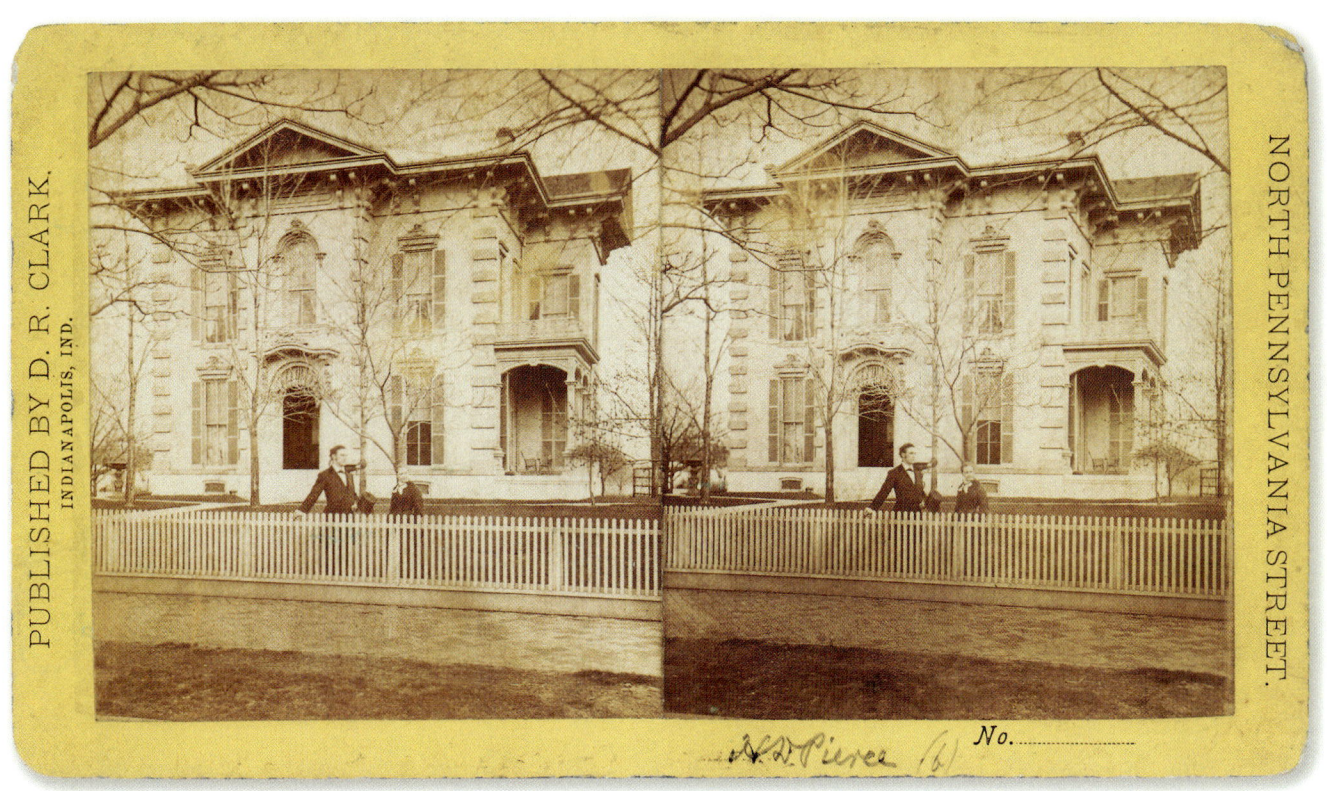

289

No.

Future Pierce residence, Indianapolis, ca. late 1870s. Photographed by D. R. Clark.
Henry Pierce and family moved to this North Meridian Street home in the mid-1880s. Another view of it appears on page 168.